Fernando Pessoa as English Reader and Writer

Tagus Press
Center for Portuguese Studies and Culture
University of Massachusetts Dartmouth
Portuguese Literary & Cultural Studies (PLCS) 28

João Cezar de Castro Rocha, Editor in Chief

Portuguese Literary & Cultural Studies is a multilingual interdisciplinary peer-reviewed journal published semi-annually by the Tagus Press in the Center for Portuguese Studies and Culture at the University of Massachusetts Dartmouth. The journal addresses the literatures and cultures of the diverse communities of the Portuguese-speaking world in terms of critical and theoretical approaches.

Manuscript Policy
Portuguese Literary & Cultural Studies welcomes submission of original and unpublished manuscripts in English, Portuguese, or Spanish appropriate to the goals of the journal. Manuscripts should be in accordance with the *MLA Style Manual and Guide to Scholarly Publishing* (latest version) with parenthetical documentation and a list of works cited. The author is responsible for the accuracy of all quotations, titles, names, and dates. Font and sizes as close as possible to the style of the previous issue of *PLCS* should be used throughout the text. All of the information must be in the same language (e.g., abstract, body of the article, bio-blurb). Updated guidelines are available at http://www.portstudies.umassd.edu/plcs/editor.htm. *PLCS* encourages submission of manuscripts in the form of a single attached MS Word document. Please send submissions to João Cezar de Castro Rocha, Editor in Chief, at jccr123@yahoo.com.br.

PORTUGUESE LITERARY AND CULTURAL STUDIES 28

Fernando Pessoa as English Reader and Writer

Edited by PATRICIO FERRARI &

JERÓNIMO PIZARRO

Tagus Press UMASS DARTMOUTH, DARTMOUTH, MASSACHUSETTS

Portuguese Literary and Cultural Studies 28
Tagus Press at UMass Dartmouth
www.portstudies.umassd.edu
© 2015 The University of Massachusetts Dartmouth
Manufactured in the United States of America
Managing Editor: Mario Pereira
Copyedited by Sara Evangelos
Designed by Richard Hendel
Typeset in Quadraat by Integrated Typesetting Solutions

For all inquiries, please contact:
Tagus Press at UMass Dartmouth
Center for Portuguese Studies and Culture
285 Old Westport Road
North Dartmouth MA 02747–2300
Tel. 508–999–8255
Fax 508–999–9272
www.portstudies.umassd.edu

ISSN: 1521-804x
ISBN: 978-1-933227-65-8 (pbk.: alk. paper)
Library of Congress Control Number: 2014955470

5 4 3 2 1

Contents

A Note from the Editor-in-Chief
"A Very Original Issue"

Fernando Pessoa as English Reader and Writer. The title of this issue of *Portuguese Literary & Cultural Studies* may intrigue the reader. Does it mean that Patricio Ferrari and Jerónimo Pizarro are concerned mainly with the reception of the Portuguese author in English-speaking countries? Does it convey the importance of literature written in English in Fernando Pessoa's own works? Does the title stress the overlapping of reading and writing as a key element in understanding the fascination provoked by Pessoa's (as well as Jorge Luis Borges's) literature?

Indeed, Pessoa and Borges have become an authentic phenomenon as far as the contemporary breadth of their readership is concerned. The fact that they *primarily* wrote, respectively, in Portuguese and Spanish does not seem to hinder the ever-increasing impact of their unique writings, and above all the strength of their disquieting worldviews, which have bewildered readers throughout the world.

Primarily, I wrote—and that makes all the difference. From their early childhood, both authors were exposed to an English-speaking environment; therefore, they were fluent in at least two languages, and this bilingual predicament is the circumstance brought to the fore by Ferrari and Pizarro in the organization of this issue, which certainly will become an indispensable reference in the work of Fernando Pessoa *in English*.

The guest editors of this issue, in fact, are accomplished and well-known researchers on the work of Fernando Pessoa. In recent years, they have emphasized Pessoa's production written directly in English as well as in French. In the course of their groundbreaking research, they have found unpublished manuscripts and also have broadened our understanding of the resonances of Pessoa's formative years in the whole of his "verse and prose"—to recall the title of one of Octavio Paz's insightful essays.

The novelty of Ferrari and Pizarro's approach makes this a very original issue—as the reader will realize, the editors have included in their selection the disturbing short story written by the young Fernando Pessoa, that is, by Alexander Search, "A Very Original Dinner."

There is, however, another reason that this issue is particularly relevant in the history of *Portuguese Literary & Cultural Studies*.

This will be the last issue published on paper. In other words, we will begin to publish the journal as an online, open-access publication from the next issue onward.

It is our hope that this decision will provide an unprecedented broadening of the community of readers of the journal.

Introduction

More than even Conrad, Tagore, and Nabokov—to name just a few late nine-teenth-century and early twentieth-century writers who went beyond the realm of the mother tongue—Fernando Pessoa (1888–1935), from childhood on, moved with great ease between Portuguese, English, and French,[1] as well as a smattering of humorous and philosophical Latin when appropriate. Publica-tions during his lifetime, along with the numerous unpublished writings in his archive housed at the Biblioteca Nacional de Portugal (National Library of Por-tugal),[2] provide ample evidence of an intense engagement with all three lan-guages, at times simultaneously. Moreover, his private library, kept at the Casa Fernando Pessoa (Fernando Pessoa House),[3] feels more like the study of an En-glish writer permanently residing in Lisbon, surrounded by many volumes of his favorite English authors, reading French texts only in the original, and pos-sessing a large number of Portuguese books, many signed by fellow writers.[4]

After Pessoa's father—a modest employee of the secretary of state, as well as music critic of the *Diário de Notícias*—died prematurely, his mother married the then Portuguese consul to South Africa. Pessoa, age seven and a half, left Lisbon to travel with her to Durban, the capital at the time of the British colony of Natal, South Africa. He would remain there for the next nine years (February, 1896–August, 1905),[5] and all his formal education would be in English. Some might say—as Eduardo Lourenço has said—that Pessoa could never have been the writer he became had he not spent his formative years undergoing what can only be de-scribed as a typical upper-middle-class education within the British Empire at the end of the Victorian era. What Pessoa gained in literary terms during those years was invaluable. He became acquainted with Milton's *Paradise Lost* long before he read the Portuguese epic poem *Os Lusíadas* (*The Lusiads*) of Camões; he admired Keats for his "love of the decorative" and "love of the natural" before coming in contact with his beloved Cesário Verde, the "poet of unpoetical things";[6] his knowledge of Shakespeare enabled him to produce a series of his own Shake-spearean sonnets in English as well as to read, appreciate, and even attempt trans-lations of Antero de Quental's sonnets.[7] In a word, what Pessoa brought back to Lisbon was something sorely needed among the Portuguese literati of the time: an

1

informed, outsider's literary perspective on Portugal and all things Portuguese capable of reinvigorating, or better, redefining, the country's literary identity.

Once back in the city of his birth, the young Pessoa never again set foot in an English-speaking country. Yet like the traveler who dreams about distant lands without actually venturing forth, he never ceased to dream about other places, other ways of feeling, knowing, being . . . He had returned home with a mind on fire, brimming with myriad projects, both literary and commercial, often conceived in English, often left unfinished, as his archive reveals. In fact, many of his poems echo this sense of endless schemes and dreams without endings:

> Tenho já o plano traçado; mas não, hoje não traço planos . . .
> Amanhã é o dia dos planos.
> Amanhã sentar-me-hei á secretaria para conquistar o mundo;
> Mas só conquistarei o mundo depois de amanhã . . . [8]

> (I've got a plan all mapped out; but no, not mapping it out today . . .
> Tomorrow is the day for plans.
> Tomorrow is the day I'll sit at my desk and take over the world;
> But I'll only take over the world the day after tomorrow . . .)

Taking over the world implied an inner conquest: a verbal, dramatized shedding of light on some uncharted land within consciousness. His lifetime's effort never really swerved from this serious pursuit of a language capable of expressing the layered, highly complex answer to the always-elusive question of personal identity in all its conceivable dimensions. And in this endeavor, Pessoa's greatest compass remained, unfailingly, his private library. His voracious appetite for books gave him all that was necessary for his poetic voyage. It took him anywhere his precocious intellectual curiosity desired to go: across Europe and all the way to the East. Even across the Atlantic Ocean—to the companionship of Emerson, Hawthorne, and Poe. And how to forget Whitman—that "universão"[9] (giant universe) whose portrait Álvaro de Campos kissed and described as "Shakespeare da sensação que começa a andar a vapor, / Milton-Shelley do horizonte da Electricidade futura!"[10] (Shakespeare of the sensation on the verge of steam propulsion, / Milton-Shelley of the dawning future of Electricity!)? Rather than ply the waters in search of new lands, Pessoa's version of the Portuguese explorer would plumb oceanic literary depths in search of the ever-changing, fathomless Self.

What initially launched Pessoa onto the world stage was his modernist epic of personal consciousness: the poetic trio of heteronyms in his "drama-em-gente" (drama-in-people).[11] From this initial whirlwind of interest, curiosity led to awareness (and translations) of his other major works in Portuguese—*Livro do desassossego* (*The Book of Disquiet*) and *Mensagem* (*Message*; the only Portuguese work published in his lifetime, a year before his death), plus the vast output of his own poetry in Portuguese (as distinct from his heteronymic poetry). Serious interest in the English side of Pessoa, on the other hand, took much longer to rouse. Only twenty years after Pessoa's death did the focus begin to shift. The publication in 1956 of Maria da Encarnação Monteiro's pioneering work, *Incidências Inglesas na Poesia de Fernando Pessoa* (*English Influences in the Poetry of Fernando Pessoa*),[12] was soon followed by a host of editions, translations, and studies by Georg Rudolf Lind, Edouard Roditi, Jorge de Sena, José Blanc de Portugal, Hubert D. Jennings, Alexandrino Severino, George Monteiro, Susan Margaret Brown, Anne Terlinder, João Dionísio, Luísa Freire, and Maria Irene Ramalho de Sousa Santos, among others.[13] More-recent works have been published by some of the contributors to this special issue: Richard Zenith, Mariana Gray de Castro, and Jorge Uribe on Oscar Wilde; Patricia McNeill on William Butler Yeats; Mariana Gray de Castro on Shakespeare; Jorge Uribe on Matthew Arnold; Jerónimo Pizarro on Khayyam-FitzGerald; and Patricio Ferrari on Pessoa's English metrics.[14]

Studying the English literary production is pertinent for many reasons, including the way it helps contextualize Pessoa more thoroughly. It is important to know that before making his literary debut in book form with *Mensagem* in 1934, he had already published some of his works in English. In 1918 two chapbooks came out in English: *Antinous*, a long poem celebrating the homoerotic love between Antinous and the Emperor Hadrian; and *35 Sonnets*, a series of Shakespearean sonnets. Three years later, in 1921, Pessoa published *English Poems I–II* (a revised version of *Antinous* and *Inscriptions*, a series of fourteen epitaphs inspired by *The Greek Anthology*, compiled and translated by W. R. Paton[15]) and *English Poems III* (*Epithalamium*, a twenty-one-poem series set in Rome and infused with explicit scenes of heterosexual love). These two slim volumes were published by Olisipo, a commercial agency and publishing house that Pessoa founded that same year. He also published two other poems: one in the well-known London-based journal *Athenaeum*, and the other in *Contemporânea*, a literary magazine created in Lisbon. In this connection, it should be mentioned that

3

the letters Pessoa wrote to English critics, publishers, and editors underscore just how serious he was about his English poetry, and just how hopeful he was about making this poetry known in England.[16]

Especially now, with Pessoa's digitized private library online, the importance of English in his formative years is irrefutable: Shakespeare, Milton, Chatterton, Blake, Wordsworth, Coleridge, Byron, Shelley, and Keats, among others, were the bedrock from which his poetic sensibility emerged. The legacy of this literary language provided him with a scope, the breadth and depth of which characterize the quality of the imagination of the true comparatist. Most of what Pessoa eventually wrote was informed by these (his) original sources. Whether his scribbled annotations in works of other authors, his own essays, poems, and fiction, or the writings attributed to his fictitious authors, the most alluring aspect of these English writings is the connections and transformations taking place within Pessoa's mind as it migrated back and forth between two linguistic homelands. As we learn how to make these connections, we begin to find significance in what was previously of little interest. What matters is not so much that his English poems, for example, are not of the highest literary quality—one of the reasons many critics have ignored them—but rather what these poems are trying to do, what they express and how they express it, and the ways they foreshadow, in part, what would subsequently take place in Portuguese.

This issue on Pessoa is divided into five themes, each of which is treated in several chapters: the Durban years; Pessoa's short and long poems; mediating Portugal; the nineteenth century and a theoretical framework for heteronymism; and Pessoa's archive. Additional short sections containing fiction, essays, translations, an interview conducted last year, and three reviews of recent editions of Pessoa round out the volume.

Because this is the first publication devoted exclusively to Pessoa as an English reader and writer, we wanted to cover a broad spectrum of topics and approaches while still maintaining cohesion. This explains our choice of contributions.

We thought it pertinent to open with writings from Pessoa's formative years in South Africa. Richard Zenith's article deals with The Barrowboy Boys, a boy's storybook serialized in a British magazine in 1903, which sparked enough interest in Pessoa that he wrote his own version in Portuguese. With the political poetry attributed to Charles Robert Anon/Alexander Search as a focal point, Stefan

Helgesson discusses the contextual circumstances of Fernando Pessoa in the Natal Colony at the time of the Anglo-Boer War and its aftermath.

George Monteiro opens his article with a new interpretation of Pessoa's "O Menino da sua mãe" ("His Mother's Child"). Reading it in the light of specific war poems written by English poets Rupert Brooke and A. E. Housman, Monteiro offers an alternative reading to João Gaspar Simões's autobiographical interpretation of the poem, and in so doing grants it a greater universality. Pauly Ellen Bothe reflects on the modernist long poem as a cosmopolitan aesthetic phenomenon by examining characteristics of both T. S. Eliot's The Waste Land and Álvaro de Campos's Ode marítima (Maritime Ode).

Patricia Silva McNeill concentrates on Pessoa's role as cultural mediator between Portugal and England. She demonstrates Pessoa's familiarity with cultural magazines published in London in the first decade of the twentieth century, and she indicates the extent to which the British avant-garde most likely influenced Pessoa's work. José Barreto transcribes and discusses Pessoa's most ambitious English prose undertaking before the age of twenty-five: "History of a Dictatorship."

In the chapter on heteronymism,[17] Mariana Gray de Castro examines Pessoa's poetic engagement with Keats, both in specific lines of verse and in the gradual theoretical development concerning the formation of Pessoa's heteronyms. Flávio Rodrigo Penteado and Caio Gagliardi use some of Pessoa's theoretical texts in order to analyze the relationship between Robert Browning's dramatic monologues and the heteronymic project.

Finally, Jorge Uribe tracks all of Pessoa's references to Walter Pater, shedding important light on the influence and the instrumental use of tradition. Bringing to light four unpublished English sonnets, Patricio Ferrari and Carlos Pittella-Leite lay to rest the erroneous idea that Pessoa stopped writing English verse in the early 1920s.

As guest editors, we were privileged to be granted the opportunity to coordinate the five short final sections.[18] The first section, on Pessoa's fiction, includes a brief introduction and a new transcription of Alexander Search's "A Very Original Dinner" by Natalia Jerez Quintero. In the section on essays, Filipa de Freitas transcribes and comments on six fragments from Pessoa's "Erostratus," an unfinished essay in English concerning artistic fame. In the section on translation Claudia J. Fischer reveals unpublished translations of lines from Dryden, Keats, Tennyson, and Browning. Following that, Maria de Lurdes Sampaio interviews Margaret Jull Costa, joint winner of the Portuguese Translation Prize in 1992 for her translation of Pessoa's *Livro do desassossego*. The volume closes with reviews by Patricia McNeill, George Monteiro, and Susan Margaret Brown of three recent Pessoa editions.

An unpublished English manuscript datable to 1904 and still extant among Pessoa's papers reads as follows:

> It has always been the custom of man to bewail the irrevocable past and look upon it as alone good, beautiful and poetic. The early Romans mourned for the Greek past, and the latter Romans in their turn sighed for the days of the birth of their State. The Middle Ages mourned the Roman days, and what they called their poetry, their loveliness and their joy. Others again did come who sighed for the times of Dante. Does not Fielding bewail days gone before, and does not Dickens bewail the times of Fielding himself? And do we ourselves not wish present again the early days of the past century; should we not love to hear the rattling of a coach into an antique yard and to see strangely dressed figures descend from it?
>
> And yet this longing for the past and thinking it alone poetic is not a little caused by the strangeness of it. We have now no toga, no Forum and therefore think it greatly poetic for a man in a toga to be strutting across a Forum.
>
> But the poetry of earth depends much also on the mind of man.[19]

Varied, contradictory, and rapidly changing, the twentieth century was a Pessoa century. In *The Western Canon*, Harold Bloom refers to Pessoa not only as the most original poet of the past century, but as one of the twenty-six writers responsible for setting the parameters of literature in the Western world.[20] And Pessoa did so as an outsider, as a writer-between-languages.

Bowler and top hats have gone out of fashion, black suits and bow ties no longer grace the streets of Lisbon, yet the aura of that ethereal silhouette that was Pessoa lurks around the corner, any corner . . . Great literature, just like nature, moves in concentric circles and is ultimately discovered.

As guest editors, our ambition will be satisfied if, in these utilitarian days, we have succeeded in putting together a volume that contributes to the enjoyment of and interest in Fernando Pessoa's bilingual output—one of the literary treasures of the past century that is yet to be unearthed.

NOTES

We wish to express our utmost gratitude to all the contributors of this issue, as well as to João Cezar de Castro Rocha, editor-in-chief; to the managing editor, Mario Pereira; to the production editor, Susan Abel; and to the copyeditor, Sara Evangelos. We also extend our acknowledgments to Fátima Lopes and Lígia Maria de Azevedo Martins for allowing us to reproduce the images from Pessoa's archive, and to Susan Margaret Brown for the careful editing of this introduction and the translations of the verses there cited. Last but not least, this issue would not be what it is without the precious help of other professors, friends, and colleagues with whom we share a long companionship with Fernando Pessoa's works: Helena Buescu, Onésimo Teotónio Almeida, Patrick Quillier, Antonio Cardiello, Paulo de Medeiros, Carmo Mota, and José Pires Correia.

1. The approximately 200 verse texts that Pessoa wrote in French were composed during three specific periods: 1906–1908, the 1910s, and 1933–1935. See Fernando Pessoa, *Poèmes français*, ed. and annotated by Patricio Ferrari in collaboration with Patrick Quillier (Paris: Éditions de la Différence, 2014).

2. Biblioteca Nacional de Portugal/Espólio 3 [National Library of Portugal/Archive 3]. Hereafter BNP/E3.

3. Jerónimo Pizarro, Patricio Ferrari, and Antonio Cardiello have co-directed the digitization of Fernando Pessoa's private library. The collection consists of more than 1,300 titles and has been available online since October 2010 (http://casafernandopessoa.cm-lisboa.pt/bdigital/index/index.htm). The site is complemented by a bilingual paper publication. See Pizarro, Ferrari, and Cardiello, *A Biblioteca particular de Fernando Pessoa* [Fernando Pessoa's Private Library] (Lisbon: D. Quixote 2010). Fernando Pessoa's private library is held at the Casa Fernando Pessoa [Fernando Pessoa House]. Hereafter CFP.

4. Pessoa's marginalia (annotations, poetry, translations, and literary reflections or other notes that Pessoa wrote in the margins, flyleaves, or other parts of his books) are in Portuguese, English, and French. *Marginalia* is a term coined by Samuel Taylor Coleridge. See George Whalley, "Editorial Practice, Conventions, and Abbreviations," *Marginalia* in *The Collected Works of Samuel Taylor Coleridge*, 16 vols. (London: Routledge & Kegan Paul Ltd., 1980), Vol. xii, Part i, cxv.

5. In August 1901, Pessoa returned to Portugal where he remained until September of the following year, when he embarked once again for Durban. In December 1904 he completed his studies at Durban High School.

6. For Pessoa's comments on Keats and Verde, see BNP/E3, 14E–69^v and 14E–39. Fernando Pessoa, *Apreciações literárias de Fernando Pessoa*, ed. Pauly Ellen Bothe (Lisbon: Imprensa Nacional–Casa da Moeda, 2013), 302, 278.

7. BNP/E3, 138A–6; in Teresa Rita Lopes, *Pessoa por conhecer*, 2 vols. (Lisbon: Estampa, 1990), Vol. II, 76–77. See also Antero de Quental, *Os Sonetos completos de Antero de Quental,*

partial English translation by Fernando Pessoa; preface to the complete sonnets by J. P. Oliveira Martins; edition and postface by Patricio Ferrari (Lisbon: Ática, 2010).

8. Fernando Pessoa, "Addiamento," A Revista da Solução Editora 1 (Lisbon, 1929), 4–5. Fernando Pessoa, Poemas de Álvaro de Campos, ed Cleonice Berardinelli (Lisbon: Imprensa Nacional–Casa da Moeda, 1990), 205. See also the latest Campos edition: Fernando Pessoa, Obra Completa de Álvaro de Campos, ed. Jerónimo Pizarro and Antonio Cardiello (Lisbon: Tinta-da-China, 2014).

9. Fernando Pessoa, Poemas de Álvaro de Campos, 362.

10. Ibid., 119.

11. See "Tábua bibliográfica" (Dec. 1928), 10. Pessoa did not employ the term heteronímia (heteronymy). He explained the difference between "duas categorias de obras" ("orthónymas" and "heterónymas") in his "Tábua bibliográfica" (Dec. 1928), 10. In this publication, the term escripto heterónymo is also used. Pessoa employed the terms heteronymismo and heteronymos (without the accent) in the famous letter to Adolfo Casais Monteiro, dated January 13, 1935, in which he revealed to the critic the genesis of the heteronyms (see Espólio/15 [Casais Monteiro's Archive held at the National Library of Portugal]; Fernando Pessoa, Cartas entre Fernando Pessoa e os directores da presença, ed. Enrico Martines [Lisbon: Imprensa Nacional–Casa da Moeda, 1998], 251–59). Note that these categories appeared only in 1928. For the different nuances underlying this matter, see Jerónimo Pizarro, "Obras ortónimas e heterónimas," in Pessoa existe? (Lisbon: Ática, 2012), 73–97.

12. Maria da Encarnação Monteiro, Incidências Inglesas na poesia de Fernando Pessoa (Coimbra: Universidade de Coimbra, 1956).

13. This chronological list is nonexhaustive, and it extends from 1963 to 2000.

14. For the references in the previous endnote, see José Blanco, Pessoana, 2 vols. (Lisbon: Assírio & Alvim, 2008). For the more recent references, see the bibliography at the end of this introduction.

15. The Greek Anthology, English trans. William Roger Paton, bilingual ed., 5 vols. (London: William Heinemann; New York: G. P. Putman's Sons, 1916–1918).

16. See, for example, the letters written in 1915–1916 to editor Frank Palmer, to one or more English critics, to the publisher John Lane, and to Harold Monroe at the Poetry Bookshop. Fernando Pessoa, Correspondência, ed. Manuela Parreira da Silva (Lisbon: Assírio & Alvim, 1998–1999). Fernando Pessoa, Sensacionismo e outros ismos, ed. Jerónimo Pizarro (Lisbon: Imprensa Nacional–Casa da Moeda, 2009). Fernando Pessoa, Provérbios Portugueses, ed. Jerónimo Pizarro and Patricio Ferrari (Lisbon: Ática, 2010).

17. See note 11.

18. The two subsections, sections that normally follow the monographic section, are "Essays" and "Reviews," both usually handled by the editor-in-chief.

19. BNP/E3, 14²–42ʳ. We thank Pauly Ellen Bothe for this transcription. "The Poetry of earth is never dead" is the opening line of Keats's "On the Grasshopper and Cricket," a sonnet penned on December 30, 1816, and underlined by Pessoa in a copy still extant in his private library. See John Keats, *The Poetical Works of John Keats* (London: Frederick Warne, 1898), 44.

20. Harold Bloom, *The Western Canon: The Books and Schools of the Ages* (New York: Harcourt, 1994), 485–92.

WORKS CITED

Blanco, José. *Pessoana*. 2 vols. Lisbon: Assírio & Alvim, 2008.

Bloom, Harold. *The Western Canon: The Books and Schools of the Ages*. New York: Harcourt, 1994.

Castro, Mariana Gray de. "Pessoa's Shakespeare." Unpublished doctoral thesis, University of London, 2010.

———. "Oscar Wilde, Fernando Pessoa and the Art of Lying." *Portuguese Studies* XXII 2 (Sept. 2006): 219–49.

Ferrari, Patricio. "Meter and Rhythm in the Poetry of Fernando Pessoa." Unpublished doctoral thesis, University of Lisbon, 2012.

Keats, John. *The Poetical Works of John Keats*. With memoir, explanatory notes, portrait, illustrations. London, New York: Frederick Warne, 1898. CFP (Casa Fernando Pessoa [Fernando Pessoa House]) 8–294.

Khayyám, Omar. *Rubáiyát of Omar Khayyám: The Astronomer Poet of Persia Rendered into English Verse by Edward Fitzgerald*. Leipzig: Bernhard Tauchnitz, 1910 (repr. 1928). "Collection of British and American Authors, n.º 4231." CFP 8–296.

Lopes, Teresa Rita. *Pessoa por conhecer*. 2 vols. Lisbon: Estampa, 1990.

McNeill, Patrícia Silva. *Yeats and Pessoa: Parallel Poetic Styles*. London: Legenda, 2010.

Monteiro, Maria da Encarnação. *Incidências Inglesas na poesia de Fernando Pessoa*. Coimbra: Universidade de Coimbra, 1956.

Paton, William Roger. *The Greek Anthology*. With an English translation by William Roger Paton. Bilingual edition. 5 vols. London: William Heinemann; New York: G. P. Putman's Sons, 1916–1918. CFP 8–235.

Pessoa, Fernando. *Poèmes français*. Edited and annotated by Patricio Ferrari in collaboration with Patrick Quillier. Preface by Patrick Quillier. Paris: Éditions de la Différence, 2014.

———. *Apreciações literárias de Fernando Pessoa*. Edited by Pauly Ellen Bothe. Fernando Pessoa's Critical Edition, Collection "Studies." Lisbon: Imprensa Nacional–Casa da Moeda, 2013.

———. *Provérbios Portugueses*. Edited by Jerónimo Pizarro and Patricio Ferrari. Lisbon: Ática, 2010.

———. *Sensacionismo e outros ismos*. Edited by Jerónimo Pizarro. Fernando Pessoa's Critical Edition, Major Series, Vol. X. Lisbon: Imprensa Nacional–Casa da Moeda, 2009.

———. *Correspondência*. Edited by Manuela Parreira da Silva. Lisbon: Assírio & Alvim, 1998–1999.

———. *Cartas entre Fernando Pessoa e os directores da presença*. Edited by Enrico Martines. Fernando Pessoa's Critical Edition, Collection "Studies." Lisbon: Imprensa Nacional–Casa da Moeda, 1998.

———. *Poemas de Álvaro de Campos*. Edited by Cleonice Berardinelli. Fernando Pessoa's Critical Edition, Major Series, Vol. II. Lisbon: Imprensa Nacional–Casa da Moeda, 1990.

———. "Addiantamento." *A Revista da Solução Editora* 1, Lisbon, 1929: 4–5.

———. "Tábua bibliográfica." *Presença* 17, Lisbon, 1928: 10.

Pizarro, Jerónimo. "From FitzGerald's Omar to Pessoa's Rubaiyat." In *Fernando Pessoa's Modernity Without Frontiers*, 87–100. Edited by Mariana Gray de Castro. Woodbridge: Tamesis, 2013.

———. "Obras ortónimas e heterónimas." *Pessoa existe?* Lisbon: Ática, 2012, 73–97.

———. "Pessoa e Khayyam." *Pessoa existe?* Lisbon: Ática, 2012, 127–49.

Pizarro, Jerónimo, Patricio Ferrari, and Antonio Cardiello. *A Biblioteca particular de Fernando Pessoa (Fernando Pessoa's Private Library)*. Acervo Casa Fernando Pessoa (Fernando Pessoa House Archive), 3 vols. Lisbon: D. Quixote, 2010, Vol. I.

Quental, Antero. *Os Sonetos completos de Antero de Quental*. With a partial English translation by Fernando Pessoa. Preface to the complete sonnets by J. P. Oliveira Martins. Edition and postface by Patricio Ferrari. Lisbon: Ática, 2010.

Uribe, Jorge. "Um drama da crítica: Oscar Wilde, Walter Pater e Matthew Arnold, lidos por Fernando Pessoa." Unpublished doctoral thesis, University of Lisbon, 2014.

Weir, Thomas Hunter. *Omar Khayyám, The Poet*. London: John Murray, 1926. "The Wisdom of the East Series." CFP 8–662 MN.

Whalley, George. "Editorial Practice, Conventions, and Abbreviations." In *Marginalia of The Collected Works of Samuel Taylor Coleridge*, Vol. I, xxiii–lv. 16 vols. London: Routledge & Kegan Paul, 1980.

Zenith, Richard. "A importância de não ser Oscar? Pessoa tradutor de Wilde." *Egoísta*, special issue (June 2008): 32–36.

PATRICIO FERRARI holds a PhD in linguistics with a dissertation on Pessoa's metrics (University of Lisbon, 2012). He has joint responsibility with Jerónimo Pizarro and Antonio Cardiello for the digitization of *Fernando Pessoa's Private Library* (online since 2010) and is co-author of *A Biblioteca particular de Fernando Pessoa* (Lisbon, D. Quixote 2010), *Os Objec-*

tos de Fernando Pessoa (Lisbon, D. Quixote 2013), and Eu sou uma antologia: 136 autores fictícios (Lisbon, Tinta-da-China 2013). He also edited Fernando Pessoa's Poèmes français
(Paris, Éd. de la Différence 2014) as well as two other volumes in the New Series of Pessoa's Works (Lisbon, Ática). He has published articles on metrics, textual criticism, and
marginalia in various peer-reviewed journals (United States, United Kingdom, France,
Spain, Germany). Since 2013, he has been a postdoctoral fellow and researcher with a
grant from the Fundação para a Ciência e a Tecnologia (Center for Comparative Studies,
University of Lisbon; the Department of Portuguese and Brazilian Studies, Brown University; and the Department of English, Stockholm University). He is currently working
on Fernando Pessoa's unpublished English poetry.

He can be reached at patricio_ferrari@brown.edu

JERÓNIMO PIZARRO is professor at the Universidad de los Andes and holds the
Camões Institute Chair of Portuguese Studies in Colombia. He has a PhD in Hispanic
literatures (Harvard University, 2008) and a PhD in Portuguese linguistics (University of
Lisbon, 2006). He contributed seven volumes to the critical edition of Fernando Pessoa's
Works, published by INCM, the last volume being the first critical edition of the Livro
do Desasocego (Book of Disquietude). A Biblioteca particular de Fernando Pessoa was published by
D. Quixote in 2010. This book was prepared with Patricio Ferrari and Antonio Cardiello,
the other two coordinators involved in digitizing Pessoa's private library with the support
of Casa Fernando Pessoa. Together with Steffen Dix, he co-edited Portuguese Modernisms in
Literature and the Visual Arts (Legenda 2011). They also co-edited a special issue of Portuguese
Studies (2008) and a book of essays, A Arca de Pessoa (Pessoa's Trunk) (2007). Pizarro was
editor-in-chief of two new Ática series (Fernando Pessoa: Works; Fernando Pessoa: Studies), and he contributed to more than ten volumes. Currently, he is in charge of Tinta-
da-China's Colecção Pessoa. In 2013, he was program director of Portugal's visit to the
International Book Fair of Bogotá, and he won the Eduardo Lourenço Prize.

He can be reached at j.pizarro188@uniandes.edu.co.

Fernando Pessoa as English Reader and Writer

Key to Symbols Used in Transcriptions

In the transcription of unpublished documents by Fernando Pessoa, we employ the following symbols:

□	blank space in phrase
[ ]	line of verse left blank or incomplete
⋆	conjectural reading by the editor(s)
/ /	passage doubted by the author
†	illegible word
< >	enclosed word(s) were crossed out
< > / \	substitution by overwriting (<phrase replaced> /replacement\)
< > [↑]	substitution by crossing out and interlinear addition in line above
[↑]	interlinear addition in line above
[↓]	interlinear addition in line below
[→]	addition in the same line
|	new paragraph in prose
/	a new verse
[word]	word supplied by the editor(s)

Words underlined by Pessoa are reproduced in italics. In the case of verse, marginal line numbers in bold italic refer to genetic notes to the poem.

RICHARD ZENITH

Barrowby, Boys' Books, and How to Make Literature

ABSTRACT: In what is commonly understood to be an autobiographical note, Fernando Pessoa wrote, "Those books which are called boys' books and deal with exciting experiences I cared little for." In fact, as a young adolescent in Durban, Fernando not only read a lot of "boys' books," he also tried to write one of his own: *Os Rapazes de Barrowby* (The Boys of Barrowby) lifted its title, the names of some characters, and various structural details from *The Barrowboy Boys*, serialized in a British magazine for boys in 1903. Pessoa completely changed the story, however, and partly subverted the genre.

KEYWORDS: boys' books, Barrowby, story papers, dime novels, *O Palrador*, Durban

Fernando Pessoa's first sustained run of creative writing occurred during the yearlong holiday he spent in Portugal when he was thirteen and fourteen years old.[1] Between March and September 1902, he produced over fifteen poems,[2] most of which were included in several homemade newspapers, *O Palrador* (The Tattler) and *A Palavra* (The Word), whose neatly handwritten columns also presented stories, anecdotes, charades, real news, and invented news. All Pessoa's poems and other writings were in Portuguese—remarkably good Portuguese, when we consider that his schooling in Durban during the previous five and a half years had been in English. The various issues of the 1902 newspapers have been reproduced, partially transcribed, and discussed by Teresa Rita Lopes,[3] Darlene Sadlier,[4] and others. I will merely mention here that *O Palrador* was the more complex of the two journalistic enterprises. It entailed a large team of fictitiously named contributors and included the names of equally fictitious editors and staff writers on its masthead.

Before his trip to Portugal, Pessoa had written at least one poem in English, "Separated from Thee,"[5] and after returning to Durban, in October 1902, he continued to write in English—almost exclusively. Anglophone preheteronyms[6] such as David Merrick, Sidney Parkinson Stool, and Charles Robert Anon emerged in 1903. On July 11, 1903, in the *Natal Mercury*, Pessoa published his first English poem, "The Miner's Song," attributed to Karl P. Effield, a preheteronym supposedly born in Boston.[7] And then, out of the blue, in that same month of July, he revived *O Palrador*, which continued to be a strictly Portuguese production, though it now resembled a magazine more than a newspaper. The masthead, in fact, advertised it as a "periódico mensal" (monthly periodical).[8] Exactly one year had passed since the last issue, made in Lisbon and dated July 5, 1902, and almost everything about the new series was different. Some of the names on the masthead remained, but their titles and duties had changed. Dr. Pancracio, literary editor of the last 1902 issue, became the pseudonym of a new staff member, Francisco Páu, responsible for the humor section. Pad Zé, formerly the pseudonym of Pedro da Silva Salles, was now the pen name of Roberto Kóla, in charge of riddles. There were nine other editors and subeditors, one handling a sports section and another a short story section. The elaborate editorial scaffold was probably conceived with future issues in mind, but these never materialized. Volume 1, Issue 1 of the new *O Palrador* was the only issue. And Pessoa wrote virtually nothing else in Portuguese until he returned to Lisbon for good, in 1905.

The Durban issue of *O Palrador* appears to be the only example of Portuguese creative writing produced by Pessoa during the years he spent in South Africa. But upon inspection, it turns out to be a conceptually English production. An introductory editor's page, signed by Silva Salles, announces the first installments of *Quatro romances interessantíssimos* (Four Fascinating Novels), a series of "pequenos contos militares" (military short stories), and other articles "de bastante interesse" (of considerable interest).[9] No articles and no army tales were written, and only two of the four promised serial novels commenced "publication." The most interesting one, *Os Rapazes de Barrowby*, subtitled *Crónica Humorística* (Humorous Story) and signed by Adolph Moscow, is about the amusing but also violent interaction of students at a boys' boarding school in an English town called Barrowby. The first chapter, to which I will return, describes the village and the school named after it. The second and last chapter of the installment narrates the rude reception that three veteran students give to several new arrivals. The story has been the object of differing critical treatments, and I will summarize some of the resulting observations and interpretations before presenting hypotheses and conclusions from my own research.

Hubert Dudley Jennings, who revealed the existence of the Durban *O Palrador*,[10] initially reported that the Barrowby School, although fictionally situated in England, exactly fit the description of Durban High School (D H S), where Pessoa studied from 1899 to 1901 and again in 1904.[11] Jennings subsequently backed off on that assertion, admitting that Pessoa had changed some details and added an astronomical observatory,[12] but he continued to view *Os Rapazes de Barrowby* as an autobiographical transposition. According to his reading, the Barrowby headmaster was a composite of the headmaster of D H S and the director of the Commercial School (where Pessoa studied in 1903), while the abuse endured by Zacharias, a new Barrowby student who is Jewish, was a caricature of what Fernando himself had endured.[13] The *Barrowby* narrator explains, for his ideal Portuguese reader, several particulars of English boys' schools, including the use of boxing as the only respectable form of fighting among students. Though the tradition of *fagging*—whereby younger schoolboys act as servants (*fags*) for the older boys—is not explained, it is illustrated by the authoritarian attitude of the older students toward Zacharias and other newcomers. Pessoa's knowledge and possible firsthand experience of fagging, as revealed by his story, led Yara Frateschi Vieira to propose it as a seed for sadomasochistic scenes in poems such as Álvaro de Campos's *Ode marítima* (*Maritime Ode*).[14]

Jennings also called attention to Pessoa's ostensibly Dickensian humor,[15] a point focused and expanded on by António Sabler, who argued that the juvenile writer's love of *The Pickwick Papers* inspired the comic descriptions of his *Barrowby* characters.[16] Sabler also found puns at work in some of the students' names, such as Godfrey Slater ("god free is later") and Donald Dowson ("Donald [wi] dow son"). In the latter name, Sabler posited a linguistic projection of Pessoa's status as the son of a mother who became a widow when he was five years old.[17]

In a chapter tracing the development of Pessoa's interest in physiognomy, phrenology, and other sciences "of the minute" grouped under "microsophy" (a Pessoan coinage), Jerónimo Pizarro offers *Barrowby* as the first example of a literary text in which the young writer mentions and exploits physiognomy.[18] Adolph Moscow, the fictitious author of *Barrowby*, refers directly to Johann Kaspar Lavater (1741–1801), the pioneering promoter of physiognomy in modern times, in order to justify reading the personalities of the Barrowby schoolboys in their facial features. Blue eyes, for instance, are said to indicate forthrightness.[19] Moscow does not associate Zacharias's large, stork-like nose with any personality trait, but Pizarro stresses the fact that Pessoa would become especially interested in the physiognomic importance of the nose. Because Pessoa's partly Jewish heritage was detectable in the shape of his own nose (so one of his

Jewish friends told him in 1913), Pizarro allows for a possible autobiographical connection between Zacharias's less than warm welcome by veteran Barrowby students and Fernando's own reception at Durban High School.[20]

Aníbal Frias, after reviewing and critiquing the contributions of the four scholars just named, remarks on the insufficient attention paid to what he considers the central theme: "un rituel de praxe entre collégiens" (a ritual of praxis among students).[21] Praxis encompasses initiation and other student rituals practiced at Portuguese institutions of higher learning, particularly at the University of Coimbra.[22] Frias's discussion of Barrowby is contained in an article on the relationship of Pessoa to Coimbra, but its relevance, as far as I can tell, is tangential. There is a slight connection between Coimbra and O Palrador, because Pad Zé (a corruption of "Padre José")—one of the names on the masthead, as previously noted—was the nickname of Alberto Costa (1877–1908), a law student at the University of Coimbra who became famous for his bohemian extravagance and quick wit. He would publish a best-selling book about his university days in 1905 and become a militant republican, but he had founded a satirical student magazine, Revista do Civil, as early as 1899 and achieved some notoriety by the time Pessoa founded O Palrador in Lisbon. The Durban issue of O Palrador had a "Director Artístico" (artistic director) whose name, Alberto Rey da Costa, may have been derived from the real name of the Pad Zé from Coimbra. There is no substantive link, however, between Coimbra and Os Rapazes de Barrowby. According to its fictional setting and to the explicit indications of Adolph Moscow, Barrowby is a story of social behaviors among English high school students. And Frias confirms this, pointing out that the atmosphere, rituals, and hierarchical relations are those of a British public school ("public" insofar as they are open to whoever can pay the tuition and fees). He suggests that Barrowby could be a hybrid name combining Harrow and Rugby, two prominent public schools.[23] He notes as well that the term newbie (a "new boy" at a public school) might be encoded in the novel's title, if we translate it into English: The Boys of Barrowby.[24]

Frias provides a thorough account of how all the Barrowby banter, name calling, and acts of violence fit into the institution of fagging as practiced at British public schools. He does not speculate on where Pessoa obtained his information—whether through reading or through direct experience—or on what motivated him to mold it into a story. If, as Jennings asserts, the experience was largely autobiographical, then that would explain both the source of Pessoa's knowledge and his motivation for converting it into literature. The problem is that DHS, back in those days, was a far cry from a British boys' boarding school such as the one described by Moscow. Only a quarter of the DHS students were boarders; the system of organizing the boys into various "houses" was introduced only in 1902 (one year after Pessoa left the school for Portugal); and testimonies from the period suggest there was not yet any formalized hierarchical division of students, much less any tradition of fagging or ritualized bullying.[25]

The Durban *O Palrador* defined itself as a magazine rather than a newspaper, but what sort of magazine did it aim to be? Its format and planned contents—which included military short stories as well as serialized novels such as *Os Rapazes de Barrowby*—reminded me specifically of the "story papers" or boys' magazines that became popular in Victorian Great Britain, spread to the United States and elsewhere, and endured until the 1960s. Further, *Os Rapazes de Barrowby* struck me as a Pessoan take on a typical boys' adventure story from the period. It occurred to me that it might actually be a doctored translation from the English, particularly because *The Boys of Barrowby* is a likely sounding title, as Frias noticed. On the Internet I quickly discovered a novel with that same title, published serially in forty-seven issues of *The Boys' Friend* magazine, beginning in April of 1903. Because it took a month for British publications to reach Durban, Pessoa could have read no more than ten installments (the eleventh was published on June 20) when he began writing his own Portuguese version for *O Palrador*. But how much of *The Boys of Barrowby*, beyond its title, did Pessoa steal? None of the forty-seven issues of *The Boys' Friend* where it was serialized is consultable online, but I managed to obtain a reproduction of the complete novel, published in 1908 as Volume 50 of *The Boys' Friend Library*.[26]

Os Rapazes de Barrowby is not a translation or even a remake of the original *The Boys of Barrowby*, which was signed by Sidney Drew, a pseudonym of Edgar Joyce Murray. Pessoa preserved the story's title, its setting, the division of Barrowby School into two rival houses, and the names of certain characters, along with a few of their salient traits, but he radically altered its plot and literary style. Donald and Richard Dowson, students and identical twins in Drew's novel, feature in Pessoa's as Donald and Ricardo Dowson. A classmate named George Honey becomes Mel, but this is only a nickname, which Moscow explains by noting that the boy has a sweet tooth. Moscow gives Mel's real name as Henry Ford. (This was a rather precocious nod at the carmaker, who had founded the Ford Motor Company just one month earlier, in June of 1903, and who did not come out with the Model T until 1908. Pessoa would write about and repeatedly allude to Ford in his adult writings.) Another school chum is called Slater in both stories, but Pessoa endows him with a first name, Godfrey, and a nickname: Gyp. A Chinese student christened Ching-Lung by Drew is inversely called Lung-Hi in Portuguese. He is a Chinese prince in both stories but holds center stage in The Boys of Barrowby, which is subtitled The Story of Ching Lung's Schooldays. Adult names are also translated. A teacher named Mr. Flint becomes Senhor Pedra, and the screw in Drew's Admiral Screwhamer is evoked in Pessoa's Almirante Saca-rolhas (Admiral Corkscrew).

The Boys of Barrowby is full of student pranks and scuffles, with some mention of fags and fagging, but with no scenes of incoming students being subjected to hazing; quite the contrary. Drew's story opens with the arrival of Ching-Lung, whose social acceptance and integration among his schoolmates is instantaneous. (He is, after all, a prince.) Os Rapazes de Barrowby is a different story. The second chapter is specifically about the harassment that Mel (Henry Ford), Lung-Hi, and Gyp (Slater) mete out to the large-nosed Jewish boy, whose full name is Zacharias Phumtumpum, and to another youngster named Ralph Tig. Both boys are newcomers to the school and newcomers to the fictional cast of characters, with no corresponding prototypes in the British Ur-story. Zacharias is intimidated but not roughed up, except for a single, ritual punch in the nose; and Ralph, refusing to be intimidated, fights Gyp and gets the better of him. It is possible that Fernando, timid and not at all athletic, was teased by other students at DHS, and perhaps knocked around by older boys, in which case Ralph may have served as a vehicle for him to get at least some literary revenge. But it seems doubtful that Fernando identified with Zacharias, who is portrayed as a ridiculous specimen of a racist Jewish stereotype. The boy is covered with phony jewelry: three fake diamond and gold rings, a gold-painted tie clasp decorated with a fake emerald, and a fake silver pocket watch.[27] If autobiography is at work here, then it is almost surely by way of denial, with Pessoa establishing a distance between his own, considerably diluted Jewishness (ancestors on his father's side) and the unflattering caricature he draws of a "real" Jew.

Whether Pessoa was actually a victim of intimidation and hazing—and there is no concrete evidence to that effect—he would have known about the practices at schools like Harrow and Rugby precisely through his readings of other serialized novels for boys. School life, in this juvenile genre, was naturally one of the major themes. And Pessoa, from early on, had the habit of schooling his readers. He used his story, as Frias has pointed out, to expound on some of the traditions of British public schools.

Pessoa also used his reinvented *Barrowby* to convey, or perhaps to show off, his newly acquired awareness of physiognomy. Pizarro is surely right to reckon that this story contains Pessoa's first reference to this technique for discovering personality. In a small memo book from his Durban years, Pessoa noted the selling price of Lavater's *Essays in Physiognomy* at Adams & Co., a Durban bookstore that still exists.[28] That was probably in late 1903 or 1904—judging by other notations on the same folio (including a list of characters for the story "The Case of the Science Master" and a signature for Charles Robert Anon)—but perhaps he had leafed through *Essays* in mid-1903, right before launching into his serial novel. Pessoa-qua-Moscow mentions not only Lavater but also a second physiognomist, an Englishman named Kisch (1821–1843), who is himself a fiction. Not only that, but the nonexistent Kisch gets a much more detailed footnote than Lavater.[29] Jorge Luis Borges would no doubt have approved.

The first chapter of Pessoa's serial novel, which has received less critical attention than the second, is just as entertaining and stylistically more characteristic. Pessoa, or Adolph Moscow, takes up several pages lamenting how much time and eyesight he has lost poring over atlases, maps, and books in an unsuccessful effort to discover the exact whereabouts of the "célebre aldeia de Barrowby" (well-known village of Barrowby).[30] Not that it really matters, finally, for Moscow is completely indifferent to "se a povoação de Barrowby se tivesse achado situada na Europa, ou na Ásia, ou na África, ou na América, ou na Oceânia, ou nas profundidades caóticas do inferno dantesco" (whether the village of Barrowby is located in Europe, in Asia, in Africa, in America, in Oceania, or in the chaotic depths of Dante's inferno).[31] For the sake of the story, he arbitrarily supposes that Barrowby is an English village not far from Brighton, being served by a port town "ao qual chamaremos Lynmouth" (that we will call Lynmouth).[32] Contrary to what that "chamaremos" (we will call) suggests, Lynmouth indeed exists on the coast a little west of Brighton. Moscow invents a location for a town about which he knows only the name (Barrowby), and he *pretends* to invent the name and location of a town about which he knows both things (Lynmouth). It's as if Pessoa were already rehearsing his poetics of *fingimento* (feigning), whereby even unquestionable reality is feigned or pretended.

The narrator's disdain of geographical detail is not surprising, given the scant attention Pessoa paid to the factual particulars of the many destinations

21

he imaginatively visited, but Pessoa must have undertaken at least some of the humorously described research to try to locate Barrowby. Without a good gazetteer at his disposal, he failed to find the village, which is in Lincolnshire County, near Nottingham, and he apparently concluded that Sidney Drew had dreamed up the place name. And he may have concluded correctly. Or, more probably, Drew had heard the name but, like Pessoa, didn't worry too much about exactly where it was. Drew situates Barrowby near two invented towns called Fapnell and Zetfield,[33] and states, in the opening scene, that several Barrowby schoolboys "could hear the musical whisper of the River Barrow as it glided towards the sea."[34] There is a River Barrow in Ireland, but none in England, and no river glides by the real village of Barrowby, which is far from the sea. Curiously, Pessoa would commit his own Barrow error many years later, when he wrote a five-sonnet sequence titled "Barrow-on-Furness" and signed by Álvaro de Campos, who is supposedly gazing at the Furness River while giving poetic expression to his existential anguish. In fact, no such river exists. Furness is a peninsula, and the correct name of the town is Barrow-in-Furness.[35]

In the same way that Pessoa, particularly as a developing writer, often used someone else's poem as his starting point to produce a very different and, with luck, superior poetic composition,[36] he took a preexisting serial novel and gutted it. He retained the title, some names, and a few structural props; but he shifted the perspective, changed the tone, added a quasi-philosophical preamble (if it has no other reality, "a aldeia de Barrowby existirá, pelo menos, nesta crónica" [the village of Barrowby will exist at least in this story], Moscow assures us[37]), delineated the characters with the aid of physiognomy, and inserted learned footnotes about this dubious science and other matters. A simple story relying on slapstick humor acquires, in Pessoa's transformation, an erudite narrator with vaguely sociological as well as philosophical pretensions. It is a largely tongue-in-cheek performance, however, written to entertain, and in the end it even resorts to a classic gag, with Gyp taking a calamitous slide on a banana peel.

Various scholars, as noted earlier, have looked at *Os Rapazes de Barrowby* from contrasting points of view, affording us a critical picture of reasonable complexity. I hope to have elucidated a few points as well, but we may all be at risk of overinterpreting. Pessoa, after all, was going for laughs, and he probably had a specific audience in mind: his immediate family. After "The Miner's Song" was printed in early July 1903, it is likely that Pessoa's parents, while enthusiastically congratulating him, also encouraged him to keep up his creative writing in Portuguese, perhaps reminding him of the mock newspapers he had created in Lisbon (O Palrador) and the Azores (A Palavra). Whatever it was that prompted Fernando to produce another issue of O Palrador, he must have shown it to his parents and siblings, for he used several blank pages in the middle of the in-progress periodical to keep score for a parlor game in which they all participated. Called "Derby," the game mimicked the Durban July Handicap, held on the first Saturday of that month. The July Handicap was and is South Africa's premier horse race. "Derby," played with dice, was Fernando's invention.[38] The family members were assigned different-colored horses, mounted by jockeys with names such as Clumsy Dick, Yreka Jim, and Tom Wallis.[39] The last of these names belongs to the protagonist of Tom Wallis: A Tale of the South Seas, a boys' adventure book published by Louis Becke in 1900. Yreka Jim is the protagonist of Yreka Jim: The Gold-Gatherer, Yreka Jim of Yuba Dam, and several other serialized boys' books.

In an autobiographical text probably written in 1907, Pessoa wrote (in English), "The earliest literary food of my childhood was in the numerous novels of mystery and of horrible adventure. Those books which are called boys' books and deal with exciting experiences I cared little for. With a healthy and natural life I was out of sympathy. My craving was not for the probable, but for the incredible, not even for the impossible by degree, but for the impossible by nature." Pessoa went on to say that he recognized in himself from an early age "an inborn tendency to mystification, to artistic lying."[40] This confessed tendency was acted on in the same text, because the writer falsely claims to have been uninterested in boys' books. In fact, Sidney Drew's The Boys of Barrowby fits squarely in the genre, and allusions to characters such as Yreka Jim and Tom Wallis suggest that he read many other similar works, both in book form and in juvenile periodicals such as The Boys' Friend. There is no evidence that Pessoa preferred novels "of horrible adventure." And wasn't his favorite novel, The Pickwick Papers, a kind of boys' book for grown-ups?

The other serial novel partially written for O Palrador is titled Os Milhões dum doido (A Madman's Millions) and signed by Marvell Kisch (a descendant of Kisch, the fictitious physiognomist?). The first and only chapter produced describes a snowy night in an aristocratic neighborhood of London, where two wealthy women—one older, one younger—exit their mansion to enter a fancy coach, at which point they are accosted by a beggar, with a baby in her arms, whom they haughtily rebuff. Jennings senses the influence of *Bleak House* in this sad wintry scene,[41] but to me, the story reads suspiciously like a Portuguese translation of the opening pages of yet another English boys' book, or possibly a girls' book. In *Os Rapazes de Barrowby*, we can feel that Pessoa's Portuguese is occasionally contaminated by English syntax;[42] in *Os Milhões* we find entire sentences directly imported from English: for instance, "Eles discutiam a advisibilidade de ter bife com cebolas para a ceia"[43] (They were discussing the advisability of having steak and onions for supper). It is conceivable that Pessoa was mocking the "lofty" tone found in a certain register of English speech, but it was unlike him to portray narrative scenes with so much carefully coordinated physical detail.

The third and fourth novels promised by the editor in *O Palrador*'s prefatory note to readers—*Em Dias de Perigo* (*In Days of Danger*) by Gabriel Keene, and *A Luta Aérea* (*The Aerial Fight*) by Sableton Kay—may also have been inspired by British (or American) models, a supposition bolstered by the English-sounding names of their unreal authors. Despite a certain appetite for the literature of story papers and dime novels (to be succeeded, in his adult years, by crime novels), Pessoa had no interest in or talent for writing effective but commonplace descriptions of rich nobles in their well-cushioned coaches and poor people shivering in the cold on snowy winter nights. His inclination, conspicuous in his spin-off of *The Barrowby Boys*—and in keeping with the thesis of "adverse," or subverted, genres recently advanced by K. David Jackson—was to transgress the traditional rules and expectations of storytelling.

Fernando had no qualms about filching a few ideas, characters, and even entire sentences from British serial novels, but an aesthetic if not ethical scruple seems to have prevented him from signing his own name to the stories that resulted from his borrowings. Though they were written in Portuguese, he preferred to attribute their authorship to fictive Englishmen such as Adolph Moscow and Marvell Kisch. (The two first names are English, and a few Durbanites were surnamed Kisch, as I discovered by consulting *The Natal Alamanac, Directory and Yearly Register* for 1897 through 1905.) It was as if counterfeit authorship served, paradoxically, as a seal of authenticity for the writing itself, with Pessoa acting as the translator of what Moscow and Kisch purportedly authored. However much he reworked or reinvented them, Pessoa's serialized novels belonged to an Anglo-American genre, a fact he apparently wished to emphasize. And perhaps he did not want his own name to be associated with the tradition of boys' books—a tradition he seemed to disdain in the aforecited autobiographical text written just four years later, in 1907.

Whatever their inspiration, Moscow and Kisch are atypical of Pessoa's pseudoauthors. Even though Moscow has a definite narrative posture that affects the tone and framing of his story, it is perhaps better not to count him or Kisch as heteronyms, preheteronyms, or fictitious personalities.[44] They were one-offs, without biographical substance, whose narrative existence began and ended with their respective stories.

NOTES

1. Pessoa arrived at Durban, South Africa, in February of 1896 with his mother, who had recently married Portugal's consul to that city. It was there that Pessoa lived and studied until July of 1901, when he embarked with his new family—which included children by the second marriage—for an extended holiday in Portugal, where they arrived in August. He returned to Durban on his own, a few months after the rest of the family, in October of 1902, and stayed there until August of 1905, when he made his final, month-long voyage back to Lisbon, where he enrolled in the Curso Superior de Letras. He completed his studies at Durban High School (Form VI) in December of 1904. See Alexandrino E. Severino, *Fernando Pessoa na África do Sul* (Lisbon: D. Quixote, 1983) and Jennings, *Os dois exílios: Fernando Pessoa na África do Sul* (Oporto: Centro de Estudos Pessoanos & Fundação Eng.º António de Almeida, 1984) for detailed information on Pessoa's Durban years.

2. Eighteen poems from this period—all written in Portuguese—can be found in Pessoa, *Obra essencial de Fernando Pessoa*, Vol. 2, ed. R. Zenith (Lisbon: Assírio & Alvim, 2006), 455–68, but it might make more sense to classify one of them, "Enigma," as a rhymed riddle rather than a bonafide poem. Two additional poems in Portuguese, written almost certainly in 1902, were transcribed and published by Jerónimo Pizarro in Fernando Pessoa, *Cadernos*, Vol. I (Lisbon: INCM, 2009), 108–9.

3. Teresa Rita Lopes, *Pessoa por conhecer* (Lisbon: Estampa, 1990), Vol. I, 89–96 ; Vol. II, 130–55.

4. Darlene J. Sadlier, *An Introduction to Fernando Pessoa: Modernism and the Paradoxes of Authorship* (Gainesville: University of Florida Press, 1998), 9–26.

5. "Separated from thee" was the first poem written in Pessoa's own hand, on May 12, 1901 (BNP/E3,16A–48; Pessoa, *Obra poética* 1960, 621). This same date has repeatedly and erroneously been attributed to the poem "Anamnesis," which belongs to *The Mad Fiddler* and was written on August 29, 1915.

6. *Preheteronyms* is a scholarly coinage for referring to literary personae invented by Pessoa before the emergence of his full-fledged heteronyms, in 1914.

7. See the "Tábua de heterónimos e outros autores fictícios," in Pessoa, *Teoria da heteronímia* (Lisbon: Assírio & Alvim, 2012), 39–110, for a chronological account of Pessoa's fictional authors and a description of their works. Pessoa, *Eu sou uma antologia: 136 autores fictícios* (Lisbon: Tinta-da-China, 2013) provides an account with additional information, additional names, and samples of their literary texts. A transcription of "The Miner's Song" was published in R. Zenith, "Karl P. Effield: O pré-heterónimo de Boston," *LER*, Feb. 2011 (Lisbon), 39, and a facsimile of the original newspaper publication in R. Zenith and J. Vieira, *Fotobiografia de Fernando Pessoa* (São Paulo: Companhia das Letras, 2011), 65. The poem can also be found in Pessoa, *Eu sou uma antologia: 136 autores fictícios*, 114–15.

8. BNP/E3, 144R–1; Fernando Pessoa, *Cadernos*, I, ed. Jerónimo Pizarro (Lisbon: Imprensa Nacional–Casa da Moeda, 2009), 69.

9. BNP/E3, 144R–1ᵛ; Pessoa, *Cadernos*, I, 69–70.

10. According to António Sabler, "The Man Who Liked Dickens," *Persona* 9 (Oct. 1983, Oporto), 47, an article by Jennings that appeared in *O Século*, Aug. 31, 1968 (Lisbon) is virtually identical to the one he published a year later in *Colóquio Artes e Letras* (Jennings, 1969). I consulted only the latter.

11. Hubert Dudley Jennings, "Alguns aspectos da vida de Fernando Pessoa na África do Sul," *Colóquio Artes e Letras* 52 (Feb. 1969, Lisbon), 65.

12. Jennings, *Os dois exílios: Fernando Pessoa na África do Sul* (Oporto: Centro de Estudos Pessoanos & Fundação Eng.º António de Almeida, 1984), 82.

13. Ibid., 83–84.

14. Yara Frateschi Vieira, *Sob o ramo da bétula: Fernando Pessoa e o erotismo Vitoriano* (Campinas: UNICAMP, 1989), 23–24.

15. Jennings, *Os dois exílios*, 80–81.

16. Sabler, "The Man Who Liked Dickens," 47–48.

17. Ibid., 48.

18. Jerónimo Pizarro, *Fernando Pessoa: Entre génio e loucura* (Lisbon: Imprensa Nacional–Casa da Moeda, 2007), 17–23.

19. BNP/E3, 144R–6; Pessoa, *Cadernos*, I, 74.

20. Pizarro, 21–23.

21. Aníbal Frias, "Pessoa à Coimbra et Coimbra dans Pessoa," *Biblos: Revista da Faculdade de Letras, Universidade de Coimbra*, Vol. 7 (2009), 372.

22. Founded in 1290 in Lisbon, the university moved to Coimbra in 1308. Portugal's other universities, most founded only in the twentieth century, are less steeped in tradition.

23. Frias, 373.

24. Ibid.

25. See E. A. Belcher and G. C. Collins, *The Durban High School Record 1866–1906* (Durban: John Singleton, 1906), 56–58.

26. Information on the story's serialization can be found at http://www.philsp.com/ homeville/fmi/s1129.htm and http://www.philsp.com/homeville/fmi/t508.htm. Information for the complete novel is at http://www.friardale.co.uk/BFL/Series%201/BFL_Series1 .htm. Professor Vincent Barletta kindly obtained and sent me a reproduction of the work, which is included in Stanford University's dime novel and story paper collection.

27. BNP/E3, 144R–7; Pessoa, *Cadernos*, I (2009), 75.

28. BNP/E3, 279D²–26ᵛ. The bookstore is located at 341 West Street, Durban.

29. BNP/E3, 144R–6ʳ; Pessoa, *Cadernos*, I, 74.

30. BNP/E3, 144R–2; Pessoa, *Cadernos*, I, 70.

31. BNP/E3, 144R–3; Pessoa, *Cadernos*, I, 71.

32. BNP/E3, 144R–3ᵛ; Pessoa, *Cadernos*, I, 72.

33. Sidney Drew, *The Boys of Barrowby* (London: Amalgamated Press, 1908), 3–4.

34. Ibid., 2.

35. The original manuscript of the Campos sonnets has been lost, and it is quite possible that Pessoa's posthumous publishers (*Poesias de Álvaro de Campos*, Lisbon: Ática, 1944) misread "in-Furness" or miscorrected it to "on-Furness." Indeed, "Barrow-in-Furness" is correctly spelled on a surviving publication plan drawn up by Pessoa (BNP/ E3, 87–95a) as well as in an open letter (with replies to a literary survey) signed by Álvaro de Campos—who refers to the time he spent in Barrow-in-Furness—and published in *A Informação*, a Lisbon newspaper, in 1926. But the geographical mistake remains. However Pessoa spelled the name of the town, references in the sonnets indicate that he believed Furness to be a river that flowed past it. See also George Monteiro, *Fernando Pessoa and Nineteenth-Century Anglo-American Literature* (Lexington: University Press of Kentucky, 2000), 33–35.

36. In 1902, for instance, he wrote the sonnet "Antígona," whose title was inspired by a letter of Shelley, and whose verses were a kind of "correction" of Elizabeth Barrett Browning's sonnet "How do I love thee? Let me count the ways." See Zenith, "A Sonnet from the English—Fernando Pessoa: 'Antígona'" (2013), 169–75.

37. BNP/E3, 144R–3ᵛ; Pessoa, *Cadernos*, I, 72.

38. Jennings, *Os dois exílios*, 114–15.

39. BNP/E3, 144R–10ᵛ; Pessoa, *Cadernos*, I, 79.

40. BNP/E3, 20–10; Pessoa, *Páginas íntimas e de auto-interpretação*, eds. Georg Rudolf Lind and Jacinto do Prado Coelho (Lisbon: Ática, 1966), 11–12. It is possible that the cited passage is autobiographical of Alexander Search rather than of Pessoa. Although the passage is not exactly signed by Search, his signature appears more than once in a corner of the manuscript, suggesting that Pessoa—who often practiced his heteronymic signatures in the margins of his texts—was in Search mode, or mood. Search's personality traits, though based on Pessoa's, were fewer in number and more sharply defined, more

accentuated. On October 2, 1907, Search signs a pact with the devil (BNP/E3, 20–93; Pessoa, *Páginas íntimas*, 10), something Pessoa would surely not do in his own name, and one could argue that it was he—not Pessoa himself—who claimed to be attracted to mystery and horror in literature.

41. Jennings, *Os dois exílios*, 80.

42. Sabler, "The Man Who Liked Dickens," 47–48.

43. BNP/E3, 144R–13; Pessoa, *Cadernos*, I, 82.

44. In a text datable to some time after 1923 and probably intended for a preface to his heteronymic works, Pessoa used the term "personalidades fictícias" to signify the imaginary playmates and alter egos he began inventing already as a child (BNP/E3, 20–74; Pessoa, *Teoria da heteronímia* [Lisbon: Assírio & Alvim, 2012], 231).

WORKS CITED

Belcher, Ernest Albert, and G. Clinton Collins. *The Durban High School Record 1866–1906*. Durban: John Singleton & Sons, 1906.

Drew, Sidney. *The Boys of Barrowby*. London: Amalgamated Press, 1908.

Frias, Aníbal. "Pessoa à Coimbra et Coimbra dans Pessoa." *Biblos: Revista da Faculdade de Letras, Universidade de Coimbra* 7, 2009: 363–87.

Jackson, K. David. *Adverse Genres in Fernando Pessoa*. New York: Oxford University Press, 2010.

Jennings, Hubert Dudley. "Alguns aspectos da vida de Fernando Pessoa na África do Sul." *Colóquio Artes e Letras* 52, Lisbon, Feb. 1969: 64–69.

———. *Os dois exílios: Fernando Pessoa na África do Sul*. Oporto: Centro de Estudos Pessoanos & Fundação Eng.º António de Almeida, 1984.

Lopes, Teresa Rita. *Pessoa por conhecer*. 2 vols. Lisbon: Estampa, 1990.

Monteiro, George. *Fernando Pessoa and Nineteenth-Century Anglo-American Literature*. Lexington: University Press of Kentucky, 2000.

Pessoa, Fernando. *Obra poética*. Edited, introduced, and notes by Maria Aliete Dores Galhoz. Rio de Janeiro: José Aguilar, 1960.

———. *Páginas íntimas e de auto-interpretação*. Edited by Georg Rudolf Lind and Jacinto do Prado Coelho. Lisbon: Ática, 1966.

———. *Obra essencial de Fernando Pessoa*. 7 vols. Edited by Richard Zenith. Lisbon: Assírio & Alvim, 2006.

———. *Cadernos*. Edited by Jerónimo Pizarro. Fernando Pessoa's Critical Edition, Major Series, Vol. XI, Tome I. Lisbon: Imprensa Nacional–Casa da Moeda, 2009.

———. *Teoria da heteronímia*. Edited by Fernando Cabral Martins and Richard Zenith. Lisbon: Assírio & Alvim, 2012.

————. *Eu sou uma antologia: 136 autores fictícios*. Edited by Jerónimo Pizarro and Patricio Ferrari. Lisbon: Tinta-da-China, 2013. Pessoa Collection coordinated by Jerónimo Pizarro.

Pizarro, Jerónimo. *Fernando Pessoa: Entre génio e loucura*. Fernando Pessoa's Critical Edition, Collection "Studies," Vol. III. Lisbon: Imprensa Nacional–Casa da Moeda, 2007.

Sabler, António. "The Man Who Liked Dickens." *Persona* 9, Oporto, Oct. 1983: 47–65.

Sadlier, Darlene J. *An Introduction to Fernando Pessoa: Modernism and the Paradoxes of Authorship*. Gainesville: University Press of Florida, 1998.

Severino, Alexandrino E. *Fernando Pessoa na África do Sul*. Lisbon: D. Quixote, 1983.

Vieira, Yara Frateschi. *Sob o ramo da bétula: Fernando Pessoa e o erotismo Vitoriano*. Campinas: UNICAMP, 1989.

Zenith, Richard. "Karl P. Effield: O Pré-heterónimo de Boston." *LER*, Lisbon, Feb. 2011: 36–40.

————. "A Sonnet from the English—Fernando Pessoa: 'Antígona.'" In *Reading Literature in Portuguese: Commentaries in Honour of Tom Earl*, 169–75. Edited by Cláudia Pazos Alonso and Stephen Parkinson (London: Legenda, 2013).

RICHARD ZENITH, an American by birth but a longtime resident of Lisbon, works as a freelance writer, translator, researcher, and critic. His recent publications include, as an editor, *Fernando Pessoa & Ofélia Queiroz—Correspondência amorosa completa, 1919–1935* (Rio de Janeiro: Capivara, 2013) and *Mensagem e outros poemas sobre Portugal*, by Fernando Pessoa (ed. with Fernando Cabral Martins; Lisbon: Assírio & Alvims, 2014); and, as a translator, *Multitudinous Heart: Selected Poems of Carlos Drummond de Andrade* (New York: Farrar, Straus and Giroux, forthcoming). He is writing a biography of Fernando Pessoa.

He can be reached at rzenith@gmail.com.

STEFAN HELGESSON

Pessoa, Anon, and the Natal Colony
Retracing an Imperial Matrix

ABSTRACT: Fernando Pessoa's years in Durban (1896–1905) have often been side-lined by critics. Conversely, the memory and reception of Pessoa in South Africa have been slight, sustained by only a few individuals. By contextualizing Pessoa's placement in the historically peculiar Natal Colony, and by reading some early work by Pessoa's English literary persona Charles Robert Anon against the backdrop of the Anglo-Boer War (1899–1902), this article adds to the emergent understanding of the Durban years as deeply formative for Pessoa's work. It is here, not least, that we can trace the early formation of the imperial view of history that also becomes a strange limitation to his thinking. The "empire" as a frame of reference, an object of desire, a cause for ridicule, and a lofty ideal, recurs repeatedly in Pessoa's writing, and even when Anon expresses severe criticism of British imperial conduct, he remains beholden to an imperial optic, almost by default restricted to a white outlook on events in southern Africa. We find thereby in the early work the makings of an imperial ambivalence that is then dispersed and refracted through multiple poetic voices in Pessoa's oeuvre.

KEYWORDS: Fernando Pessoa, Charles Robert Anon, Roy Campbell, Natal Colony, Anglo-Boer War, imperialism

This article is written under the shadow of a double elusiveness. One concerns the traces of Fernando Pessoa in South Africa, the other the traces of South Africa in Fernando Pessoa. To what extent, we must ask ourselves, do the two cross paths in a meaningful way?

The external facts are familiar enough: after his mother remarried, Pessoa's family settled in Durban, where his stepfather worked in the Portuguese consulate. Between 1896 and 1905, young Fernando would live in this subtropical coastal town, with a population of under 30,000 at the time. He attended, famously, Durban High School (DHS), a boys' school founded in 1866. At the age of seventeen, having failed to secure an Oxford scholarship, Pessoa returned to Portugal, where he lived for the remaining thirty years of his life.[1]

In other words, Pessoa the individual intersects with South Africa during the most impressionable years of any young person's life. And yet a common impression has been that little remains of this experience, both in public memory in South Africa and in the work of Pessoa himself. The poet Roy Campbell (1901–1957), probably the first of the few South Africans who have publicized Pessoa's significance as a poet to an English-speaking audience, even saw this period as completely immaterial to Pessoa's work: "His ten years in Durban, where he learnt the English language so well, that he had no trace of a colonial accent, and where he stripped most of the school-prizes from his British colonial competitors, left absolutely no trace on his writings except that he corresponded for twenty years with his friend, Mr. Ormond."[2]

Campbell was himself a Durbanite and a DHS boy, and some of the most evocative passages in his sketch of Pessoa's life concern his own recollections of early twentieth-century Durban. He remembers that the name "F. Pessoa" was carved into the lid of his own desk at DHS, and waxes nostalgic about the city of yore:

Nowhere in the world were there more beautiful gardens, though most of the houses had ugly corrugated iron roofs. In those days, each house reposed amidst several acres of fruit trees and flowers. Flowering trees, Jacaranda, Tulip-trees, Flame-trees, Golden Shower, Flamboyants, Kaffirboom (the most brilliant of all) and Mimosa succeed each other throughout the year (like phoenixes taking fire from each others ashes) to culminate in the gorgeous blaze of the winter-flowering Kaffirboom [a contentious name; now it is called "coral tree"]. As the Pessoas were neighbours of ours, on the Berea, they must have had a house and garden very much like ours.[3]

This is about as close as we will get to the sensuous immediacy of young Pessoa's surroundings in Durban. In his own work, "impersonal" from the beginning, the city is mostly filtered out, displaced, or transcoded, hence lending credence to the perception that Durban left no, or at least very few, traces on his writing. (A rare exception would be the late poem "Un Soir à Lima," with its powerful evocation of a domestic interior in Durban.)[4]

Against this, given not only our more detailed and thorough understanding of Pessoa's oeuvre today, but also a greater preparedness to think outside the boxes of national and European literary historiography, one could list a number of general as well as specific reasons that the Durban years should be granted prominence in Pessoa scholarship. The first and most obvious is the reason mentioned by Campbell: the persistence of the English language throughout Pessoa's life. He corresponded with English journals, published poetry in English, and continued above all to write and read in English. As George Monteiro and Irene Ramalho Santos, among others, have shown, the importance of English-language poetry in Pessoa's work, from Shakespeare to Walt Whitman, can hardly be overstated.[5] Even in Pessoa's Lusophone poetry—for instance, Álvaro de Campos's *Ode marítima* and "Ultimatum"—English words and phrases appear. It is barely conceivable that this intellectual commerce with the Anglophone world would have occurred without those childhood years in Durban.

In a similar vein, it may be argued that Pessoa would never have become *Pessoa* without the migrant experience of being a Portuguese child in exile, educated in the most excessively British, colonial part of southern Africa, not just at the peak of the British high-imperial period, but also during the dramatic years of the Anglo-Boer War (1899–1902). The very conservative brand of Britishness of the Natal Colony, which contrasts both with the white liberalism of the Cape Colony and the Afrikanerdom of Transvaal and the Orange Free State, should be highlighted in this context. If the colonial histories of other parts of South Africa had been rather checkered, and the boom town of Johannesburg (founded in 1886) was rapidly becoming a cosmopolitan metropolis, the Natal Colony—where segregationist policies were implemented very early—was staunchly and self-consciously a part of the British Empire.[6] It is for good reason that Pietermaritzburg, the administrative capital of Natal (and of KwaZulu-Natal today), 70 kilometers inland from Durban, bears the popular slogan "the last outpost of the empire."[7] If what passed for "English" identity in much of South Africa took shape against the Boer (or Afrikaner) other, in Natal it was mainly the Zulu nation that provided a foil for Englishness. Add to this the fact that South Africa was formed as a political union only in 1910, after Pessoa's departure. In other words, it was a very specific, and specifically English, colonial African setting that Pessoa entered as a child.

Here we can trace the early formation of the imperial view of history that is so prominent in his work and, in its way, also becomes a strange limitation to his thinking. The *empire* as a frame of reference, an object of desire, a cause for ridicule, and a lofty ideal, would recur again and again in his writing. This is commonly read as a poetic conceit serving to promote the notion of an "empire of culture" rather than "actual" imperialism, but the historical basis of Pessoa's rarefied idea of empire cannot be ignored.[8] In notes that he prepared for *Mensagem* (*Message*), for example, he states the following: "Foi a civilização moderna creada pela concentração e europeização da alma antiga, e isso foi obra da Italia; pela abertura de todas as portas do mundo, e o descobrimento d'elle, e isso foi a obra de Portugal; e pela restituição da idéa de Grande Imperio, e isso foi obra de Inglaterra. Tudo o mais é de segunda ordem." (Modern civilization was created by the concentration and Europeanization of the spirit of antiquity, which was the achievement of Italy; by the discovery of the world and the opening of all its harbors, which was done by Portugal; and by the restitution of the idea of the Grand Empire, which was achieved by England. Whatever remains is of a second order.)[9]

This emphasis on a European—and particulary English and Portuguese—imperial history as a keystone of modern civilization is foreshadowed, refracted, and reformulated across Pessoa's unruly oeuvre. We recognize it in his musings in *Mensagem* and elsewhere about Portugal as the "Fifth Empire" (after "Greece, Rome, Christianity and Europe");[10] but also, in Álvaro de Campos's wild (to say the least) diatribe against all of contemporary Europe and the Americas in his 1917 "Ultimatum,"[11] the imperial frame of reference structures much of the poem, mainly to lament the lack of imperial grandeur in contemporary Europe:

Tu, ambição italiana, cão de collo chamado Cesar!
[. . .]
Tu, organização britannica, com Kitchener[12] no fundo do mar desde o principio da guerra!
[. . .]
Tu, cultura alemã, Sparta pôdre com azeite de christismo e vinagre de nietzschização, colmeia de lata, transbordeamento imperialoide de servilismo engatado!
[. . .]
Nenhuma idéa grande, ou noção completa ou ambição imperial de imperador-nato!
Nenhuma idéa de uma estructura, nenhum senso do Edificio, nenhuma ansia do Organico-Creado!

Nem um pequeno Pitt, nem um Goethe de cartão, nem um Napoleão de
Nürnberg!

(You, Italian ambition, lap-dog called Caesar!
[. . .]
You, British organization, with Kitchener in the bottom of the sea from the
beginning of the war!
You, German culture, putrid Sparta with oil of Christianity and vinegar of
Nietzscheanisation, tin-can beehive, imperialoid trangression of misguided
servility!
[. . .]
Not a single grand idea, nor a complete notion or imperial ambition of the
born emperor!
Not a single idea of a structure, no sense of an Edifice, no longing for
Organic-Creation!
Not even a small Pitt, not even a cardboard Goethe, not even a Nuremburg
Napoleon!)[13]

Even South Africa—through the imperial mediation of Kipling—enjoys a
brief, derogatory mention in "Ultimatum": "Fóra tu, mercadoria Kipling, homem-
practico do verso, imperialista das sucatas, epico para Majuba e Colenso, Empire-Day do calão das fardas, tramp-steamer da baixa immortalidade!" (Out with
you, you merchant-like Kipling, practical-man of poetry, pig-iron imperialist,
epic bard of Majuba and Colenso, Empire-Day of the slang of the uniforms,
tramp-steamer of base immortality! [Majuba and Colenso were the sites of two
Anglo-Boer battles]).

Pessoa's early work from his South African years helps us notice the very ma-
trix of this imperial thinking. To substantiate this, let us look briefly at a small
set of early texts: his 1905 letter to the *Natal Mercury*, the sonnets that accompanied this letter, and the newly discovered fragmentary poem "Steal, Steal, Steal"
dated 1906. Pessoa was at this time experimenting with the literary persona
Charles Robert Anon, who would later merge with Alexander Search. The latter
would become Pessoa's most prominent Anglophone persona, but critics today
agree that Search emerged after the Durban years; the first evidence we have
of his name dates from 1906.[14] The letter to the *Natal Mercury* is signed Charles
Robert Anon, and although the accompanying sonnets in manuscript form extant in Pessoa's archive bear the name Alexander Search, this is a later addi-

tion. There is another minor equivocation: in the letter, Anon says that he is attaching three sonnets, but there are four sonnets that clearly belong together thematically—two of them called "To England." I will treat all four as connected to the concerns expressed in the letter.

Despite the lack of an explicit reference to the Russo-Japanese War (1904–1905), we can safely assume that this is what prompted Pessoa/Anon to express his dissatisfaction in July 1905: "I have been somewhat astonished, in the perusal of the 'Natal Mercury,' and especially of your column, to perceive how meanly, and in what slavish way, sarcasm and irony are heaped on the Russians, on their army, and on their Emperor."[15]

His complaint concerns, above all, the lack of tact and delicacy in the face of another's defeat, and a concomitant refusal to realize that "grief and misery ennoble." This compassionate and humanistic rejoinder is nonetheless combined with the Realpolitik of geopolitical considerations: "It is quite clear, I believe, that our hearty amusement may be constructed [sic], not even by one malicious, into a joy from the relief we now have from fears of an Indian disturbance. Russia does not now threaten our Eastern possession; and is it therefore that we laugh?"[16]

It was indeed the case that Japan, which emerged victorious from the war, had been allied with Britain, and that Russia was a contender in the "Great Game" of imperial rule in Asia. Anon's complaint is in that respect motivated and even perceptive, but what is particularly interesting is the speaking position that he constructs for himself in the letter. Anon speaks unequivocally of "us, Englishmen" and the mention of India as "our Eastern possession" is hardly ironic. The problem is certain attitudes and the conduct of the British, not the British Empire or imperial ambitions. In this respect, Pessoa/Anon seems typical of his time: another European foreigner in the British Empire, Joseph Conrad, would similarly voice criticism of colonial conduct, but without questioning the imperial system.[17] More important, Pessoa, with Anon as his mouthpiece, is displaying how powerful the interpellation of British imperial subjects in Durban could be. Even as a Portuguese child, Pessoa's schooling enabled him to identify (and made him want to identify) as English.

These observations are borne out by the sonnets and the poem "Steal, Steal, Steal." As mentioned, two of the sonnets bear the title "To England"; the other two are called "Joseph Chamberlain" and "Liberty."[18] Geopolitically, only one of the "To England" sonnets concerns itself directly with the Russo-Japanese

War: "Our enemies are fallen; other hands / Than ours have struck them, and our joy is great / To know that now at length our fears abate / From hint and menace on great Eastern lands."[19] The other three either speak idealistically in the abstract of the conduct of nations and men, or move closer to home by thematizing aspects of the Anglo-Boer War. In "Liberty," we read,

> Oh, sacred Liberty, dear mother of Fame!
> What are men here that they should expel thee?
> What right of theirs, save power, makes others be
> The pawns, as if unfeeling, in their game?
>
> Ireland and the Transvaal, ye are a shame
> On England and a blot! Oh, shall we see
> For ever crushed and held who should be free
> By human creatures without human name?[20]

And "Joseph Chamberlain" begins like this: "Their blood on thy head, whom the Afric waste / Saw struggling, puppets with unwilful hand, / Brother and brother: their bought souls shall brand / Thine own with horrors. [. . .]"[21] Finally, the rediscovered unfinished poem is also locally inflected and no less harsh in its judgement:

> Steal, steal, steal
> Wherefore are ye strong
> Steal, steal, steal
> The weak are ever wrong
>
> Englishmen remember all
> The example your nation doth deal
> Scotland, Ireland, the Transvaal
> Many a land [   ]
> So steal, steal, steal!
>
> Wherefore strength if not to oppress
> Wherefore might if not to make distress
> Wherefore [   ]
> So, men of England, continue your work
> And steal, steal, steal![22]

Pessoa, "Steal, Steal, Steal." BNP/E3, 49A¹–28ʳ.

July 1906.

Steal, steal steal
Wherefore are ye strong
While ye are strong and others
?. ?. ?. weak
The weak are ever wrong
Steal steal steal!

Englishmen remember all
The example your nation
doth deal
Scotland, Ireland, the Transvaal
Many a land
To steal steal steal!

Wherefore strength if not
t' oppress
Wherefore might – if not to
make distress

Wherefore
So, men of England continue
your work
And steal steal steal.

How should we assess these instances of rhetorical *accusatio* against Britain? It is evident, first, that Pessoa/Anon is animated more by the Anglo-Boer War of 1899–1902 than the Russo-Japanese War. This is hardly surprising, given Pessoa's geographical positioning. The Anglo-Boer had been a moment of deep crisis for the British Empire and a Pyrrhic victory—in retrospect, the first decisive turning

37

point in the empire's fortunes. Although it deserves repeating that Pessoa's Durban years coincided with the high point of empire, we see how the poems also register the seismic shock of this crisis. If colonial propaganda, predictably, supported the war, as the stepson of a Portuguese consul, Pessoa would also have been exposed to the more common continental European perception that this was an unjust act of aggression against a small, freedom-loving people (i.e., the Boers).[23] The lines "Ireland and the Transvaal, ye are a shame / On England and a blot!" convey thereby the damage wrought by the war on the *image* of the British Empire. Irish volunteers had fought on the Boer side, identifying not with the Afrikaner ambition to maintain a quasi-feudal racist order, but with the nationalist David struggling against the imperialist British Goliath.

There was indeed little doubt, even on the British side, that the annexation of Transvaal had to do with anything other than economic interest. The conflict had been preceded by the infamous Jameson raid, a failed attempt in 1895 to take control of Johannesburg and the Transvaal. It had not directly involved British troops, but the scheme had been devised by a group of influential British politicians and capitalists (most prominent among them Cecil Rhodes) and was aimed at provoking an interstate conflict. We know today, of course, that not only was the raid carried out with the tacit blessing of Joseph Chamberlain—then British secretary of state for the colonies—but its ultimate outcome would be the outbreak of the war in October 1899.[24]

We begin to see, in other words, how the poems draw on a web of contemporary political references, all of them emerging from a British imperial frame of reference, but that they do so with a critical purpose. Chamberlain is likened to a puppet-master, and British aggression is seen in terms of naked power politics: "Wherefore strength if not to oppress." Articulating such criticism while adopting a fully English persona and mastering the meters and rhythms of English verse, often perfectly, is of course an ambivalent performance by the teen-aged Pessoa. Consider, for example, the flawless iambic pentameter of "Joseph Chamberlain" in lines such as "To know that now at length our fears abate," or the carefully rendered ictic verse of "Steal, Steal, Steal" which—recalling Tennyson's "Break, Break, Break"—relies on three or four beats per line rather than stresses to form a dynamic rhythm.[25] This is the work of a young poet wanting to display his mastery of his acquired language, English, even if the performance sometimes strikes an odd and antiquated note (especially on a lexical level) to an English ear. The letter, as can be seen in the earlier quotation, uses "constructed" in a strange way, and the lines in "Liberty" about Ireland and Transvaal being a "shame" and "a blot" not only employ the archaic "ye," but also read back to front at first, as though the poet were criticizing Ireland and Transvaal rather than England. The ventriloquizing aspect of Anon's letter and these poems cuts both ways: even as Pessoa is being ventriloquized by the English language, he himself is ventriloquizing the English persona of Anon and subtly, probably unintentionally, infusing Anon's English with a slight foreignness.

The ambivalence of this early work deepens yet further if we consider that the essay that won Pessoa the Queen Victoria Memorial Prize in 1903—at the age of fifteen—was nothing less than a critical appraisal of the work of Thomas Babington Macaulay, these days routinely identified as a key figure in the articulation of British imperialist ideology.[26] His "Minute on Indian Education" (1835) promoted, notoriously, the formation of "a class of persons, Indian in blood and colour, but English in taste, in opinions, in morals, and in intellect."[27] Besides what his engagement with Macaulay tells us of Pessoa's deep exposure to a British imperial outlook, however, we should recognize the uncanny resonance between Macaulay's words in "Minute" and Pessoa's early heteronymic experiments, wherein English and Portuguese elements mix and contrast with each other. Through Anon, he endeavored to be "English in taste, in opinions, in morals, and in intellect," while still cultivating a remaining sense of otherness and estrangement toward Englishness.

There are four provisional conclusions we can draw from the discussion thus far. One is that from the young to the mature Pessoa, there is a consistent preoccupation with empires as political, supranational, and imagined constructs. This vindicates earlier claims by George Monteiro, Irene Ramalho Santos, António Sousa Ribeiro and Onésimo Almeida, although the Anon pieces make it difficult to transpose this exclusively to an apolitical, literary realm, or what Ribeiro calls a "fiction of a decentred centre."[28] One could say that insofar as Pessoa did concern himself with geopolitics, empires were the main organizing principle by which he made sense of the wider world.

The second conclusion is that this imperial preoccupation, already in Durban, is critical and contradictory. Empire, in Pessoa's view, can be based on strength as well as culture, or spirit, and his writings tend to favor the idealistic notion of an empire of the spirit. I would call this *imperial ambivalence*, and it is played out between heteronyms (or preheteronyms) as well as between heteronyms and the orthonymic poetry of Pessoa. This is demonstrated convincingly in Monteiro's discussion of "O Menino da sua mãe," with its compassionate and elegiac view of the "webs of empire," as opposed to the imperial aggressiveness of Álvaro de Campos. Pessoa's imperial ambivalence, one could say, is dispersed across the multiple voices that make up his work.

The third conclusion is that—adopting a term from Laura Doyle—Pessoa already at an early age cultivated an *inter-imperial* outlook. Doyle develops her idea of inter-imperiality from within a deep-time view of world history, and explains that it "lays a certain kind of stress on art's foundational entanglement in a multilateral and sedimented geopolitics [. . .] Situating the institutions and conventions of literature within such geopolitical histories, an inter-imperial analysis tracks the signs of that *political* history in texts—not to reduce them to political treatises but rather to reveal the dynamic onto-political conditions of their production and circulation" (original emphasis).[29]

This, it seems to me, is of great explanatory value in our reading of Pessoa. The inter-imperial dimension is apparent in the letter to the *Mercury*, as well as in the notes for *Mensagem* and the rant of "Ultimatum": Pessoa makes sense of the world as a Great Game between British, Russian, Portuguese, French, and other imperial powers. Even the title "Ultimatum" recalls the ultimatum of 1890 when Britain, as part of the ongoing scramble for Africa, challenged Portuguese claims to imperial sovereignty over territories that today comprise Zimbabwe and Zambia. This inter-imperial political crisis—which was completely oblivious to the will and fate of the African populations in these regions—must undoubtedly have reverberated in the memory of the small Portuguese community in Durban in Pessoa's day, and nurtured the type of imperial ambivalence we can detect in Anon's sonnets.

Yet this also leads to the fourth conclusion: Pessoa's outlook on the world was ultimately and fatally limited by this early imperial conditioning in Durban. If we see the Anglo-Boer War as a foundational if curiously refracted event in Pessoa's life, we need to recall that it was fought, as T. R. H. Davenport puts it, "to determine which *white* authority held real power in South Africa" (emphasis added).[30] There is no evidence in Pessoa's early poems that he was aware of anything other than white concerns in southern Africa. Anon speaks of "Afric waste," as though the continent were an empty playing field for white interests. And although Pessoa was in Durban at the same time that Mahatma Gandhi lived there, publishing *Indian Opinion* and promoting the rights of Indians in Natal, this does not enter his frame of reference at the time.[31] When Pessoa does write about Gandhi later in his life—and extols him as a saintly figure—this is evidently in response to international reporting on Gandhi.[32]

I am not claiming that Pessoa was unusual. On the contrary, he was—much like Roy Campbell—a fully representative product of Durban, in which white society created its own world, resolutely set apart from the African reality around it. This stakes out with grim finality the limits of the criticism articulated by the poems discussed in this article. But as other work produced by white South African writers in the colonial era shows, from the abolitionist and egalitarian poetry of Thomas Pringle in the 1820s to Olive Schreiner's scathing denunciation of Cecil Rhodes's conquest of Zimbabwe in *Trooper Peter Halket of Mashonaland* (1897), these limits should not falsely be taken as impermeable. Given that Pessoa related to the world through writing and reading, one could well imagine that had he stayed longer in Durban, these more trenchant literary critiques of the colonial order in southern Africa would eventually have caught his attention. But this is speculation. What we can say is that Durban made Pessoa *imperial* but never sufficiently *colonial* to engage seriously with the political and ethical dynamics of Natal and southern Africa.

This, in turn, also serves to explain why Pessoa is and probably will remain such a minority interest in South Africa itself. A handful of South African critics and writers, from Roy Campbell and Hubert Jennings to Charles Eglington and Stephen Gray, have kept the memory of Pessoa alive in South Africa and the English-speaking world.[33] However, the fact that all are white males does tell us something about the historical compartmentalization of South African literature, and the fact that so few local readers have engaged directly with Pessoa's Lusophone poetry also tells us something about the limits of multilingualism in South Africa. Campbell produced some good translations of Pessoa, but his memory has been compromised by his lapse into fascism.[34] (He died in Portugal in 1957 as an enthusiastic supporter of both Franco and Salazar.) Jennings, as we have seen, was instrumental in reconstructing the memory of Pessoa's years at DHS, although this too was done from within the tight enclosure of Durbanite whiteness. Gray, who belongs to a younger generation, is a different case: a highly respected critic, his key contribution to literary studies in southern Africa has been to conceive of literature on a regional rather than a racial or linguistic basis. This has enabled him to include both Camões and Pessoa in his numerous anthologizing projects, such as *The Penguin Book of Southern African Verse*.[35] Arguably the finest South African tribute to Pessoa has been, however, the set of poems that Charles Eglington (1918–1971) wrote in response to some of Pessoa's poetry in Portuguese. Here is Eglington's "Horizon," written as a counterpart to Pessoa's "Horizonte":[36]

The early mariners perhaps
Were first to understand the pure
Aesthetic of horizons: chart
And instrument were insecure
Against the treacheries of sky
And ocean; often as they watched
They saw the ancient portents fade
On winds of promise, or reveal
Their shining menace; then, afraid
Because they found no hallowed sign
To prosper them, they sought in awe
The low horizon's thin, cold line.[37]

It is in the elusive horizons of this finely wrought iambic tetrameter, we might say, that Pessoa and South Africa cross paths most meaningfully. Insofar as Pessoa is one of the strongest examples we have of life being usurped by writing, then it is also through language and verse that it becomes possible to meet Pessoa on his own terms. Eglington the poet achieves in that way what critics, forced to approach Pessoa from the outside, will be unable to match. For that reason, I also read Eglington's lines in a cautionary vein, directed at what I have been attempting to explain here. This is true, not only because this article cannot pretend to be more than a footnote to Pessoa studies, but more pointedly because my "chart / And instrument" of contextual critique will easily risk misreading the "sky / And ocean" of Pessoa's work. If I embrace this risk openly, it is for the simple reason that we cannot afford to ignore the cold historical horizon of my reading: the conflicted world that is the legacy of European imperialisms. The imperial backdrop to Pessoa's oeuvre needs to be taken seriously, therefore, not in a narrowly moralistic sense, but as its problematic onto-political condition of possibility.

NOTES

1. The most informative account of Pessoa's DHS years I have come across is in Hubert D. Jennings, *The D. H. S. Story, 1866–1966* (Durban: Durban High School and Old Boys' Memorial Trust, 1966), 99–110.

2. George Monteiro, "Fernando Pessoa: An Unfinished Manuscript by Roy Campbell," *Portuguese Studies* 10 (1994), 152. It should be noted that the correspondence between Ormond and Pessoa has disappeared, if indeed it ever existed.

3. Monteiro, "Fernando Pessoa," 149.

4. Fernando Pessoa, *Novas poesias inéditas*, ed. Maria do Rosário Marques Sabino and Adelaide Maria Monteiro Sereno (Lisbon: Ática, 1973), 137; and Fernando Pessoa, *Poemas de Fernando Pessoa: 1934–1935*, ed. Luís Prista (Lisbon: Imprensa Nacional–Casa da Moeda, 2000), 232–41.

5. George Monteiro, *Fernando Pessoa and Nineteenth-Century Anglo-American Literature* (Lexington: University Press of Kentucky, 2000); Irene Ramalho de Sousa Santos, *Atlantic Poets: Fernando Pessoa's Turn in Anglo-American Modernism* (Hanover: University Press of New England, 2002).

6. T. R. H. Davenport, *South Africa: A Modern History* (London: Macmillan, 1991), 101–8; Saul Dubow, *The Commonwealth of Knowledge: Science, Sensibility, and White South Africa 1820–2000* (Oxford: Oxford University Press, 2006), 18–35.

7. Obvious nuances can be added to this picture. The Cape Colony had been British ever since the early nineteenth century, and Grahamstown in the eastern Cape was also a markedly British "outpost." But the Dutch colonial legacy in the Cape was mostly absent in Natal.

8. Irene Ramalho de Sousa Santos, "An Imperialism of Poets: The Modernism of Fernando Pessoa and Hart Crane," *Luso-Brazilian Review* 29.1 (1992), 90.

9. BNP/E3, 14^2–69^r; cf. Fernando Pessoa, *Mensagem* (Lisbon: Relógio d'Água, 2013), 29.

10. Pessoa, *Mensagem*, 125.

11. First published in *Portugal Futurista* in 1917. Fernando Pessoa, *Sensacionismo e outros ismos*, ed. Jerónimo Pizarro (Lisbon: Imprensa Nacional–Casa da Moeda), 2011. See also *Obra completa de Álvaro de Campos (Álvaro de Campos's Complete Works)* Pessoa, 2014.

12. There exists a fragmentary sonnet titled "Kitchener" (BNP/E3, 49B^1–100^v), datable from 1907, that opens, "Oh hireling son of tyranny & hate." We thank Carlos Pittella-Leite for this finding. Editors' note.

13. My translation.

14. See João Dionísio, "Introdução," in Fernando Pessoa, *Poemas Ingleses: Poemas de Alexander Search*, Tome II, ed. João Dionísio (Lisbon: Imprensa Nacional–Casa da Moeda, 1997), 7–21. It should be noted that Anon transformed into Search sometime around 1906, and then Search was retrospectively imposed on part of Anon's work, so these two personae are to a great extent virtually interchangeable. See Fernando Pessoa, *Eu sou uma antologia*, ed. Jerónimo Pizarro and Patricio Ferrari (Lisbon: Tinta-da-China, 2013), 139–44, 227–33.

15. BNP/E3, 114^I–52^r to 55^r. Fernando Pessoa, *Pessoa inédito*, ed. Teresa Rita Lopes (Lisbon: Livros Horizonte, 1993), 168.

16. Ibid.

17. This can be seen in the much-debated case of Conrad's *Heart of Darkness*.

18. "Liberty" also appears in one of the three existing lists for the book *Death of God* (BNP/E3, 48C–9^v).

19. Pessoa, *Poemas Ingleses*, 303.

20. Ibid., 301.

21. Ibid., 304.

22. BNP/E3, 49A^I–28^r. Transcribed by Patricio Ferrari. Poem dated July 1906. Although unsigned, this poem appears in one of the three lists existing for the book titled *Death of God* (BNP/E3, 48C-11^r). In one of these, the list bears Charles Robert Anon's seal (BNP/E3, 48C-9^r). The third list may be found in BNP/E3, 48C-10. In 49A^1–28a^r we find three lines that could be either the continuation of this poem or the beginning of yet another unfinished piece: "Murder and rapine hallows / How many a hero, were there no wars / Had ended in the gallows."

23. Davenport, *South Africa*, 195.

24. Ibid., 188–92.

25. For a discussion of ictic verse, see Martin J. Duffell, *A New History of English Metre* (London: Legenda, 2008), 65–66.

26. For more on the essay, see Jennings, *The D. H. S. Story*, 90–110.

27. Thomas Babington Macaulay, "Minute on Indian Education," in *Selected Writings*, eds. John Clive and Thomas Pinner (Chicago: University of Chicago Press, 1972), 249.

28. António Sousa Ribeiro, "'A Tradition of Empire': Fernando Pessoa and Germany," *Portuguese Studies* 21 (2005), 203.

29. Laura Doyle, "Inter-Imperiality," *Interventions* 16 (2014), 183.

30. Davenport, *South Africa*, 198.

31. Isabel Hofmeyr, *Gandhi's Printing Press: Experiments in Slow Reading* (Cambridge: Harvard University Press, 2013). In a recent article, Leela Gandhi makes a point similar to mine but deliberately juxtaposes Pessoa and Gandhi, to see how Pessoan heteronymy and a Gandhian conception of democracy may resonate with one another. Leela Gandhi, "Pessoa's Gahndi: Meditating on a Lost Heteronym," in *Gender, Empire, and Postcolony: Luso-Afro-Brazilian Intersections*, ed. Hilary Owen and Anna M. Klobucka (New York: Palgrave Macmillan, 2014), 19–32.

32. Jerónimo Pizarro, Patricio Ferrari, and Antonio Cardiello, "Os Orientes de Fernando Pessoa," *Cultura Entre Culturas* 3 (2011), 166–67. See also Gandhi, "Pessoa's Gahndi.

33. For a thorough bibliographical account of the English-language (including South African) reception of Pessoa, see José Blanco, "Fernando Pessoa's Critical and Editorial Fortune in English: A Selective Chronological Overview," *Portuguese Studies* 24.2 (2008), 13–32.

34. Roy Campbell, *Collected Works II: Poetry Translations* (Johannesburg: Ad Donker, 1985).

35. Stephen Gray, ed., *The Penguin Book of Southern African Verse* (London: Penguin, 1989), 1–26, 167–70.

36. Pessoa, *Mensagem*, 52.

37. Charles Beaumont Eglington, *Under the Horizon* (Cape Town: Purnell, 1977), 3.

WORKS CITED

Almeida, Onésimo Teotónio. *Pessoa, Portugal e o Futuro*. Lisbon: Gradiva, 2014.

Blanco, José. "Fernando Pessoa's Critical and Editorial Fortune in English: A Selective Chronological Overview." *Portuguese Studies* 24.2 (2008): 13–32.

Campbell, Roy. *Collected Works II: Poetry Translations*. Johannesburg: Ad Donker, 1985.

Davenport, T. R. H. *South Africa: A Modern History*. London: Macmillan, 1991.

Doyle, Laura. "Inter-Imperiality." *Interventions* 16 (2014): 159–96.

Dubow, Saul. *The Commonwealth of Knowledge: Science, Sensibility, and White South Africa 1820–2000*. Oxford: Oxford University Press, 2006.

Duffell, Martin J. *A New History of English Metre*. London: Legenda, 2008.

Eglington, Charles Beaumont. *Under the Horizon*. Cape Town: Purnell, 1977.

Gandhi, Leela. "Pessoa's Gahndi: Meditating on a Lost Heteronym." In Hilary Owen and Anna M. Klobucka, eds., *Gender, Empire, and Postcolony: Luso-Afro-Brazilian Intersections*. New York: Palgrave Macmillan, 2014.

Gray, Stephen, ed. *The Penguin Book of Southern African Verse*. London: Penguin, 1989.

Jennings, Hubert Dudley. *The D. H. S. Story 1866–1966*. Durban: Durban High School and Old Boys' Memorial Trust, 1966.

Macaulay, Thomas Babington. *Selected Writings*. Edited by John Clive and Thomas Pinner. Chicago: University of Chicago Press, 1972.

Monteiro, George. "Fernando Pessoa: An Unfinished Manuscript by Roy Campbell." *Portuguese Studies* 10 (1994): 122–54.

———. *Fernando Pessoa and Nineteenth-Century Anglo-American Literature*. Lexington: University Press of Kentucky, 2000.

Pessoa, Fernando. *Mensagem*. Lisbon: Parceria António Maria Pereira, 1934.

———. *Novas poesias inéditas*. Edited by Maria do Rosário Marques Sabino and Adelaide Maria Monteiro Sereno. Lisbon: Ática, 1973.

———. *Pessoa inédito*. Edited by Teresa Rita Lopes. Lisbon: Livros Horizonte, 1993.

———. *Poemas Ingleses: Poemas de Alexander Search*. Fernando Pessoa's Critical Edition, Major Series, Vol. V, Tome II. Edited by João Dionísio. Lisbon: Imprensa Nacional–Casa da Moeda, 1997.

———. *Poemas de Fernando Pessoa: 1934–1935*. Vol. I, Tomo V. Edited by Luís Prista. Fernando Pessoa's Critical Edition, Major Series, Vol. I, Tome V. Lisbon: Imprensa Nacional–Casa da Moeda, 2000.

———. *Sensacionismo e outros ismos*. Edited by Jerónimo Pizarro. Fernando Pessoa's Critical Edition, Major Series, Vol. X. Lisbon: Imprensa Nacional–Casa da Moeda, 2009.

———. *Eu sou uma antologia: 136 autores fictícios*. Edited by Jerónimo Pizarro and Patricio Ferrari. Lisbon: Tinta-da-China, 2013. Pessoa Collection coordinated by Jerónimo Pizarro.

———. *Mensagem*. Edited by Teresa Sobral Cunha. Lisbon: Relógio d'Água, 2013.

———. *Obra Completa de Álvaro de Campos*. Edited by Jerónimo Pizarro and Antonio Cardiello. Lisbon: Tinta-da-China, 2014. Pessoa Collection coordinated by Jerónimo Pizarro.

Pizarro, Jerónimo, Patricio Ferrari, and Antonio Cardiello. "Os Orientes de Fernando Pessoa." *Cultura Entre Culturas* 3, Spring-Summer, Lisbon, Âncora (2011): 148–85.

Ribeiro, António Sousa. "'A Tradition of Empire': Fernando Pessoa and Germany." *Portuguese Studies* 21 (2005): 201–9.

Santos, Irene Ramalho "An Imperialism of Poets: The Modernism of Fernando Pessoa and Hart Crane." *Luso-Brazilian Review* 29.1 (1992): 83–95.

———. *Atlantic Poets: Fernando Pessoa's Turn in Anglo-American Modernism*. Hanover: University Press of New England, 2002.

STEFAN HELGESSON is professor of English at Stockholm University. He has published widely on southern African literature in English and Portuguese, Brazilian literature, postcolonial theory, translation theory, and theories of world literature. He is the author of *Transnationalism in Southern African Literature* (Routledge 2009), and is currently editing a volume (with Pieter Vermeulen) called *Institutions of World Literature: Writing, Translation, Markets*, to be published by Routledge in 2015.

He can be reached at stefan.helgesson@english.su.se.

GEORGE MONTEIRO

World War I
Europe, Africa, and "O Menino da sua mãe"

ABSTRACT: Written in the midst of World War I, the over-psychologized poem "O Menino da sua mãe" ("His Mother's Child") can be best read as Fernando Pessoa's most efficient antiwar poem. Among its antecedents is the antimilitary poetry of the English poet A. E. Housman, whose *A Shropshire Lad*, though first published in 1896, achieved its first great dissemination and popularity during the Anglo-Boer War (1899–1902), an event that took place during Pessoa's long stay in South Africa. Important to the overall argument of this essay, also, is the large-scale public reaction to the unsettling death of the young "war" poet Rupert Brooke, a death that occurred, ironically, while he was aboard a ship transporting British forces to Gallipoli.

KEYWORDS: A. E. Housman, *A Shropshire Lad*, "Epitaph on an Army of Mercenaries," "O Menino da sua mãe," Rupert Brooke, Emma Lazarus, "1879" (sonnet), "Ultimatum," Henry James, Homer, *Iliad*, Anglo-Boer War

At the outset of his review of the collective volume of the poetry of Wilfred Owen, the English poet killed in France in the final days of the Great War, Philip Larkin works out a singular definition of the true "war poet" and what he deems the nature of this poet's work:

> A "war poet" is not one who chooses to commemorate or celebrate a war but one who reacts against having a war thrust upon him: he is chained, that is, to a historical event, and an abnormal one at that. However well he does it, however much we agree that the war happened and ought to be written about, there is still a tendency for us to withhold our highest praise on the grounds that a poet's choice of subject should seem an action, not a reaction. "The Wreck of the Deutschland," we feel, would have been markedly inferior if Hopkins had been a survivor from the passenger list. Again, the first-rank

poet should ignore the squalid accident of war: his vision should be powerful enough to disregard it. Admittedly, war might come too close for this vision to be maintained. But it is still essentially irrelevant.[1]

Larkin's observation raises an interesting specter. After all, Homer was not a participant in the war he wrote about in the *Iliad*, nor was Shakespeare at Agincourt. Without making any attempt to come out on either of the two sides of this issue, one can still note that the poets whose names come up in the discussion that follows were not participants in the battles referred to more or less directly in their poems. Besides Homer, the poets whose poems are examined in this discussion of Fernando Pessoa's "O Menino da sua mãe" ("His Mother's Child") include Emma Lazarus, A. E. Housman, and Rupert Brooke.[2]

In one way or another, the West's war poetry as a whole derives from Homer's *Iliad*. The Greek poet's grand poem about the ways of warfare and the heroism of warriors stands as the beginning design and, in my opinion, remains the benchmark for all that has followed. Not unexpectedly, Homer's work has had several major English-language translations. The best known of these and, perhaps, the most influential—even to those with a knowledge of the original languages—were done, first, by George Chapman, and then in the next century, by Alexander Pope. It was Chapman's Homer that John Keats first read and then celebrated in the equally well-regarded sonnet "On First Reading into Chapman's Homer."

Chapman's translation lasts as a straightforward expression in naturalistically brutal language, in which Homer excels, that is evocative of dramatic deeds, as, for example, in Achilles's taunting of the dying Hector in Book 22, boasting that his body, unburied, will be left to the unkindness of dogs and birds: "And now the dogs and fowles in the foulest use / Shall teare thee up, thy corse exposed to all the Greeks' abuse."[3] Contrast this speech with the quite different vow that the same Achilles addresses to the body of Patroclus, his friend and fellow warrior:

O my Patroclus, for thy Corse before I hither bring
The armes of Hector, and his head, to thee for offering.
Twelve youths, the most renown'd of Troy, I'le sacrifise beside
Before thy heape of funerall, to thee unpacifide.
In meane time, by our crooked sternes lye drawing teares from me;
And round about thy honour'd Corse these dames of Dardanie

And Ilion with the ample breasts (whom our long speares, and powres,
And labours purchast from the rich and by-us-ruined towres
And cities strong and populous, with divers-languag'd men)
Shall kneele, and neither day nor night be licenst to abstaine
From solemne watches, their toil'd eyes held ope with endless teares.
This passion past, he gave command to his neare souldiers
To put a Tripod to the fire, to cleanse the festred gore
From off the person. They obeyd, and presently did powre
Fresh water in it, kindl'd wood, and with an instant flame
The belly of the Tripod girt till fire's hote qualitie came
Up to the water. Then they washt and fild the mortall wound
With wealthy oyle of nine yeares old, then wrapt the body round
In largenesse of a fine white sheete, and put it then in bed [. . .]⁴

Within the Homeric tradition overall, there is a noteworthy place, perhaps surprisingly so, for the American poet Emma Lazarus (1849–1887), a descendant of the first Portuguese Sephardic Jewish settlers in what would become known as New York, and whose continuing fame outside of Jewish circles rides on the fact that she is the author of "The New Colossus," the poem quoted on the pedestal of the Statue of Liberty standing on Ellis Island in New York Harbor. Less well known is her sonnet "1879," the second poem comprising a diptych titled "Destiny":

Born to the purple, lying stark and dead,
Transfixed with poisoned spears, beneath the sun
Of brazen Africa! Thy grave is one,
Fore-fated youth (on whom were visited
Follies and sins not thine), whereat the world,
Heartless howe'er it be, will pause to sing
A dirge, to breathe a sigh, a wreath to fling
Of rosemary and rue with bay-leaves curled.
Enmeshed in toils ambitious, not thine own,
Immortal, loved boy-Prince, thou tak'st thy stand
With early doomed Don Carlos, hand in hand
With mild-browed Arthur, Geoffrey's murdered son.
Louis the Dauphin lifts his thorn-ringed head,
And welcomes thee, his brother, 'mongst the dead.⁵

very good.   XI.

ON FIRST LOOKING INTO CHAPMAN'S HOMER.

Much have I travelled in the realms of gold,
  And many goodly states and kingdoms seen ;
  Round many western islands have I been
Which bards in fealty to Apollo hold.
Oft of one wide expanse had I been told
  That deep-browed Homer ruled as his demesne ;
  Yet did I never breathe its pure serene
Till I heard Chapman speak out loud and bold :
Then felt I like some watcher of the skies
  When a new planet swims into his ken ;
Or like stout Cortez when with eagle eyes
  He stared at the Pacific—and all his men
Looked at each other with a wild surmise—
  Silent, upon a peak in Darien.

Keats, "On First Looking into Chapman's Homer," *The Poetical Works of John Keats*, London / New York: Frederick Warne, 1898, 42. CFP 8–294. Pessoa jotted "Very good."

Tempting though it might be to see echoes and traces of this poem lamenting the violent death of a historical celebrity, Prince Imperial Bonaparte (1856–1879), the last of the Bonaparte line, in the stanzas of Pessoa's decidedly more ironic poem "O Menino da sua mãe"—the corpse of a young soldier, lying "beneath the sun" of "brazen Arica"—one need not infer that Pessoa was acquainted with Lazarus's poem, for the link may be only that it is reminiscent (as is Pessoa's own poem) of the death of Portugal's young king Sebastian in a sixteenth-century African battle. Similarly, it would be less than plausible to think, for that matter, that Pessoa was comfortable enough with ancient Greek to take on Homeric poetry in the original in any appropriative way. But he knew English well enough, naturally, to recognize the importance to the English literary canon of the translations of Homer's poetry by Chapman or Pope.

Pessoa should have known just where his own war poetry fit in as well as differed from those model works lamenting the death of kings and princes and other historic heroes—all traceable to Homer's great poetry. His soldier has met his death, his name silenced.

Forty-three years ago, Georg Rudolf Lind identified and analyzed Pessoa's small cache of antiwar poems written during World War I.[6] Pessoa wrote war-time poems he attributed to the heteronyms Ricardo Reis, Alberto Caeiro, and Álvaro de Campos ("Ode marcial" ["Martial Ode"]). He also wrote "Salute to the Sun's Entry into Aries," "Tomámos a vila depois de um intenso bombardea-mento" ("We Took the Town after Heavy Bombardment"), and "O Menino da sua mãe," poems he attributed not to heteronyms but to his orthonymic self.

The last of these poems is central to this essay: a poem that was written, most likely, sometime before the Portuguese government, succumbing to British political pressure and in defiance of Portuguese public opinion, agreed to send troops to support the English and the French in their war against the Germans and their allies.[7] For some unknown reason, however, the poem remained un-published for a decade, until it appeared in the May 1926 issue of the Lisbon periodical *Contemporânea*.[8] It is my contention that reading "O Menino da sua mãe" in light of specific poems written by the English poets Rupert Brooke (1887–1915) and A. E. Housman (1859–1936) will take it out of the realm of disguised autobiography (as João Gaspar Simões would have it)[9] and reveal its greater universality.

Following is undoubtedly Pessoa's most frequently declaimed and oft-quoted lyric, "O Menino da sua mãe":

No plaino abandonado
Que a morna brisa aquece,
De balas trespassado—
Duas, de lado a lado—,
Jaz morto, e arrefece.

Raia-lhe a farda o sangue.
De braços estendidos,
Alvo, louro, exangue,
Fita com olhar langue
E cego os céus perdidos.

Tão jovem! que jovem era!
(Agora que idade tem?)
Filho único, a mãe lhe dera

Um nome e o mantivera:
"O menino da sua mãe."

Caiu-lhe da algibeira
A cigarreira breve.
Dera-lhe a mãe. Está inteira
E boa a cigarreira,
Ele é que já não serve.

De outra algibeira, alada
Ponta a roçar o solo,
A brancura embainhada
De um lenço . . . Deu-lh'o a criada
Velha que o trouxe ao colo.

Lá longe, em casa, há a prece:
"Que volte cedo, e bem!"
(Malhas que o Império tece!)
Jaz morto e apodrece
O menino da sua mãe.[10]

(On a deserted plain
Heated by a warm breeze,
Drilled clean through—
By two bullets—
He lies, dead, turning cold.

Blood steeps his uniform.
Blond, white, bloodless,
His arms extended,
He stares listlessly and
Unseeingly at lost skies.

He was so young! So young.
[And now how old is he?]
An only son, his mother
Had called him "Mother's
Boy." The name stuck.

Anon from his pocket
Falls his cigarette-case,
A gift from his mother.
The case is intact and in
Good shape. He is not.

From the other pocket, a
Dangling edge, the hemmed
White of a handkerchief flicking
The ground—a gift from the old
Nurse who carried him about.

Far off, at home, there is prayer:
"Return him soon—safe, sound."
[Webs that the Empire weaves!]
He lies dead, and rots,
This mother's boy.)[11]

In late July 1914, the result of political and diplomatic events that began with the assassination in Sarajevo of Archduke Franz Ferdinand, heir to the Austrian-Hungarian throne, warfare broke out in Europe. Within days, England was deeply involved. Patriotism ran high. Despite Portugal's long-standing alliance with England, the smaller country did not enter the war until March 9, 1916, sending troops to the front no earlier than February 1917. Portugal's quarrels with Germany were not such that the country felt it needed to immediately join England's side. In fact, if Pessoa's views at the time are any indication, there was much to be said in Germany's favor, at least until Germany declared war on Portugal in 1916. Pessoa's references to Germany, especially before 1916—in his political, sociological, and historical writing—indicate a comparatively favorable view of the role the Germans were made to play in the Great War.

Yet Pessoa did not hold any brief for warfare itself. In fact, it was likely in 1916 that he wrote the most famous of his three or four great antiwar poems. His view of warfare, revealed in the figure of a dead soldier, is in sharp contrast, as I will demonstrate, with that of the English poet Rupert Brooke—so sharp a contrast, in fact, that one is tempted to see "O Menino da sua mãe" as something of an answer to the public sentimentality exemplified in the young Brooke's last poetry. But that Pessoa sets the young soldier's death in Africa recalls the fact that at a certain point in the war, Portugal had an army in East Africa where, along with Great Britain and Belgium, it fought successfully to take over Germany's colonial possessions, a situation that gives precise historical meaning to Pessoa's exasperation—"Malhas que o Império tece!" ("Webs that the Empire weaves!").[12] There was irony in the fact that the hunger to increase their "Empires" in Africa had led Portugal to join forces not only with Belgium, but also with Great Britain, the international power that in 1890 had directed its famous "ultimatum" against Portugal's claims in Africa. There were still bitter memories of the British "mapa de rosa" (their "red map"), a move in accordance with Great Britain's desire to colonize Africa from Cairo to Cape Town, one that humiliated Portugal into backing down. It was no accident that Álvaro de Campos issued his own "Ultimatum" (in the first and only issue of *Portugal Futurista*, in September 1917), not merely against Great Britain and the Allies, but against the whole of modern Europe's history and culture at just about the same time that Pessoa wrote "O Menino da sua mãe."[13]

Before Pessoa registered his reactions to the war being waged in Africa as well as Europe, in December 1914, Rupert Brooke placed five poems in *New Numbers*, a journal of small circulation. Grouped under the title "1914," they soon became known as the "War Sonnets" and were widely circulated. Two of the poems—"The Dead" and "The Soldier"—were reprinted on March 11, 1915, in the London *Times Literary Supplement*; and on April 4 (Easter Sunday), "The Soldier" was read from church pulpits. But it was Brooke's death less than three weeks later, on April 23, 1915, that turned "The Soldier," a stirring feat of bravado in which he celebrated his own death and burial as gestures of an ultimate patriotism, into the British national anthem par excellence.

If I should die, think only this of me:
That there's some corner of a foreign field
That is for ever England. There shall be
In that rich earth a richer dust concealed;
A dust whom England bore, shaped, made aware,
Gave, once, her flowers to love, her ways to roam,
A body of England's, breathing English air,
Washed by the rivers, blest by suns of home.

And think, this heart, all evil shed away,
A pulse in the eternal mind, no less

Gives somewhere back the thoughts by England given;
Her sights and sounds; dreams happy as her day;
And laughter, learnt of friends; and gentleness,
In hearts at peace, under an English heaven.[14]

Notably, in "The Soldier," Brooke does not write about the soldier's death in battle or anything similar. Rather, he conveys the meaning that the soldier at eternal rest—the buried soldier—will always have for his country. It is in "The Dead" that Brooke talks about the aftermath of the soldier's sacrifice in losing his life for his country. They are the dead, in his words—"the rich Dead."

Blow out, you bugles, over the rich Dead!
There's none of these so lonely and poor of old,
But, dying, has made us rarer gifts than gold.
These laid the world away; poured out the red
Sweet wine of youth; gave up the years to be
Of work and joy, and that unhoped serene,
That men call age; and those who would have been,
Their sons, they gave, their immortality.

Blow, bugles, blow! They brought us, for our dearth,
Holiness, lacked so long, and Love, and Pain.
Honour has come back as a king, to earth,
And paid his subjects with a royal wage;
And Nobleness walks in our ways again;
And we have come into our heritage.[15]

There is no question that it was Brooke's deep-seated desire (or foolhardy wish, some would say) to prove his mettle by risking his life in combat, even dying a hero's death. This was not to be, however, for on April 23, 1915, the would-be warrior "died of septicæmia in a French hospital ship in the Ægean, and was buried the same day on the island of Scyros,"[16] at some distance from Gallipoli, where the ship carrying the young naval officer was headed and where England (and her allies) were destined to suffer disastrous naval defeats in a long and unsuccessful campaign to take the Dardanelles Strait. Brooke's death had at least spared him that dispiriting experience.

As might well be imagined, the circumstances surrounding the poet-soldier's untimely death were not the most propitious for launching a real-life hero into the midst of propaganda for the war. The London *Times* notice of Brooke's untimely death begins with a substantial quotation from "W. S. C.," not otherwise identified. It offered the right sentiments, obviously, in the right words:

> During the last few months of his life, months of preparation in gallant comradeship and open air, the poet-soldier told with all the simple force of genius the sorrow of youth about to die, and the sure triumphant consolations of a sincere and valiant spirit. He expected to die; he was willing to die for the dear England whose beauty and majesty he knew; and he advanced towards the brink in perfect serenity, with absolute conviction of the rightness of his country's cause and a heart devoid of hate for fellow-men.
>
> The thoughts to which he gave expression in the very few incomparable war sonnets which he has left behind will be shared by many thousands of young men moving resolutely and blithely forward into this, the hardest, the cruelest, and the least-rewarded of all the wars that men have fought. They are a whole history and revelation of Rupert Brooke himself. Joyous, fearless, versatile, deeply instructed, with classic symmetry of mind and body, ruled by high undoubting purpose, he was all that one would wish England's noblest sons to be in days when no sacrifice but the most precious is acceptable, and the most precious is that which is most freely proffered.[17]

Such propaganda was wildly successful, so much so that the *Fortnightly Review*, in the months following the outbreak of war, felt the need to describe Brooke as "almost too good to be true," as "certainly one of those whom the gods love," for he died young, at the age of twenty-seven.[18] Pessoa himself would invoke the same notion—"he dies young whom the Gods love" ("morre jovem o que os Deuses amam")—when memorializing his friend, the poet Mário de Sá-Carneiro, who died in his twenty-sixth year.[19] But in Brooke's case, it fell to Henry James, the renowned Anglo-American novelist who had thrown himself into the war effort—including efforts to raise money for American voluntary ambulances, as well as renouncing his American citizenship to become a British citizen as a supportive gesture of the British cause (not to mention its being a complaint against the reluctance of the United States to enter the war on the side of the Allies)—to place the sacrificed life of the poet-warrior Rupert Brooke at the center of the exemplary ethos the British nation had imagined for itself and confirmed in Brooke's meaningful death. In the preface he contributed to Brooke's posthumously published *Letters from America*, James defined that meaning, indulging himself in the fullness of his own late style in the really unearned (and thus exaggerated) poignancy of Brooke's death, not in combat but on a ship making its way to a future scene of battle:

The event [death] came indeed not in the manner prefigured by him in the repeatedly perfect line, that of the received death-stroke, the fall in action, discounted as such; which might have seemed very much because even the harsh logic and pressure of history were tender of him at the last and declined to go through more than the form of their function, discharging it with the least violence and surrounding it as with a legendary light. He was taken ill, as an effect of blood-poisoning, on his way from Alexandria to Gallipoli, and, getting ominously and rapidly worse, was removed from his transport to a French hospital ship, where, irreproachably cared for, he died in a few hours and without coming to consciousness. I deny myself any further anticipation of the story to which further noble associations attach, and the merest outline of which indeed tells it and rounds it off absolutely as the right harmony would have it. It is perhaps even a touch beyond any dreamt-of harmony that, under omission of no martial honour, he was to be carried by comrades and devoted waiting sharers, whose evidence survives them, to the steep summit of a Greek island of infinite grace and there placed in such earth and amid such beauty of light and shade and embracing prospect as that the fondest reading of his young lifetime could have suggested nothing better. It struck us at home, I mean, as symbolizing with the last refinement his whole instinct of selection and response, his relation to the overcharged appeal of his scene and hour. How could he have shown more the young English poetic possibility and faculty in which we were to see the freshest reflection of the intelligence and the soul of the new generation? The generosity, I may fairly say the joy, of his contribution to the general perfect way makes a monument of his high rest there at the heart of all that was once noblest in history.[20]

Of course, behind James's characterization of a heroic, if noncombat, death such as Brooke's was the idea that everyone, not just the military, could contribute heroically to the British cause. Like James himself—to evoke something of the spirit of John Milton—"they also serve who only stand and wait."

However, there were those few who, unlike James, demurred when Brooke was apotheosized in this way, but significantly, they did not choose to go public with their reservations or complaints. But one of those who did privately question the young poet's "attitudinizing" was a fellow poet. Writing at the time of Brooke's death, Charles Sorley complained that his "War" sonnets were overpraised:

> He [Brooke] is far too obsessed with his own sacrifice, regarding the going to war of himself (and others) as a highly intense, remarkable and sacrificial exploit, whereas it is merely the conduct demanded of him (and others) by the turn of circumstances, where non-compliance with this demand would have made life intolerable. It was not that "they" gave up anything of that list in one sonnet: but that the essence of these things had been endangered by circumstances over which he had no control, and he must fight to recapture them. He has clothed his attitude in fine words: but he has taken the senti- mental attitude.[21]

But the younger poet's words were meant for private ears only, as has been noted, and so they remained. For when almost immediately after Brooke's death his publisher brought out 1914 & Other Sonnets, the English embraced the book so eagerly that in 1915 alone, it was reprinted eleven times. Eager to cash in on Brooke's new and greater prominence, his publisher managed to bring out Col- lected Poems in the same year. A copy of the 1926 "The Augustan Books of Poetry edited by Edward Thompson" edition of Brooke's poems survives in Pessoa's private library.[22]

Pessoa's first knowledge of war in his time came while he was living with his stepfather, mother, and half-siblings in Durban, South Africa, at some distance from the conflicts. The Anglo-Boer War, waged between the farmers of the small Boer republics and British troops in the years 1899–1902, evoked from the fourteen-year-old Fernando Pessoa, in the guise of his English preheteronym Charles Robert Anon, the following poetic complaint, which he submitted to the Natal Mercury.

[. . .]
The fallen lion every ass can kick,
 That in his life, shamed to unmotioned fright,
 His every move with eyes askance did trace.

Ill scorn beseems us, men of war and trick,
 Whose groaning nation poured her fullest might
 To take the freedom of a farmer race.[23]

The *Natal Mercury* did not publish this sonnet, nor the other two (compare these sonnets as discussed in Stefan Helgesson's article in this volume).

The Anglo-Boer War, as history would deem, brought fresh attention in a far less singular way, to a small book of poems published in England at its author's own expense in 1896, three years before the fighting broke out in South Africa. Although A. E. Housman did not participate in the wars of his time—the Anglo-Boer War, the Great War—he nevertheless included in *A Shropshire Lad* several poems about the fate of the young soldier at war. Modestly presented (and mostly untitled), Housman's poetry was slow to gain readers at first, but about a dozen years after publication, according to Paul Fussell's *The Great War and Modern Memory*, Housman's *A Shropshire Lad* was "'in every pocket' just before the war," and thus "the book was on the spot (as was Rupert Brooke) to take advantage of the increase of interest in poetry brought about by 1914."[24] Not incidentally, that the poetry of Housman and of Brooke was immediately available to the English-language reader (such as Pessoa) at the outbreak of war answers Georg Rudolf Lind's question, "How does the poet, living in a pacific Lisbon, become inspired by bellicose motives, knowing nothing about war other than what the newspapers told him?" ("Como é que o poeta, morando na pacífica Lisboa, se teria inspirado em motivos bélicos, não conhecendo mais sobre a guerra do que aquilo que os jornais relatavam?").[25]

In fairness, it should be noted that Housman's own credibility as an anti-military poet was later compromised by the popular success of "Epitaph on an Army of Mercenaries," a poem recalling the British army's defeat at Ypres in 1914 that he published in 1915. Caught up in home front controversies over whether soldiers should receive payment for their service, Housman supplied a defense of the English mercenary that was adopted as a patriotic rallying poem, celebrating the grit and courage of the British soldier. Useful as propaganda, it was reprinted on anniversaries of the otherwise disastrous defeat. In later years, well aware of how the poem had been employed during the war, Housman refused to let it be reprinted or anthologized. Yet it was not the wrongly or rightly perceived patriotism of "Epitaph on an Army of Mercenaries" that appealed to Pessoa, but Housman's antimilitary ethos, especially as it is expressed in this early *A Shropshire Lad* poem:

On the idle hill of summer,
Sleepy with the flow of streams,

Far I hear the steady drummer
Drumming like a noise in dreams.

Far and new and low and louder
On the roads of earth go by,
Dear to friends and food for powder,
Soldiers marching, all to die.

East and west on fields forgotten
Bleach the bones of comrades slain,
Lovely lads and dead and rotten;
None that go return again.

Far the calling bugles hollo,
High the screaming fife replies,
Gay the files of scarlet follow:
Woman bore me, I will rise.[26]

In "O Menino da sua mãe," Pessoa goes so far as to draw on this Housman poem for particulars. When he writes, "On the deserted plain" the young soldier "lies dead, and is rotting," he echoes Housman's lines "on fields forgotten / Bleach the bones of comrades slain, / Lovely lads and dead and rotten." If Housman's poem works more generally, its naturalistic detail—the corpse left to rot on the deserted battlefield—serves as a poetic gift from Housman to Pessoa contradicting Horace's notion that *dulce et decorum est pro patria mori*—the overarching theme of Rupert Brooke's "War" sonnets. In the poetry written during the war, body parts—usually referred to, with a strong trace of Victorian delicacy, as "limbs"—were lost and heroically dead bodies were interred under fields of red poppies and blooming roses, but it was not noted that myriad corpses, unclaimed for burial, lay rotting on the battlefields where they died.[27] Housman and Pessoa knew better, even if Brooke did not, or would not.

Interesting, too, is the discrepancy between the fate of the corpse in Brooke's poem—it is "claimed," so to speak, and is, of course, buried—and in Pessoa's. The corpse in Pessoa's poem lies on an abandoned field, unburied. It does not take a classicist of Housman's stature and wide learning to recall here the Greek theme of the crime committed against the righteous Antigone when she is denied the right to claim her brother's body for burial, to keep his rotting corpse from becoming food for dogs and scavenging birds. This tragic note is sounded by Pessoa by his singling out, metonymically, the unburied, rotting body of one lad (as Housman would have called him), who was a "mother's boy."[28] Yet, touching history, Pessoa's dead soldier serves as a sign of what was already happening on a then unheard-of scale in astonishing numbers. It is estimated that "some 400,000 British soldiers would have no known grave," according to a recent report, "their bodies swallowed in shell-torn mud, sometimes emerging to this day when a plow strikes bones."[29]

NOTES

1. Philip Larkin, *Required Writing: Miscellaneous Pieces 1955–1982* (New York: Farrar Straus Giroux, 1984), 159.

2. Several other aspects of Pessoa's poem—theme, image, and so on—are discussed by Monteiro in a chapter titled "Webs of Empire: Caroline Norton, Rimbaud, and Others," in *Fernando Pessoa and Nineteenth-Century Anglo-American Literature* (Lexington: University Press of Kentucky, 2000), 129–44. Relevant to this kind of literary scholarship is the American poet Elizabeth Bishop's testimony that "it takes probably hundreds of things coming together at the right moment to make a poem and no one can ever really separate them out and say this did this, that did that." Elizabeth Bishop, *Conversations with Elizabeth Bishop* (Jackson: University Press of Mississippi, 1996), 88.

3. Allardyce Nicoll, ed., *Chapman's Homer: The Iliad* (Princeton, NJ: Princeton University Press, 1998), 448. In Alexander Pope's later translation (published in 1715–1720), these lines are rendered: "While cast to all the Rage of hostile Pow'r, / Thee, Birds shall mangle, and the Dogs devour." Reuben A. Brower and W. H. Bond, eds., *The Iliad of Homer*, trans. Alexander Pope (New York / London: Macmillan / Collier-Macmillan, 1965), 501.

4. Nicoll, ed., 380–81. Pope's version of Achilles's address to the body of Patroclus reads as follows: "Yet, my Patroclus! yet a space I stay, / Then swift pursue thee on the darksome way. / E'er thy dear Relicks in the Grave are laid, / Shall Hector's Head be offer'd to thy Shade; / That, with his Arms, shall hang before thy Shrine, / And twelve, the noblest of the Trojan Line, / Slain by this Hand, sad Sacrifice! expire; / Their Lives effus'd around thy flaming Pyre. / Thus let me lie till then! thus, closely prest, / Bathe thy cold Face, and sob upon thy Breast! / While Trojan Captives here thy Mourners stay, / Weep all the Night, and murmur all the Day: / Spoils of my Arms, and thine; when wasting wide, / Our Swords kept time, and conquer'd side by side. // He spoke, and bid the sad Attendants round / Cleanse the pale Corse, and wash each honour'd Wound. / A massy Caldron of stupendous Frame / They brought, and plac'd it o'er the rising Flame: / Then heap the lighted Wood; the Flame divides / Beneath the Vase, and climbs around the Sides; / In its wide Womb they pour the rushing Stream; / The boiling Water bubbles to

the Brim: / The Body then they bathe with pious Toil, / Embalm the Wounds, anoint the Limbs with Oyl; / High on a Bed of State extended laid, / And decent cover'd with a linen Shade; / Last o'er the Dead the milkwhite Mantle threw; / That done, their Sorrows and their Sighs renew" (Brower and Bond, eds., 432).

5. Emma Lazarus, *The Poems of Emma Lazarus* (Boston / New York: Houghton Mifflin, 1889), I, 213.

6. Georg Rudolf Lind, "Fernando Pessoa perante a primeira guerra mundial," in *Estudos sobre Fernando Pessoa* (Lisbon: Imprensa Nacional–Casa da Moeda, 1981), 425–58.

7. On October 19, 1916, this widely published paragraph appeared in the *New York Times*: "A Madrid dispatch to the Cologne Gazette says no Portuguese troops will be sent to France until two new divisions have been made ready to preserve order in Portugal. Travelers reaching Vigo from Portugal, the dispatch says, declare most of the Portuguese people are opposed to war and many arrests are being made. At Oporto a crowd attacked the barracks, and 130 persons, including soldiers, were arrested," in "Asserts Portuguese Oppose War," *New York Times*, Oct. 19, 1916, 2. Note that these events in Portugal are reported in a Spanish dispatch to a newspaper in Germany. That these details were deemed newsworthy to readers in the United States indicates that what Portugal would do—and when—regarding the war was of interest to more than just the Germans, French, or British.

8. It was reprinted two years later in *O Notícias Illustrado*, on November 11, 1928, marking the tenth anniversary of the true armistice that led to the end of the long war. João Rui de Sousa, *Fotobibliografia de Fernando Pessoa* (Lisbon: Imprensa Nacional–Casa Moeda / Biblioteca Nacional, 1988), 159. And it was published, with minor alterations, also in May 1930 (*Cancioneiro—I Salão dos Independentes*). The poem reproduced in this article is from this last publication.

9. See João Gaspar Simões, *Vida e obra de Fernando Pessoa: História de um geração* (Lisbon: Bertrand, 1950), I.

10. Fernando Pessoa, *Cancioneiro—Iº Salão dos Independentes* (Lisbon, May 10 1930), 1–2.

11. Fernando Pessoa, "His Mother's Child" ["O Menino da sua mãe"], in *Self-Analyses and Thirty Other Poems*, trans. George Monteiro (Lisbon: Calouste Gulbenkian Foundation, 1988), 25.

12. See, for example, "German Colonies," 4.

13. Pessoa was careful to point out that Campos's "Ultimatum" was "not pro-German" but "anti-everything, Allied and German." BNP/E3, 21–121; Fernando Pessoa, *Sensacionismo e outros ismos* (Lisbon: Imprensa Nacional–Casa da Moeda, 2009), 275.

14. Rupert Brooke, *Collected Poems* (New York: John Lane, 1916), 64.

15. Ibid., 66.

16. Geoffrey Keynes, "Preface," in Brooke, The Poetical Works of Rupert Brooke (London: Faber and Faber, 1946), 5.

17. "Death of Mr. Rupert Brooke: Sunstroke at Lemnos," London Times, Apr. 26, 1915, 5.

18. S. P. B Mais, "Rupert Brooke," Fortnightly Review 98 (Aug. 1915), 348. Highly romanticized notions of the heroism of Brooke's life and death persisted. For an example of this, see "The Gods' Beloved," Athenaeum 4632 (Aug. 1918), 354–55.

19. Fernando Pessoa, "Mario de Sá-Carneiro (1890–1916)," Athena 1 (Nov. 1924), 41.

20. Henry James, "Preface," in Letters from America by Rupert Brooke (New York: Scribner's, 1916), xl–xlii.

21. Quoted in John Lehmann, The Strange Destiny of Rupert Brooke (New York: Holt, Rinehart & Winston, 1980), 137–38.

22. Jerónimo Pizarro, Patricio Ferrari, and Antonio Cardiello, A Biblioteca particular de Fernando Pessoa I (Lisbon: D. Quixote, 2010), 201; call number CFP 8–69.

23. BNP/E3, 77–80r; Fernando Pessoa, Poemas Ingleses II (Lisbon: Imprensa Nacional–Casa da Moeda, 1997), 303.

24. Paul Fussell, The Great War and Modern Memory (New York: Oxford University Press, 1979), 282.

25. Lind, "Fernando Pessoa perante a primeira guerra mundial," 425.

26. A. E. Housman, A Shropshire Lad (London: K. Paul, Trench, Trubern, 1896), 41–42.

27. Siegfried Sassoon was the notable exception. In "Counter-Attack," he describes the World War I battlefield: "The place was rotten with dead; green clumsy legs / High-booted, sprawled and groveled along the saps / and Trunks, face downward, in the sucking mud / [. . .]" Sassoon, "Counter-Attack," in The Penguin Book of First World War Poetry (London / New York: Penguin, 1996), 68. See also Sassoon's poem sympathetic to the German dead, "'The rank stench of those bodies haunts me still'" (London / New York: Penguin, 1996), 124–26.

28. By an odd coincidence, Philip Larkin concludes that "the fundamental biographic fact" about Wilfred Owen is that he was "his mother's boy." Larkin, Retired Writing, 231.

29. Geoffrey Wheatcroft, "Hello to All That!," New York Review of Books 58 (June 23, 2011), 28–31.

WORKS CITED

"Asserts Portuguese Oppose War." New York Times, Oct. 19, 1916: 2.

Bishop, Elizabeth. Conversations with Elizabeth Bishop. Edited by George Monteiro. Jackson: University Press of Mississippi, 1996.

Brooke, Rupert. The Poetical Works of Rupert Brooke. Edited by Geoffrey Keynes. London: Faber & Faber, 1946.

Brower, Reuben A., and W. H. Bond, eds. *The Iliad of Homer*. Translated by Alexander Pope. New York / London: Macmillan / Collier-Macmillan, 1965.

"Death of Mr. Rupert Brooke: Sunstroke at Lemnos." *London Times*, Apr. 26, 1915: 5.

Fussell, Paul. *The Great War and Modern Memory*. New York: Oxford University Press, 1979.

"German Colonies to Be Divided Up: Britain, France, Belgium, and Portugal Likely to Readjust their African Possessions." *New York Times*, Feb. 23, 1917: 4.

"The Gods' Beloved." *Athenaeum* 4632 (Aug. 1918): 354–55.

Housman, A. E. *A Shropshire Lad*. Waterville, ME: Colby College Library, 1946.

James, Henry. "Preface," in *Letters from America by Rupert Brooke*, ix–xlii. New York: Scribner's, 1916.

Keats, John. *The Poetical Works of John Keats*. London / New York: Frederick Warne, 1898. CFP 8–294.

Keynes, Geoffrey. "Preface," in *The Poetical Works of Rupert Brooke*, 5–10. London: Faber & Faber, 1946.

Larkin, Philip. *Required Writing: Miscellaneous Pieces 1955–1982*. New York: Farrar Straus Giroux, 1984.

Lazarus, Emma. "Destiny." In *The Poems of Emma Lazarus*. 2 vols. Boston and New York: Houghton Mifflin, 1889.

Lehmann, John. *The Strange Destiny of Rupert Brooke*. New York: Holt, Rinehart & Winston, 1980.

Lind, Georg Rudolf. "Fernando Pessoa perante a primeira guerra mundial." In *Estudos Sobre Fernando Pessoa*, 425–58. Lisbon: Imprensa Nacional–Casa da Moeda, 1981.

Mais, S. P. B. "Rupert Brooke." *Fortnightly Review* 98 (Aug. 1915): 348–62.

Monteiro, George. *Fernando Pessoa and Nineteenth-Century Anglo-American Literature*. Lexington: University Press of Kentucky, 2000.

Nicoll, Allardyce, ed. *Chapman's Homer: The Iliad*. Princeton, NJ: Princeton University Press, 1998.

Pessoa, Fernando. *Sensacionismo e outros ismos*. Edited by Jerónimo Pizarro. Fernando Pessoa's Critical Edition, Major Series, Vol. X. Lisbon: Imprensa Nacional–Casa da Moeda, 2009.

———. *Poemas Ingleses: Poemas de Alexander Search*. Edited by João Dionísio. Fernando Pessoa's Critical Edition, Major Series, Vol. V, Tome II. Lisbon: Imprensa Nacional–Casa da Moeda, 1997.

———. "His Mother's Child" ["O Menino da sua mãe"]. In *Self-Awareness and Thirty Other Poems*, 25. Translated by George Monteiro. Lisbon: Calouste Gulbenkian Foundation, 1988.

————. "O Menino da sua mãe." In *Cancioneiro do I Salão dos Indepenctentes* (Dedicado êste Cancioneiro à memória dos precursores Cesario Verde Camillo Pessanha Angelo de Lima e Mario de Sá-Carneiro), Lisbon, May 10, 1930.

————. "Mario de Sá-Carneiro (1890–1916)." *Athena* 1 (Nov. 1924): 41–42.

Pizarro, Jerónimo, Patricio Ferrari, and Antonio Cardiello. *A Biblioteca particular de Fernando Pessoa (Fernando Pessoa's Private Library)*. Acervo Casa Fernando Pessoa (House of Fernando Pessoa's Collection). 3 vols. Lisbon: D. Quixote, 2010, Vol. I.

Sassoon, Siegfried. "'The rank stench of those bodies haunts me still.'" In *The Penguin Book of First World War Poetry*, 124–26. Edited by Jon Silkin. London / New York: Penguin Group, 1996.

————. "Counter-Attack." In *Collected Poems 1908–1956*, 68. London: Faber and Faber, 1961.

Severino, Alexandrino E. "Was Pessoa Ever in South Africa?" *Hispania* 74 (Sept. 1981): 526–30.

Simões, João Gaspar. *Vida e obra de Fernando Pessoa: História de um geração*. 2 vols. Lisbon: Bertrand, 1950.

Sousa, João Rui de. *Fotobibliografia de Fernando Pessoa*. Lisbon: Imprensa Nacional–Casa da Moeda / Biblioteca Nacional, 1988.

Wheatcroft, Geoffrey. "Hello to All That!" *New York Review of Books* 58 (June 23, 2011): 28–231.

GEORGE MONTEIRO continues to serve as adjunct professor of Portuguese and Brazilian studies at Brown University, Providence, Rhode Island. In recent years he has published *Elizabeth Bishop and Brazil: A Poetic Career Transformed* (McFarland 2012) and *As Paixões de Pessoa* (Atica 2013), as well as co-editing, with Alice R. Clemente, *The Gávea-Brown Book of Portuguese-American Poetry* (Gávea-Brown, 2013). His latest book, *Robert Frost's Poetry of Rural Life* (McFarland) will be published in 2015. His ongoing research on Fernando Pessoa complements *Pessoa Chronicles*, a multivolume collection of original poems still under way.

He can be reached at George_Monteiro@brown.edu.

Notes on the Modernist Long Poem in the Writings of Fernando Pessoa's Heteronym Álvaro de Campos and T. S. Eliot

---

ABSTRACT: Starting from Edgar Allan Poe's assertion that there is no such thing as a long poem, several modernist poets discovered the lyrical potential of a new poetical form in which extension is possible if one follows an analogous principal to that in music: base the poem not on narration, but on a concert of images or emotions that pursue a new language, a language we could say begins with Mallarmé and resolves itself in modern poems of very diverse natures, such as T. S. Eliot's *The Waste Land* and *Four Quartets*, and *Ode marítima* by Fernando Pessoa's heteronym Álvaro de Campos.

The purpose of this reflection is to compare the way Eliot and Pessoa, representing differing contemporary literary traditions, created, each in his own way, the modernist long poem. The result, I hope, may enhance our understanding of this poetic manifestation, not as a national but as a cosmopolitan phenomenon, which may explain its success throughout the last century.

KEYWORDS: Álvaro de Campos, T. S. Eliot, modernist long poem

> That is why Mallarmé, who is so complex and confused, is clearer than Bocage, than Tennyson, than Victor Hugo. Mallarmé unifies his complexity; he knows how long his poems must be and how the insane essence must be developed. He knows what method he must put in his madness.
> —Fernando Pessoa

The modernist long poem is a poetical form that pursued unity in extension, not in the traditional manner—that is, subordination to a narrative or dramatic form—but in the lyrical sense of creating states of mind—emotions, sensations— that correspond to each other and are understood as a single form, as happens in music. In the following pages, I intend to briefly compare the way in which T. S.

Eliot and Fernando Pessoa, modernist poets from differing literary traditions—
American English and Portuguese (with an English insight)—found their way
to the definition and creation of what we now consider modernist long poems.
The result, I hope, may enhance our understanding of this poetic manifestation.

Modernist long poems have been studied and may be understood in many
different ways. For instance, M. L. Rosenthal and Sally Gall, in the 1980s, considered T. S. Eliot's poems *The Waste Land* and *Four Quartets* as modern poetic se-
quences: "a grouping of mainly lyric poems and passages, rarely uniform in
pattern, which tend to interact as an organic whole."[1] I think this definition may
be misleading, especially when comparing these poems with their counterparts
at other latitudes, such as *Ode marítima* (1915) by Pessoa's heteronym poet Álvaro
de Campos. I prefer to understand modernist long poems in a different way,
more as Brian McHale understood them in his essay "Telling Stories Again: On
the Replenishment of Narrative in the Postmodernist Long Poem." McHale
shows us one of the most salient characteristics of the modernist poetic form,
and points out the importance of Ezra Pound and the imagist group for its conformation: "If a prohibition on narrative did not, in fact, figure among Ezra
Pound's 'A Few Don'ts by an Imagist' of 1913, it might as well have, so decisive
was imagism's interdiction of narrative in poetry; and the image, as Joseph Riddel reminds us, 'remains the irreducible element of the modern long poem.'"[2]
Further on, McHale mentions, "Modernism's legacy, then, amounts to a classic
double bind: you must write long poems; but you must not narrate, hence, in
effect, you must not write long poems. Out of this double bind have emerged
the characteristic modernist and postmodernist non-narrative forms of the long
poem."[3]

This interdiction of narrative did not happen only in English-speaking countries. In Spain, the well-known poet Federico García Lorca had encountered the
origin of modern lyrical poems in Góngora's famous *Soledades*. García Lorca,
calling Góngora the "father of modern lyricism," explains in a conference from
1926 that

> Góngora tuvo un problema en su vida poética y lo resolvió. Hasta entonces,
> la empresa se tenía por irrealizable. Y es: hacer un gran poema lírico para
> oponerlo a los grandes poemas épicos que se cuentan por docenas. Pero
> ¿cómo mantener una tensión lírica pura durante largos escuadronados ver-

sos? ¿Y cómo hacerlo sin narración? Si le daba a la narración, a la anécdota, toda su importancia, se le convertiría en épico al menor descuido. Y si no narraba nada, el poema se rompía por mil partes sin unidad y sin sentido. Góngora elige entonces su narración y se cubre de metáforas. Ya es difícil encontrarla. Está transformada. La narración es como un esqueleto del poema envuelto en la carne magnífica de las imágenes. Todos los momentos tienen idéntica intensidad y valor plástico, y la anécdota no tiene ninguna importancia, pero da con su hilo invisible *unidad* al poema. Hace el gran poema lírico de proporciones nunca usadas . . . Las *Soledades*.

(Góngora had one problem in his poetic life and he resolved it. Until then, the task had been considered unattainable. That is: make a great lyrical poem to oppose it to the great epical poems which were counted by dozens. But how to maintain a pure lyrical tension during long squadrons of verse? And how to do it without narration? If he gave narration, anecdote, all the importance, it would turn into epic at any moment. And if he did not narrate at all the poem would split into a thousand pieces without unity or sense. Góngora then selects his narration and covers it with metaphors. Now it is difficult to find. It is transformed. The narration is like the skeleton of the poem wrapped in the magnificent flesh of the images. Every moment has equal intensity and plastic value, and the anecdote has no importance, but it gives, with its invisible thread, *unity* to the poem. He makes the great lyrical poem of never seen proportions . . . The *Soledades*.)[4]

In Portugal, Fernando Pessoa, in an early unpublished manuscript, an essay he was writing—but never completed—around 1912 on the major Portuguese epic poet Luís Vaz de Camões,[5] gives us his account of the matter when he approaches a definition of lyricism: "Construir uma obra qualquér—seja qual fôr o seu caracter ou extensão—sobre um *sentimento* pessoal (e não propriamente concebido □ como artistico) é fazer obra lyrica." (To construct any sort of work—whatever its character or extension—on a personal *sentiment* [and not properly conceived □ as artistic] is to make a lyrical work.)[6] Pessoa remarks in this essay that Camões's epic poem "Os Lusíadas" has a lyrical base, because, he argues, "A poesia epica baseia-se n'um poder de imaginação constructora, ao paso que a poesia dramatica se apoia na d'uma imaginação □, e a lyrica assenta em ser de uma imaginação egoistica, egocentrica, pessoal." (Epical poetry is based on a power of imagination that constructs, whereas dramatic poetry rests on a □

imagination, and the lyric is based on being an egoistic, egocentric, personal imagination.)[7] This is important to understand, because even when Pessoa may appear to contradict himself elsewhere, as will be apparent later, in this definition he refers to lyricism as something possible not only in a short composition, but also in compositions that involve extension.

Taking into consideration not only the comments just cited and his other prose writings on the matter, but the publication of his first long poems in 1915 (*Ode triunfal* ["Triumphal Ode"] and *Ode marítima* [*Maritime Ode*]), Pessoa in the personality of his heteronym Álvaro de Campos seems to have been working on the form of the long poem quite early—more or less at the same time that Ezra Pound may have started working on *The Cantos* and published his "Don'ts."[8] Unfortunately, Pessoa's poems did not reach many readers at his time; it is unlikely that Eliot, or, for that matter, any well-known modernist poet in the world, had heard of them. Thus, the form did not have its origin in one specific place or language from which it may have extended to others, but instead it seems to have emerged simultaneously in different latitudes. Its origin, still, seems to have responded to a unique and cosmopolitan challenge made to poetry by the French symbolists, which is not directly linked to the poetic sequence as understood in an English poetic context.

I would like to start tracing the account of this challenge in Edgar Allan Poe's assertion: "I hold that a long poem does not exist. I maintain that the phrase, 'a long poem,' is simply a flat contradiction in terms."[9] We know this is a common idea now, but I am still surprised to find, among the writings of the poets here brought to our attention, the same passage of Poe's prose discussed, perhaps in an—unconscious?—response to the challenge Poe hints at after explaining his own claim: "If, at any time, any very long poem *were* popular in reality, which I doubt, it is at least clear that no very long poem will ever be popular again."[10]

Eliot, in an essay written around 1948, referring to Poe's observation, reacts with these words: "Poe has a remarkable passage about the impossibility of writing a long poem—for a long poem, he holds, is at best a series of short poems strung together. What we have to bear in mind is that he himself was incapable of writing a long poem."[11] The context of this observation shows us something about the manner in which Eliot differed with Poe: "He could conceive only a poem which was a single simple effect: for him, the whole of a poem had to be in one mood. Yet it is only in a poem of some length that a variety of moods can be expressed; for a variety of moods requires a number of different themes or subjects, related either in themselves or in the mind of the poet. These parts can form a whole which is more than the sum of the parts; a whole such that the pleasure we derive from the reading of any part is enhanced by the grasp of the whole."[12]

As a reaction to Poe's claim, Eliot defines the architecture of the modern long poem. We may complete this definition by adding some lines from Eliot's essay "The Music of Poetry," where the attention shifts—without abandoning Poe's claim—to music as a unifying element: "Just as, in a poem of any length, there must be transitions between passages of greater and less intensity, to give a rhythm of fluctuating emotion essential to the musical structure of the whole; and the passages of less intensity will be, in relation to the level on which the total poem operates, prosaic—so that, in the sense implied by that context, it may be said that no poet can write a poem of amplitude unless he is a master of the prosaic."[13]

Pessoa also commented on Poe's claim. In an early (c. 1915), unpublished fragment intended to be part of a preface to *An English Lyric Anthology* (Appendix I), Pessoa wrote, "When Edgar Allan Poe, cutting the garments of theory from the body of practice, wrote that a poem should be short, he spoke too much from his temperament to let his analysis be free to /qualify/ his critical statement. For if he had analyzed it, he would have qualified it. He would have easily seen that objectively the only species of poems that is of necessity short is the lyrical species; and, subjectively, that it was because he was exclusively a lyrical poet that he had betrayed his intellect into a generality when the whole man of him as poet so clearly lay revealed."[14]

Years later, around 1920, in one of his notes for an unfinished and posthumously published essay called "Erostratus," Pessoa recalls Poe's dictum again, announcing, "Our age is not that of long poems, for the sense of proportion and construction are the qualities that we have not got. Our age is the age of small poems, of short lyrics, of sonnets and of songs."[15] The essay addresses the posthumous celebrity of literary works, and seems to openly agree with Poe. Why, then, would Pessoa have engaged in writing not one, but several long poems? At the moment when Pessoa hinted at the necessity of short lyrics, his famous long poems had already been written and published, or perhaps Pessoa changed his mind on this matter, or he had indeed created his heteronym Álvaro de Campos with a different idea in mind. This personality had a very interesting perspective when venturing into the definitions of art. Consider, for instance, this document, published in 1936, but dating from much earlier. When Campos here refers to a symphonic poem, he seems to recognize not only the modernist long poem, but all hybrid art, so popular in our day:

> Toda a arte é uma forma de literatura, porque tôda a arte é dizer qualquer coisa. Há duas formas de dizer—falar e estar calado. As artes que não são a literatura são as projecções de um silêncio expressivo. Há que procurar em toda a arte que não é a literatura a frase silenciosa que ela contém, ou o poema, ou o romance, ou o drama. Quando se diz "poema sinfónico" fala-se exactamente, e não de um modo translato e fácil. O caso parece menos simples para as artes visuais, mas, se nos prepararmos com a consideração de que linhas, planos, volumes, côres, juxtaposições e contraposições, são fenómenos verbais dados sem palavras, ou antes por hieroglifos espirituais, compreenderemos como compreender as artes visuais, e, ainda que as não cheguemos a compreender ainda, teremos, ao menos, já em nosso poder o livro que contém a cifra e a alma que pode conter a decifração. Tanto basta até chegar o resto.

> (All art is a form of literature, because all art says something. There are two ways of saying something—to speak and to remain silent. The arts that are not literature are the projections of an expressive silence. It is necessary to look in all art that is not literature for the silent phrase it contains, or the poem, or the novel, or the drama. When one says "symphonic poem" one speaks exactly, and not in a figurative and easy way. The case seems less simple for the visual arts, but, if we prepare ourselves with the consideration that lines, surfaces, volumes, colours, juxtapositions and contrapositions are verbal phenomena given without words, or better even spiritual hieroglyphs, we will understand how to understand the visual arts, and, even if we still don't understand them then, we will, at least, have in our power the book that has the cipher and the soul that may contain a key to decipher them. So much must do until the rest arrives.)[16]

However short or long, as he mentions in his essay "Erostratus," Pessoa believed a poem should achieve something he attributed to Milton's *Lycidas* when identifying the elements that may, so to say, redeem a poem: "There is a note of immortality, a music of permanence subtly woven into the substance of some rhythms and the melodies of some poems. There is a rhythm of another speech in which the careful ear can detect the note of a god's confidence in his godship."[17]

As we have seen, both poets, in responding to Poe's words, defended and defined their own poetic practice: the incursion in the uncertain territory of the modern long poem, giving us a clue as to its origin.

A knowledge of French symbolist poetry is fundamental to understanding the conformation of modernist poetics. France represented the poetical vanguard and, as Eliot said, anyone interested in creating a style for himself, any young poet, was attracted to that scenario of innovation: "And at that stage [1908], Poe and Whitman had to be seen through French eyes."[18]

Eliot, who met Paul Valéry, wrote about Valéry's ideas and his poetry;[19] for example, in "From Poe to Valéry," he indicates in what sense Poe's influence led Valéry to his particular consciousness of language. Eliot mentions in this essay that Baudelaire, Mallarmé, and Valéry "[r]epresent the beginning, the middle and the end of a particular tradition in poetry."[20] And, he continues, this tradition involves "[t]he development and descent of one particular theory of the nature of poetry through these three poets and it is a theory which takes its origin in the theory, still more than in the practice, of Edgar Poe."[21] Every one of these poets, Eliot explains, was influenced by Poe, resulting in "[t]he most original development of the aesthetic verse made in that period as a whole."[22] Eliot remarks that Poe, in his essays—especially "The Philosophy of Composition"—might have suggested to Valéry "[a] method and an occupation—that of observing himself write."[23] Eliot did not consider Poe a great poet, and this made him question what it was that these French poets found in Poe that escaped most English readers. His answer: something that was not there at all.

The high point in this genealogy, I want to emphasize, is Mallarmé's "Crise de vers."[24] Mallarmé, as he was introducing free verse, also had insights about the form in which such a verse may happen: a symphony. And it is also in music that Mallarmé found, as Baudelaire had before him,[25] the possibility of a new poetical syntax. Pessoa was well aware of Mallarmé's acute observation. We may note this, for instance, in another unpublished fragment written around 1912, where he states, "Our intellect is Greek, our sensibility modern. Our intellect is as old as Homer, in whose Unity we learn; our sensibility is of the same ages as our verses, which may be but a moment old. | That is why Mallarmé, who is so complex and confused, is *clearer* than Bocage, than Tennyson, than Victor Hugo. Mallarmé unifies his complexity; he knows how long his poems must be and how the insane essence must be developed. He knows what method he must put in his madness. Neither Bocage, Tennyson nor Hugo—to take three examples—are aware of the existence of method, of self-Control, of □."[26]

What I want to stress is that just as Pessoa found in the French poets, Eliot found between Poe and Valéry a series of evolving ideas that would bring about the modern long poems, each in its precise moment and place.

A final note: Donald Davie, in his essay "Pound and Eliot: A Distinction," remarks, "If Laforgue was the presiding genius of Eliot's earlier poems, no figure presided more insistently over the later ones than Valéry, deliberately Mallarmé's disciple, and like his master as much high-priest of symbolist theory as a writer of symbolist poems." [27] And Davie continues:

> We cannot but suppose, therefore, that it is Valéry, bringing with him the whole symbolist endeavour to make poetry approximate to music, who stands behind the title—*Four Quartets*—by which Eliot explicitly indicates a musical analogy for the work which crowns his maturity. And we shall not be surprised to find that 'Burnt Norton,' the first of the Quartets, is a poem very much à la Valéry—a poem in the first place about itself and about the writing of poetry, even (more narrowly) about poetry and music and the specifically close relation between these two arts among the others.[28]

Pessoa's *Ode marítima* also reveals a symphonic design,[29] and, even if it is not as pure an example as the *Four Quartets*, it also deals with literature, with the journey of writing. The difference may be understood to take into account that Pessoa's relation to French Symbolism had two fronts, a friendly and an unfriendly one: Pessoa, like the French poets, searched for the unity, the oneness of the poem or book—as in Mallarmé; but on the other hand, Pessoa was completely against what he called the unreadable vagueness of the symbolists. Pessoa, with the voice of his heteronym Álvaro de Campos, would refer to Mallarmé: "Escrevia em versos rigorosamente 'clássicos,' tinha a mesma nebulosidade de sentido, compelindo o leitor a decifrar charadas sem conceito ao mesmo tempo que procurava senti-las."[30] In the first lines of another of the many unfinished essays that Pessoa left behind, called "A Vigaria" ("The Swindle"), he remarks, "Acabo de não poder ler *La Jeune Parque* de Paul Valéry. Egual coisa me tem succedido com outros versos d'este poeta, de sorte que a minha incomprehensão não me foi novidade. Desejo, porém, para minha tranquilidade mental, analysar essa incomprehensão. É o que vou fazer, de Mallarmé para cá, pois o poeta de nossos dias não é mais que a continuação identica do celebre symbolista." (I am just finished with not being able to read "The Young Fate" of Paul Valéry. The same thing has happened to me with other verses of this poet, in such a way that my incomprehension was no novelty. I wish, thus, on behalf of my mental tranquility, to analyze this incomprehension. And that is what I will do, from Mallarmé to the present day, because poets nowadays are nothing else than the identical continuation of the famous symbolist.)[31] This double admiration and rejection may explain why his poetry participates in the musical innovations of the symbolist poets, but without exploiting symbolist syntax to the same degree that Eliot does.

T. S. Eliot and Fernando Pessoa, reading through the symbolist tradition that started with Poe and ended with Valéry, found inspiration for the form and content of their great poems, each of them molding, with their own personality, as Álvaro de Campos would have said,[32] a style in the cosmopolitan spirit of their time: the modernist long poem.

Appendix I

Preface to *An English Lyric Anthology*

When Edgar Allan Poe, cutting the garments of theory from the body of practice, wrote that a poem should be short, he spoke too much from his temperament to let his analysis be free to /qualify/ his critical statement. For if he had analysed it, he would have qualified it. He would have easily seen that objectively the only species of poems that is of necessity short is the lyrical species;[33] and, subjectively, that it was because he was exclusively a lyrical poet that he had betrayed his intellect into a generality when the whole man of him as poet so clearly lay revealed.[34]

Granted that all poetry is a direct product of the faculty called imagination, let us consider of what it is indirectly the product, that is to say, what inspirational faculties underlie the directly creative faculty of imagination. There are but two that can do so and a third resulting from the combination or interpenetration of these two. Those two are feeling and thought. /The combination of these is twofold: either feeling is thought or thought is felt before being imagined into verse./

Feeling to imagination: Shelley: Asia song.
Intellect to imagination: Anthero: sonetos.
Feeling thought—to im[agination]——Browning: Prospice–(?)
Thought feeling—to im[agination][35]——Tennyson: Higher Pantheism[36]

Anthero does not, strictly speaking, feel what he thinks. He feels *imaginatively* what he thinks, which is a diff[eren]t thing. In the man who, properly speaking, *feels* what he thinks we find the thought merged in the feeling. In Anthero, on the contrary, the thought remains clear in the imagination (even if symbolic) garb. The garments of imagination lie close to the body of thought and give entirely its shape.

Although to feel what one thinks is not, to a strict analysis, the same is thinking what one feels, yet after passing through imagination into Verse, the effect becomes the same. Besides the man whose temperament is feeling his thoughts, or thinking his feelings, will in the first case, if he feels, think his feelings, in the mind, if he then feels his thoughts. The connection between feeling and thought is the essential basis: thus Tennyson thinks his feelings in such a poem as □, and feels his thoughts in such a poem as "The Higher Pantheism." The result is more

Pessoa, "Preface to *An English Lyric Anthology*," 1, BNP/E3, 14⁴-94ʳ.

"Preface to *An English Lyric Anthology*," 2, BNP/E3, 14⁴–94ᵛ.

or less the same, [because] the mental processes involved, though superficially diverse, are essentially manifestations of the same temperament—one in which the *conversion of feeling into thought or thought into feeling is natural and easy.

The highest kind of poetry is that in which there is no preparation for imagination; where feeling *as* thought spontaneously passes into imagination and so break their selves into verse. The process of conversion of thought into feeling or f[eeling] into th[ought] indicates a slowness of the imagination faculty in assimilating the inspirational matter.

NOTES

Epigraph: Fernando Pessoa, *Apreciações literárias de Fernando Pessoa*, ed. Pauly Ellen Bothe (Lisbon: Imprensa Nacional–Casa da Moeda, 2013), 175.

1. M. L. Rosenthal and Sally M. Gall, *The Modern Poetic Sequence: The Genius of Modern Poetry* (New York: Oxford University Press, 1983), 9.

2. Brian McHale, "Telling Stories Again: On the Replenishment of Narrative in the Postmodernist Long Poem," in *The Yearbook of English Studies* XXX (2000), 250. Riddel's quote is from "A Somewhat Polemical Introduction: The Elliptical Poem," *Genre* II (1978), 459–77 (476).

3. McHale, "Telling Stories Again," 251.

4. Federico García Lorca, "La imagen poética de don Luis de Góngora" in *Prosa* (Madrid: Alianza Editorial, 1969), 121–22. All translations in this article, unless otherwise mentioned, are mine.

5. Several years later, Pessoa actually published a short article on Camões—*Diario de Lisboa* 3, 866 (Feb. 4, 1924), 3—but quite distant from the one he projected around 1912, and from which several manuscript fragments remain. See also Pauly Ellen Bothe's article "A Superstição Camoneana," *Pessoa Plural* 2 (Fall 2012), 271–80.

6. Fernando Pessoa, *Apreciações literárias*, 85.

7. Ibid.

8. Ezra Pound, *Literary Essays of Ezra Pound*, ed. with an intro. by T. S. Eliot (London: Faber & Faber, 1954). "A Few Don'ts by an Imagiste" was first published in March 1913, in *Poetry* I, 6, 200–206, a review edited by Harriet Monroe in Chicago.

9. Edgar A. Poe, "The Poetic Principle," in *The Choice Works of Edgar Allan Poe: Poems, Stories, Essays*, intro. by Charles Baudelaire (London: Chatto & Windus, 1902), 642.

10. Ibid.

11. T. S. Eliot, "From Poe to Valéry," in *To Criticize the Critic and other Writings* (New York: Farrar, Straus & Giroux, 1965), 34.

12. Ibid.

13. T. S. Eliot, "The Music of Poetry," in *On Poetry and Poets* (London: Faber & Faber, 1957), 32.

14. From Fernando Pessoa's legacy at the Portuguese National Library (BNP/E3, 14⁴–94). The word between slashes indicates doubt, and it was marked by Pessoa himself, who probably intended to change this word for some other one.

15. Fernando Pessoa, *Páginas de estética e de teoria e crítica literárias*, eds. Georg Rudolf Lind and Jacinto do Prado Coelho (Lisbon: Ática, 1967), 282. Manuscript, c. 1920.

16. Fernando Pessoa, "Um inédito de Álvaro de Campos" ["An Unpublished Document of Álvaro de Campos"], in *Presença* II, 48, dir. and eds. João Gaspar Simões, José Régio, and Casais Monteiro (July 1936, Coimbra), 3.

17. Fernando Pessoa, *Páginas de estética*, 283.

18. T. S. Eliot, *Inventions of the March Hare: Poems 1909–1917*, ed. Christopher Ricks (New York: Harcourt Brace, 1996), 388.

19. For a broader scope of what Eliot wrote on Valéry, see James Torrens, "T. S. Eliot and the Austere Poetics of Valéry," *Comparative Literature* XXIII, 1 (Winter 1971), 1–17.

20. Eliot, "From Poe to Valéry," 28.

21. Ibid.

22. Ibid., 29.

23. Ibid., 41.

24. "Le moderne des météores, la symphonie, au gré ou à l'insu du musicien approche la pensée; qui ne se réclame plus seulement de l'expression courante" ["The symphony, the modern meteor, which following or not the musicien approaches thought"]. Stéphane Mallarmé, *Divagations* (Geneva: Les Éditions du Mont-Blanc, 1943), 250.

25. Charles Baudelaire, "Richard Wagner et Tannhäuser à Paris," in *L'Art Romantique: Littérature et Musique*, ed. Lloyd James Austin (Paris: GF Flammarion, 1968), 267–93.

26. Fernando Pessoa, *Apreciações literárias*, 175.

27. Donald Davie, *Modernist Essays: Yeats, Pound, Eliot*, ed. with an intro. by Cliver Wilmer (London: Carcanet, 2004), 85.

28. Ibid.

29. "[E]sta ode se divide em andamentos, como as sinfonias" ["This ode is divided in movements, as symphonies are"]. António Coimbra Martins, "De Castilho a Pessoa: Achegas para uma poética histórica Portuguesa," *Bulletin des Etudes Portuguaises* XXX (Institut Français du Portugal, 1969), 225–26.

30. "He wrote strictly in 'classical' verse, had the same nebulous sense, compelling the reader to decipher charades without concept at the same time as he tried to feel them." Fernando Pessoa, *Poemas completos de Alberto Caeiro*, ed. and annotated by Teresa Sobral Cunha (Lisbon: Presença, 1994), 272.

31. From Fernando Pessoa's legacy at the Portuguese National Library (BNP/E3, 14E–27ʳ).

32. "O limite que temos é a nossa própria personalidade; é o sermos nós e não a vida inteira." ["The limit we have is our own personality; it is our being ourselves and not the whole of life."] Pessoa, *Poemas completos de Alberto Caeiro*, 272.

33. the only species of poems that are [↑ is] of necessity short are [↑ is] the lyrical species.

34. when his <*len> whole man of [↑ the whole man of him as] poet so clearly lay revealed.

35. "(indistinguishable)" Cf. p. 76 (bottom center of facsimile).

36. "effect produced is the same." Cf. p. 76 (lower right margin of facsimile).

WORKS CITED

Baudelaire, Charles. "Richard Wagner et Tannhauser à Paris." In *L'Art Romantique: Littérature et Musique*, edited by Lloyd James Austin. Paris: GF Flammarion, 1968.

Bothe, Pauly Ellen. "A Superstição Camoneana." *Pessoa Plural: A Journal of Fernando Pessoa Studies* 2 (Fall 2012): 271–80. www.pessoaplural.com.

Davie, Donald. *Modernist Essays: Yeats, Pound, Eliot*. Edited with an introduction by Cliver Wilmer. London: Carcanet, 2004.

Eliot, T. S. *Inventions of the March Hare: Poems 1909–1917*. Edited by Christopher Ricks. New York: Harcourt Brace, 1996.

———. *To Criticize the Critic and other Writings*. New York: Farrar, Straus & Giroux, 1965.

———. *On Poetry and Poets*. London: Faber & Faber, 1957.

García Lorca, Federico. *Prosa*. Madrid: Alianza Editorial, 1969.

Mallarmé, Stéphane. *Divagations*. Geneva: Les Éditions du Mont-Blanc, 1943.

Martins, António Coimbra. "De Castilho a Pessoa: Achegas para uma poética histórica Portuguesa." *Bulletin des Etudes Portuguaises* XXX (Institut Français du Portugal, 1969): 223–345.

McHale, Brian. "Telling Stories Again: On the Replenishment of Narrative in the Postmodernist Long Poem." *Yearbook of English Studies* XXX (2000): 250–62.

Pessoa, Fernando. *Apreciações literárias de Fernando Pessoa*. Edited by Pauly Ellen Bothe. Fernando Pessoa's Critical edition, Collection "Studies." Lisbon: Imprensa Nacional–Casa da Moeda, 2013.

———. *Poemas completos de Alberto Caeiro*. Edited by Teresa Sobral Cunha. Lisbon: Presença, 1994.

———. *Páginas de estética e de teoria e crítica literárias*. Edited by Georg Rudolph Lind and Jacinto do Prado Coelho. Lisbon: Ática, 1967.

———. "Um Inédito de Álvaro de Campos." *Presença* II, 48, directed and edited by João Gaspar Simões, José Régio, and Casais Monteiro (July 1936, Coimbra): 3.

Poe, Edgar A. *The Choice Works of Edgar Allan Poe: Poems, Stories, Essays.* Introduction by Charles Baudelaire. London: Chatto & Windus, 1902.

Pound, Ezra. *Literary Essays of Ezra Pound.* Edited with an introduction by T. S. Eliot. London: Faber & Faber, 1954.

———. "A Few Don'ts by an Imagiste." *Poetry* I, 6, edited by Harriet Monroe (Mar. 1913, Chicago): 200–206.

Rosenthal, M. L., and Sally M. Gall. *The Modern Poetic Sequence: The Genius of Modern Poetry.* New York: Oxford University Press, 1983.

Torrens, James. "T. S. Eliot and the Austere Poetics of Valéry." *Comparative Literature* XXIII, 1 (Winter 1971): 1–17.

PAULY ELLEN BOTHE earned a doctorate in literature from the Universidad Nacional Autónoma de México (UNAM) and a master's degree in comparative literature from the University of Lisbon. She did postdoctoral research at the Linguistic Center of the University of Lisbon (CLUL) between 2010 and 2012, editing *Apreciações literárias de Fernando Pessoa* (Fernando Pessoa's Literary Appreciations [INCM 2013]). She currently teaches Portuguese literature at UNAM and collaborates with the Centro de Literaturas e Culturas Lusófonas e Europeias (CLEPUL) and CLUL.

She can be reached at paulybothe@hotmail.com.

PATRICIA SILVA MCNEILL

Mediating Transnational Reception in Portuguese Modernism
Fernando Pessoa and the English Magazines

ABSTRACT: This essay argues that Fernando Pessoa played a key role as a cultural mediator between English and Portuguese modernist movements, presenting new findings about the importance of literary and cultural magazines for his reception of English Modernism. An examination of sources present in Pessoa's archive, mentioned in his writings on modernist aesthetics and correspondence or relating to works in his private library, shows that Pessoa was familiar with important cultural magazines published in London in the first decade of the twentieth century. Additionally, such an examination traces Pessoa's reception of writers, works, and movements featured in English magazines from the 1910s, and analyzes his engagement with the British avant-garde in his critical writings and literary production for Portuguese magazines.

KEYWORDS: Fernando Pessoa, Álvaro de Campos, poetry, heteronym, literary magazine, *Blast*, *Orpheu*, Cubism, Futurism, Imagism, Sensationism, Vorticism

The introduction to the third volume of *The Oxford Critical and Cultural History of Modernist Magazines*, devoted to Europe, highlights "the networked exchange across borders characterizing European Modernisms and the role of magazines in articulating and mobilising these."[1] This observation aptly describes the reception of British Modernism in Portugal by one of the key figures of Portuguese Modernism, Fernando Pessoa, which to a large extent relied on the mediating role of literary and cultural magazines, and therefore can be regarded as an exemplary case study of transnational exchange between European Modernisms. This subject has not hitherto received much scholarly attention due to the scant information about Pessoa's sources. However, a thorough examination of Pessoa's correspondence alongside new evidence that has come to light as a result of the comprehensive mapping of Pessoa's archive, which has generated an expanded textual and paratextual Pessoan corpus, shows that the Portuguese poet was kept abreast of contemporary literary trends in Britain in the first decade of the twentieth century largely through literary and cultural magazines. Given that Pessoa came into contact with English literary and cultural magazines during the crucial years of the creation of the main triad of heteronyms and of intense cultural activity as a producer of *Orpheu*—the principal cultural magazine of the first Portuguese Modernism—the scrutiny of their reception is particularly pertinent.

Pessoa's interest in modern artistic movements in Britain undoubtedly originates in the fact that he regarded British culture as part of his heritage, having received a formal education in the English language while he lived in South Africa, from ages seven to seventeen. After returning to Portugal at age seventeen to proceed with his studies at the University of Lisbon in 1905,[2] he continued to closely follow developments in the London literary scene by ordering periodicals and publishers' catalogs and buying recently published books by contemporary writers.[3] This was not merely to stay informed of contemporary aesthetic developments and to synchronize his literary production and that of his Lisbon coterie of young writers with the European trends, but it was also with a view to making their works known in the cosmopolitan English publishing milieu, as attested by several letters Pessoa wrote to English publishers between 1912 and 1917. Evidence found in Pessoa's archive shows that he was familiar with several contemporary literary and cultural magazines, ranging from the lowbrow *Tit-Bits* and middlebrow *Pearson's Weekly*, *T.P.'s Weekly*, and *Strand Magazine*, to the highbrow *Athenaeum*, *English Review*, *Poetry Review*, and even the avant-garde magazine *Blast*.[4]

One of Pessoa's chief sources during this period appears to have been *T.P.'s Weekly*, an inexpensive and popular literary magazine with a commendable level of quality, which acquainted him with significant cultural magazines such as the *Poetry Review* and *Blast*; with the work of Yeats, Synge and Chesterton; and with movements such as Imagism and Vorticism.[5] The absence of full issues of the magazine in Pessoa's archive and private library is likely due to its intrinsically ephemeral nature, meaning that the issues would have been discarded once the relevant information about the latest authors, works, and tendencies had been collected. Similarly, no copies of contemporary monthly literary magazines have been found in his archive or private library. Because these magazines were more expensive, it is possible that Pessoa could have read them in a public library, as seems to have been the case with the *Athenaeum*.[6] The exception to this is *Blast* (1914–1915), whose two issues Pessoa kept in his private library.[7] This suggests that *Blast* had a greater impact on his literary and cultural production than did the other magazines, which is corroborated by further evidence discussed at length in this essay.

T.P.'s *Weekly* is mentioned in a letter from December 26, 1912, addressed to the Poetry Society in London, as the source where Pessoa claims to have seen an advertisement for the *Poetry Review*.[8] In it, he enquires about membership in the society and expresses an interest in receiving the magazine issues "from its beginning" or a sample issue, in order to "obtain a nearer knowledge of such currents as must exist in the contemporary English poetry."[9] He adds a further purpose, which consists of "the desire and hope to obtain a channel of some sort through which to carry into some approach to internationality, the extremely important and totally ignored movement represented, exclusively as yet, by contemporary Portuguese poetry."[10] Therefore, Pessoa offers to submit "(not in any way for publishing, but for your personal appreciation)" English poems of his authorship representative of "the state of mind of what is high and poetic in contemporary Portuguese souls," which he compares to "the Elizabethan state of mind," echoing his claims in the articles "A nova poesia Portuguesa" ("The New Portuguese Poetry") published in *A Águia* in 1912.[11] This was Pessoa's roundabout way of trying to secure publication in *Poetry Review*; he likely boasted of having succeeded in a contemporary letter to Mário de Sá-Carneiro that elicited the following reply in a letter from January 7, 1913: "Alegrou-me a sua colaboração nessa revista inglesa" (I was pleased to hear of your contribution to that English magazine).[12]

Because *Poetry Review* had been founded in January 1912, and the Poetry Society had a policy of sending new subscribers the annual volume, it is likely that Pessoa received all the issues for that year. In the annual volume, Pessoa would have read an article by James H. Cousins, titled "William Butler Yeats: The Celtic Lyrist," published in the fourth issue of the magazine dating from April 1912, as argued elsewhere.[13] This special issue devoted to "Modern English Poetry" included a series of brief articles under the heading "Six Living Poets," one of which was Cousins's piece on Yeats. The other articles were titled "Robert Bridges: The Classical Poet," "T. Sturge Moore: The Idyllist," "William Watson: The Poet of Public Affairs," "John Masefield: The Realist in Poetry," and "Rudyard Kipling: The Poet of Reality." As the titles indicate, the series sought to represent the different facets of modern English poetry based on the output of contemporary poets. The coincidence between the epithets applied to these poets—"classical," "idyllist," "realist"—and the aesthetic stances of Ricardo Reis, Alberto Caeiro, and Álvaro de Campos raises the question of whether the typology of modern poets outlined in *Poetry Review* provided a conceptual model for Pessoa's main heteronyms. If Pessoa received the complete volume of the magazine for 1912, it would have been no earlier than January 1913 in view of his letter to the Poetry Society dating from late December. At this time, he was, by his own admission, experiencing a period of intense creativity, which eventually led to the conception of the main triad of heteronyms.

In a letter from February 1, 1913, to his literary associate, Mário Beirão, Pessoa speaks of a crisis of "over-abundance," which resulted in "verses in English, in Portuguese, reflections, ideas, projects."[14] In this letter, Pessoa calls his prolific output during this period "a whole literature," an expression he uses in relation to "the work of Caeiro-Reis-Campos" in another letter from January 19, 1915, to his friend, Armando Côrtes-Rodrigues, suggesting that part of that output was the incipient production of the heteronyms.[15] If Pessoa did not receive the annual volume of the *Poetry Review*, the affinities between the set of articles on contemporary English poets and the subsequent output of his heteronyms—comprising the modern pastoral poet Alberto Caeiro, the neoclassical lyricist Ricardo Reis, and the singer of modern reality Álvaro de Campos—show that he was attuned to contemporary trends in modern poetry outside of Portugal, likely through his attentive reading of literary magazines.

Another name that recurred in the pages of T.P.'s *Weekly* and other magazines throughout 1913 and 1914 was that of Ezra Pound, particularly with regard to his involvement with Imagism. The March 1914 issue of the magazine announces the publication of an "Anthologie des Imagistes," explaining that "*Imagisme* [. . .] is the name given to a new school of English poetry," expounding its chief tenets.[16] The June issue of the same year advertises a second anthology of imagist poetry "*Des Imagistes*," which, according to the reviewer, expresses "that imaginative view of life peculiar to the American poet, Ezra Pound and his followers or co-thinkers."[17] Additionally, Pessoa would have encountered work by several imagists in the special issue of the *Egoist* dedicated to Imagism (May 1915), which he is thought to have received.[18] This would have acquainted him with the aesthetic tenets of the "school" of Imagism, as set out by Harold Monro in the essay "The Imagists Discussed" and with essays by Richard Aldington, editor of the *Egoist* at the time, on the poetry of Ezra Pound and F. S. Flint. The essays in the *Egoist* likely led him to acquire copies of Richard Aldington's *Images* and F. S. Flint's *Cadences* when they were published by the Poetry Bookshop in 1915, and to write to Harold Monro, the proprietor of the Poetry Bookshop and former editor of the *Poetry Review*, to whom he had previously written in 1912 enquiring about that magazine.

In the letter to Monro from May 1915, Pessoa mentions Aldington's and Flint's books and unabashedly claims that "in my own language, Portuguese, I am far more advanced than the English Imagists."[19] He uses the term *intersectionist* to characterize the poems in English that he claims to enclose in the letter alongside his own translation into English of "Chuva oblíqua" ("Slanting Rain"), the series of poems published in the second issue of *Orpheu*.[20] He further explains that "intersectionist is not the distinction of a school or current, like 'futurist' or 'imagist,' but a mere definition of process," claiming that his intention in those poems has been "to register, in intersection, the mental simultaneity of an objective and of a subjective image."[21] Pessoa's definition of the "intersectionist" process of composition resembles Pound's description of his own imagist poetry in an essay titled "Vorticism," wherein—providing as example the hokku-like "The apparition of these faces in the crowd: / Petals, on a wet, black bough."—he claims that in "a poem of this sort one is trying to record the precise instant when a thing outward and objective transforms itself, or darts into a thing inward and subjective."[22] Described in this manner, Intersectionism and Imagism (as a style of poetry theorized by Pound) can be seen as comparable poetic experiments with the binary subjectivity-objectivity in the modern lyric.

Pessoa's Intersectionism and Pound's Imagism display clear analogies to the cubist or simultaneist methods of painting. Pound's goal in the essay mentioned earlier was to foreground the continuities between the practices of the vorticist artists in their unique synthesis of Cubo-Futurism and the expression of a similar aesthetic in poetry, which he termed Imagism. Pessoa also adopted a pictorial language inspired by Cubism to describe the Sensationist (his coinage) aesthetic that Intersectionism (his coinage) is said to stylistically realize, in a fragment in English:

Every sensation (of a solid thing) is a solid body bounded by planes, which are *inner images* (of the nature of dreams—two-dimensioned), bounded themselves by lines (which are ideas, of one dimension only). *Sensationism pretends, taking stock of this real reality, to realise in art a decomposition of reality into its psychic geometrical elements.* [. . .] What is the process to be adopted to realise sensationism? [. . .] Intersectionism realised it by attempting to realise the deformation which every cubic sensation suffers by the deformation of its planes. Now every cube has six sides: these sides, looked at from the sensationist standpoint, are: the sensation of the exterior object as object, quâ object; the sensation of the exterior object quâ sensation; the objective ideas associated to this sensation of an object; the subjective ideas associated to this sensation—i.e., the "state of mind" through which the object is seen at the time; the temperament and fundamentally individual mental attitude of the observer; the abstract consciousness behind that individual temperament.[23]

This passage shows that Pessoa was knowledgeable about the European visual avant-gardes, resorting to the cubist terminology of geometrical decomposition. This is corroborated by his correspondence from 1912 through 1915 with Sá-Carneiro, who kept him informed on the latest artistic developments in Paris and sent him magazines and exhibition catalogs. Indeed, Cubism features repeatedly in their letters, as in Sá-Carneiro's letter from March 16, 1913, in which he claims to be impressed with his friend's knowledge about Cubism, which encompassed the work of Amadeo de Sousa Cardoso.[24] Pessoa also read with interest the vorticists' critique of contemporary artistic movements in *Blast*, judging from the fact that he marked and underlined passages on Futurism, Cubism, and Expressionism in his copies of the first and second issues of the magazine, especially in Wyndham Lewis's "A Review of Modern Art" (*Blast* 2, 40–44). See the first two figures that follow.

Pessoa most likely encountered references to *Blast* and Vorticism in *T.P.'s Weekly* (or possibly the *Poetry Review*). The June 1914 issue announces the launch of the new magazine thus:

This week Mr. Wyndham Lewis commences to "blast" the Futurists. [. . .] on Thursday, "Blast," a new illustrated quarterly, edited by Mr. Lewis and published my Mr. John Lane [. . .] appeared. "It is the Manifesto of the Vorticists," I am told. Surely the correct name for their organ should be "Whirlpool." "The English Parallel Movement to Cubism and Expressionism. Imagism in poetry. Death Blow to Impressionism and Futurism and all the Refuse of Naif Science." The capitals are placed by Vorticists and reproduced by the printers.[25]

the same as Impressionism, largely dosed in many cases with a Michaelangelizing of the every-day figure or scene. (Metzinger's " Femme à la Tasse," etc.) For the great licence Cubism affords tempts the artist to slip back into facile and sententious formulas, and escape invention.

IV.

The other link of CUBISM with IMPRESSIONISM is the especially scientific character of it's experiments. Matisse, with his decoration, preceded the Cubists in reaction against scientific naturalism. But CUBISM, as well, though in a sense nearer the Impressionists than Matisse, rejects the scentless, invertebrate order of Nature seen en petit. Any portion of Nature we can observe is an unorganized and microscopic jumble, too profuse and too distributed to be significant. If we could see with larger eyes we should no doubt be satisfied. But to make any of these minute individual areas, or individuals, too proudly compact or monumental, is probably an equal stupidity. Finite and god-like lines are not for us, but, rather, a powerful but remote suggestion of finality, or a momentary organization of a dark insect swarming, like the passing of a cloud's shadow or the path of a wind.

The moment the Plastic is impoverished for the Idea, we get out of direct contact with these intuitive waves of power, that only play on the rich surfaces where life is crowded and abundant.

We must constantly strive to ENRICH abstraction till it is almost plain life, or rather to get deeply enough immersed in material life to experience the shaping power amongst its vibrations, and to accentuate and perpetuate these.

So CUBISM pulled Nature about with her cubes, and organized on a natural posed model, rather than attempting to catch her every movement, and fix something fluent and secret. The word CUBISM at once, for me, conjures up a series of very solid, heavy and usually gloomy Natures Mortes,—several bitter and sententious apples (but VERY GOOD WEIGHT) a usually pyramidal composition of the various aspects of a Poet or a Man with a Mandoline, Egyptian in static solemnity, a woman nursing disconsolately a very heavy and thoughtful head, and several bare, obviously tremendously heavy objects crowded near her on a clumsy board,—a cup and saucer and probably apples.

I admire some of these paintings extremely. Only we must recognize that what produced these paintings was a marvellous enterprise and enthusiastic experimentation, and that if we are to show ourselves worthy of the lead given us by two or three great painters of the last fifteen years, we must not abate in our interrogation.

V.

The FUTURISTS, briefly, took over the plastic and real, rather than the scientific, parts of the practice of the Cubists. Only they rejected the POSED MODEL, imitative and static side of CUBISM, and substituted the hurly-burly and exuberance of actual life. They have not brought a force of invention and taste equal to the best of the Paris group to bear on their modification of the Cubist formulas. Their work is very much prejudiced by Marinetti's propaganda, which is always too tyrannically literary, and insists on certain points that are not essential to their painting and is in itself rather stupid. His "Automobilism" is simply an Impressionist pedantry. His War-ravings is the term of a local and limited pugnacity, romantic and rhetorical. He is a useful figure as a corrective of very genuine character. But the artist is NOT a useful figure, though he may be ornamental. In fact the moment he becomes USEFUL and active he ceases to be an artist. We most of us nowadays are forced to be much more useful than we ought to be. But our painting at least should be saved the odour of the communistic platform or the medicine chest.

None of the Futurists have got, or attempted, the grandness that CUBISM almost postulated. Their doctrine, even, of maximum fluidity and interpenetration precluded this. Again, they constituted themselves POPULAR ARTISTS. They are too observant, impressionist and scientific; they are too democratic and subjugated by indiscriminate objects, such as Marinetti's moustache. And they are too banally logical in their exclusions.

VI.

The EXPRESSIONISTS finally, and most particularly Kandinsky, are ethereal, lyrical and cloud-like,—their fluidity that of the Blavatskyish soul, whereas the Futurist's is that of 19th century science. Kandinsky is the only PURELY abstract painter in Europe. But he is so careful to be passive and medium-like, and is committed, by his theory, to avoid almost all powerful and definite forms, that he is, at the best, wandering and slack. You cannot make a form more than it is by the best intentions in the world. In many of his abstract canvasses there are lines and planes that form the figure of a man. But these accidents are often rather dull and insignificant regarded as pieces of representation. You cannot avoid the conclusion that he would have done better to ACKNOWLEDGE that he had (by accident) reproduced a form in Nature, and have taken more trouble with it FOR IT'S OWN SAKE AS A FRANKLY REPRESENTATIVE ITEM. A dull scribble of a bonhomme is always that and nothing else.

In the first show the FUTURISTS held in London, in the same way, from their jumble of real and half-real objects, a perfectly intelligible head or part of a figure would stick up suddenly. And this head or part of a figure, where isolated and mak-

Pessoa's reader's marks of the section on futurists, Kandinsky, and Expressionism in Wyndham Lewis's "A Review of Modern Art" in his copy of *Blast* 2 (40).

32. In any heroic, that is, energetic representations of men to-day, this reflection of the immense power of machines will be reflected.

33. But, in the first place, Picasso's structures are not ENERGETIC ones, in the sense that they are very static dwelling houses. A machine is in a greater or less degree, a living thing. It's lines and masses imply force and action, whereas those of a dwelling do not.

34. This deadness in Picasso, is partly due to the naturalistic method, of "cubing" on a posed model, which I have referred to before, instead of taking the life of the man or animal inside your work, and building with this life fluid, as it were.

35. We may say, this being so, that in Picasso's portrait the forms are those of masonry, and, properly, should only be used for such. They are inappropriate in the construction of a man, where, however rigid the form may be, there should be at least the suggestions of life and displacement that you get in a machine. If the method of work or temperament of the artist went towards vitality rather than a calculated deadness, this would not be the case.

36. A second point to underline is the disparity between the spectator's and the artist's capacity for impersonal vision, which must play a part in these considerations.

37. A Vorticist, lately, painted a picture in which a crowd of squarish shapes, at once suggesting windows, occurred. A sympathiser with the movement asked him, horror-struck, "are not those windows?" "Why not?" the Vorticist replied. "A window is for you actually A WINDOW: for me it is a space, bounded by a square or oblong frame, by four bands or four lines, merely."

38. The artist, in certain cases, is less scandalized at the comprehensible than is the Public.

39. And the fine artist could "represent" where the bad artist should be forced to "abstract."

40. I am not quite sure, sometimes, whether it should not be the Royal Academy where the severity of the abstract reigns, and whether we should not be conspicuous for our "Life" and "Poetry"—always within the limits of plastic propriety. Life should be the prerogative of the alive.

41. To paint a recognisable human being should be the rarest privilege, bestowed as a sort of "Freedom of Art."

D.

1. The human and sentimental side of things, then, is so important that it is only a question of how much, if at all, this cripples or perverts the inhuman plastic nature of painting.

If this could be decided we should know where we were. For my part I would put the maximum amount of poetry into painting that the plastic vessel would stand without softening and deteriorating : the poetry, that is to say, that is inherent in matter.

2. There is an immense amount of poetry, and also of plastic qualities as fine as Rembrandt's, in Vincent Van Gogh. But they remain side by side, and are not assimilated perfectly to each other.

3. On the other hand, Kandinsky's spiritual values and musical analogies seem to be undesirable, even if feasible; just as, although believing in the existence of the supernatural, you may regard it as redundant and nothing to do with life. The art of painting, further, is for a living man, and the art most attached to life.

4. My soul has gone to live in my eyes, and like a bold young lady it lolls in those sunny windows. Colours and forms can therefore have no DIRECT effect on it. That, I consider, is why I am a painter, and not anything else so much as that.

5. The eyes are animals, and bask in an absurd contentment everywhere.

6. They will never forget that red is the colour of blood, though it may besides that have a special property of exasperation.

7. They have a great deal of the coldness of the cat, its supposed falsity and certain passion.

8. But they like heat and the colour yellow, because it warms them : the chemicals in the atmosphere that are good for the gloss of their fur move them deeply ; and the "soul" sentimentalizes them just so much as it may without causing their hair to drop out.

9. This being so, the moonlight and moon-rack of ultra-pure art or anything else too pure "se serait trompé de guichet" if it sought to move me.

10. But I have no reason to believe that any attempt of this sort has been made.

11. So much for my confession. I do not believe that this is only a matter of temperament. I consider that I have been describing the painter's temperament.

12. When I say poetry, too, I mean the warm and steaming poetry of the earth, of Van Gogh's rich and hypnotic sunsets, Rembrandt's specialized, and golden crowds, or Balzac's brutal imagination. The painter's especial gift is a much more exquisite, and aristocratic affair than this female bed of raw emotionality. The two together, if they can only be reconciled, produce the best genius.

44

This excerpt highlights two important characteristics of Blast: first, its status as an avant-garde magazine, evident both in its iconoclasm and in its typographical innovation; second, its antagonistic relationship to Futurism, in an effort by London-based artists and writers to dissociate themselves from the "futurist" label applied to avant-garde artists and movements to develop a home-grown aesthetic.

Pessoa would have been interested in a magazine that sought to agitate the English literary establishment and counter the dominance of international Futurism, especially because at that time, he and Sá-Carneiro were planning to launch a literary magazine that sought to produce an equally strong and original impact on the Portuguese literary scene. Discussing the nature of the magazine in a letter to Pessoa from May 14, 1913, Sá-Carneiro states, "A sua ideia sobre a revista entusiasma-me simplesmente. É, nas condições que indica, perfeitamente realizável materialmente, disso mesmo me responsabilizo. Claro que não será uma revista perdurável. Mas para *marcar* e *agitar* basta fazer sair uma meia dúzia de números." (I am simply thrilled with your idea for a magazine. In the terms you describe, it is perfectly feasible materially; I'll take full responsibility for it. Of course it won't be a lasting magazine. But to *make a mark* and *agitate* we only need half a dozen issues.)[26] The fact that Blast sought and achieved this very effect on the English readership, as gathered from contemporary reviews in T.P's Weekly, might explain why Pessoa acquired the two issues of the English magazine.

The first issue of Orpheu (March 1915) was jointly edited by Pessoa and Sá-Carneiro, although it listed as directors and representatives in Portugal and Brazil respectively Luís de Montalvor and Ronald Carvalho, who had idealized the launch of a Luso-Brazilian magazine in partnership with the Lisbon duo and who had suggested its name.[27] This issue had a predominantly post-symbolist quality epitomized by its cover, which was echoed by most of its content, with the exception of "Ode triunfal" ("Triumphal Ode") by Pessoa's heteronym Álvaro de Campos. However, the second issue of Orpheu (June 1915) displays striking parallels with the first issue of Blast in terms of layout, iconography, and content. If Pessoa acquired his copy of Blast 1 following the magazine's publication in June 1914 or in early 1915, it is possible that the English magazine could have influenced certain aspects of the second issue of Orpheu, largely produced by Pessoa.

Although no precise date of purchase of the two issues of the magazine has been determined, Pessoa mentioned it to his fellow editor of Orpheu, who had returned to Paris in July 1915. In a letter from August 10, 1915, Sá-Carneiro alludes to a comment in Pessoa's letter from August 6 about "uma revista inglesa [. . .] quase do tamanho duma mesa" (an English magazine [. . .] almost the size of a table), which is an unmistakable reference to Blast.[28] Because Pessoa's letters to Sá-Carneiro have been lost, it is impossible to know what else he said about the English magazine, apart from the remark on its size that caught his friend's attention. However, the fact that Pessoa mentioned Blast in the same letter in which he discussed the second issue of Orpheu with his friend indicates that he had established some form of connection between the two magazines. In the same letter, Sá-Carneiro congratulates Pessoa for the type of paper and of lettering that he chose for Orpheu 2, which he describes as "tão Álvaro de Campos e, ao mesmo tempo, tão inglesa?" (so Álvaro de Campos and, at the same time, so English?).[29] He asks where Pessoa had sourced them and had the magazine issues printed, which proves that Pessoa had complete editorial control over those aspects of production.[30] Sá-Carneiro's remark also shows that the link Pessoa had established between Orpheu and Blast was probably related to typographic features, which was one of the most distinctive features of the English magazine. Indeed, the block capital letters in bold and the number on the front cover of Orpheu 2 resemble somewhat the block letters on the cover of the first issue of Blast and the numbers in bold that appear in the first vorticist manifesto. The block letters resurface in Sá-Carneiro's "Manucure," a poem that displays a variety of types and sizes that likely elicited his congratulatory remark on Pessoa's editorial choices.

Another significant innovation of the second issue of Orpheu was the introduction of reproductions of cubo-futurist paintings by the Portuguese painter Santa Rita Pintor, rather like the reproductions of vorticist paintings, etchings, drawings, and sculptures in Blast, which also denote the combined influence of Futurism and Cubism. According to Reed Dasenbrock, "Blast from the first was thought of as a magazine involved with both literature and the visual arts."[31] José de Almada Negreiros, one of the contributors to Orpheu and a leading writer and visual artist of the first Portuguese Modernism, ascribes a similar goal to the Portuguese magazine, claiming that it "era já o resultado da convergência da literatura e da pintura" (it was already the result of a convergence of literature and painting).[32]

However, the parallels between the British and the Portuguese magazines are not restricted to formal and iconographic aspects, but also encompass their literary content. Despite being primarily a poetry magazine, *Orpheu* also included other types of texts, such as Pessoa's static drama *O Marinheiro* (*The Sailor*) and Almada Negreiros's poetic prose "Frisos" ("Friezes") in the first issue, and Raul Leal's short story "Atelier" in the second one, recalling the textual diversity of *Blast* that comprised poems, a play, prose fiction, and reviews. What is conspicuously missing in the two issues of *Orpheu* is a manifesto, and this absence is one reservation posited by some critics to considering it an avant-garde magazine, because it lacked the interventionist element characteristic of this type of publication.[33] However, the extreme reaction that *Orpheu* elicited from the Portuguese press and general public, ranging from disapproval to outright slander, attained the "slap in the face of public taste" effect of the avant-garde magazine while stridently announcing the birth of Portuguese Modernism.

Margarida Pereira ascribes a greater aesthetic aggressiveness to the second issue of *Orpheu*, epitomized by Santa Rita Pintor's paintings, Sá-Carneiro's futurist "Manucure," Campos's *Ode marítima*, and Pessoa's intersectionist "Chuva oblíqua."[34] Although this increased aggressiveness undoubtedly derived from the extreme public reaction to the first issue of the magazine, it could also have been inspired by the notoriously combative rhetoric of the first issue of *Blast*, if Pessoa acquired the magazine before the publication of *Orpheu* 2. That a more aggressive posture was intended is corroborated by the fact that the editorial pages of *Orpheu* 2 announce a "Manifesto of the New Literature" in the third issue of the magazine, a likely reference to Álvaro de Campos's "Ultimatum" planned for this issue—which was never published due to lack of funds—and published several years later in *Portugal Futurista* (1917).

Although *Orpheu* did not adopt as aggressive a rhetoric as *Blast*, the Portuguese magazine shared with *Blast* a common goal of launching a national artistic movement as a reaction to international Futurism. In his study of the English avant-garde movement, Dasenbrock claims that "the impetus behind the creation of Vorticism was largely Lewis' need to find a distinctive term for his art *as opposed to* that of Cubism and Futurism."[35] However, as Dasenbrock notes, "planned and announced before the birth of Vorticism, *Blast* was initially announced as a 'Discussion of Cubism, Futurism, Imagism and all Vital Forms of Modern Art'" in the advertisement that appeared in the *Egoist* on April 15, 1914, and "[o]nly in May or June 1914 did Pound and Lewis come up with that new word, Vorticism, to describe their own art in contra-distinction to other isms of modern art, Cubism, Futurism, Expressionism, and Imagism."[36]

Virtually around the same time, Pessoa was himself in search of a distinctive term to describe the multifaceted poetry he was writing and the Portuguese artistic movement he was about to found through the launch of a new magazine. Pessoa eventually called this movement Sensationism, with *Orpheu* as the mouthpiece of the Portuguese Sensationist Movement. In her study of Sensationism and Vorticism, Pereira argues that "the way in which both aesthetics struggle for an originality that reflects the national element from which they arise" could be due to "a possible influence of Vorticism, of which Pessoa was aware, over Sensationism," though her study is inconclusive due to lack of evidence.[37] Access to the issues of *Blast* that had been in the possession of Pessoa's heirs, made possible through their recent digitization as part of the project to catalog Pessoa's private library, has revealed new evidence in support of this hypothesis.[38]

The focus of analysis will be restricted to the first issue of *Blast* (1914), which preceded both issues of *Orpheu*, and will center on the contribution to the second issue of *Orpheu* by the heteronym Álvaro de Campos, the greatest exponent of Sensationism in Pessoa's coterie of poets, who coined its key tenet, "Sentir tudo de todas as maneiras" ("To feel everything in every way").[39] The comparative examination of the first issue of *Blast* and Campos's *Ode marítima* (*Maritime Ode*), published in *Orpheu* 2, suggests that the two manifestos written by Lewis with Pound's collaboration could have provided the inspiration for Campos's poem. Adopting the "blast" and "bless" structure of Apollinaire's "Futurist Anti-Tradition Manifesto" published in *Lacerba*, Manifesto-I blesses England "for its ships," "seafarers," and "ports" in point 1 of the section titled "Bless."[40] Similarly, Manifesto-II states that "the English character is based on the Sea," which endows it with its "particular qualities and characteristics," in paragraphs 6 through 8 of the third part, which were marked by reading signs in Pessoa's copy of the magazine (see figure that follows).[41]

Thus, it would appear that, in *Ode marítima*, Campos takes these statements as a starting point to revisit and revise the maritime cultural imaginary, emulating the tradition of the heroic poem by adopting the triadic structure of the Pindaric ode. The poem begins on a pier by the river Tagus, where the speaker observes the movement of ships at the port of Lisbon and meditates on the psychic and metaphysical implications of sea travel in what constitutes the first section of the poem, corresponding to the strophe in the Pindaric ode.

The speaker's invocation to "nautical things" for poetic inspiration soon launches him on a reverie through "[a]s épocas marítimas todas sentidas no will be always actual, and springs of Creation for these two peoples.

6 The English Character is based on the Sea.

7 The particular qualities and characteristics that the sea always engenders in men are those that are, among the many diagnostics of our race, the most fundamentally English.

8 That unexpected universality as well, found in the completest English artists, is due to this.

35

Pessoa's reader's marks of section of Manifesto-II on the English and the sea in his copy of *Blast* 1 (35).

passado" (every seafaring age there ever was),[42] which constitutes the second and longer section of the poem, corresponding to the antistrophe in the Pindaric ode:

Homens do mar actual! homens do mar passado!
Comissários de bordo! escravos das galés! combatentes de Lepanto!
Piratas do tempo de Roma! Navegadores da Grécia!
Fenícios! Cartaginêses! Portuguêses [. . .]

(Men of today's ocean! Men of yesterday's ocean!
Pursers! Galley slaves! Combatants at Lepanto!
Pirates from Roman times! Mariners from Greece!
Phoenicians! Carthaginians! Portuguese [. . .])[43]

Despite the array of past maritime ages evoked in these verses, the prevalent cultural references associated with this maritime imagery belong to the English literary heritage. Hence, the speaker's guide to "the ancient sea life" is an English sailor:

Tu, marinheiro inglês, Jim Barns meu amigo, fôste tu
Que me ensinaste êsse grito antiquíssimo, inglês,
Que tão venenosamente resume
Para as almas complexas como a minha
A voz inédita e implícita de todas as cousas do mar,
Dos naufrágios, das viagens longinquas, das travessias perigosas.
Esse teu grito inglês, tornado universal no meu sangue, [. . .]
(Fingias sempre que era por uma escuna que chamavas,
E dizias assim, pondo uma mão de cada lado da bôca,
Fazendo porta-voz das grandes mãos cortidas e escuras:
Ahò-ò-ò-ò-ò-ò-ò-ò-ò-ò—yyyy . . .
Schooner ahò-ò-ò-ò-ò-ò-ò-ò-ò-ò-ò—yyyy . . .)

(It was you, Jim Barnes, English sailor and my friend,
Who taught me that ancient English cry
Which so virulently sums up
For complex souls like mine
The confused call of the waters,
The uncanny, implicit voice of all maritime things,

95

Of shipwrecks, of long voyages, of dangerous crossings.
That English cry of yours, which in my blood becomes universal, [. . .]

[You always pretend to be calling a schooner,
Cupping your large, dark and weathered hands
On the sides of your mouth to make a megaphone, crying:
Aho-o-o-o-o-o-o-o-o-o-o—yyyy . . .
Schooner aho-o-o-o-o-o-o-o-o-o-o-o-o—yyyy . . .])[44]

The sailor's name was possibly inspired by characters from short stories in W. W. Jacobs's *Sailors' Knots* (1909).[45] The traditional English nautical call of mariners is evoked, as is the dying song of Captain Flint, the notorious pirate from Robert Louis Stevenson's *Treasure Island* (1883):

E estala em mim, feroz, voraz,
A canção do Grande Pirata,
A morte berrada do Grande Pirata a cantar
Até meter pavor plas espinhas dos seus homens abaixo.
Lá da ré a morrer, e a berrar, a cantar:
Fifteen men on the Dead Man's Chest.
Yo-ho-ho and a bottle of rum!
E depois a gritar, numa voz já irreal, a estoirar no ar:
Darby M'Graw-aw-aw-aw-aw!
Darby M'Graw-aw-aw-aw-aw-aw-aw-aw!
Fetch a-a-aft the ru-u-u-u-u-u-u-u-um, Darby!

(And from deep within booms the *savage* and insatiable
Song of the Great Pirate,
The bellowing death of the Great Pirate,
Whose singing sends a chill down the spine of his men.
Astern he dies, howling his song:
Fifteen men on the Dead Man's Chest.
Yo-ho-ho and a bottle of rum!
And then yells in a blasting, unreal voice:
Darby M'Graw-aw-aw-aw-aw!
Darby M'Graw-aw-aw-aw-aw-aw-aw-aw!
Fetch a-a-aft the ru-u-u-u-u-u-u-u-um, Darby!)[46]

The savage epithet that Campos ascribes to the song of the Great Pirate, and which is signaled by the onomatopoeic freedom of the lines conveying the lyrics, encapsulates the condition to which Campos aspires, echoing the vorticist tenet that "the artist of the modern movement is a savage," expounded in paragraph 9 of the second section of Manifesto-II.[47] This praise expands into a long hymn celebrating the violent exploits of the pirates and their fearless and feared domination of the sea in an emotional crescendo that functions as a climax to the second section of the ode.

By claiming that the sailor's English cry has become universal in his blood in the first excerpt (emphasized line), the speaker identifies universality as a collective character trait belonging to the Portuguese race, metonymically encapsulated in the epithet "my blood." In doing so, Campos counters the vorticists' claim that the "universality" of English artists is due to the fact that the "English Character is based on the Sea" in the sections of Manifesto-II mentioned earlier, highlighted by Pessoa in his copy of the magazine. Campos's appropriation and subversion of a key vorticist principle can be seen as a historical revisionist gesture that reclaims cultural hegemony of the sea and all things maritime for the Portuguese, collectively represented by the speaker of the poem, who fashions himself as a modern Camões and sings the illustrious Lusitanian maritime past in the lines "Portuguêses atirados de Sagres / Para a aventura indefinida, para o Mar Absoluto, para realizar o Impossível!" ("Portuguese launched from Sagres / Into an uncertain adventure, onto the Absolute Sea, to achieve the Impossible!").[48]

Possibly taking the cue from the vorticists, in a text in English drafted as a preface to an "Anthology of Sensationist Poets" (1916), Campos claims that "the Portuguese temperament is universal" and that "[t]he Portuguese Sensationists are original and interesting because, being strictly Portuguese, they are cosmopolitan and universal."[49] However, he highlights the cosmopolitanism of the Portuguese sensationists seemingly by contrast to the vorticists, who define their aesthetic as "native art" in the fifth part of Manifesto-II.[50] Their claim that this indigenous "ENGLISH art" is an instance of "Northern Art" and, therefore, is opposed to that practiced by "the Romance peoples" of the "South" betrays a nationalist and regionalist bias,[51] to which Campos opposes the "temperamental nonregionalism" of the Portuguese, which, in his view, warrants the originality of the Portuguese Sensationists.[52]

97

6   To believe that it is necessary for or conducive to art, to "improve" life, for instance—make architecture, dress, ornament, in "better taste," is absurd.

7   The Art-instinct is permanently primitive.

8   In a chaos of imperfection, discord, etc., it finds the same stimulus as in Nature.

9   The artist of the modern movement is a savage (in no sense an "advanced," perfected, demo-cratic, Futurist individual of Mr. Marinetti's limited imagination): this enormous, jangling, journalistic, fairy desert of modern life serves him as Nature did more technically primitive man.

10   As the steppes and the rigours of the Russian winter, when the peasant has to lie for weeks in his hut, produces that extraordinary acuity of feeling and intelligence we associate with the Slav; so England is just now the most favourable country for the appearance of a great art.

33

Pessoa's reader's marks of section of Manifesto-II on the modern artist as "savage," *Blast* 1 (33).

On the other hand, in other texts from Blast that are not as concerned as the manifestos with distinguishing Vorticism from other contemporary movements such as Futurism, the nationalist claims become more ambivalent, as in Lewis's observation that "the universal artist, in fact, is in the exactest sense national. He gathers into one all the types of humanity at large that each country contains" in "The Art of the Great Race."[53] This turn of phrase calls to mind Campos's articulation of the sensationist desire for ubiquity encapsulated in the closing line of "Ode triunfal" ("Triumphal Ode"): "Ah não ser eu toda a gente e toda a parte!" ("Ah if only I could be all people and all places!").[54] The cosmopolitanism celebrated in this line and throughout the whole poem is further reinforced by the fact that Campos places its composition in London and dates it June 1914, coinciding with the place and date of publication of Blast, thus paying homage to his Anglophone aesthetic affiliations.

Awoken from his reverie by the cry of the English sailor, the speaker finds himself once again on the pier and in present-day reality. In the third section of the poem, corresponding to the epode of the Pindaric ode, he meditates on modern maritime life, describing it as sanitized, healthy, and efficient by contrast to the savagery of the past. Still, he claims, not without irony,

Nada perdeu a poesia. E agora há mais as máquinas
Com a sua poesia também, e todo o novo género de vida
Comercial, mundana, intelectual, sentimental,
Que a era das máquinas veio trazer para as almas.

(Nothing has lost its poetry.
And now there are also machines
With their poetry, and this entirely new kind of life,
This commercial, worldly, intellectual and sentimental life
Which the machine age has conferred on our souls.)[55]

This section of the poem denotes the influence of the futurist cult of the machine. However, Campos praises not only their beauty, like "The Founding and Manifesto of Futurism" (1909), but also the efficiency of the ships and of their machine parts:

Todas as peças das máquinas, todos os navios pelos mares, [. . .]
Tão maravilhosamente combinando-se

Que corre tudo como se fôsse por leis naturais,
Nenhuma cousa esbarrando com outra!

(All the machine parts, all oceangoing vessels, [. . .]
So perfectly integrated
That everything seems to happen by natural laws
Nothing ever colliding with anything else!)[56]

By juxtaposing the commercial efficiency of modern ships with ancient maritime epics such as Homer's *Odyssey*, the speaker contrasts the new values associated with capitalist modernity to the old world order, which he had so nostalgically evoked in the preceding section. His praise of the efficiency of the machines in modern ships resembles the importance ascribed to machine-like efficiency by the vorticists. In "A Review of Contemporary Art," Lewis criticizes Picasso's structures for not being "energetic" (a comment that Pessoa highlighted in his copy of the magazine), claiming that "in our time it is natural that an artist should wish to endow his 'bonhomme' when he makes one in the grip of an heroic emotion, with something of the fatality, grandeur and efficiency of the machine."[57] Lewis is here evoking a drawing he had published in the first issue of *Blast*, titled "Timon of Athens," which consists of a graphic representation of Lewis's remarks in its depiction of the homonymous character from Shakespeare's tragedy.[58] Similarly, in his manifesto, Pound defines the *vortex* as "the point of maximum energy," which "represents, in mechanics, the greatest efficiency," underscoring the technical quality of his acceptation of the term.[59]

Accordingly, whereas the self-induced depersonalizing reverie in the second part of *Ode marítima* leads the speaker to experience the sailors' heroism and the pirates' savagery, in the alert state of the final section, he describes his feelings as "naturais e comedidos como gentlemen, / [. . .] práticos, longe de desvairamentos" ("natural and discreet like gentlemen, / [. . .] practical and free of hysteria").[60] These emotions are more in accordance with the temperament and mindset of his regular self: "Eu o engenheiro, eu o civilizado, eu o educado no estrangeiro" ("I the engineer and sophisticate who studied abroad").[61] Significantly, Pessoa's choice, in fictional biographical notes, to depict Álvaro de Campos as a naval engineer educated in Glasgow might have something to do with the vorticists' claim, in Manifesto-II of the first issue of *Blast*, that industrialized England was the bedrock of "the Modern World" and that it could convey "the new possibilities of expression in present life" better than any other European nation.[62]

"Ode triunfal," published in *Orpheu* 1, is often considered the instance of reception of Futurism by Campos, whereby the heteronym dialogues with a major European avant-garde movement, and reconfigures its underlying principle of celebration of modernity and the machine in the context of his own aesthetic concerns. Campos himself, who publicly claims that he is not a futurist in a letter to *Diário de Notícias* from June 4, 1915, concedes that "A minha 'Ode Triunfal,' no 1º número do *Orpheu*, é a única coisa que se aproxima do futurismo. Mas aproxima-se pelo assunto que me inspirou, não pela realização" ("My 'Triumphal Ode' is the only thing that comes close to Futurism, though it does so for its object of inspiration, not for its execution").[63] In turn, *Ode marítima*, published in *Orpheu* 2, would be more accurately described as Campos's dialogue with Vorticism, an avant-garde movement that emerged as a local response to international Futurism in Britain.

The scrutiny of *Blast* and *Orpheu* undertaken in this essay has revealed illuminating parallels between the English and the Portuguese modernist magazines, which shed light on the potential impact of Vorticism on the First Portuguese Modernism. These points of contact are particularly salient in Pessoa's self-fashioned Sensationism, which informs both the content and structure of the second issue of *Orpheu*. Judging from Pessoa's reading marks, he became aware of close affinities between the vorticist principles proposed in *Blast* and his own aesthetic tendencies and, therefore, could have incorporated some of them into his theorization of Sensationism and his poetic practice. This would have been in accordance with the syncretism underlying "[t]he sensationist movement (represented by the Lisbon quarterly 'Orpheu') [which] represents the final synthesis. It gathers into one organic whole [. . .] the several threads of modern movements, extracting honey from all the flowers that have blossomed in the gardens of European fancy."[64]

Aside from Pessoa's productive and highly original dialogue with Vorticism, this essay has also established significant parallels between Pessoa's aesthetic theories and poetic practices and those of important contemporary movements such as Imagism and figures such as Ezra Pound. Most significantly, it has underscored the importance of cultural magazines as a resource for Pessoa, and the key role they played in his reception of British Modernism and, through his mediation, its reception in Portugal. This exercise was particularly fruitful in light of the fact that Pessoa was the leading figure of the first generation of Portuguese modernists and was involved, as managing editor or major contributor, in the production of several Portuguese magazines from that generation, having also produced a substantial and significant aesthetic discourse on Portuguese Modernism. All this makes him a major cultural agent in Portugal in the first decades of the twentieth century, as well as a disseminator of modern British artistic culture in a country whose knowledge and contact in that respect was extremely limited. The elements Pessoa gleaned from these cultural magazines circulated among the *Orpheu* circle and inspired the creative production of several of his contemporaries. Indeed, the mapping of Pessoa's reception and dissemination of British Modernism undertaken in this article, and the comparative exploratory readings carried out, incite further reappraisals of his own works and those of other figures of the first generation of Portuguese modernists in light of the new findings.

NOTES

1. Peter Brooker, "Introduction," in *The Oxford Critical and Cultural History of Modernist Magazines, Volume III: Europe 1880—1940*, ed. Peter Brooker, Sascha Bru, Andrew Thacker, and Christian Weikop (Clarendon: Oxford University Press, 2013), 21.

2. See Luís Prista, "Pessoa e o curso superior de letras," in various authors, *Memórias dos afectos: Homenagem da cultura Portuguesa ao Prof. Giuseppe Tavani* (Lisbon: Edições Colibri, 2001), 157–85.

3. See Antonio Cardiello, "Selos [Stamps]," *Biblioteca digital de Fernando Pessoa* (Casa Fernando Pessoa website, bilingual article, 2010), 1. http://casafernandopessoa.cm-lisboa .pt/bdigital/index/selos.htm. And see Patricio Ferrari, "Genetic Criticism and the Relevance of Metrics in Editing Pessoa's Poetry," *Pessoa Plural* 2 (Fall 2012), 9.

4. I wish to thank Patricio Ferrari for the information about references to some of these publications found in Pessoa's archive. *T.P.'s Weekly* and the *English Review* are mentioned in a note in which Pessoa criticizes Masefield's and Kipling's high number of votes in a plebiscite held by *T.P.'s Weekly* in 1913, included in the critical apparatus of *Apreciações literárias de Fernando Pessoa*, ed. Pauly Ellen Bothe (Lisbon: Imprensa Nacional– Casa da Moeda, 2013), 548, 293.

5. The *Poetry Review* is announced as connected to the Poetry Society and described as "an improvement upon previous journals dealing with poetry" in the February 1912 issue of *T.P.'s Weekly* (20: 71). *Blast* is advertised as a "new illustrated quarterly" in the June 1914 issue of *T.P.'s Weekly* (23: 788). Yeats is often mentioned throughout the 1912 and 1913 issues of *T.P.'s Weekly*, including in an article titled "Mr. W. B. Yeats: Poet and Mystic,"

published in the April 1913 issue of the magazine. In light of Pessoa's interest in mysticism, this facet of the Irish poet might have led him to acquire a volume of Yeats's poetry, *A Selection from the Poetry of W.B. Yeats* (Tauchnitz, 1913). The anthology of Synge's plays (Maunsel, 1912) found in Pessoa's personal library is advertised in the June 1912 issue of *T.P.'s Weekly* (20: 744). Chesterton's *The Victorian Age in Literature* (1913), a copy of which also exists in Pessoa's private library, is reviewed in the March 1913 issue of *T.P.'s Weekly* (21: 329). The two imagist anthologies published in London in 1914 are announced in the March and June issues of *T.P.'s Weekly*.

6. I wish to thank Jorge Uribe for drawing my attention to Pessoa's annotation to read the *Athenaeum* in the Library of the Academy of Sciences in the page of a diary from 1913 (BNP / E3, 28–94).

7. Fernando Pessoa, *Escritos autobiográficos, automáticos e de reflexão Pessoal*, ed. Richard Zenith (Lisbon: Assírio & Alvim, 2003), 272. Fernando Pessoa, *Sensacionismo e outros ismos*, ed. Jerónimo Pizarro (Lisbon: Imprensa Nacional–Casa da Moeda, 2009), 656, 658.

8. Fernando Pessoa, *Correspondência*, ed. Manuela Parreira da Silva, 2 vols (Lisbon: Assírio & Alvim, 1999), Vol. I: 1905–1922, 59.

9. Pessoa, *Correspondência*, I, 59. In the catalog of Pessoa's private library, the editors mention "a list of tasks, presumably from 1913," which includes a reference to "The Poetry Society" and the annotations "Ask for a specimen of H[arold] Monro's journal, and the Poetry Bookshop catalog" and "Order papers, books, etc." (Jerónimo Pizarro, Patricio Ferrari, and Antonio Cardiello, eds., *A Biblioteca particular de Fernando Pessoa [Fernando Pessoa's Private Library]* I [Lisbon: D. Quixote, 2010], 14.) The list is transcribed in Appendix II of the book, with the full identification of the manuscripts in Pessoa's archive (BNP/E3, 28A–9r, 28–95, 28–94), and described as torn from a 1913 diary (Pizarro, Ferrari and Cardiello, *Biblioteca*, 428). Because the date on the diary page refers to January 5, 1913, this document is likely related to a letter Pessoa drafted to the Poetry Society on December 26, 1912 (Pessoa, *Correspondência*, I, 58–61). In the diary entry, under the heading "The Poetry Society—entrar para" [The Poetry Society—enter], Pessoa wrote "(concurso de poesia da 'The Poetry Review')" [poetry competition of the *Poetry Review*], which shows that Pessoa intended to enter this competition.

10. Pessoa, *Correspondência*, I, 59. The movement Pessoa is referring to (which he dates back to 1898) is the Renascença Portuguesa, of which he provides an overview, referring to Guerra Junqueiro's *Pátria* and *Oração à luz* (without mentioning their names) as its greatest achievements (Ibid., 60).

11. Ibid.

12. Mário de Sá-Carneiro, *Cartas de Sá-Carneiro a Fernando Pessoa*, ed. Manuela Parreira da Silva (Lisbon: Assírio & Alvim, 2001), 28.

13. Patricia Silva McNeill, *Yeats and Pessoa: Parallel Poetic Styles* (Oxford: Legenda, 2010), 2. An alternative or additional source for the reception of Yeats by Pessoa is G. H. Mair's *English Literature: Modern*, which Pessoa likely acquired in 1912, after reading the publication notice in the January issue of T.P.'s *Weekly* (19: 67). That Pessoa read this book is corroborated by the reading marks in the section on Yeats as the leader of the Celtic Revival in the existing copy of the book in Pessoa's personal library (Mair 241–42). Pessoa also read about J. M. Synge in Mair's study, which praised the Irish playwright as the "great dramatist" of the "Irish school of drama," comparing him to "the great masters of drama," including Shakespeare (247, 249). The critic's encomiastic remarks about Synge and his comparison of the Irish playwright to Shakespeare and other greats clearly caught Pessoa's attention, because he underlined and marked these sections in his copy of the book. This likely led him to acquire the anthology of Synge's plays announced in a later issue that year of T.P's *Weekly*.

14. Fernando Pessoa, *A Centenary Pessoa*, ed. Eugénio Lisboa and L. C. Taylor (New York: Routledge, 2003), 132.

15. Ibid. See also Darlene J. Sadlier, *An Introduction to Fernando Pessoa: Modernism and the Paradoxes of Authorship* (Gainesville: University Press of Florida, 1998), 5.

16. T.P.'s *Weekly* 23 (1914), 306.

17. Ibid, 815.

18. Pessoa, *Sensacionismo*, 385.

19. Pessoa, *Sensacionismo*, 387.

20. Ibid. The critical apparatus includes a draft of an "Interseccionist poem" in English dated March 25, 1914 (Ibid., 449–50), therefore contemporary with "Chuva oblíqua," in which objective and subjective images intersect. I wish to thank Jerónimo Pizarro for drawing this draft to my attention.

21. Ibid., 387.

22. Ezra Pound, "Vorticism," in *Ezra Pound and the Visual Arts*, ed. Hariet Zinnes (New York: New Directions, 1980), 204.

23. Pessoa, *Sensacionismo*, 153–54.

24. Sá-Carneiro, *Cartas de Sá-Carneiro*, 59.

25. T.P.'s *Weekly* 23, 788.

26. Sá Carneiro, *Cartas de Sá-Carneiro*, 91. This idea subsequently matured, and most likely around the time Pessoa wrote the first intersectionist poems in 1914, it materialized as a plan and table of contents for a magazine titled *Europa: Revista Orgão do Interseccionismo* (Pessoa, *Sensacionismo*, 36–37).

27. Mário da Silva Brito, *História do modernismo Brasileiro*, 3rd ed. (Rio de Janeiro: Civilização Brasileira/INL, 1971), 38.

28. Sá-Carneiro, *Cartas de Sá-Carneiro*, 189.

29. Ibid., 188.

30. Ibid.

31. Reed Way Dasenbrock, The Literary Vorticism of Ezra Pound and Wyndham Lewis: Towards the Condition of Painting (Baltimore / London: Johns Hopkins University Press, 1985), 14.

32. José de Almada Negreiros, Textos de intervenção (Lisbon: Imprensa Nacional–Casa da Moeda, 1986), 174.

33. Margarida Isabel Esteves da Silva Pereira, A Vanguarda historica na Inglaterra e em Portugal: Vorticismo e futurismo (Braga: Universidade do Minho / Centro de Estudos Humanisticos, 1998), 102–3.

34. Ibid., 97.

35. Dasenbrock, The Literary Vorticism, 3.

36. Ibid., 13–14.

37. Pereira, Vanguarda, 154.

38. CFP 0–29MN.

39. Fernando Pessoa, Poemas de Álvaro de Campos, ed. Cleonice Berardinelli (Lisbon: Imprensa Nacional–Casa da Moeda, 1990), 263; Fernando Pessoa, Fernando Pessoa & Co: Selected Poems, ed. and trans. Richard Zenith (New York: Grove Press; Atlantic Monthly Press, 1999), 146.

40. Blast 1, ed. Wyndham Lewis (London: Thames & Hudson, 2009 [repr. 1914]), 23.

41. Ibid., 35.

42. Pessoa, Poemas de Álvaro de Campos, 87. Pessoa, A Little Larger Than the Entire Universe: Selected Poems, ed. and trans. Richard Zenith (London / New York: Penguin, 2006), 173.

43. Pessoa, Poemas de Álvaro de Campos, 89; Pessoa, A Little Larger, 175.

44. Pessoa, Poemas de Álvaro de Campos, 87; Pessoa, A Little Larger, 173 (emphases added).

45. Pessoa had this and several other books by Jacobs in his private library and, in a personal note in English estimated to be from 1910, he claimed to "have read Mr. W. W. Jacobs' books," which centered for the most part on marine life, "several times over" (Pessoa, Páginas íntimas e de auto-interpretação, ed. Georg Rudolf Lind and Jacinto do Prado Coelho [Lisbon: Ática, 1966], 20).

46. Pessoa, Poemas de Álvaro de Campos, 92; Pessoa, A Little Larger, 178 (emphasis added).

47. Blast 1, 33. This paragraph is also marked in Pessoa's copy of the magazine.

48. Pessoa, Poemas de Álvaro de Campos, 89; Pessoa, A Little Larger, 175.

49. Pessoa, Sensacionismo, 218.

50. Blast 1, 37.

51. Ibid., 38, 41, 42. Pessoa also highlighted passages about this topic in Part VII of Manifesto-II (par. 5, 6).

52. Pessoa, *Sensacionismo*, 218. Pessoa was equally critical of another foreign cultural movement that had inspired his literary nationalism at an early stage of his career, namely the Celtic Revival, which he dissociates from Sensationism in a fragment in English, thought to be from 1914: "We do not fall into the narrowness of regionalist movements and such like; we must not be confounded with things like the 'Celtic Revival' or any Yeats fairynonsense. We are not Portuguese writing for Portuguese; [. . .]. We are Portuguese writing for Europe, for all civilisation; we are nothing as yet, but even what we are now doing will one day be universally known and recognised" (McNeill, *Yeats and Pessoa*, 77).

53. *Blast 2*, ed. Wyndham Lewis (Santa Rosa, CA: Black Sparrow Press, 2000 [reed. 1915]), 72.

54. Pessoa, *Poemas de Álvaro de Campos*, 73; Pessoa, *A Little Larger*, 160.

55. Pessoa, *Poemas de Álvaro de Campos*, 104–5; Pessoa, *A Little Larger*, 191–92.

56. Pessoa, *Poemas de Álvaro de Campos*, 104; Pessoa, *A Little Larger*, 191.

57. *Blast 2*, 44, 43.

58. *Blast 1*, fig. v.

59. Ibid., 153.

60. Pessoa, *Poemas de Álvaro de Campos*, 105; Pessoa, *A Little Larger*, 192.

61. Pessoa, *Poemas de Álvaro de Campos*, 86; Pessoa, *A Little Larger*, 172.

62. *Blast 1*, 39, 41.

63. Pessoa, *Sensacionismo*, 376.

64. Ibid., 159.

WORKS CITED

A Biblioteca particular de Fernando Pessoa (Fernando Pessoa's Private Library). Vol. I. Edited by Jerónimo Pizarro, Patricio Ferrari, and António Cardiello. Lisbon: D. Quixote, 2010.

Blast 1. Edited by Wyndham Lewis. London: Thames & Hudson, 2009 (reed. 1914).

Blast 2. Edited by Wyndham Lewis. Santa Rosa, CA: Black Sparrow Press, 2000 (repr. 1915).

Brito, Mário da Silva. *História do modernism brasileiro*. 3rd ed. Rio de Janeiro: Civilização Brasileira/INL, 1971.

Brooker, Peter. "Introduction." In *The Oxford Critical and Cultural History of Modernist Magazines, Volume III: Europe 1880—1940*, edited by Peter Brooker, Sasha Bru, Andrew Thacker, and Christian Weikop. Clarendon: Oxford University Press, 2013.

Cardiello, Antonio. "Selos [Stamps]." *Biblioteca digital de Fernando Pessoa*. Fernando Pessoa House Site. Bilingual article. 2010. http://casafernandopessoa.cm-lisboa.pt/bdigital/index/selos.htm.

Dasenbrock, Reed Way. *The Literary Vorticism of Ezra Pound and Wyndham Lewis: Towards the Condition of Painting*. Baltimore / London: Johns Hopkins University Press, 1985.

Ferrari, Patricio. "Genetic Criticism and the Relevance of Metrics in Editing Pessoa's Poetry." Pessoa Plural 2 (Fall 2012). www.pessoaplural.com.

Mair, G. H. *English Literature: Modern*. London: Williams and Norgate; New York: Henry Holt and Company, 1911.

McNeill, Patricia Silva. *Yeats and Pessoa: Parallel Poetic Styles*. Oxford: Legenda, 2010.

Monro, Harold. *Poetry Review* I (London: St. Catherine Press, Feb. 1912): 2.

Negreiros, José de Almada. *Textos de intervenção*. Lisbon: Imprensa Nacional–Casa da Moeda, 1986.

Pereira, Margarida Isabel Esteves da Silva. *A vanguarda histórica na Inglaterra e em Portugal: Vorticismo e futurismo*. Braga: Universidade do Minho/Centro de Estudos Humanísticos, 1998.

Pessoa, Fernando. *A Centenary Pessoa*. Edited by Eugénio Lisboa and L. C. Taylor. New York: Routledge, 2003.

———. *A Little Larger than the Entire Universe: Selected Poems*. Edited and translated by Richard Zenith. London and New York: Penguin, 2006.

———. *Correspondência*. Edited by Manuela Parreira da Silva. Vol. I: 1905–1922. 2 vols. Lisbon: Assírio & Alvim, 1999.

———. *Escritos autobiográficos: Automáticos e de reflexão Pessoal*. Edited by Richard Zenith. Lisbon: Assírio & Alvim, 2003.

———. *Fernando Pessoa & Co: Selected Poems*. Edited and translated from the Portuguese by Richard Zenith. New York: Grove Press, 1999.

———. *Páginas íntimas e de auto-interpretação*. Edited by George Rudolf Lind and Jacinto do Prado Coelho. Lisbon: Ática, 1966.

———. *Poemas de Álvaro de Campos*. Edited by Cleonice Berardinelli. Fernando Pessoa's Critical Edition, Major Series, Vol. II. Lisbon: Imprensa Nacional–Casa da Moeda, 1990.

———. *Sensacionismo e outros ismos*. Edited by Jerónimo Pizarro. Fernando Pessoa's Critical Edition, Major Series, Vol. X. Lisbon: Imprensa Nacional–Casa da Moeda, 2009.

Pound, Ezra. "Vorticism." In *Ezra Pound and the Visual Arts*, edited by Hariet Zinnes, 199–209. New York: New Directions, 1980.

Prista, Luís. "Pessoa e o curso superior de letras." In various authors, *Memórias dos Afectos: Homenagem da cultura Portuguesa a Giuseppe Tavani*, 157–185. Lisbon: Colibri, 2001.

Sá-Carneiro, Mário. *Cartas de Sá-Carneiro a Fernando Pessoa*. Edited by Manuela Parreira da Silva. Lisbon: Assírio & Alvim, 2001.

Sadlier, Darlene J. An *Introduction to Fernando Pessoa: Modernism and the Paradoxes of Authorship*. Gainesville: University Press of Florida, 1998.

PATRICIA SILVA MCNEILL is a postdoctoral research fellow at the Centre for Social Studies (CES), University of Coimbra and Queen Mary, University of London. Her project centers on Anglo-Euro-American and Luso-Brazilian transatlantic cultural exchanges during the modernist period and is funded by the Portuguese Foundation for Science and Technology. She holds a PhD in Portuguese and Brazilian studies from King's College London, was visiting research fellow at the School of Advanced Study, University of London, and has taught at the University of Cambridge and University College London. She is the author of *Yeats and Pessoa: Parallel Poetic Styles* (2010). Recent publications include "'The Alchemical Path': Esoteric Influence in the Works of Fernando Pessoa and W. B. Yeats," in *Fernando Pessoa's Modernity without Frontiers: Influences, Dialogues, Responses* (2013); "Echoes of Albion: The Reception of Darwin by Eça de Queiroz" in *The Reception of Charles Darwin in Europe: Literary and Cultural Reception* (2014); and "'The Last City of the Future': Perspectives on Brasília in Literature and Film" in *Alternative Worlds: Blue-Sky Thinking Since 1900* (2014).

She can be reached at psm@ces.uc.pt or p.silva-mcneill@qmul.ac.uk.

JOSÉ BARRETO
Translated by Mario Pereira

"History of a Dictatorship"
An Unfinished Political Essay by the Young Fernando Pessoa

ABSTRACT: The first part of this article reviews the materials from Pessoa's literary remains associated with the book project from 1909 to 1910 titled "History of a Dictatorship." These materials remain little known and mostly unpublished. The second part examines some central themes and theses of this unfinished political work and places them within the evolution of Pessoa's thought.

KEYWORDS: Fernando Pessoa, Portuguese monarchy, João Franco dictatorship, Portuguese Republic, national decay, nationalism, Sebastianism

Materials from Pessoa's Literary Remains Related to the "History of a Dictatorship" Project

Between 1907 and 1910, the final years of the monarchy in Portugal, the young Fernando Pessoa produced a notable quantity of writings on political sociology and "psychological history," as he called it. These writings are dispersed throughout a series of book projects and essays, some in English and others in Portuguese, that the author left unfinished or only in outline form, a practice which would later become the norm. Pessoa's literary estate includes hundreds of pages of text and myriad notes and annotations related to these projects. These comprise a vast collection of political writings in prose that remain even today mostly unpublished.[1] Among these projects, readers should note the following: "The Portuguese Regicide and the Political Situation in Portugal," 1908; "A Psychose [or Nevrose] adeantativa" ("The Advancing Psychosis [or Neurosis]"), 1908–1909; "History of a Dictatorship," 1909–1910; and "Da dictadura á republica" ("From the Dictatorship to the Republic"), begun at the end of 1910 and continued into 1911.

The dictatorship of João Franco (1907–1908) was a prominent theme of these projects, with particular attention given to the actions and personality of this ruler. The young Pessoa intended to undertake a historical, political, sociological, and psychological analysis of this period, with some forays into the realm of psychiatric analysis. Also dating from this period, from 1909 or the beginning of 1910, is the project titled "O Iconoclasta" ("The Iconoclast"), a radical republican and anticlerical publication[2] that Pessoa planned to publish in Íbis, his unsuccessful publishing and typographic business. "The Iconoclast" followed another project, "O Phosphoro" ("The Match"), a title that was perhaps too incendiary and for this reason abandoned in 1909.[3]

Although many political and sociological reflections, predating the projects just mentioned, can be found among Pessoa's papers, the writings from the years 1907 to 1910 reveal that Pessoa, who was around twenty years old at the time, followed Portuguese politics closely with the intention of publishing various works on it: first, works that were primarily aimed at an imaginary English-speaking public, and then works for a no less imaginary Portuguese-speaking public. These writings likewise express an intermediate stage of Pessoa's political thought, somewhere between the libertarian ideas of his adolescence, which he claimed to have abandoned when he was about seventeen years old (1905), and the conservative and increasingly elitist and antidemocratic ideas that he began to develop during the decade following the Republican Revolution of October 5, 1910.

Between ages nineteen and twenty-two, Pessoa was, politically, an independent republican with radical and anticlerical tendencies and a fervent nationalist, who considered the corrupt and oppressive monarchy and the harmful influence of the Catholic Church as the two major causes of Portugal's centuries-long decline. At the same time, he was a harsh critic of the "errors of diagnosis of social issues" (the title of another project from this period) and of the "fanatical" and "degenerative" political solutions of the anarchists and socialists. As a republican nationalist, Pessoa was in sharp opposition to another form of nationalism then existing in Portugal, represented by the Nationalist Party, a Catholic and monarchical party that had been founded in 1903 but became defunct in 1910 after the establishment of the Portuguese Republic. Republican nationalism made its first strong showing during the commemorations of the tricentennial of the death of Camões in 1880, and then from 1890 its influence increased notably as a result of the national humiliation stemming from the Portuguese monarchy's government conceding to the British Ultimatum.[4] The nationalist reaction triggered by the ultimatum provided a great stimulus for the propaganda of the Republican Party, and also found expression in literary works, principally in *Finis patriae* (1890) and *Pátria* (1896) by Guerra Junqueiro, which made a powerful impression on the young Pessoa.[5] According to one scholar, *Pátria* should be considered of seminal importance to Pessoa's poetical project, originally titled "Portugal" during the decade of the 1910s, but which would come to fruition only in 1934 in the book *Mensagem*.[6]

Many important events occurred during the years 1907 to 1910, a period characterized by great political instability and republican agitation. These include the academic events of 1907, which witnessed a student strike that originated in Coimbra and spread to the rest of the country; the laws regarding the press passed by João Franco's government, which unleashed strong protests; the closing of parliament by the king and the beginning of the Franco dictatorship in May 1907; the question of illegal advances to the royal family and the highly controversial solution presented by the dictator in August 1907; the failed republican revolutionary attempt of January 28, 1908; the regicide of February 1, 1908, which involved the assassinations of King D. Carlos I and of the heir to the throne, Prince Luís Filipe, and the end of the Franco dictatorship; a series of monarchical governments that were incapable of generating confidence in the country; the Republican Party's success in the legislative and municipal elections of 1908; an outbreak in 1909 of labor and syndicalist agitation, unlike anything that had occurred before in Portugal; and, finally, the successful Republican Revolution of October 5, 1910.

During this period of great unrest, Pessoa passed through his so-called third adolescence on his way to adulthood, when he abandoned his university studies, ceased to live in the house of relatives, and tried to initiate his career as a writer and editor. The political climate in which Pessoa was living inflamed his feelings of patriotism and aroused his desire to intervene as a political writer and to contribute to the revolution, which since 1909 he had felt was both necessary and inevitable.

In 1907 and the beginning of 1908, before the regicide of February 1, Pessoa had already prepared notes on the character of João Franco, the leader of the government, and on his dictatorship,[7] a theme that he would later develop after the assassination of the king. In 1907 the republican doctor Artur Leitão had published a book, titled *A Case of Epileptic Madness* (*Um caso de loucura epiléptica*), on João Franco's personality—a book that the nineteen-year-old Pessoa (as Alexander Search) read and annotated in the margins. This work made a strong impression on Pessoa, inspiring him to write on João Franco and *franquismo*, even though he disagreed with Leitão on some points. Nevertheless, there is no trace in Pessoa's papers from 1907 and 1908 of the project titled "History of a Dictatorship," which, according to all available evidence, was initiated only in 1909, as will be explained in this essay.

We know from a note from September 1908 that Pessoa continued with his readings, which he had begun in 1907, of Max Nordau and of works of psychology, psychiatry, and other fields, while he was simultaneously trying to write a book on the political situation in Portugal in indignant reaction to what had been written abroad about Portugal since the regicide. This book was not named in the manuscript note written in English, but because of the date, it almost certainly refers to the project titled "The Portuguese Regicide and the Political Situation in Portugal," a book that was intended for a foreign readership and whose authorship was attributed to Alexander Search.[8] Enlivened by an ardent patriotism, the note likewise reveals the author's inclination to Messianism and Sebastianism:

5th September 1908.

God give me the strength to draw, to understand the whole synthesis of the psychology and psychological history of the Portuguese nation!

Every day the papers bring me news of facts that are humiliating, □ to us, the Portuguese. No one can conceive how I suffer with them. No one can imagine the deep despair, the mighty pain that seizes me at this. Oh, how I dream of that Marquis of Tavira who should come and redeem the nation—a saviour, a true man, great and bold that would put us right. But no suffering can equal that when I bring myself to understand that this is no more than a dream.

I am never happy, neither in my selfish, nor in my unselfish moments. My solace is reading Anthero de Quental. We are, after all, brother-spirits. Oh, how I understand that deep suffering that was his.

I must write my book. I dread what the truth may be. Yet, be it bad, I have to write it. God get the truth be not bad!

I should like to have written this in better style, but my power of writing is gone.[9]

In addition, notes from the same year (after February 1, 1908) belong to another project, "A Psychose adeantativa,"[10] which deals with the question of the illegal advances made by the government to the royal house. It was still an active project during the second half of 1909 and was even included as a title to be published in a pamphlet series issued by Íbis under the new title "A Nevrose adeantativa."[11] There also exists an incomplete text in English on the same topic, titled "Psychopathology of the Advance Decree,"[12] which could be either an autonomous essay or a chapter for the book "History of a Dictatorship."

The title "The Portuguese Regicide and the Political Situation in Portugal" appears in the group of projects Pessoa called "Book of Tasks,"[13] dating from the first half of 1908 (again, after the regicide of February 1). On another contemporaneous list of projects titled *Books*, Pessoa planned the execution of this work from June through October of 1908.[14] In the note just transcribed, from September 5, Pessoa writes, "I must write my book," without naming the book, though he could only be referring to "The Portuguese Regicide." Almost two months later, Pessoa drafted a text, signed by Alexander Search and dated October 30, 1908, in which he recounts the enormous difficulties he was facing in carrying out his plans, or, more precisely, his "patriotic projects" with which he intended "to provoke a revolution" in Portugal. The Portuguese regicide is mentioned in this text, which, because of its importance to a number of titles, I have transcribed here:[15]

No soul more loving or tender than mine has ever existed, no soul so full of kindness, of pity, of all the things of tenderness and of love. Yet no soul is so lonely as mine—not lonely, be it noted, from exterior, but from interior circumstances. I mean this: together with my great tenderness and kindness an element of an entirely opposite kind enters[16] into my character, an element of sadness, of self-centredness, of selfishness therefore, whose effect is two-fold: to warp and hinder the development and full *internal* play of those other qualities, and to hinder, by affecting the will depressingly, their full *external* play, their manifestation. One [day] I shall analyse this, one day I shall examine better, discriminate, the elements of my character, for my curiosity of all things, linked to my curiosity for myself and for my own character, leads to one attempt to understand my personality.

It was on account of these characteristics that I wrote, describing myself, in the "Winter Day":

One like Rousseau . . .
A misanthropic lover of mankind.

I have, as a matter of fact, many, too many affinities with Rousseau. In certain things our characters are identical. The warm, intense, inexpressible love of mankind, and the portion of selfishness balancing it—this is a fundamental characteristic of his character and, as well, of mine.

My intense patriotic suffering, my intense desire of bettering the condition of Portugal provoke in me—how to express with what warmth, with what intensity, with what sincerity!—a thousand plans which, even if one man could realise them, he had to have[17] one characteristic which in me is purely negative—the power of will. But I suffer—on the very limit of madness, I swear it—as if I could do all and was unable to do it, by deficiency of will. The suffering is horrible. It holds me constantly, I say, on the limit of madness.

And then ununderstood. No one suspects my patriotic love, intenser than that of everyone I meet, of everyone I know. I do not betray it; how do I then know they have it not? how can I tell their care is not such as mine?[18] Because in some cases, in most, their temperament is entirely different; because, in the other cases they speak in a way which reveals the non-existence at least of a warm patriotism. The warmth, the intensity—tender, revolted and eager, of mine I shall never express, so as not to be believed, if ever express[ed] at all.

Besides my patriotic projects—writing of "P[ortuguese] Reg[icide]"—to provoke a revolution here, writing of Portuguese pamphlets, editing of older national literary works, creation of a magazine, of a scientific review, etc.—other plans, consuming me with the necessity of being soon carried out—Jean Seul projects, critique of Binet-Sanglé, etc.—combine to produce an excess of impulse that paralyses my will. The suffering that this produces I know not if it can be described as on this side of insanity.

Add to all this other reasons still for suffering, some physical, others mental, the susceptibility to every small thing that can cause pain (or even that to a normal man could not cause any pain), add this to other things still, complications, money difficulties—join this all to my fundamentally unbalanced temperament and you may be able to *suspect* what my suffering is.

A. Search—30–10–08—

There are no further references to "The Portuguese Regicide" project after this text, just transcribed, which means the plan for writing this work must have been abandoned in the fall or following winter in favor of the new "History of a Dictatorship" project, which was motivated by the same extreme patriotism and by the same desire to contribute to the Republican Revolution in Portugal.

The title "The Portuguese Regicide" never appears on lists of projects together with "History of a Dictatorship," which suggests, because of the thematic similarity between the two projects, that the latter project not only succeeded the former, but likely incorporated it. It is possible that Pessoa had simply decided to change the title of the projected work and introduce some changes to its structure, eventually preferring to give less emphasis to the specific theme of regicide and to limit discussion of it to one chapter. In this way, "The Portuguese Regicide and the Political Situation in Portugal" and "History of a Dictatorship" would have to be considered successive stages of the same project and same work. Although no document from Pessoa's literary remains expressly confirms this hypothesis, there is no evidence that disproves it.

Few texts conserved in Pessoa's remains are explicitly connected to "The Portuguese Regicide" project.[19] However, sufficient evidence does exist for us to conclude that it followed a plan that was distinct from that of "History of a Dictatorship," even though the two projects had many topics in common. For example, the theme of an introduction that Pessoa wrote for "The Portuguese Regicide" is the same as the first chapter ("National and Institutional Decay") of Part I of the work that would come to be identified as "History of a Dictatorship." Although no document proves the continued attribution of authorship of this chapter to Alexander Search, it seems logical that it could have been maintained.

The new "History of a Dictatorship" project appears on a list of "work to be done" from June 1909, a list that also named the autonomous project "A Psy-

PART I.

E X T E N T   A N D   C A U S E S   O F   P O R T U G U E SE

D E C A Y .

CHAPTER I.

NATIONAL AND INSTITUTIONAL DECAY.

Bichât defined life as the sum-total of functions which resist death. The definition - all admit - is correct, though it is not ex- plicit nor has the clearness that is required in a definition. But it is pregnant. What is necessary is to define, or, at least, to give a shadow of a definition of death. In itself death is nothing, that is, cannot be defined so as to be understood; absolute extinction, unless it be the absolute extinction of form, which we derive from experience, cannot enter into our comprehension. From a material standpoint, death can almost be defined as decay. When an organism decays it tends to die. Death is more: it consists in <u>absolute</u> decay. Decay means disintegration. Death means absolute, pure disintegra- tion, disintegration <u>unintegrated</u>.

We are now in a position to understand what the French medical philosopher meant by his definition: that life is the sum-total of functions that resist total disintegration. If for "life" we put "vitality", the definition is, naturally, little changed: Vitality is the sum total of functions (or, of activities) that resist dis- integration, not now <u>total</u> disintegration, but any disintegration at all. Disintegration, of course, can be translated by "decay".

./.

Pessoa, "Extent and Causes of Portuguese Decay," typescript, BNP/E3, 92N–1ʳ.

chose adeantativa."[20] Other lists from 1909 include "A Psychose adeantativa" in a group of "Portuguese Books" and the "History of a Dictatorship" project in a list of "English Books."[21] As has been said, none of the 1909 lists mentions "The Portuguese Regicide." Consequently, the beginning of the "History of a Dictatorship" project, appearing hereafter as the abbreviated title H. of a D. (and sometimes H. of D.), seems to date from the first half of 1909. There is no indication that H. of a D. was initiated in 1908.[22] Meanwhile, the pamphlet project "A Psychose adeantativa" would similarly not receive mention in 1910, and it is possible that its subject was incorporated into H. of a D, which occupied the author throughout 1909 and 1910.

In 1909 Pessoa received an inheritance from his grandmother Dionísia, and in the second half of this year, he established his publishing and typographic business Íbis, which enjoyed a short life. It is possible that the launching of Íbis gave Pessoa additional impetus to write and edit his "patriotic" work. Unlike the young Pessoa's other projects, which sometimes took the form of summary plans and fragmentary texts and other times never went beyond being mere titles in lists, H. of a D. reached a relatively advanced state of realization. Indeed, this was Pessoa's first continuous and persistent attempt to write and publish a book—and significantly, it was on a political topic.

In addition to hundreds of scattered notes bearing the title H. of a D., we have in Pessoa's remains a collection of more than 200 pages of text in English. Evidence seems to indicate that despite the lack of a title for the work, this collection should be identified as almost the entirety of Part I of "History of a Dictatorship" as well as a series of texts belonging to the ending of Part I and to Parts II, III, and IV.[23] The first ninety pages of this collection, comprising the first four chapters of Part I, titled "Extent and Causes of Portuguese Decay," exist as typescript copy (carbon copies) numbered sequentially and with some emendations and manuscript additions. There also exists in Pessoa's remains the original typescript of these ninety pages without manuscript annotations. Almost all of the remaining pages of this collection are in manuscript form and are numbered sequentially within each chapter only. The typescript and manuscript are not characterized by separate notes and fragmentary texts, but rather are composed of running text divided into chapters. This was a book intended for an English-speaking audience not only because of the language in which it was written, but also because of certain kinds of explanations that the author provided for his readers, and because of the way he refers to Portugal.

The title of the entire work is not present on the first page of Part I, which has only the title of this section. In fact, the general title of the work is not to be found anywhere on the manuscript and typescript, which helps to explain why they have not been previously identified as the unfinished text of "History of a Dictatorship." Moreover, the materials are undated, and their date can only be determined indirectly.[24] Nevertheless, the central theme of the work is indisputably the dictatorship of João Franco, for on page 50 Pessoa declares that the dictator is "the hero, so to speak, of this book"—or, preferably, the anti-hero.[25]

This collection of texts—composed of finished text in typescript and draft text in manuscript, exclusive of individual notes—constitutes the most extensive work of essay writing that Pessoa ever did, even though, as would become habitual, he never brought it to completion.

Pessoa seems to have vacillated several times over the division of "History of a Dictatorship" into parts and chapters. In what seems to be the initial plan of the work, the book was to have an introduction and five parts, although Part II was not specified, which was likely an oversight.[26] According to this plan with five parts (which in reality listed only four), Part I was to have nine chapters, the last dealing with the reign of D. Carlos, begun in 1891. Part III (which was Part II) was to be composed of only three chapters, which would address antecedents of the dictatorship and person of João Franco. Part IV (which was Part III) would deal exclusively with Franco's dictatorship, and the theme of Part V (or IV) was "problems of the future." In a later manuscript,[27] from the end of 1910 or beginning of 1911, Pessoa writes that the "Hist[oria] de uma dict[adura]," a title that he now references in Portuguese, had only three parts, a comment that does not correspond to the division of the typescript and manuscript texts, which comprised four parts. In the typescript text of Part I of "History of a Dictatorship," the reign of D. Carlos is discussed in Chapter IV, which reveals a rather different arrangement from the initial plan of four parts. As was mentioned earlier, this plan included an introduction of a theoretical nature, divided into five points, which Pessoa failed write, at least in this format. The first three chapters of Part I of this plan, which was theoretical or general in nature, did not correspond thematically with the text of Part I as it was actually written. Some correspondence between the plan and the themes of the typescript text appear in the following chapters dealing with the periodization of the history of the monarchy and with the phases of its alleged decline.

The Part I of "History of a Dictatorship" that was actually written and titled "Extent and Causes of Portuguese Decay" comprised four chapters, though the fourth chapter was unfinished. These four chapters consist of typescript pages with relatively few handwritten emendations, were given a title, and were numbered with Roman numerals. The rest of the work, including Parts II, III, and IV, is in manuscript form and is clearly a draft. These parts lack titles and consist of an indeterminate number of chapters, which themselves only rarely have titles. In addition, there are gaps in the numbering of manuscript chapters (five manuscript chapters are unnumbered), but within this group are chapters numbered XIV, XV, and XVII, which gives a sense of the extent of the book.

In addition to this main group of texts pertaining to the work itself, Pessoa wrote copious scattered notes and comments of all kinds under the title H. *of a D.* throughout 1909 and 1910. Among other means of dating these notes—such as the use of Íbis letterhead (1909–1910), references to information from the newspapers from 1910, and postmarks from this same year[28]—there are numerous notes for H. *of a* D. that had been written on the back of small sheets taken from a 1910 day calendar from January to the end of August. In total, Pessoa's remains hold over 700 pages of text related to this project, including the text divided into chapters and the individual notes. From that time, the project began to be named occasionally with a Portuguese designation, "Historia de uma dictadura," but the abbreviated title H. *of a* D. continued to appear in English throughout 1910 and even in notes written after the establishment of the Portuguese Republic.[29] The contents of this multitude of individual notes, comments, and brief theoretical reflections are varied: religious themes, history of literature, sociology, psychology, psychiatry, legislation, politics, ancient and contemporary history, European and Portuguese history, and so on.

It is sometimes difficult to imagine how these notes and comments would relate to the principal subject of "History of a Dictatorship." The title H. *of a* D. appears in many of these notes, together or alternating with other titles associated with other contemporaneous projects, such as "Errors of Diagnosis of Social Isssues" ("Erros de diagnostico [em questões sociaes]");[30] "Jeshu ben Pandira," a legendary personality who was identified by some with the historical figure of Jesus;[31] "Foundations of a Republican Constitution" ("Bases [de uma Constituição Republicana]");[32] "Ic[onoclasta]"[33] and "Sursum corda!"[34] The diffusion of all of these projects seems to signal Pessoa's inability or lack of persistence in bringing the project H. *of a* D. to completion. Nevertheless, "History of a Dictatorship" undoubtedly constitutes the principal mobilizing focus of Pessoa's essay writing between 1909 and 1910, concentrating or touching on multiple themes, which comprised corresponding subjects of interest and of reading. Pessoa seems to have not resisted the somewhat juvenile temptation to introduce into a project with a specific theme all of the materials which then interested him and which were the subject of his varied readings.

The concern for a scientific character, the multiplicity of viewpoints, and some originality of approach do not succeed in concealing the obvious naivety of various aspects of the contents of the work. The frequent invocation of "sociological," "psychological," and even "psychiatric" arguments—which led him to present his work in a preface that he wrote for H. of a D. as the first historical study, not just in Portugal but also internationally, that was founded on the sciences of psychology and psychiatry[35]—clashed with the manifest political bias of the book, which was close to views expressed in republican propaganda, including the anticlericalism of its radicals. In this respect, there is a glaring contrast between the texts by the young Pessoa and the book by Sampaio Bruno, A Dictadura (The Dictatorship), written in 1908 and published in the beginning of 1909, which is a contemporary study of the same topic by an independent republican intellectual, a man with a great critical spirit and vast culture who wrote the book during the final phase of his life. It should be noted that Pessoa never refers to this work by Bruno, perhaps because he did not yet know it, although he included Bruno's O Brasil mental (1898) in a list datable to 1910 of bibliographic references for his own book.[36]

The fact that "History of a Dictatorship" had been imagined for an English-speaking public, which had little knowledge about the political situation in Portugal and about Portugal itself, meant that Pessoa was disinclined to develop or exhaustively detail his analysis. This problem of the intended public for the work must have been appreciated and considered by Pessoa, who was at that moment in the midst of a period of transition during which he began to write increasingly less in English and more in Portuguese.[37] The title of the planned work, "History of a Dictatorship," would certainly not be the most appropriate for a book intended for an English-speaking audience for whom the personality of João Franco and the circumstance rendering his government "dictatorial"—the temporary closing of Parliament—would have been far less interesting than the fact of the regicide. The initial project from 1908—"The Portuguese Regicide and the Political Situation in Portugal"—had a title that just might have been adequately appealing to this readership. As Pessoa himself would write in a note after the establishment of the republic, perhaps from 1911, the regicide and the Republican Revolution were the two events that most attracted international attention to Portugal: "The Regicide and, then, the Revolution were the two phenomena that attracted to us, though imperfectly, attention from abroad. That is to say: instead of being unknown, we became poorly known. Previously, nothing was known about us; then it happened that entirely false things were learned about us. The knowledge that foreigners have about us fluctuates between nothing and error."[38]

Even less appealing to an international audience would be the fact that "History of a Dictatorship" is a work of pure republican propaganda. To write in English or in Portuguese? To write for an international audience or a Portuguese one? To write with the scientific impartiality of a sociologist and historian, or with the commitment of a republican revolutionary? These surely were some of the dilemmas confronting Pessoa at this time.

The changes of title, theme, and time range of his political essays from this period, the transition to writing in Portuguese, and, finally, the apparent disappearance of the British pseudonym Alexander Search as author indicate that Pessoa was in the process of moving toward a Portuguese reading public and a greater desire for personal involvement in the life of the nation, as though only around 1910, five years after his return from Durban, did he begin to feel fully integrated into his Portuguese milieu. We should recall his contemporaneous plan to create a publishing house with a typographic office—the unsuccessful Íbis—which theoretically would have enabled the publication of his works, including especially "History of a Dictatorship," without having to rely on the doubtful acceptance of the manuscript by an English publisher. After the financial ruin of Íbis, which occurred between November 1909 and the early months of 1910,[39] and during which time Pessoa squandered most of the inheritance from his grandmother Dionísia,[40] he nevertheless continued throughout the year to work on this English-language project.

After the establishment of the republic, Pessoa began to develop other political essay projects, which focused more on recent and contemporary history, but whose themes, nevertheless, partially extended or overlapped those of "History of a Dictatorship." It is true that among the set of individual texts grouped under the designation "Post-Revolutionary Considerations" ("Considerações post-revolucionarias") from 1910 to 1911, there are some with the title H. of a D.[41]

This is the case principally with the project "From the Dictatorship to the Republic" ("Da dictadura á republica"; abbreviated *Da D. á R.*), which seems to constitute a new version, now intended for a Portuguese-speaking public, of part of "History of a Dictatorship," but which considers a broader range of time, incorporating the first months of the republic, and suggests with its new title a causal connection between João Franco's dictatorship and the victorious Republican Revolution. In an unpublished text, mentioned earlier, from the end of 1910 or the beginning of 1911, which seems to be the preface to the projected book "From the Dictatorship to the Republic," Pessoa wrote, "The book which we present is actually the third part of a work on which we have been working for some time—Hist[ory] of a Dicta[torship] [. . .] Indefinitely delayed, this study could become dated, because perhaps it was preceded by the proclamation of the Republic; which would essentially not invalidate the first and second parts of the book, but which would certainly invalidate the third—the part which we are now presenting."[42]

In the already mentioned short bibliography for H. *of a D.*, which Pessoa prepared in 1910,[43] there appears a Spanish work, published in February 1908, by Luis Morote about the crisis of the monarchy in Portugal and the prospect of establishing the republican regime. The title of this book, *From the Dictatorship to the Republic (De la dictadura á la república)*[44] was identical to the title Pessoa gave his project, "From the Dictatorship to the Republic" ("Da dictadura á republica"). A copy of Morote's book was found in Pessoa's private library, and in addition to Alexander Search's ownership signature, the copy contains underlining and notes in pencil.[45] Evidence would indicate that Pessoa appropriated the title of Morote's book for his own new project, which emerged during the second half of 1910 after the Republican Revolution.

The projects *H. of a D.* and *Da D. á R.*, dedicated to partially overlapping themes, coexisted independently for some time. In Pessoa's remains there are sheets with multiple passages, some with the title *H. of a D.* and others with the title *Da D. á R.*[46] On a composition from the end of 1910 or beginning of 1911 in which he makes an appraisal of the decrees of the provisional republican government, Pessoa characteristically places four alternative titles at the top of the text—"Ic[onoclast] or H. of a D. or [Post-Revolutionary] Cons[iderations] or From the D[ictatorship] to the R[epublic]"—though he later crossed out the second title in the list.[47] In theory, the two works by Pessoa, one in English and the other in Portuguese, were not mutually redundant, despite their largely similar themes, apparently because they were intended for different (imagined) publics. Although the project Da D. á R. retained its title, the project H. of a D., after some hesitations, seemed to take on the English title "The Decline and Fall of the Portuguese Monarchy," which is how it appeared in a list of "Publications" along with "From the Dictatorship to the Republic: Sociological Study of the Final Years of the Monarchy in Portugal" (title in Portuguese).[48]

An unpublished manuscript[49] confirms that the themes of the two works, Portuguese and English, were for the most part comparable, for it contains under the title "From the Dictatorship to the Republic" (1906–1910)—note the chronological range indicated—a summary plan of the Portuguese work in which Pessoa in Part I, the introductory section, intended to divide the political history of Portugal from the sixteenth century to 1906 into periods, exactly as he had planned to do in "History of a Dictatorship." This first part of "From the Dictatorship to the Republic" is significantly titled "Extensão e causas da decadencia Portugueza," which is a translation into Portuguese of the title that he had already given to Part I of "History of a Dictatorship": "Extent and Causes of Portuguese Decay." The periodization of Portugal's centuries-long decline was also one of the themes of the new project "Post-Revolutionary Considerations" ("Considerações post-revolucionarias").[50] Finally, during the year 1911, the surviving project Da D. á R. would itself disappear, yielding its place to other projects that were more focused on contemporary politics, such as "The Oligarchy of Beasts" ("A Oligarchia das bestas"), a project that was begun at the start of 1911 and that remained apparently on hold for many years.[51] Meanwhile, the essay project in English, now titled "The Decline and Fall of the Portuguese Monarchy," remained alive in 1911, for it appears on two lists of projects from that year, along with "The Oligarchy of Beasts."[52]

The final crisis of the Portuguese monarchy ceased being the main subject of Pessoa's political writings around 1911–1912, when it was replaced by analysis and "sociological" criticism of the revolution and of the republican governments, radical republicanism, afonsismo, anarchism, and socialism (Pessoa had begun writing critically on the last two topics around 1906), and also by criticism of the monarchical and Catholic reactions to the Portuguese Republic. However, the political essay projects that Pessoa began to work on at this time, such as "The Oligarchy of Beasts," were not the object of a persistent effort nor, apparently, did Pessoa show as great a desire to publish these projects as he had in previous years, in 1908 to 1910. In 1912 Pessoa finally published his first essays in the second series of the magazine *A Águia*, but these were on literary and not specifically political themes: the "sociological" and "psychological" analysis of new Portuguese poetry, though this did not hinder him from expressing some political opinions.

On the Central Themes and Some Theses of "History of a Dictatorship"

I will not attempt here to analyze or describe the totality of the work that Pessoa composed, because of the number of manuscript pages and the herculean efforts required to decipher them as well as the number of individual notes related to the project. Nevertheless, some of Pessoa's principal theses and the theoretical principles on which they are based are formulated in the first ninety pages of the work, which consist of typescript pages with very few corrections.

Pessoa immediately cautions that "History of a Dictatorship" is not a historical treatise, and further explains, "It is not our intention to attempt the history of Portugal. It is sufficient that we show by what degrees the Portuguese people, victim of their institutions, fell into a state of deep depression, from which however they are striving to rise."[53] The work by the young Pessoa belongs to this struggle against the institutions of the declining Portuguese monarchy.

The book begins by considering, in general terms, the concept of *decadence* or *decay*, the central theme of its analysis of the Portuguese situation, and then moves on to define and delimit two types of decay: institutional and national.[54] From the outset Pessoa reveals an adherence to a markedly organicist concept of society, which was indebted to sociological concepts derived from Comte and Spencer, but which was also inspired by the biological notion of degeneration that Pessoa, following in the footsteps of Max Nordau, applied to society in order to express the process opposed to the evolution of society. In Pessoa's text, decadence (or decay) and degeneration are used as nearly interchangeable terms. The first pages are dedicated to defining the basic concepts of life and death. These considerations and the medical-biological concepts of vitality, health, sickness, a dying state, and so on, are applied not only to living organisms, including human beings, but also to "those other species of organisms—societies and nations," whose "cells" are individuals.[55] In a nation or society, as in a living organism, two opposing forces are active, one of integration and the other of disintegration.[56] The existence of public opinion and of collective will, normally represented by the government of a state, would manifest this integrating force. The excessive individualization of opinion or the splintering into parties and factions would expose the contrary, disintegrating force, which would have a negative influence on government, rendering it incapable of performing its normal functions. In a free state, in which the collective will determines the government which represents it, the decline of government would be connected to the decline of the nation itself; in a state that is not free, the decay of political power or of institutions could or could not relate to the decay of the nation because in this case, power is not representative of the nation, of its opinion or the people.[57]

Young Pessoa's thought was characterized by a firm belief in progress and democracy. This is seen in his conception of the political evolution of societies as a process of ascending degrees of power, which, historically, was based at the outset on force, on the will of the strongest, and then evolved to power based on authority, and finally to power based on opinion, that is, on the public will or democracy. It should be noted that Pessoa returned to this same evolutionary typology of forms of power in a work of his maturity, "O Interregno" ("The Interregnum"), from 1928.[58] With the formation of the monarchy and the aristocracy, power based on mere force became authority, and the superstition of primitive peoples became religion. However, because the original source of authority, and even its essence, continued to be force, Pessoa declared that "the authoritarian or conservative spirit has three forms: it is monarchical, it is religious and it is militarist." The following stage is degeneration of the system of power based on authority, which would gradually give way to the formation of the system of power based on opinion—the popular will—the stage that by historical experience, Pessoa claimed, would be reached only through a revolution.[59]

The Portuguese constitutional monarchy (1820–1910), similar to other constitutional monarchies of its time, was merely, according to Pessoa, "a fraudulent mixture of the system of authority and of opinion," a kind of hybrid organism that would reveal an atavistic tendency for the reverse, for the regression to absolutism.[60] In this process of degeneration, "monarchy and aristocracy become imbecile, base and cruel." Institutions were corrupted and entered into an accelerated decline. The corruption of some and the oppression of all were the means by which the system of authority tried to compensate for its loss of prestige and loss of control over the people, but "the clearer-sighted of the rising middle classes," who could not be bought, would embody, despite being oppressed by power, the spirit of the public good against the decay of institutions. The revolution then showed on the horizon as the solution for the evolution of society into a new stage, democracy.[61] In these considerations the theoretical skeleton of the book emerges, as does the role the author awards to himself, which is *the clear-sighted and incorruptible element of the rising middle class*, embodying the revolutionary spirit of resistance against the decline of institutions.

In a *decaying nation*, the more selfish and criminal interests of people and politicians prevail over the public good, a value which would have to rule in a *healthy nation*.[62] Personal ambition, a thirst for power, and a tendency to fanaticism and to oppression predominate with political conservatives. On the other hand, certain representatives of the people, who are equally indifferent to the public good and to the effects on the masses of their utopian and dangerous doctrines, possess only the ambition to lead and to gain prestige as orators. The country flounders in these extremes of selfishness, personal ambition, and indifference, revealing what Pessoa calls national decay.[63] The organicistic relation between collective decay and the individual degeneration of politicians is emphasized in a manuscript text that Pessoa wrote for Part II of the book: "Abnormal times call abnormal people into existence. Abnormal times bring abnormal figures to the fore. The abnormal and degenerative conditions of [the] Portuguese monarchy called forth many strange creatures to public life."[64] He was obviously referring to the "degenerate" and "born-criminal" João Franco, the dictator who emerged during the final stage of the decline of monarchical institutions.

Institutional—or political—decay might or might not reflect, according to Pessoa, a process of decay of the nation or society. The distinction between *institutional* decay and *national* decay, on which Pessoa repeatedly insisted, corresponded with the distinction between free and unfree nations, according to whether political power had its origins in opinion—the people—or whether it was granted by a king with absolute powers. If there is political decay in a *free* nation, in which the institutions and government reflect the will of the nation, then this is because the decay is also national (or social), and this is what produces political decay. If there is political decay in an *unfree* nation, then it does not necessarily follow that the people, the nation, or society are decadent, although the source of political power, which is the absolute monarch or king, certainly is. However, in an *unfree* nation with an absolute or semi-absolute government, political decay would tend to cause the decay of society. Within the concept of national or social decay, Pessoa also included economic, commercial, and moral decay.[65]

These considerations on institutional and national decay tend to sustain Pessoa's thesis—as well as the larger conclusion of the work—that the causes of Portuguese decline were primarily institutional (the monarchy and Catholic Church), thereby demonstrating that the overthrow of institutions was the solution for the ills affecting the nation.[66] But for this to happen, it was still necessary to have sufficient elements of regeneration in the nation, in order to avoid a situation of complete national decadence, characterized by the absence of public opinion and popular protest or by the existence of a disjointed opposition mistaken in its purpose and dominated solely by feelings of hatred or revenge. As bad as the country's situation was, if "the majority of the people" displayed sentiments of citizenship and showed their devotion to the public good, then the power that governed against the nation would have no other option than to submit or be overthrown.

However, it was indispensable to have an organized and disciplined "body of men" who were animated by a sound spirit with coherent and attainable aspirations, and who were capable of exerting increasing pressure on the monarchy's government. This necessary spirit—as the young sociologist Pessoa could not refrain from indicating—was the revolutionary republican sentiment, and its objective had to be the establishment of the republican regime.[67] In 1909–1910, according to Pessoa, Portugal would have been at the height of a centuries-long process of institutional decay with its corrupt, oppressive, and practically moribund monarchy. However, Portugal would still not have have been in a situation of *complete* national decay, even though the monarchy had profoundly contaminated the entire life of the nation. For this reason, it was urgent that the country accelerate the process of transforming its institutions and securing internal liberty "by the establishment of a republic."[68] Proof of the vitality that in the midst of decline nevertheless endured in Portugal was the existence of a large Republican Party, which in those years had fostered such strong action. "There is yet hope. All is not lost," Pessoa commented.[69]

This conveys the general sense of the book "History of a Dictatorship," a nationalistic work that tries to demonstrate the need to establish the republic in order to save the moribund nation from the threat of complete and fatal decay or, in other words, death.

The book does not historically locate the beginning of the Portuguese monarchy's decline with the loss of independence in 1580, but even earlier during the golden age of maritime expansion under D. Manuel I, the monarch with whom Pessoa identified the stigma of degeneration and who, citing the historian Alexandre Herculano, would have ripped up, while invoking "divine right," hundreds of *cartas de privilégio, forais*, and other charters and statutes in which the ancient rights, liberties, and exemptions of the people and cities were written.[70] The delivery or sale of the country to the Spanish by the high nobility and clergy in 1580, after the African disaster of Alcácer-Quibir (1578), would prove the existence of a prior degenerative process.[71] Pessoa also associates the Spanish occupation with the oppressive influence of the church, because the loss of independence to Castile had occurred during the reign of Cardinal D. Henrique and had been blessed by the pope. After the Spanish occupation (which Pessoa mistakenly claims had lasted eighty instead of sixty years), the spirit of adventure, conquest, and expansion, which had generated the glorious past of the nation, would have completely vanished.

The malign influence of the church and the church's role throughout the long process of Portuguese decline are constantly noted in this work, and this specific theme is the focus of the second chapter of Part I.[72] The Catholic Church, by its nature, would be compatible only with an absolute monarchy,[73] and the church would be the only entity capable of producing the two types of decay—institutional and national—that were occurring in Portugal.[74] Following in the footsteps of the pamphletary writings of Alexandre Herculano and of *Causas da decadência dos povos peninsulares* by Antero Quental, the young Pessoa maintains that moral sense had been transformed by the church in Portugal into religious sense, a characteristic specific to the faith of southern Europe (Pessoa calls them "the Southerners"), and that this religious sense was transformed in Portugal and Spain into an *institution* contrary to what had occurred in northern Europe and, particularly, in England.[75]

Pessoa also considers the *degeneration* of the royal family and of the aristocracy (caused by consanguinity, which he claims had been studied by Júlio Dantas, a "distinguished Portuguese author") another contributing factor to the decline of the monarchy, though it was not the primary cause. There was an even stronger and more profound degenerative effect than the one eventually caused by biological blood relation, and this was the effect caused by the "moral consanguinity" of all royal families resulting from the exercise of power. (Pessoa cites in support of this thesis a work on human selection by the Russian psychiatrist and anthropologist Paul Jacoby.[76]) However, the main cause of the *moral* degeneration of Portuguese monarchs and nobles was, in Pessoa's opinion, "fanaticism," that is, "religion, the Roman Catholic faith."[77] In a Catholic nation, the absolutist, authoritarian, and oppressive influence of the church would be particularly harmful among monarchs and nobles who were already "naturally predisposed to all kinds of evils and aberrations" by the exercise of power and inbreeding.[78] It would have been the church that, during the constitutional monarchy as well as before it, "rooted in the souls of the monarchs and of the nobility the ideas of absolute government." This was because the church was by nature absolutist and despotic: "The Catholic Church has an absolutist constitution, far more despotic and oppressive than any absolutism that has been, far more cruel than any political cruelty in its bad moments, and far less excusable because doing all these things for the glory of God and, of course, in the name of Jesus."[79]

The Catholic Church likewise exercised a malignant influence on the masses, even though the people, thanks to their "good sense," mental sanity, and "human morality," had avoided the worst effects of this religious contamination. This demonstrated the strength of the Portuguese race at its core for having preserved its existence under such negative influences, thus preventing the decline of the country from being much greater.[80] In any case, in southern Europe (and here Pessoa cites Lombroso and an unnamed Portuguese scientist), the individuals most lacking in moral sense, the "born-criminals" and "born-prostitutes," were "characteristically religious, devoted to the Catholic Church."[81] This relation between an atavistic tendency to crime and a no less atavistic type of religious devotion were not characteristic of other religions, which generated less superstition and moral laxity. "The best part of religion is that which keeps the moral sense in activity," Pessoa affirms, thereby inferring "the enormous superiority of the Protestant religion to the Catholic." He then comments, "The further from dogma, from pomp, from superstition, the better for a religion."[82]

The radical anti-Catholicism expressed in many of these pages from 1909–1910 would be, on the whole, maintained by Pessoa throughout his life, though with nuances and variations in some of his old positions. After abandoning his negative vision of absolute monarchy in the period after World War I, Pessoa naturally no longer accused the detested Catholic Church of being the mentor of absolutism in Portugal, though he never ceased emphasizing the church's "oppressive" nature and its role as "corruptor of souls"[83] as well as its responsibility for "two centuries of monkish and jesuitical education."[84] In addition, his position on religious dogma would be revised. Around 1930, Pessoa criticized the Portuguese Freemasons, accusing them of having a Catholic mentality, even though they were irreligious: "For what reason do you reject Catholic dogma, which is inoffensive and lofty, and retain the Catholic mentality, which is an intellectual and moral perversion of civilized state of mind?"[85]

Even before recounting in detail the recent antecedents (1906–1907) and succession of events of João Franco's dictatorship (1907–1908), which were addressed in the following parts of the book, Part I of "History of a Dictatorship" extensively reviews the successive phases of Portuguese decline from the beginning of absolutism. During the epoch of absolutism, only the actions of the Marquis of Pombal, whom Pessoa describes as "one of the greatest statesmen in the world," were distinguished, for Pombal was motivated by ideas of public good and of national regeneration, but he had revealed himself to be even more absolutist than absolute monarchs. After the liberal revolution of 1820, Pessoa believed that constitutional monarchy was truly initiated only in 1851 with the regeneration of Fontes Pereira de Melo, an idea Pessoa had taken from the counselor Augusto Fuschini, a liberal politician with vaguely socialist ideas who during the 1890s had written two famous books on Portuguese politics, which Pessoa abundantly cites in his book.[86]

The period of the constitutional monarchy is divided by Pessoa into two phases: the first from 1851 until 1890, which he paradoxically designates "Unconstitutional monarchy," and the second from 1890 onward, which he no less paradoxically designates "Constitutional anarchy."[87] From the liberal revolution until the time when he wrote the book, Pessoa, following Fuschini,[88] always refused to grant the Portuguese monarchy the attribute of being constitutional because he felt that it never attained an equilibrium between sovereignty with popular origins and the prerogatives of the crown, an equilibrium that was difficult to obtain and that had only been possible, according to Pessoa, in England and in other countries of northern Europe because they were not subject to the influence of the Catholic Church. Not only was the Carta Constitutional (1826) of an "ultraconservative spirit," because it maintained instruments of the king's absolute power (the dissolution of parliament by D. Carlos two years before Pessoa was writing seemed to confirm this) and because it maintained Catholicism as the state religion, but so were the politicians, who were elected under the carta, even when they were of popular origins, and who became increasingly immersed in the general climate of corruption and venality, which royal power itself favored and fomented, and they rarely represented the interests of their people.

The central themes of Part I of "History of a Dictatorship" are national decay and the possibility of Portugal's regeneration. Let us first consider the social forces and dynamics that the young Pessoa, in 1909–1910, considered essential for the Portuguese nation to resist decline and start down the path of regeneration. Second, let us examine how his thinking on these questions developed as he matured.

In the organism of the nation, which he sometimes also calls the state, the young republican Pessoa indicates the sickly organs, responsible for national decay and for the "moribund" state of the Portuguese monarchy—the monarchs, the aristocracy, the Catholic Church, and the political bosses—as a whole, corrupt and corrupting enemies of the public good. Foreign influence is also singled out as a cause of decline, though years later Pessoa would rather focus on the process of *denationalization*. If these determining causes were removed, "what was physiologically social below this would improve," Pessoa wrote in his proposed conclusions to the work.[89] For Pessoa, in fact, the healthy part of the nation was the people in general and the middle classes in particular, a term that for him encompassed the various social strata between the nobility and the proletariat. Even though they were subjected to the harmful influence of the church and the corrupting system of monarchy, the people—or at least the part of the people who were saved from these contaminating influences— constituted for the young author the healthy basis of the nation, the main foundation of resistance to disintegration and decline. The people had common sense and were the guardians of *human* moral sentiment that was independent of (Catholic) religion, a surprising statement when we consider the author's thoughts on the religiosity of the Latin peoples.

In this work, Pessoa uses the concepts of democracy, popular will (or government founded on the people), and popular opinion (or government based on opinion) synonymously. As bad as institutions might be, if the *majority of the people* (according to his democratic credo at the time) possessed a sense of citizenship and demonstrated devotion to the public good, government would have to submit or be overthrown.[90] However, in other passages of the text, this sense of citizenship and of devotion to the public good, the conditions for national regeneration, seem to have been conferred not on the majority of the people, but instead on specific entitities. Thus, as was mentioned earlier, Pessoa distinguished from the mass of the people "the discerning elements of the rising middle classes," which were the bourgeoisie and the intellectual elite; he also noted the indispensable existence of an organized and orderly "body of men," animated by a healthy spirit and coherent aspirations with a realistic and attainable program—in other words, the Republican Party.[91]

Basing his considerations on the analysis of psychiatrist Júlio de Matos (who in 1904 translated *The Socialist Superstition* by Raffaele Garofalo, founder of criminology and luminary of positivism), Pessoa believed that socialists, anarchists, and workers' leaders did not belong to the healthy part of the people and nation. The emphasis Pessoa placed on the clear-sighted and incorruptible elements of the rising middle classes evokes the decisive importance he would later attribute to the elites, to an "aristocracy" not of blood, but of merit, intelligence, and ethical sense. Thus, in a phase in which Pessoa still spoke much about the people and "the majority of the people" as a natural reserve of the nation, he nevertheless began to show embryonic signs of his future elitist thinking, which would lead him years later to formulate the doctrine of an "aristocratic republic" and, in 1919–1920, in a climate of great social and political instability following the government of Sidónio Pais (1917–1918), to reject entirely the value of democracy and to speak of the majority of the people almost always with contempt.

In addition, Pessoa's notion of public opinion changed with time: when Pessoa was twenty years old, he thought that the *government of opinion* was the government of the people, the government of the majority. When he was in his thirties, he conveyed in such works as "O Interregno" (1928) the idea that a government founded on public opinion could not be a "democracy"—at least as it was then understood—because public opinion was the opinion of minorities, and because the wills and opinions of the majority of individuals could not be merged. In his youth, as already mentioned, he criticized egoism and individual ambition, whereas in his thirties he considered these characteristics, as a whole, the most solid pillar of society and civilization.

In conclusion, let us briefly examine the persistence of the themes of national decay and regeneration in Pessoa's political, literary, and prophetic work from his youth until death—themes that he had basically recovered from previous generations of intellectuals.

As has been established, the theme of national decline is treated in "History of a Dictatorship" according to an organicist, evolutionist, and rigid historicist paradigm, a rather schematic and simplistic approach that is not surprising in a kind of radical political manifesto by a young author. Pessoa did not intend to distinguish his work by its theme alone, nor by its conclusions, but rather by its pretense to a scientific approach, which was very much influenced by works written by psychiatrists, criminologists, and some exponents of positivist thinking.[92] The theme of decay, whether it referred to the monarchy or to Portuguese society itself, had long been commented on by the intellectual elite of Portugal. National decay had been previously discussed in differing tones and with more or less hope of regeneration by Alexandre Herculano, Antero de Quental, Oliveira Martins, Eça de Queirós, Ramalho Ortigão, Guerra Junqueiro, Fialho de Almeida, Sampaio Bruno (who was less apocalyptic in his diagnosis of decline), and other patriotic intellectuals, such as Augusto Fuschini, the most cited author in "History of a Dictatorship." Indeed, Pessoa could have imbibed the notion of a *moribund nation* from Fuschni, Oliveira Martins, or Guerra Junqueiro. Fuschini was perhaps the most pessimistic of all, ultimately believing that the people and the Portuguese race itself had been "poisoned" by "centuries of physical decay and moral corruption."[93]

As we have seen, Pessoa believed that the people constituted the healthy segment and the moral reserve of the nation, and that "the Portuguese race" had been in the past, and was still, "a strong race, the strongest in the South."[94] Pessoa also followed in the path of those who cultivated the theme of Portugal's decadence, a compulsory motto of elite thinking during the second half of the nineteenth century. But—following other patriotic thinkers, such as Oliveira Martins, Guerra Junqueiro, and Sampaio Bruno (also author of *O Encoberto* from 1904)—Pessoa augmented this theme early on with messianic mysticism and Sebastianism. We should recall the focus of Pessoa's hope in 1908 when he was twenty years old: "A savior, a true man, great and bold that would put us right." The diagnosis of national decline, originating in the belief in a mythic national golden age (essentially, the period of discoveries and overseas expansion), had as its natural complement, in the young Pessoa's Sebastianist mysticism,[95] the prophecy of a messianic redemption or savior. It seems defensible to state that Pessoa's Sebastianism first crystallized around the idea of the republic as savior, and that "History of a Dictatorship" is the work that announces its coming.

Pessoa's political thought during the years following the revolution of 1910 tended toward a self-professed conservative republicanism, though he always maintained his independence, a stance that would characterize him from youth until death. In his political writings, he was soon diverted from the study of national decline as a process related specifically to the monarchy, and he ended by projecting the phenomenon, with no discontinuity, onto the period of the First Republic (1910–1926). This process of further "radicalizing," "anarchizing," and "denationalizing" the declining nation would have pushed Portuguese society into a period of supposed "degeneration," a term used in a pejorative sense that goes beyond simple decay or denationalization, indicating a pathological or "moribund" state in a regressive process.[96] For Pessoa, the First Republic ultimately revealed the continuation and worsening, even without the monarchy, of the vices that he had diagnosed in the constitutional monarchy.

After his disappointment with the democratic republic, which since 1911 was clearly seen in the fragments that he wrote for "Oligarchy of Beasts," in collaboration from 1912 with the magazine A Águia,[97] and in various other writings, Pessoa created or adhered to other self-professed messianic and Sebastianist models, and to other "Desejados": the "supra-Camões" (announced in A Águia[98]); the redeeming figure of "President-King Sidónio Pais" (created after his death in Pessoa's collaboration with the Sidonist journal Acção in 1919–1920); the Fifth Empire (a biblical myth that Pessoa reelaborated, beginning in the mid-1920s, inspired by António Vieira's seventeeth-century interpretation published in his History of the Future); and, from May 1926, the more realistic military dictatorship (to which Pessoa offered his messianic perspective with the publication of "The Interregnum"). All of these prophetic models were associated with diagnoses of decline and ideas of national regeneration, glory, and future greatness of Portugal—the "super-Portugal of tomorrow" as he called it in A Águia in 1912.[99]

Thus, the theme of national decline accompanied Pessoa throughout this life, whether it was with the hope of redemption, as in Mensagem, a work written and rewritten through his maturity ("Tudo vale a pena se a alma não é pequena," "É a Hora!"); or whether it was finally without hope, as in the pessimistic poem "Elegia na sombra," a declaration of the despair and disbelief of a mystic and messianic nationalist, written in 1935, months before his death ("Quem nos roubou a alma?," " . . . nada vale a pena").

NOTES

1. Some of these were inventoried by Jerónimo Pizarro, who gave priority to contents related to the themes of genius and madness in Pessoa's writings. See Fernando Pessoa, Escritos sobre génio e loucura, Vols. I, II, ed. Jerónimo Pizarro (Lisbon: INCM, 2006); and Jerónimo Pizarro, Fernando Pessoa: Entre génio e loucura (Lisbon: INCM, 2007).

2. Outlines of the program and presentation of "O Iconoclasta" can be found in BNP/ E3, 87–53^r to 57^r and 92B–30^r.

3. "Let up *O Phosporo*" is the annotation in a list of things to do in 1909 (BNP/E3, 48H-49^r).

4. With the publication of the "Pink Map" (c. 1886), Portugal claimed sovereignty over the territory between Angola and Mozambique, allegedly against Cecil Rhodes's "Cape to Cairo" projects. The dispute resulted in the British Ultimatum (Jan. 11, 1890), to which the Portuguese kingdom conceded, fostering a wave of republican nationalism. The Portuguese national anthem, adopted in 1910 by the new republican government, had been composed in 1890 in the wake of the British Ultimatum.

5. In response to an enquiry by Boavida Portugal published in the newspaper *República* (n. 1161, Apr. 7, 1914) about the "most beautiful Portuguese book of the last thirty years," Fernando Pessoa suggested *Pátria* by Guerra Junqueiro, which, in his opinion, was "not only the best work of the past thirty years, but until now the foremost work in our literature." In an unpublished text, a chapter in English on Guerra Junqueiro that Pessoa wrote in 1909–1910, according to our identification, for "History of a Dictatorship," Pessoa highly praised the author of *Patria, Finis patriae, A Morte de D. João*, and *A Velhice do padre eterno*, and considered this last title, which he translated as *God's Old Age*, as "his best work (at some points, at least)." Guerra Junqueiro is here described as "the greatest of Portuguese contemporary poets." The title of this unfinished chapter by Pessoa is "Words to Remain in History: A Poet's Trial," and it discusses the sentence passed on Guerra Junqueiro in April 1907 (BNP/E3, 14C–30^r–35^r).

6. See Maria Teresa Pinto Coelho, *Apocalipse e regeneração: O Ultimatum e a mitologia da pátria na literatura finissecular* (Lisbon: Cosmos 1996), 164, 191–92.

7. Jerónimo Pizarro, *Fernando Pessoa: Entre génio e loucura*, 91; and Fernando Pessoa, *Escritos sobre génio e loucura*, 234.

8. BNP/E3, 79A–71 (title page of the manuscript of the work to which was attached an unfinished draft of the introduction and little else).

9. BNP/E3, 138A–6, published for the first time in Teresa Rita Lopes, *Pessoa por conhecer* (1990), Vol. II, 76–77, with transcription errors corrected by Jerónimo Pizarro in *Fernando Pessoa: Entre génio e loucura*, 132. The Marquis of Tavira (and not of Távora, as T. R. Lopes read it) referred to in the text is a fictitious person created by the Spanish dramaturge José Zorrilla (1817–1893) in this piece "Traidor, inconfeso y mártir," supposedly inspired by the historical figure Cristóvão de Távora, the favorite of King D. Sebastião, who accompanied the king to Alcácer Quibir and was at his side when he died.

10. BNP/E3, 48C–3^r, list of projects attributed to the pseudonym "Pantaleão (if necessary give true name)," and 92H-16^r, "A Psychose adeantativa," published in Fernando Pessoa, *Escritos sobre génio e loucura*, 238.

11. Pessoa, *Escritos sobre génio e loucura*, 241. Some texts actually written for this project are found on pp. 238–40.

12. BNP/E3, 92P–10. The "decreto dos adiantamentos" (Aug. 30, 1907), signed by João Franco after the government had closed Parliament, annuled the debts of the Royal House with an accounting maneuver, which unleashed a wave of discontent, disparaging the king and the monarchy.

13. BNP/E3, 48C–1^r to 5^r (the title in question is on 48C–2^r, list of projects of Alexander Search).

14. BNP/E3, 49C^1–48^v.

15. BNP/E3, 20–1^r to 6^r, published for the fist time, with errors and lacunae in Fernando Pessoa, *Páginas íntimas e de auto-interpretação*, ed. Jacinto Prado Coelho and Georg Rudolf Lind (Lisbon: Ática, 1966), 3–6, and with corrections in Fernando Pessoa, *Escritos autobiográficos, automáticos e de reflexão Pessoal*, ed. Richard Zenith (Lisbon: Assírio & Alvim, 2003), 84–88. The transcription just mentioned ends after the line with signature and date.

16. enter<ed>/s\

17. Richard Zenith, in his transcription of the text, corrected the English to "he would have to have." See Pessoa, *Escritos autobiográficos*, 86.

18. This question mark is lacking in the original.

19. The principal texts are the already mentioned introduction with the subtitle "National and Institutional Decay" (BNP/E3, 79A–71 to 82), which apparently remained unfinished, and the three initial pages of Part I (BNP/E3, 92W–70^r to 72^r). The introduction was translated into Portuguese and published without explicit reference to the fact that it was an introduction to "The Portuguese Regicide and the Political Situation in Portugal," in [Ana Cristina Assunção,] "Ensaio político inédito: O Regicídio Português e a situação política em Portugal," *Jornal de Letras, Artes e Ideias* 177 (Nov. 26, 1985), 14–15.

20. BNP/E3, 48–24^r, published in Fernando Pessoa, *Escritos sobre génio e loucura*, 240–41.

21. BNP/E3, 144D–3^r and 6^r.

22. Cf. the differing opinion of Jerónimo Pizarro expressed in his *Fernando Pessoa: Entre génio e loucura*, 44, and in Fernando Pessoa, *Escritos sobre génio e loucura*, 822. It cannot be confirmed that "History of a Dictatorship" was a bilingual work (Pizarro, *Fernando Pessoa: Entre génio e loucura*, 122), because the chapters actually written, whether typescript or manuscript, were always in English, and Pessoa himself classified the work either as an "English essay" or as an "English book." (BNP/E3, 144D–6^r). For the project *H. of a D.*, although scattered notes were written in Portuguese, some additional notes were written in English.

23. The whole is mostly divided between numbers 92N, 920, and 92P of the literary remains, as well as numbers 92Q, 92R, 92S, and 92Y. A typescript chapter, also unfin-

ished, which appears to be Chapter IX of Part II, is located in another section of the remains (BNP/E3, 14C–30ʳ to 35ʳ).

24. We know, for example, that the work was written during the monarchy (before Oct. 5, 1910) from the following phrase: "the Portuguese monarchy [. . .] is at present very low, very weak—dying, we may say" (BNP/E3, 92N–40ʳ).

25. BNP/E3, 92N–93ʳ.

26. BNP/E3, 92L–19 to 20, published by Pizarro in Fernando Pessoa, *Escritos sobre génio e loucura*, 260–61. In addition to this plan and part of a preface, fifty-one texts by Pessoa associated with the project "History of a Dictatorship" are transcribed in this work (259–302).

27. BNP/E3, 92S–54.

28. See Fernando Pessoa, *Escritos sobre génio e loucura*, 822, with caution regarding the assertion that Pessoa would have already begun "History of a Dictatorship" in 1908; this claim cannot be confirmed.

29. For example, BNP/E3, 108A–75 to 79ʳ, under the title H. *of a D.*, is a text dated after the fall of the monarchy.

30. BNP/E3, 108A–40 and 108A–65 to 66.

31. BNP/E3, 108–46 and 47. Pessoa also wrote *Ieshu* and *Jeschú*.

32. BNP/E3, 108–20 to 26, 108–50, 108–95.

33. BNP/E3, 92E–26 to 29.

34. BNP/E3, 108A–91.

35. BNP/E3, 92S–42 and 43. The author here writes, "This is, we believe, the first clearly historical work in which the principles of a psychology based upon science, in which even the principles of psychiatric science are applied." This preface was partially transcribed by Jerónimo Pizarro in Fernando Pessoa, *Escritos sobre génio e loucura*, 259.

36. BNP/E3, 93–48ʳ, under the title "Livros para escrever a H. of a D.," reproduced in Fernando Pessoa, *Escritos sobre génio e loucura*, 291. This bibliography included a book by João de Barros published in 1910, *La Littérature Portugaise*, which enables us to date it from this year.

37. See Jerónimo Pizarro, *Fernando Pessoa: Entre génio e loucura*, 123.

38. BNP/E3, 92Q–97r.

39. António Mega Ferreira, *Fazer pela vida* (Lisbon: Assírio & Alvim, 2005), 59–60.

40. In a still unpublished letter from Pretoria dated January 12, 1913, Fernando Pessoa's mother speaks of the "cinco contos de réis" from the inheritance of his grandmother which had disappeared, leaving her son a debt of 350,000 réis to pay. His mother attributed these events to the failed typographic business: "A tua má cabeça, metendo-te em negócios de que nada entendias, levou tudo por água abaixo." The cause of every-

thing, according to his mother, was "tuas ideias da tipografia, para publicar livros teus, os quais tu próprio confessas, ainda nem hoje estão escritos."

41. For example, BNP/E3, 108A–22 to 23 and 108A–25^r.

42. BNP/E3, 92S–54^{r-v}.

43. Pessoa, "Livros para escrever a H. of a D."

44. Luis Morote, *De la Dictadura á la república: La vida política en Portugal* (Valencia: F. Sempere, n.d. [1908]). The ambiguity of the title and the fact that the edition was undated have produced confusion regarding the publication date of this book, which has generally been considered to be after October 5, 1910. Morote's book recounts the history of the dictatorship of João Franco and its antecedents, concluding with a brief note written at the last minute: "Tragedia final: derrumbamiento de un regímen" (281–82), which refers in two pages to the regicide (Feb. 1, 1908) and the accession to the throne of King D. Manuel II. Morote does not, then, actually discuss the fall of the monarchy, but only his conviction that the republic was about to be established. Patricio Ferrari correctly dates the work to 1908 in "A Biblioteca de Fernando Pessoa na génese dos heterónimos," in Jerónimo Pizarro, coord., *Fernando Pessoa: O Guardador de papéis* (Alfragide: Texto, 2009), 195.

45. Jerónimo Pizarro, Patricio Ferrari, and Antonio Cardiello, *A Biblioteca particular de Fernando Pessoa* I (Lisbon: D. Quixote, 2010), 138–39, 142.

46. For example, BNP/E3, 108–10.

47. BNP/E3, 92B–63.

48. BNP/E3, 48H–33^r. The new title of the essay in English also appears in the list on 48H–7^r and 58^r, with its authorship being here attributed for the first time to Fernando Pessoa. This list enumerates nine titles under the heading "Estudos Contemporaneos" (a collection of books?) and the title "Da Dictadura á republica" does not figure in it.

49. BNP/E3, 92C–71^r.

50. BNP/E3, 92C–82: "Cons[ideração]s post-rev[olucionarias] e (?) / ou Da D. á R."

51. Curiously, the idea of writing *A Oligarchia das bestas* emerges during the writing of a note for *Cons[ideração]s post-rev[olucionarias]* (BNP/E3, 92F–27^r). *A Oligarchia das bestas* is here described as "A Pamphlet against our radicals, against A[fonso] C[osta], etc."

52. BNP/E3, 48H–58^r, under the title *Politica e sociologia*, and 48H–7^r, cited earlier, seems to be the project for a collection of studies titled *Estudos contemporaneos*. This project is datable to 1911, because the title *A Coroação de Jorge Quinto* (the coronation of George V took place in June 1911) figures among the projected studies.

53. Fernando Pessoa, "Extent and Causes of Portuguese Decay" (text that we here identify with Part I of "History of a Dictatorship"), 18 (BNP/E3, 92N–35^r).

54. Pessoa, "Extent and Causes of Portuguese Decay." The first chapter of Part I is titled "National and Institutional Decay" (BNP/E3, 92N–1^r to 17^r). As has been said, "Na-

tional and Institutional Decay" was also the subtitle of the introduction that Pessoa wrote for "The Portuguese Regicide and the Political Situation in Portugal" (BNP/E3, 79A–71 to 82).

55. Pessoa, "Extent and Causes of Portuguese Decay," 92N–4.

56. The pair of concepts of integration and disintegration, which Herbert Spencer first employed in *First Principles* to describe organic processes as well as social processes, was then used in the sociological work of Émile Durkheim. Pessoa had direct or indirect knowledge of the work of both, and was particularly influenced by Spencer, whom he had read before 1910. See José Barreto, "Fernando Pessoa racionalista, livre-pensador e individualista: A influência liberal Inglesa," in S. Dix, J. Pizarro, eds., *A Arca de Pessoa: Novos ensaios* (Lisbon: ICS, 2007), 109–27; Jerónimo Pizarro, *Fernando Pessoa: Entre génio e loucura* (Lisbon: INCM, 2007), 50–54; and S. Dix and J. Barreto, "Um sociólogo oblíquo: A Função social da religião e da arte e as reflexões políticas em torno de Fernando Pessoa," in P. A. Silva and F. C. Silva, eds., *Ciências sociais: Vocação e profissão—Homenagem a Manuel Villaverde Cabral* (Lisbon: ICS, 2013), 181–205.

57. Pessoa, "Extent and Causes of Portuguese Decay," 5.

58. See José Barreto, "A publicação de *O Interregno* no contexto político de 1927–1928," *Pessoa Plural* 2 (Fall 2012), 191, n. 19.

59. Pessoa, "Extent and Causes of Portuguese Decay," 6–8.

60. Ibid., 2.

61. Ibid., 8–9.

62. Ibid., 11.

63. Ibid., 10–11.

64. BNP/E3, 92R–75^r.

65. Pessoa, "Extent and Causes of Portuguese Decay," 12–13.

66. See BNP/E3, 108B–5^r, under the title H[istoria] *de uma Ditadura—Conclusões*. Other factors of national decline would be foreign influence, the oligarchy of political bosses, and the decline of Western civilization itself.

67. Pessoa, "Extent and Causes of Portuguese Decay," 15–16.

68. Ibid., 17.

69. Ibid., 37–38.

70. Ibid., 19.

71. Ibid., 38.

72. Ibid., Chapter II, "Origin of Portuguese Decadence: Influence of the Roman Catholic Church," 18–43.

73. Pessoa, "Extent and Causes of Portuguese Decay," 44.

74. Ibid., 23.

75. Ibid., 22.

76. Ibid., 28. This is the book *Etudes sur la sélection dans ses rapports avec l'hérédité chez l'homme* (1881) by Paul Jacoby; Pessoa could have had been aware of this book through the work of John F. Nisbet, *Marriage and Heredity* (1908), which he had read.

77. Pessoa, "Extent and Causes of Portuguese Decay," 29.

78. Ibid., 33.

79. Ibid., 22.

80. Ibid., 37.

81. Ibid., 30.

82. Ibid., 31.

83. BNP/E3, 55F–17^r, 55F–18^r to 20^r, extract from an unpublished response to an inquiry from around 1930.

84. BNP/E3, 55I–23^r, extract from an unpublished response to an inquiry from around 1930, published for the first time in *Sobre Portugal*, 84–85.

85. BNP/E3, 129A–3^r, extract from an unpublished response to an inquiry from around 1930, published for the first time in Fernando Pessoa, *Associações secretas e outros escritos*, ed. José Barreto (Lisbon: Ática, 2011), 190.

86. The works most cited by Pessoa throughout Part I of "History of a Dictatorship" are *O Presente e o futuro de Portugal* by Fuschini, originally published in 1899, and *Manual político do cidadão Português* by Trindade Coelho, published in 1906.

87. These two periods are analyzed in Chapters III and IV of Part I, titled "Unconstitutional Monarchy" and "Constitutional Anarchy." See Pessoa, "Extent and Causes of Portuguese Decay," 44–76, 77–89. The author also uses for the first expression the variant of "constitutional absolutism" (Ibid., 55).

88. Pessoa, "Extent and Causes of Portuguese Decay," 41.

89. BNP/E3, 108B–5^r, H[istoria] *de uma Dictadura—Conclusões*.

90. Pessoa, "Extent and Causes of Portuguese Decay," 16.

91. Ibid., 15–16.

92. Among others, Pessoa cites in support of his theses works by Paul Jacoby, Cesare Lombroso, Júlio de Matos, Júlio Dantas, and the physiologist Xavier Bichat (1771–1802), one of the great inspirations of Auguste Comte.

93. Augusto Fuschini, *Liquidações políticas* (Lisbon: Companhia Tipográfica, 1896), 149.

94. Pessoa, "Extent and Causes of Portuguese Decay," 25.

95. Obviouly, mystical Sebastianism did not prevent Pessoa from judging King D. Sebastião's African adventure as a catastrophe that led to the loss of Portugal's independence in 1580. In his opinion, the young king had scorned all prudent counsel, subjected as he was to the influence of the church: "the sole cause of the madly audaciuous condition of minds" would have been religion (Pessoa, "Extent and Causes of Portuguese Decay," 26).

96. See the text "A desorientação em que temos vivido, a decadência em que temos vegetado . . ." (BNP/E3, 92D–37ʳ), published for the first time in Fernando Pessoa, *Sobre Portugal: Introdução ao problema nacional*, ed. Joel Serrão (Lisbon: Ática, 1979), 130.

97. Fernando Pessoa, "Reincidindo . . . ," *A Águia* 5 (May 1912), 143.

98. Fernando Pessoa, "A Nova poesia Portuguesa sociologicamente considerada," *A Águia* 4 (Apr. 1912), 107.

99. Ibid.

WORKS CITED

Assunção, Ana C. "Ensaio político inédito: O Regicídio português e a situação política em Portugal." *JL—Jornal de Letras, Artes e Ideias*, 177 (Nov. 26, 1985), 14–15.

Barreto, José. "A publicação de *O Interregno* no contexto político de 1927–1928." *Pessoa Plural—A Journal of Fernando Pessoa Studies* 2 (2012): 174–207.

———. "Fernando Pessoa racionalista, livre-pensador e individualista: A Influência liberal inglesa." In Steffen Dix, Jerónimo Pizarro, eds., *A Arca de Pessoa: Novos ensaios*, Lisbon, ICS, 2007. 109–27.

Coelho, M. Teresa Pinto. *Apocalipse e regeneração: O Ultimatum e a mitologia da pátria na literatura finissecular*. Lisbon: Cosmos, 1996.

Dix, Steffen, and José Barreto, "Um sociólogo oblíquo: A Função social da religião e da arte e as reflexões políticas em torno de Fernando Pessoa." In P. A. Silva, F. C. Silva, eds., *Ciências sociais: Vocação e profissão. Homenagem a Manuel Villaverde Cabral*. Lisbon: ICS, 2013, 181–205.

Lopes, Teresa Rita. *Pessoa por conhecer*. 2 vols. Lisbon: Estampa, 1990.

Ferrari, Patricio. "A Biblioteca de Fernando Pessoa na génese dos heterónimos." In Jerónimo Pizarro (ed.), *Fernando Pessoa: O Guardador de papéis*. Alfragide: Texto, 2009. 191–213.

Ferreira, António Mega. *Fazer pela vida*. Lisbon: Assírio & Alvim, 2005.

Fuschini, Augusto. *Liquidações políticas*. Lisbon: Companhia Tipográfica, 1896.

Morote, Luis. *De la dictadura á la República (la vida política en Portugal)*. Valencia: F. Sempere y Compañía, [1908].

Pessoa, Fernando. *Associações secretas e outros escritos*. Edited by José Barreto. Lisbon: Ática, 2011.

———. *Escritos sobre génio e loucura*. 2 vols. Edited by Jerónimo Pizarro, Lisbon: Imprensa Nacional–Casa da Moeda, 2006.

———. *Escritos autobiográficos, automáticos e de reflexão pessoal*. Edited by Richard Zenith. Lisbon: Assírio & Alvim, 2003.

———. *Sobre Portugal: Introdução ao problema nacional*. Edited by Joel Serrão. Lisbon: Ática, 1979.

———. *Páginas íntimas e de auto-interpretação.* Edited by Jacinto Prado Coelho and Georg Rudolf Lind. Lisbon: Ática, 1966.

———. "Reincidindo . . . ." *A Águia* 5 (May 1912), 137–44.

———. "A Nova Poesia portuguesa sociologicamente considerada." *A Águia* 4 (April 1912), 101–7.

Pizarro, Jerónimo. *Fernando Pessoa: Entre génio e loucura.* Collection "Studies." Lisbon: Imprensa Nacional–Casa da Moeda, 2007.

Pizarro, Jerónimo, Patricio Ferrari, and Antonio Cardiello. *A Biblioteca particular de Fernando Pessoa.* Lisbon: D. Quixote, 2010.

JOSÉ BARRETO, a historian with training in economics and sociology, has worked as a researcher at the Instituto de Ciências Sociais da Universidade de Lisboa (ICS–UL, Institute of Social Sciences, University of Lisbon) since the 1970s. In the past eight years, he has dedicated himself mainly to the study of the sociological and political writings of Fernando Pessoa. His publications include "O Fascismo e o salazarismo vistos por Fernando Pessoa" in *Estudos Italianos em Portugal* (2013); "António Ferro: Modernism and Politics" in *Portuguese Modernisms* (Legenda, 2011); and "Nacional-catolicismo: Origens e carreira de um conceito" in C. Gaspar et al., *Estado regimes e revolução* (ICS, 2012). His articles in *Pessoa Plural* include "Mar Salgado: Fernando Pessoa perante uma acusação de plágio," "O Núcleo de Acção Nacional em dois escritos desconhecidos de Fernando Pessoa," "A Publicação de O Interregno no contexto político de 1927–1928," "Fernando Pessoa e Raul Leal contra a campanha moralizadora dos estudantes em 1923," "Mussolini é um louco: Uma entrevista desconhecida de Fernando Pessoa com um antifascista italiano," and "O Mago e o louco: Fernando Pessoa e Alberto da Cunha Dias." His books include *Misoginia e anti-feminismo em Fernando Pessoa* (Ática, 2011); and Fernando Pessoa, *Associações secretas e outros Escritos* (Ática, 2011, ed. José Barreto).

He can be reached at jose.barreto@ics.ulisboa.pt.

MARIANA GRAY DE CASTRO

Pessoa and Keats

ABSTRACT: This article examines the dialogue between Fernando Pessoa and the English romantic poet John Keats (1795–1821). It begins by exploring Pessoa's poetic engagement with Keats's verse, before moving on to an analysis of his assimilation of Keats's most influential aesthetic ideas, above all those of the *chameleon poet* and *negative capability*, which I argue were a significant, yet hitherto largely unexplored, influence on Pessoa's heteronymic invention.

KEYWORDS: influence, Pessoa, Keats, private library

Several of Fernando Pessoa's poems, particularly his adolescent production in English, as well as his ideas about poetry, are indebted to his immersion in English Romantic era literature during his formative years. This article will explore Pessoa's creative and theoretical debt to the poet-critic John Keats (1795–1821), following in the footsteps of pioneering studies about this fertile dialogue by such critics as George Monteiro, Maria Irene Ramalho de Sousa Santos, and António M. Feijó.[1] It will begin by examining an instance of poetic influence, before going on to consider Pessoa's wider assimilation, in the context of his thinking on the heteronyms, of Keats's aesthetic ideals.

Pessoa's reading diary of 1903, when he was fifteen and sixteen years old, reveals his voracious consumption of Keats over several months, and in the same year he selected Keats's *Poetical Works* as part of a school prize.[2] This book is still present in his personal library, together with a number of critical studies of romantic literature, plus a biography of Keats.[3]

Pessoa's marginalia in these books, together with his few existing writings about Keats, reveal that he was particularly drawn to his famous odes and to his long poem "Hyperion"; Pessoa listed three of Keats's odes in a poetry anthology, partially translated at least one of them into Portuguese,[4] and used "Hyperion" as a model for his own epic poem *Mensagem* (*Message*),[5] as Santos and Feijó have shown.[6]

The earliest Portuguese example of Pessoa's poetic engagement with Keats is his 1908 poem "A Keats," ("To Keats") which provides us with a good window into his appraisal of Keats's art. "A Keats" bears the note, or subtitle, "Depois de ler o seu soneto: 'When I have fears that I may cease to be'" (After reading his sonnet: "When I have fears that I may cease to be").[7]

Here is Keats's relevant sonnet, of 1818:

When I have fears that I may cease to be
　Before my pen has gleaned my teeming brain,
Before high-pilèd books, in charact'ry,
　Hold like rich garners the full-ripened grain;
When I behold upon the night's starred face,
　Huge cloudy symbols of a high romance,
And think that I may never live to trace
　Their shadows with the magic hand of chance;
And when I feel, fair creature of an hour!
　That I shall never look upon thee more,
Never have relish in the faery power
　Of unreflecting Love!—then on the shore
Of the wide world I stand alone, and think,
Till Love and Fame to nothingness do sink.

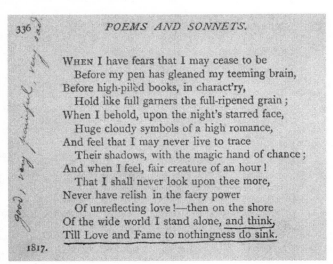

Keats, "When I have fears that I may cease to be," *The Poetical Works*, 1898, 336.

Keats's use of capitals and punctuation is notoriously haphazard; this is the version of the poem as it appears in Pessoa's personal copy of his verse. In it, Pessoa underlined the the final words: "and think, / Till Love and Fame to nothingness do sink," and he wrote what is for him strong praise in the margin next to the poem, describing it as "good; very painful, very sad."[8]

Pessoa responded to Keats's good, very painful, very sad sonnet with a poem of his own:

A KEATS

> (Depois de ler o seu soneto:
> "When I have fears that I may cease to be")

Estatuário da poesia, tu disseste:
"Ah, se eu morrer sem pôr em verso ardente
Tudo—sim, tudo—que a minha alma sente!"
E morreste, e em pouco! Súbito horror!
Se comigo assim for!
Se eu também não puder dizer ao mundo
O meu sentir atónito e profundo!
Se eu morrer dentro em mim guardando fria
A minha inspiração e a minha dor,
Como tu, Estatuário da poesia![9]

(TO KEATS

> [After having read your sonnet:
> "When I have fears that I may cease to be"]

Sculptor of poetry, you said
"Ah, if I die before I put into ardent
Poetry all—yes, all—that my soul feels."
And you died—right afterwards. Sudden horror!
If that's the way it will with me!
Of my astonished and profound feelings!
If I die holding coldly within me
My inspiration, my pain,
Like you, Sculptor of poetry!)[10]

The way in which Pessoa addresses Keats, in this poem, is representative of his attitude toward Keats, as evidenced in his prose texts and marginalia. Keats is, according to Pessoa, a great "estatuário da poesia" (statuary sculptor of poetry), whose carefully crafted, formally constructed odes he will later praise in "Erostratus" (late 1920s), an essay about artistic greatness and what will survive into succeeding ages.[11] Keats's odes were created with the same attention to form that one might use in creating statues, and in this light they are similar to many poems penned by the orthonym and heteronym Ricardo Reis. "Autopsicografia" ("Autopsychography")[12] famously speaks of the poet as being a "fingidor" (feigner), but the Latin word *fingere*, at the root of the Portuguese verb *fingir* (to feign), also refers to molding or forming, thus carrying with it a subsidiary meaning as applicable to the art of sculpture as to the art of poetry.

At the same time, Pessoa is attracted to what he considers to be the moving, sensuous, emotional charge of Keats's poetry, as his attempt to inject strong feeling into his own poem makes clear. This is corroborated by a prose text he wrote in the same year:

> I cannot think badly of the man who wrote the "Ode to a Nightingale," nor of him who, in that "to the Grecian Urn," expresses so human an idea as the heart-rending untimeness of beauty. We all have felt that tearful sensation. Mothers, how many of ye, in looking at your bright children and at their heavenly fairness, have not wished such small, lovely forms could be preserved for ever and unchanged. Lover, when looking upon the form of thy mistress hast thou not felt thy heart oppressed because such beauty should one day be no more, nay, should grow old and, may hap, unbeautiful. Have we not all wished the immortality of someone that we know, have we all not felt that same pain at feeling that none are immortal.[13]

One might be forgiven for thinking these words must have come from the pen of a romantic poet, rather than a budding modernist one—further evidence of Pessoa's literary diet during his teenage years.

In his poem to Keats, Pessoa ponders the anguishing thought that he, too, may die before being able to transform all of his thoughts and feelings into poetry, which is a common romantic topos.

Keats, in his sonnet, appears to tragically foretell his early death:

> When I have fears that I may cease to be
> Before my pen has gleaned my teeming brain

Pessoa translates Keats's opening lines:

Ah, se eu morrer sem pôr em verso ardente
Tudo—sim, tudo—que a minha alma sente!

However, as Monteiro points out, Pessoa makes no genuine effort to translate Keats's actual words.[14] He replaces the mind with the soul; Keats's "teeming brain" becomes "tudo que a minha alma sente" (everything which my soul feels), even though ending the line with "mente" (mind) would have provided just as good a rhyme for "ardente" (ardent).

Throughout his poem, Pessoa addresses Keats directly and informally, employing the second person singular (tu) to establish a personal, familiar connection between the two men, not only in relation to their desire to glean poetry from their teeming brains (Keats) or the emotion in their souls (Pessoa), but also in the context of Pessoa's fear that he too may succumb to his predecessor's fate:

E morreste, e em pouco! Súbito horror!
Se comigo assim for!

As we can see from these lines, Pessoa's poem is melodramatic in tone. It also lacks subtlety: notice how Keats expertly avoids the word *death*, while Pessoa directly refers to dying three times. Pessoa's poem is self-aggrandizing and self-indulgent. It carries undertones of what George Orwell calls, in reference to some of T. S. Eliot's poetry, a "twilight-of-the-gods feeling," and a soppy emphasis on the speaker's personal emotions: "O *meu* sentir atónito e profundo! [. . .] A *minha* inspiração e *a minha* dor" (my astonished and profound feelings! [. . .] My inspiration, *my* pain). This is poetic egotism of the sort Keats vehemently condemned in writers such as William Wordsworth, as we shall see. An uncharitable reader might conclude that in his poem, Pessoa is attempting to outdo the power of emotion present in Keats's heartbreaking sonnet, while a more charitable reader may consider his poem the immature product of a promising young poet who has not yet struck the ideal balance he so admires in Keats—the art of crafting a sculptural poem and infusing it with just the right amount of sentiment.

Interestingly, Pessoa's poem to Keats does not mention love, which in Keats's sonnet is one of the two things (the second being literary immortality) that the speaker fears he may not fully experience before he dies (see the second half of the sonnet, from "fair creature of the hour" onward).

In Pessoa's poem, the speaker's "sentir atónito e profundo" (astonished and profound feelings), his "inspiração" (inspiration) and "dor" (pain), the things his "alma sente" (soul feels), may well be the feelings traditionally stirred by a love object, but they may simply be the necessary raw materials for the making of romantic poetry, mere objects to be transformed into the "verso ardente" (ardent verse). In other words, these powerful emotions may here be chiefly of interest to Pessoa as themes and subjects for poetry, rather than, as in Keats's poem, desirable feelings to be experienced in real life. (T. S. Eliot, who shared so many of Pessoa's aesthetic beliefs, agreed with him on this point: "impressions and experiences which are important for the man may take no place in the poetry, and those which become important in the poetry may play quite a negligible part in the man."[15])

Twenty years later, Pessoa would explain to his girlfriend Ophélia Queiroz that everything assumed second place in his life, relative to his literary ambition:

> A minha vida gira em torno da minha obra literária—boa ou má, que seja, ou possa ser. Tudo o mais na vida tem para mim um interesse secundário: há coisas, naturalmente, que estimaria ter, outras que tanto faz que venham ou não venham. É preciso que todos, que lidam comigo, se convençam de que sou assim, e que exigir-me os sentimentos, aliás muito dignos, de um homem vulgar e banal, é como exigir-me que tenha olhos azuis e cabelo louro.

> (My life revolves around my literary work—good or poor as it may be, or might be. Everything else in life is of secondary importance to me: there are things, of course, I would like to have, others I don't mind whether or not they come to be. All those who deal with me must accept that this is the way I am, and that demanding me to have the feelings of a common, ordinary man, however worthy they may be, is like demanding me to have blue eyes and blond hair.)[16]

On the evidence of these words, harsh when addressed to a supposed beloved, together with the absence of any direct reference to love in Pessoa's poetic response to Keats's sonnet, it would appear that as a young poet, Pessoa already considered earthly love and artistic success to be incompatible, perhaps even mutually exclusive, at least in his own case. "A Keats" therefore supports the widely held notion that, for Pessoa, the world of literature was always more worthy of investment than his actual day-to-day life, just as artistic emotion was more important than real-life passion. (Keats's life story, which fascinated Pessoa, appears to highlight the dangers of a life lived with too much real emotion: toward the end, his doctors urged him not to overexert himself by reading and writing poetry, or seeing his girlfriend Fanny Browne.[17])

Monteiro, in his book *Pessoa and Nineteenth-Century Anglo-American Literature*,[18] suggests a further instance of Pessoa's poetic engagement with Keats, his even earlier poem "On Death" ("Sobre a morte"), written in 1904. Monteiro analyzes this poem as a response to not only Keats's "When I have fears that I may cease to be," but also John Milton's "On His Blindness" and Emily Bronte's "Last Lines."[19]

It is conceivable that "Tabacaria" ("Tobacco Shop"), written over twenty years later and attributed to the heteronym Álvaro de Campos, also contains a teasing echo of one of Keats's poems.

Keats's "Ode to a Nightingale" explores the themes of transience and mortality, like "Ode on a Grecian Urn." [20] In the poem, the speaker's sense of his inevitable demise is contrasted with the nightingale's immortality ("Thou wast not born for death, immortal Bird!"). The bird is thus a portal to immortality, a land of fantasy and imagination, via its eternal song, which through the ages "Charm'd magic casements, opening on the foam / Of perilous seas, in faery lands forlorn."

"Tabacaria" is also concerned with the speaker's mortality versus the immortality of art; in this case, poetry rather than music. It contains no birdsong; instead, when the speaker himself sings the "cantiga do Infinito" (song of the Infinite), he does so, ironically, in a "capoeira" (chicken coop), which does not even appear to be populated with chickens: "Serei sempre o que [. . .] cantou a cantiga do Infinito numa capoeira" (I'll always be the one who [. . .] / sang the song of the Infinite in a chicken coop).[21] Pessoa may here be transposing the nightingale's song, which is the bird's way of achieving immortality, into the poet's art, which the speaker, arguably like all artists, banks on for his own immortality.

Granted, the speaker declares that his poetry will, like everything else, eventually cease to exist:

[o dono da tabacaria] morrerá e eu morrerei.
Ele deixará a tabuleta, eu deixarei os versos.
A certa altura morrerá a tabuleta também, os versos também.

Depois de certa altura morrerá a rua onde esteve a tabuleta,
E a língua em que foram escritos os versos.

(the tobacco shop owner will die and I will die.
He'll leave his signboard, I'll leave my poems.
His sign will also eventually die, and so will my poems.
Eventually the street where the sign was will die,
And so will the language in which the poems were written.)[22]

However, as these lines make clear, the speaker is convinced that his poetry will outlive him. "A caligrafia rápida destes versos," like the nightingale's song, opens "magic casements" to an imaginary, everlasting world ("faery lands") beyond the death of the speaker and the physical world around him. Poetry becomes, in Pessoa's poem, another "pórtico partido para o Impossível." (broken gateway to the Impossible).[23]

Pessoa not only made good use of Keats as a model for some of his poems; more significantly, he also assimilated his predecessor's most influential ideas about poetry for his thinking on the heteronyms.

Keats's aesthetic ideals appear chiefly in his striking letters. Unlike Pessoa, Eliot was never a huge fan of Keats's poetry, yet he wrote that these letters were "the most notable and most important ever written by any English poet," because he considered that they contained hardly a statement about poetry that was not "true."[24]

In one letter, Keats proclaims his longing for feeling over intellect: "O for a life of Sensations rather than of Thoughts!" These words are cited in a book Pessoa owned, and he underlined them.[25] Sensacionismo (derived from *sensação*; sensation), the modernist movement Pessoa and Mário de Sá-Carneiro adapted from Futurism, has more than a little in common with Keats's romantic plea for feeling over intellect. Keats's words foreshadow the sensationist experiments of the heteronyms Álvaro de Campos and Alberto Caeiro, who both attempt to lead a life of sensations rather than thoughts, with very different results. Caeiro's life of sensations is experienced through his eyes: he desires to depend on his sense of sight, almost exclusively, to show him things as they truly are. He consequently wishes to see only what is shown to him through his senses, probing no hidden or symbolic interpretations in the world around him: "O meu olhar é nítido como um girasol" (My gaze is as clear as a sunflower).[26]

Campos's sensationist goal, in contrast, is not to see things as they are, but as they make him feel: he wishes to feel through his five senses, Walt Whitman–like, often simultaneously, and through every nerve in his body.

Pessoa, like Keats, is averse to excessive intellectual thought, which he cannot, unfortunately, escape. This leads to the "dor de pensar" (pain of [over]thinking) that infuses so much of his poetry. Unfortunately, however desirable it may be to lead a sensationist life rather than an intellectual one—the orthonym—Campos and Soares find it ultimately impossible to escape their rational makeup: their neurasthenic introspection leads to a Hamlet-like melancholy.[27] This is precisely what Keats had warned against in "Ode to a Nightingale": "to think is to be full of sorrows / And leaden-eyed despairs."[28]

Keats's model for the ideal poet was the same as Pessoa's: William Shakespeare.[29] His vision of Shakespeare was profoundly informed by that of his fellow Romantic era poets and critics, most notably Samuel Taylor Coleridge (1772–1834) and William Hazlitt (1778–1830).

In a letter from 1802, Coleridge had written of Shakespeare's uncanny ability to imagine himself as someone else: "It is easy to clothe Imaginary Beings with our own Thoughts and Feelings; but to send ourselves out of ourselves, to think ourselves in to the Thoughts and Feelings of Beings in circumstances wholly and strangely different from our own / hoc labor, hoc opus / and who has achieved it? Perhaps only Shakespeare."[30]

Hazlitt, in his first London lecture on Shakespeare in 1817 (which Keats did not attend, but later heard about), described Shakespeare in similar terms, as being "just like any other man, but that he was like all other men. He was the least of an egoist that it was possible to be. He was nothing in himself; but he was all that others were, or that they could become. He not only had in himself the germs of every faculty and feeling, but he could follow them by anticipation, intuitively, into all their possible ramifications, through every change of fortune, or conflict of passion, or turn of thought [. . .] When he conceived of a character, whether real or imaginary, he not only entered into all its thoughts and feelings, but seemed instantly, and as if by touching a secret spring, to be surrounded with all the same objects."[31]

In his *Characters in Shakespeare's Plays*,[32] Hazlitt went on to venture that Shakespeare's ability to travel through his dramatic characters at will left him with a "scarcely [. . .] an individual existence of his own."[33]

Inspired by these words, a year later Keats coined the memorable image of the "chameleon poet" who was "continually in for and filling [sic] some other Body," the effect of which was to leave him with "none, no Identity" of his own.[34]

Various critics have mentioned Keats's chameleon poet in the context of Pessoa's work, but always in passing, and without drawing attention to the direct nature of his influence on Pessoa's heteronymic theory and practice. Pál Ferenc, for instance, touches on the connection when he writes that Keats's idea of the chameleon poet prompted Pessoa to don his heteronymic masks: "É muito provável que [. . .] a ideia de 'Camelion Poet' de John Keats [. . .] o incitariam a ocultar-se atrás de figuras de poetas heterónimos" (It is very probably that Keats's "Chameleon Poet" idea prompted Pessoa to hide himself behind heteronymic poet characters).[35] Ferenc does not appear to be aware, however, that Pessoa read this letter, or at least a part of it, and drew a line next to it in his copy of Colvin's biography of Keats.[36]

Colvin's rendition of Keats's letter is truncated, and it leaves out memorable lines and phrases from other editions, so it is worth citing a more complete version of Keats's letter about the chameleon poet:

As to the poetical Character itself, (I mean that sort of which, if I am any thing, I am a Member; that sort distinguished from the wordsworthian or egotistical sublime; which is a thing per se and stands alone) it is not itself— it has no self—It has no character—it enjoys light and shade; it lives in gusto, be it foul or fair, high or low, rich or poor, mean or elevated—It has as much delight in conceiving an Iago as an Imogen. What shocks the virtuous philosopher, delights the camelion Poet. [. . .] A Poet is the most unpoetical of any thing in existence; because he has no Identity—he is continually in for—and filling some other Body—The Sun, the Moon, the Sea and Men and Women who are creatures of impulse are poetical and have about them an unchangeable attribute—the poet has none, no identity—he is certainly the most unpoetical of all God's Creatures. [. . .] It is a wretched thing to confess: but is a very fact that not one word I ever utter can be taken for granted as an opinion growing out of my identical nature—how can it, when I have no nature? When I am in a room with People if I am free from speculating on creations of my own brain, then not myself goes home to myself: but the identity of every one in the room begins to so press upon me that, I am in a very little time annihilated—not only among Men; it would be the same in a Nursery of children.

But even now I am perhaps not speaking from myself; but from some character in whose soul I now live. I am sure however that this next sentence is from myself. [37]

Such haunting words of authorial impersonality were instrumental in shaping the artistic ideals of the modernist generation to which Pessoa belonged, and consequently their literary practice too. The modernists came to regard impersonality as one of the hallmarks of artistic genius; Eliot's seminal essay "Tradition and the Individual Talent" argues that the best part of a poet's work is "a continual self-sacrifice, a continual extinction of personality," and his own identity is so elusive in his poems that he was labeled "The Invisible Poet" by biographer Hugh Kenner in 1959.[38] James Joyce similarly envisions the perfect author as being "like the God of creation, [. . .] within or behind or beyond or above his handiwork, refined out of existence, indifferent, paring his fingernails."[39] Pessoa's continual ontological meditations on the nature of his authorial existence—or, more commonly, nonexistence—is wonderfully illustrated when he has Álvaro de Campos declare, "Fernando Pessoa não existe, propriamente falando" (Fernando Pessoa does not, strictly speaking, exist).[40]

Keats viewed the impersonality of the "poetical character" in dramatic terms—not least because his ideal poet, Shakespeare, was a dramatist. Such a character was adept at projecting itself into, or assuming, the identities of others: "[the poetical character] is not itself—it has no self [. . .] it has no character [. . .] It has as much delight in conceiving an Iago as an Imogen." Pessoa and his fellow modernists would also consider the greatest poetry to be necessarily dramatic, with all the impersonality the genre entails. Joyce, in *A Portrait of the Artist as a Young Man*, has Stephen Dedalus theorize that in the movement from lyric to epic to dramatic, the personality of the poet, "at first a cry or a cadence or a mood and then a fluid and lambent narrative, finally refines itself out of existence, impersonalises itself, so to speak."[41] Pessoa similarly explains, in "Os graus da poesia lírica" ("The Levels of Lyric Poetry"), that the ascending progression of poetry, from lyric to dramatic, is characterized by increasing degrees of impersonality: "O quarto grau da poesia lírica é aquele, muito mais raro, em

IX.]   CHARACTER AND GENIUS.   215

of the poet's " want of decision of character and power of will," and says that "never for two days did he know his own intentions," his criticism is deserving of more attention. This is only Haydon's way of describing a fact in Keats's nature of which no one was better aware than himself. He acknowledges his own "unsteady and *Infirmity* vagarish disposition." What he means is no weakness *of will!* of instinct or principle affecting the springs of conduct in regard to others, but a liability to veerings of opinion and purpose in regard to himself. "The Celtic instability," a reader may perhaps surmise who adopts that hypothesis as to the poet's descent. Whether the quality was one of race or not, it was probably inseparable from the peculiar complexion of Keats's genius. Or rather it was an expression in character of that which was the very essence of that genius, the predominance, namely, of the sympathetic imagination over every other faculty. Acute as was his own emotional life, he nevertheless belonged essentially to the order of poets whose work is inspired, not mainly by their own personality, but by the world of things and men outside them. He realised clearly the nature of his own gift, and the degree to which susceptibility to external impressions was apt to overpower in him, not practical consistency only, but even the sense of a personal identity.

"As to the poetic character itself," he writes, "(I mean that sort, of which, if I am anything, I am a member; that sort distinguished from the Wordsworthian, or egotistical sublime; which is a thing *per se*, and stands alone), it is not itself—it has no self—it is everything and nothing—it has no character—it enjoys light and shade—it lives in gusto, be it foul or fair, high or low, rich or poor, mean or elevated,—it has as much delight in conceiving an Iago as an Imogen. A poet is the most unpoetical of anything in existence,

Annotated page from Sidney Colvin, *Keats*, London: Macmillan, 1899, 2nd ed., 215.

que o poeta, mais intelectual ainda mas igualmente imaginativo, entra em plena despersonalização. Não só sente, mas vive, os estados de alma que não tem directamente." (The fourth level of lyric poetry is much more rare: when the poet, even more intellectual but just as imaginative, becomes completely impersonal. He not only feels, but lives, the states of mind he does not directly possess.)[42]

Eliot, Joyce, and Pessoa are the all posthumous siblings of Keats's chameleon poet, and in Pessoa's case, the family resemblance is particularly striking. Many of his critical texts, describing himself as the creator of a "drama em gente" (drama in people), the heteronyms, as well as his letters, particularly those to Adolfo Casais Monteiro, call to mind Keats's description of the ideal "poetical character," which, having no ego or identity of its own, dramatically assumes, chameleon-like, the identities of other characters, whether imaginary or real ("Iago"; "every one in the room"). Richard Woodhouse, the recipient of Keats's letter about the chameleon poet, made some notes later in the same year offering his interpretation of Keats's meaning: "The highest order of Poet [. . .] will have so high an imagination that he will be able to throw his own soul into any object he sees or imagines, so as to see, feel, be sensible of or express—& he will speak out of that object so that his own self with the Exception of the Mechanical part be "annihilated."—and it is of the excess of this power that I suppose Keats to speak, when he says he has no identity."[43]

Woodhouse reported that often, after Keats had written down some thought or expression, it "struck him with astonishment and seemed rather the production of another person than his own [. . .] It seemed to come by chance or magic—to be as it were something given to him."[44] Compare this to Pessoa's letter to Casais Monteiro about the genesis of the heteronyms, in which he claims to receive his fictional characters' poems ready-made, as if he were not their author but their medium: "em tudo isto me parece que fui eu, criador de tudo, o menos que ali houve. Parece que tudo se passou independentemente de mim. E parece que assim ainda se passa. [. . .] Eu *vejo* diante de mim, no espaço incolor mas real do sonho, as caras, os gestos de Caeiro, Ricardo Reis e Álvaro de Campos." (in all of this it seems that I, the creator of everything, was the least important thing there. It seems it all happened independently of me. And it seems to happen like that still. [. . .] I *see* before me, in the colorless but real space of dreams, the faces, the gestures of Caeiro, Ricardo Reis and Álvaro de Campos.)[45]

In the same letter, Pessoa claimed that he could sometimes feel imaginary passions more acutely than real ones: "ao escrever certos passos das Notas para recordação do meu Mestre Caeiro, do Álvaro de Campos, tenho chorado lágrimas verdadeiras."[46] (writing certain passages of the Notes for the Memory of My Master Caeiro, by Álvaro de Campos, I have cried real tears). This curious phenomenon had been awarded fuller expression in an earlier letter to his future biographer João Gaspar Simões, in words that support the conclusion, based on my reading of Pessoa's 1908 poem to Keats, that for him, imaginary passions—those contained in, and of use for, his poetry—held greater interest than real-life emotions:

Nunca senti saudades da infância; nunca senti, em verdade, saudades de nada. Sou, por índole, e no sentido directo da palavra, futurista. Não sei ter pessimismo, nem olhar para trás. Que eu saiba ou repare só a falta de dinheiro (no próprio momento) ou um tempo de trovoada (enquanto dura) são capazes de me deprimir. Tenho, do passado, somente saudades de pessoas idas, a quem amei; mas não é saudade do tempo em que as amei, mas a saudade delas, queria-as vivas hoje, e com a idade que hoje tivessem, se até hoje tivessem vivido. O mais são atitudes literárias, sentidas intensamente por instinto dramático, quer as assine Álvaro de Campos, quer as assine Fernando Pessoa. São suficientemente representadas, no tom e na verdade, por aquele meu breve poema que começa, "O sino da minha aldeia . . ." O sino da minha aldeia, Gaspar Simões, é o da Igreja dos Mártires, ali no Chiado.[47]

(I never missed my childhood; I never, in truth, missed anything. I am, by nature, and in the immediate sense of the word, a futurist. I don't know how to be pessimistic, or how to look back. As far as I am aware or notice, only a lack of money [when it's needed] or stormy weather [while it lasts] are able to depress me. From the past, I only miss people who are now gone, whom I loved; but I don't miss the time when I loved them, I miss them, I would like them to be alive today, at the age they would be now, if they were still alive. Everything else is a literary pose, felt intensely by dramatic instinct, whether I sign the work Álvaro de Campos or Fernando Pessoa. These attitudes are sufficiently represented, in tone and in truth, by my short poem which begins, "Oh church bell of my village . . ." The church bell of my village, Gaspar Simões, is the bell of the Church of the Martyrs in the Chiado.)

Keats offers us a wonderful explanation, in one of his letters, of why fictional emotions may be felt more strongly than real ones: "I am as far from being unhappy as possible. Imaginary grievances have always been more my torment than real ones. [. . .] This is easily accounted for. Our imaginary woes are conjured up by our passions, and are fostered by passionate feeling; our real ones come of themselves, and are opposed by an abstract exertion of mind. Real grievances are the displacers of passion."[48]

If real grievances are the displacers of passion, this would account for the otherwise surprisingly controlled tone of some of Keats's love letters to Fanny Brawne. Nichola Deane draws attention to the way Keats "plays the lover" with Fanny, dramatizing his feelings with literary allusions to Rousseau and quotations from Shakespeare.[49] Andrew Motion argues that Keats "used his separation from Fanny as a chance to dramatise his anguish [. . .] always mindful of the attitude he strikes."[50] Such role-playing resulted in delightfully humorous passages:

> I have been writing with a vile old pen the whole week, which is excessively ungallant. The fault is in the Quill: I have mended it and still it is very much inclin'd to make blindness. However these last lines are in a much better style of penmanship though a little disfigured by the smear of black current jelly; which has made a little mark on one of the Pages of Brown's Ben Jonson, the very best book he has. I have lick'd it but it remains very purple—I did not know whether to say purple or blue, so in the mixture of the thought wrote purplue which may be an excellent name for a colour made up of those two, and would suit well to start next spring.[51]

Pessoa famously played the role of Hamlet when he met his Ophelia, declaring his love for the first time by usurping the prince's words.[52] And he could be just as detached and jocular as Keats in his love letters—so much so that he signed some of these letters as Álvaro de Campos, referring to himself, Pessoa, in the third person.[53]

In a letter, Keats mentions—for the first and only time—another essential attribute of the highest order of poet: "I had not a dispute but a disquisition with Dilke, on various subjects; several things dovetailed in my mind, & at once it struck me, what quality went to form a Man of Achievement especially in Literature & which Shakespeare possessed so enormously—I mean *Negative*

Capability, that is when a man is capable of being in uncertainties, Mysteries, doubts, without any irritable reaching after fact & reason."[54] He coined the memorable phrase "negative capability" to describe the greatest artists' (such as Shakespeare's) receptiveness to the world and its natural marvels, separating these artists from those who, like Dilke, Coleridge (who was, Keats thought, too much of a critic), or Wordsworth (too much of an egotist), searched for a single, higher-order truth or unifying solution to the mysteries of the world. This idea, too, derived largely from Hazlitt, who believed the mind to be naturally "disinterested."[55] Primarily pitted against the writings of Hobbes, Mandeville, and others who argued that the basis of human action is self-interest, Hazlitt had claimed in his *Essay on the Principle of Human Action: Being an Argument in Favour of the Natural Disinterestedness of the Human Mind* (a book Keats owned at his death) that our ability to think about our future selves depends on a power of self-projection no different from that required to think ourselves into the lives of others.

Pessoa's heteronyms and other dramatic voices argue against each other and express alternative, often contradictory beliefs, penning radically different, often diametrically opposed bodies of work. The heteronymic universe is one with no final authority, least of all the authority of Pessoa "himself," whose lifelong distrust of any single, overriding, knowable truth is evidenced by his esoteric leanings, his ontological questioning, and his interest in many different strains of philosophy. Negative capability is required for the creation of the heteronymic universe, which embodies the same quality in its fictional existence.

Keats's ideal, chameleon poet, so impersonal and lacking in identity that he could expertly inhabit fictional others at will, and with a negative capability that meant he did not believe in any single truth, but rather explored different possible truths, was thus a further fertile source, to add to the long list of sources already documented by scholars, for the genesis of Pessoa's heteronyms.

NOTES

1. George Monteiro, *Fernando Pessoa and Nineteenth-Century Anglo-American Literature* (Lexington: University Press of Kentucky, 2000); Maria Irene Ramalho S. Santos, "A Hora do poeta: O *Hyperion* de Keats na *Mensagem* de Pessoa," *Revista da Universidade de Coimbra* 37 (1992), 389–99; and António M. Feijó, "Uma explicação de *Mensagem*" (unpublished article, 2013).

2. See Fernando Pessoa, *Cadernos*, I, ed. Jerónimo Pizarro (Lisbon: Imprensa Nacional–Casa da Moeda, 2009), 217. For details of Pessoa's reading of Keats, see Monteiro, *Fernando Pessoa and Nineteenth-Century Anglo-American Literature*, 45.

3. John Keats, *The Poetical Works of John Keats* (London: Frederick Warne, 1894); Sidney Colvin, *Keats*, ed. John Morley (London / New York: Macmillan, 1899).

4. See the translation section in this issue.

5. Pessoa, *Mensagem* (Lisbon: Parceria Antonio Maria Pereira, 1934).

6. See Patricio Ferrari, "Meter and Rhythm in the Poetry of Fernando Pessoa" (unpublished doctoral thesis, University of Lisbon, 2012), 385; Pessoa, *Fernando Pessoa poeta-tradutor de poetas: Os Poemas traduzidos e o respectivo original*, ed. Arnaldo Saraiva (Oporto: Lello Editores, 1996), 85; S. Santos, "A Hora do poeta"; and Feijó, "Uma explicação de *Mensagem*."

7. Unless otherwise stated, all translations are my own.

8. See Keats, *Poetical Works*, 336.

9. George Lind, "Die Englische Jugenddichtung Fernando Pessoas." In *Portugiesische Forschungen des Görresgesellschaft* (Münster: 1966), 136.

10. Monteiro, *Fernando Pessoa and Nineteenth-Century Anglo-American Literature*, 48. For a comparative rhythmic study of the two poems, see Ferrari, "Meter and Rhythm in the Poetry of Fernando Pessoa," 302.

11. "It does not take a very long consideration to perceive the immortality of Vigny's *Moïse*, *La Colère de Janson*, *La Mort du Loup*, nor of Keats' Odes to a Nightingale, to a Grecian Urn, to Autumn, to Melancholy. These poems are as fine as *Lycidas* and shall live when *Venus and Adonis* and *The Rape of Lucrece* shall have gone to human limbo to which all immature beauty is consigned" (BNP/E3,19–83ᵛ; Pessoa, *Páginas de estética e de teoria e crítica literárias*, ed. Georg Rudolf Lind and Jacinto do Prado Coelho (Lisbon: Ática, n.d. [1966]), 287. This fragment is part of "Erostratus." See the essays section in this issue.

12. *Presença*, 1932.

13. BNP/E3, 19–98; Pessoa, *Páginas de estética*, 331.

14. Monteiro, *Fernando Pessoa and Nineteenth-Century Anglo-American Literature*, 48.

15. T. S. Eliot, *The Sacred Wood: Essays on Poetry and Criticism* (London: Methuen, 1920), 50–51.

16. Pessoa, *Cartas de amor*, ed. David Mourão Ferreira (Lisbon: Ática, 1994), 23.

17. See, for example, John Keats, *Selected Letters*, ed. Robert Gittings (Oxford: Oxford University Press, 2009), 338–39.

18. Monteiro, *Fernando Pessoa and Nineteenth-Century Anglo-American Literature*.

19. Ibid., 45–48.

20. John Keats, *Selected Poetry*, ed. Elizabeth Cook (Oxford: Oxford University Press, 1994), 176–79.

21. Pessoa, *Forever Someone Else*, ed. and trans. Richard Zenith (bilingual edition) (Lisbon: Assíro & Alvim, 2008), 164–65.

22. Ibid., 168–69.

23. Ibid., 164–65.

24. Cited in Andrew Motion, *Keats* (London: Faber & Faber, 1997), 577.

25. Colvin, *Keats*, 184.

26. Pessoa, "O Guardador de rebanhos," in *Poemas de Alberto Caeiro*, ed. João Gaspar Simões and Luiz de Montalvor (Lisbon: Ática, 1993), 24.

27. See Mariana Gray de Castro, *Fernando Pessoa's Shakespeare* (unpublished doctoral thesis, King's College London, 2010), 107–8.

28. Keats, *Selected Poetry*, 177.

29. See Castro, *Fernando Pessoa's Shakespeare*.

30. Samuel Taylor Coleridge, *Collected Letters of Samuel Taylor Coleridge*, ed. Earl Leslie Griggs, 6 vols. (Oxford: Clarendon, 1971), 810.

31. Cited in Motion, *Keats*, 227.

32. Hazlitt, 1817.

33. Cited in Jonathan Bate, ed., *The Romantics on Shakespeare* (London: Penguin, 1992), 7.

34. Keats, *Selected Letters*, ed. Robert Gittings. (Oxford: Oxford University Press, 2009), 147–48. This passage is sometimes rendered as "continually in, for, and filling" or "continually informing and filling."

35. Fernando Pessoa, *Arc többes számban*, ed. Pál Ferenc, trans. Csaba Csuday, Endre Kukorelly, Ferenc Szőnyi, Zsuzsa Takács, and Szabolcs Várady (Budapest: Helikon, 1988), 37. Translation into Portuguese by Pál Ferenc.

36. These pages were first reproduced by Patricio Ferrari in notes that accompany the digital edition of Pessoa's personal library. See Ferrari, "Anotações" ["Annotations"], in *Biblioteca digital de Fernando Pessoa* (2010). http://casafernandopessoa.cm-lisboa.pt/bdigital/index/index.htm.

37. Keats, *Selected Letters*, 147–49.

38. Eliot, *The Sacred Wood*, 40.

39. James Joyce, *A Portrait of the Artist as a Young Man* (London: Penguin, 2000), 233.

40. Fernando Pessoa (Álvaro de Campos), *Notas para a recordação do meu Mestre Caeiro*, ed. Teresa Rita Lopes (Lisbon: Estampa, 1997), 75. See also Pessoa, *Prosa de Álvaro de Campos*, ed. Jerónimo Pizarro and Antonio Cardiello, with the collaboration of Jorge Uribe (Lisbon: Ática, 2012).

41. Joyce, *A Portrait*, 214.

42. Pessoa, *Páginas de estética*, 67.

43. Cited in Motion, *Keats*, 228.

44. Cited in M H. Abrams, *The Mirror and the Lamp: Romantic Theory and the Critical Tradition* (London / Oxford / New York: Oxford University Press, 1971), 214.

45. Pessoa, *Correspondência 1923–1935*, ed. Manuela Parreira da Silva (Lisbon: Assírio & Alvim, 1999), 342. See also Pessoa, *Cartas entre Fernando Pessoa e os directores da presença*, ed. Enrico Martines (Lisbon: Imprensa Nacional–Casa da Moeda, 1998).

46. Pessoa, *Correspondência*, 343.

47. Ibid., 253.

48. Keats, *Selected Letters*, 282.

49. Nichola Deane, "Keats's Lover's Discourse and the Letters to Fanny Brawne," *Keats-Shelley Review* 13 (1999), 105–14.

50. Motion, *Keats*, 414.

51. Keats, *Selected Letters*, 334.

52. See Castro, *Fernando Pessoa's Shakespeare*, 173–74.

53. See, for example, Pessoa's letter to Ophélia of September 25, 1929, signed by "*Álvaro de Campos, eng. Naval*" [Álvaro de Campos, naval engineer], in Pessoa, *Correspondência 1923–1935*, ed. Manuela Parreira da Silva. Lisbon: Assírio & Alvim, 1999), 164. See also Pessoa, *Prosa de Álvaro de Campos*, ed. Jerónimo Pizarro and Antonio Cardiello; with the collaboration of Jorge Uribe (Lisbon: Ática, 2012).

54. Keats, *Selected Letters*, 41–42.

55. See Motion, *Keats*, 218.

WORKS CITED

Abrams, M. H. *The Mirror and the Lamp: Romantic Theory and the Critical Tradition*. London / Oxford / New York: Oxford University Press, 1971.

Bate, Jonathan, ed. *The Romantics on Shakespeare*. London: Penguin, 1992.

Castro, Mariana Gray de. "Fernando Pessoa's Shakespeare." Unpublished doctoral thesis, King's College London, 2010.

Coleridge, Samuel Taylor. *Collected Letters of Samuel Taylor Coleridge*. Edited by Earl Leslie Griggs. 6 vols. Oxford: Clarendon, 1971.

Colvin, Sidney. *Keats*. Edited by John Morley. London / New York: Macmillan, 1899.

Deane, Nichola. "Keats's Lover's Discourse and the Letters to Fanny Brawne." *Keats-Shelley Review* 13 (1999): 105–14.

Eliot, T. S. *The Sacred Wood: Essays on Poetry and Criticism*. London: Methuen, 1920. 42–53.

Feijó, António M. "Uma explicação de *Mensagem*." Unpublished article, 2013.

Ferrari, Patricio. "Anotações [Annotations]." *Biblioteca digital de Fernando Pessoa* (Fernando Pessoa's Digital Library), 2010. http://casafernandopessoa.cm-lisboa.pt/bdigital/index/index.htm.

———. "Meter and Rhythm in the Poetry of Fernando Pessoa." Unpublished doctoral thesis, University of Lisbon, 2012.

Joyce, James. *A Portrait of the Artist as a Young Man*. London: Penguin, 2000.

Keats, John. *The Poetical Works of John Keats*. London: Frederick Warne, 1898.

———. *Selected Letters*. Edited by Robert Gittings. Oxford: Oxford University Press, 2009.

———. *Selected Poetry*. Edited by Elizabeth Cook. Oxford: Oxford University Press, 1994.

Lind, George. "Die englische Jugenddichtung Fernando Pessoas." *Portugiesische Forschungen des Görresgesellschaft* (Münster, 1966): 229–36.

Monteiro, George. *Fernando Pessoa and Nineteenth-Century Anglo-American Literature*. Kentucky: University Press of Kentucky, 2000.

Motion, Andrew. *Keats*. London: Faber & Faber, 1997.

Pessoa, Fernando. *Arc többes számban*. Edited by Pál Ferenc. Translated by Csaba Csuday, Endre Kukorelly, Ferenc Szőnyi, Zsuzsa Takács, and Szabolcs Várady. Budapest: Helikon, 1988.

———. *Cadernos*. Edited by Jerónimo Pizarro. Lisbon: Imprensa Nacional–Casa da Moeda, 2009.

———. *Cartas de amor*. Edited by David Mourão Ferreira. Lisbon: Ática, 1994.

———. *Cartas entre Fernando Pessoa e os directores da presença*. Edited by Enrico Martines. Lisbon: Imprensa Nacional–Casa da Moeda, 1998.

———. *Correspondência 1923–1935*. Edited by Manuela Parreira da Silva. Lisbon: Assírio & Alvim, 1999.

———. *Fernando Pessoa poeta-tradutor de poetas: Os poemas traduzidos e o respectivo original*. Edited by Arnaldo Saraiva. Oporto: Lello Editores, 1996.

———. *Forever Someone Else*. Edited and translated by Richard Zenith. Bilingual edition. Lisbon: Assírio & Alvim, 2008.

———. *Mensagem*. Lisbon: Parceria Antonio Maria Pereira, 1934.

———. *Notas para a recordação do meu Mestre Caeiro*. Edited by Teresa Rita Lopes. Lisbon: Estampa, 1997.

———. *Páginas de estética e de teoria e crítica literárias*. Edited by Georg Rudolf Lind and Jacinto do Prado Coelho. Lisbon: Ática, 1967.

———. *Poemas de Alberto Caeiro*. Edited by João Gaspar Simões and Luiz de Montalvor. Lisbon: Ática, 1993.

———. *Prosa de Álvaro de Campos*. Edited by Jerónimo Pizarro and Antonio Cardiello with the collaboration of Jorge Uribe. Lisbon: Ática, 2012.

Santos, Maria Irene Ramalho S. "A hora do poeta: O *Hyperion* de Keats na *Mensagem* de Pessoa." *Revista da Universidade de Coimbra* 37 (1992): 389–99.

MARIANA GRAY DE CASTRO is a postdoctoral research fellow at the University of Lisbon and the University of Oxford, working on Fernando Pessoa's English influences. She regularly teaches at both universities, and her publications include the chapter "Fernando Pessoa and Modernism" in *Companion to Portuguese Literature* (2010); numerous articles in the United Kingdom, Portugal, and Brazil; the edited volume *Fernando Pessoa's Modernity Without Frontiers: Influences, Dialogues and Responses* (2013); and the Portuguese anthology *Amo como o amor ama: escritos de amor de Fernando Pessoa* (2013).

She can be reached at mariana.decastro@gmail.com.

FLÁVIO RODRIGO PENTEADO AND CAIO GAGLIARDI

Translated by Luciano de Souza and Serena Rivera

The Art of Drama According to Browning and Pessoa

ABSTRACT: In this article we analyze Robert Browning's and Fernando Pessoa's inter-pretations and understandings of the concept of *drama*. Both writers, other than privileging the dramatic procedure of creation in literature, explored the limits of literary genres in their attempts to establish themselves as dramatic poets. Through an analysis of theoretical texts by Browning and Pessoa, we verify the points at which their conceptions both converge and diverge. To conclude, we discuss the re-lation of the English writer's dramatic monologues to the heteronymic project.

KEYWORDS: dramatic monologue, Fernando Pessoa, Robert Browning

1.

I shall live by forgetting myself. This assertion could be applied to the poetic projects of some of the main exponents of modern poetry. Such an assertion is founded on impersonality, defined as when the poet expresses the individuality of other selves, which should not be confused with their own. Accordingly, the statement that begins this section could also relate to Fernando Pessoa, whose conception of flight from personality led him to formalizing in heteronymy (or heteronymism[1]) his detachment from any pretense of unity of the individual. However, the assertion does not refer to any particular poet of modernity, de-spite being formulated by one. In fact, it is a verse from the poem "Browning resuelve ser poeta"[2] ("Browning Decides to be a Poet") in which the mechanism of lyrical expression to which the persona of Jorge Luis Borges's poem aspires is synthesized: he endeavors to assume the position of different personae in order to make clear that the voice materialized in the poem does not correspond to the author's.

Writers have already begun to explore the affinity between Browning's and Pessoa's writings; they include Adolfo Casais Monteiro[3] and Georg Rudolf Lind,[4] as well as Georges Güntert,[5] based on brief statements made by Jacinto do Prado Coelho,[6] who devoted himself to the topic. More recently, George Monteiro[7] has dedicated a short essay solely to this subject, and Odorico Leal de Carvalho Júnior has provided an analysis in a chapter of his master's thesis.[8] What has been concluded thus far is that, on the one hand, the bond reflects the position of the Victorian poet as a common precursor of Pessoa and the generation of Eliot, Pound, and Yeats, which is also characterized by the systematic use of literary masks as a means to problematize the authorial stance. On the other hand, this affinity highlights a specific element in the two writers' relation to one another: the fact that both Browning and Pessoa, besides favoring the dramatic procedure of literary creation, aimed at establishing themselves as dramatic poets. But what does this designation mean? What concept of drama does it mobilize? With this in mind, the purpose of this essay is to analyze the notion of drama fostered by the two writers by verifying its ramifications in Pessoa's theoretic horizon—bearing in mind that the Portuguese poet used Browning's work as one of his references. We will thus try to offer a closer view of the adjective *dramatic* as used by Pessoa, as well as the way in which he characterized himself: "sou um poeta dramático" (I'm a dramatic poet).[9]

2.

In the introduction to the *Poetical Works of Robert Browning*, of which Pessoa possessed a copy, Charles Forward notes that the dramatic element is almost always predominant in his poems.[10] Not only did Browning's contemporaries share a similar opinion, but the author himself also suggested this, as indicated in the publication of his second book, *Paracelsus* (1835). The time period when this book was published aligned with Browning's initial emphasis on the presence of the dramatic element in the structure of his work. Here, the adjective does not define what concerns the most current concept of *drama* (a dramaturgic text to be staged); it is seen rather as a principle guiding literary creation. Taking this into account, it is crucial to make a further examination of the aspects of this notion by focusing on the concise preface accompanying the first edition of the text.

Initially, Browning anticipates the possible restrictions to which *Paracelsus* could be subject as a result of the peculiar notion of drama it bears: "I am anxious that the reader should not, at the very outset—mistaking my performance for one of a class with which it has nothing in common—judge it by principles on which it was never moulded."[11] There is a reason for such a disclaimer. Apparently, the text preserves a rather traditional dramaturgical structure, especially with its presentation consisting of five parts that could be related to the acts of a Shakespearean tragedy. As Browning explains shortly thereafter, the work constitutes "an attempt [. . .] to reverse the method usually adopted by writers [. . .]; instead of having recourse to an external machinery of incidents to create and evolve the crisis I desire to produce, I have ventured to display somewhat minutely the mood itself in its rise and progress."[12]

In other words, *Paracelsus* does not refuse the fundamental principle of drama—the action—but rather dislocates it: no longer a product of external events, the conflict arises from previous tensions whose development and explosion are expressed by the characters through speech rather than actions. As we shall see, Pessoa's static theater dialogues with this dramatic model.

So far, the fundamentally lyrical conception of theater is clear. The problem is that, according to Browning's assertions, we do not necessarily have a play before our eyes: "I have endeavoured to write a poem, not a drama"; nor would it be a dramatic poem in the sense of a drama in verses to be staged: "I do not very well understand what is called a Dramatic Poem."[13] In spite of the external appearance and even the text dynamics, far from the standard dramaturgical model without denying it as a whole, Browning conceives *Paracelsus* solely as a poem. It is possible to see some arbitrariness in this procedure, which is thought of, above all, as a strategy to depart from the tradition of a genre and, therefore, liberate the poet from observing certain principles inherent in it. Curiously, the theoretical assumptions to which the writer alludes fail to contradict the current ideas in Europe during the first decades of the nineteenth century.

Clyde de L. Ryals[14] argues that the philosophical empirical tradition, appealing to causality during investigations of moral and physical phenomena, changed the way dramatic action was conceived. When the absolute nature of external events was questioned, the relation between the action and character came to be inverted: the first element ceases to embody the second and thus becomes subject to it. In other words, the action, although not negated, is seen as deprived of meaning when the mental states that prompted it are not considered. As stated by John Henry Newman in 1829, "The action then will be more justly viewed as the vehicle for introducing the personages of the drama, than as the principal object of the poet's art; it is not in the plot, but in the characters, sentiments, and diction, that the actual merit and poetry of the composition are found."[15]

Although Browning feared *Paracelsus* would be misunderstood, the play was well received. John Forster published his extensive review, "Evidences of a New

Genius for Dramatic Poetry,"[16] and the renowned actor William Charles Macready was soon in touch with the writer, encouraging him to devote himself to drama. The fact that Macready assumed management of Covent Garden in 1837 was a key event that motivated Browning to write his first play in the strict sense of the term, *Strafford: A Tragedy*, which would be staged in that theater.

The first edition of this play was also accompanied by a brief preface, whose beginning inverts the previous premise: "I had for some time been engaged in a Poem of a very different nature, when induced to make the present attempt."[17] Even though *Strafford* assumes the form of a drama to be staged, Browning once again establishes the strategy of relativizing the tradition of a genre. If in *Paracelsus* the reader is confronted with a text that resembles a play but is, in fact, a poem, the situation now involves an actual play that wishes to be understood *also* as a poem. Thus, a decrease in boundaries between the genres is produced, and was fully attained in *Dramatic Lyrics* (1842). This experiment was foreseen, in a way, when Browning anticipated the failure of his first foray into theater: "While a trifling success would much gratify, failure will not wholly discourage me from another effort: experience is to come, and earnest endeavours may yet remove many disadvantages."[18]

In fact, *Strafford* was very far from the success the playwright originally desired, as the play saw only five presentations. Despite the existing affinity between Browning's dramatic conception and those of his contemporaries, the play's failure revealed the distinguishing characteristic of the author's work: the emphasis on the development of a soul[19] that weakened the plot beyond the public's acceptable limit. Regardless of the diminished nature of the action, the lyrical intensity, a focal point of actors and playwrights when creating a character, still presupposed the construction of the plot. This is highlighted by James Patton McCormick, when contrasting Browning's next experience in the theater, with specific regard to *King Victor and King Charles* (1842), and to successful plays such as *Richelieu* (1839), by Edward Bulwer-Lytton. McCormick notes in this contrasting analysis that what separates Browning from his contemporaries is that Bulwer-Lytton's work is characterized by "misplaced letters, mistaken identities, the cloak-and-dagger intrigue of courtiers trying to usurp the throne, and several subplots involving romantic love surging violently across the stage."[20] Regarding Browning's work, this series of intrigues is never fully accomplished onstage, but is rather symbolically present in the scenes throughout the play, suggested by the narration of the characters. This often results in the audience members' displeasure, because they are unable to see the characters' intense mental action reflected in physical action, such as with fights involving guns, for example.

Browning owes most of his failure as a popular playwright to these factors. Let us hold back, however, one last aspect of the preface to *Strafford*, which dialogues more clearly with the purpose achieved in his book *Dramatic Lyrics*: the idea that this play would be one of "Action in Character rather than Character in Action."[21] The notion of soul-in-development pervades a great deal of Browning's literary efforts. This is most evident in the body of poems he would later gather for *Dramatic Lyrics*, in which the introduction reads, "Such Poems as the majority in this volume might also come properly enough, I suppose, under the head of 'Dramatic Pieces'; being, though often Lyric in expression, always Dramatic in principle, and so many utterances of so many imaginary persons, not mine."[22]

By convention, readers are accustomed to referring to these poems as *dramatic monologues*. But the author himself, in fact, never actually used that term; nor did he adhere to the generic designation of "dramatic lyrics," as can be seen from the following titles: *Dramatic Romances* (1845), *Men and Women* (1855), and *Dramatis Personae* (1864). The expression is, thus, a critical category, used not because of its previous theorization by the poet, but as a result of the clarifying power it grants to the reading of those poems. There is no consensus as to what effectively constitutes these texts that unite lyrical and dramatic elements; therefore, it is necessary to accurately determine the conception of dramatic monologue. Because our purpose is not to set critical parameters for its understanding, we will discuss some fundamental characteristics of the form by comparing the poetics of Browning and Pessoa. But first, we will analyze the question of "drama" as it is developed in the work of Pessoa.

3.

There are several allusions to the dramatic element of Pessoa's poetry in his letters and critical-theoretical texts, as well as in his "Tábua bibliográfica" (Bibliographical table), published in 1928, which allows for the elucidation of specific aspects of his notion of drama. Regarding his letters, three are noteworthy: in the first, Pessoa mentions to Armando Côrtes-Rodrigues the "propósito de lançar pseudonimamente a obra Caeiro-Reis-Campos," whose speech "é sentido na pessoa de outro; é escrito dramaticamente, mas é sincero [. . .] como é sincero o que diz o Rei Lear, que não é Shakespeare, mas uma criação dele."[23] In a different letter to João Gaspar Simões, Pessoa clarifies: "O ponto central da minha personalidade como artista é que sou um poeta dramático; tenho, continuamente, em tudo quanto escrevo, a exaltação íntima do poeta e a despersonalização do dramaturgo" (The central point of my personality as an artist is that I'm a dramatic poet; in everything I write, I always have the poet's inner exaltation and the playwright's depersonalization).[24] Finally, the poet declares to Adolfo Casais Monteiro, "O que sou essencialmente—por trás das máscaras involuntárias do poeta, do raciocinador e do que mais haja—é dramaturgo" (What I am essentially—behind the involuntary masks of poet, logical reasoner and so forth—is a dramatist).[25]

Besides these three, another letter is equally relevant, written to Francisco Costa. In it, Pessoa states his belief that both men share the same aesthetic criterion:

Pouco importa que sintamos o que exprimimos; basta que, tendo-o pensado, saibamos fingir bem tê-lo sentido.

Não é Shakespeare, talvez, o maior poeta de todos os tempos [. . .] mas é o maior expressor que houve no mundo, o mais insincero de quantos poetas tem havido, sendo por isso mesmo que exprimia com igual relevo todos os modos de ser e de sentir [. . .]

Para mim, pois, a arte é essencialmente dramática, e o maior artista será aquele que, na arte que professa—porque em todas as artes, condicionado isto pela "matéria" delas, se podem fazer dramas, isto é, sentir dramaticamente—mais intensa—profusa e complexamente viver tudo quanto não é ele, isto é, que mais intensa, profusa—e complexamente exprimir tudo quanto em verdade não sente, ou, em outras palavras, sente apenas para exprimir.[26]

What is presented here is the characteristic Pessoan idea that, in art, expressing a sentiment is not equivalent to feeling it. In art, the sentiment is thought of and then pretended—that is, it is felt by means of imagination. Therefore, it is no surprise that Pessoa highlights Shakespeare as "o mais insincero de quantos poetas tem havido." This sincerity he claims for the poetic craft is aesthetic and not factual. It is also important to note the assertion that "a arte é essencialmente dramática," in the sense that in any sort of artistic manifestation, it is possible to write dramas, even though they are not shaped as a dramaturgical text. This is because, according to this notion, writing dramas is fundamentally

O primeiro grau da poesia lyrica é aquelle em que
o poeta, de temperamento intenso e emotivo, exprime es-
pontanea ou reflectidamente esse temperamento e essas
emoções. É o typo mais vulgar do poeta lyrico; é tambem
o de menos merito, como typo. A intensidade da emoção
procede, em geral, da unidade do temperamento; e assim
este typo de poeta lyrico é em geral monocordio, e os
seus poemas giram em torno de determinado numero, em geral pequeno, de emoções. Porisso, neste genero de poetas,
é vulgar dizer-se, porque com rasão se nota, que um é
"um poeta do amor", outro "um poeta da saudade", um terceiro "um poeta da tristeza".

O segundo grau da poesia lyrica é aquelle em que
o xxxxxxxxxxxxxxxxxxxxx por mais intellectual ou imaginativo, pode ser mesmo que só por mais culto, não tem já a
simplicidade de emoções, ou a limitação d'ellas, que dis-
tingue o poeta do primeiro grau. Este será tambem typica-
mente um poeta lyrico, no sentido vulgar do termo, mas
já não será um poeta monocordio. Os seus poemas abrange-
rão assumptos diversos, unificando-os todavia o temperamento e o estylo. Sendo variado nos typos de emoção, não
o será na maneira de sentir. Assim um Swinburne, tem monocordio no temperamento e no estylo, pode comtudo escrever
com egual relevo um poema de amor, uma alegia morbida, um
poema revolucionario.

O terceiro grau da poesia lyrica é aquelle em que
o poeta, ainda mais intellectual, começa a despersonalizar-
se, a sentir, não já porque sente, mas porque pensa que
sente; a sentir estados de alma, que realmente não tem,
simplesmente porque os comprehende. Estamos na antecamara
da poesia dramatica, na sua essencia intima. O temperamento do poeta, seja qual fôr, está dissolvido pela intelligencia. A sua obra será unificada só pelo estylo, ultimo
reducto da sua unidade espiritual, da sua coexistencia com-
sigo mesmo. Assim é x xxxxxxxxxxxxxxxxxxxxx Tennyson,
escrevendo por egual Ulysses e The Lady of Shalott; assim,
e mais, é Browning, escrevendo o que chamou "poemas drama-
ticos", que não são dialogados, mas monologos revelando almas diversas, com que o poeta não tem identidade, não a
pretende ter e muitas vezes não a quere ter.

O quarto grau da poesia lyrica é aquelle, muito mais
raro, em que o poeta, mais intellectual ainda mas egual-
mente imaginativo, entra em plena despersonalização. Não
só sente, mas vive, os estados de alma que não tem directamente. Em grande numero de casos, cahirá na poesia dramatica, propriamente dita, como fez Shakespeare, poeta sub-
stancialmente lyrico erguido a dramatico xxix pelo espanto-
so grau de despersonalização que attingiu. Num ou noutro

Pages of typescript with an essay on the degrees of lyric poetry, BNP/E3, 18–50r.

caso, continuará sendo, embora dramaticamente, um poeta
lyrico. É esse o caso de Browning, etc (ut supra). ...
Nem já o estylo xxxxxx define a unidade do homem: áx só
o que no estylo ha de intellectual a denota. Assim é em
Shakespeare, em quem o relevo inesperado da phrase, a sub-
tileza e a complexidade do dizer, são a unica coisa que
approxima o fallar de Hamlet do do Rei Lear, o de Falstaff
do de Lady Macbeth. E assim é Browning atravez dos Men
and Women e dos Dramatic Poemxs.

Supponhamos, porém, que o poeta, evitando sempre a
poesia dramatica, externamente tal, avança ainda um passo
na escala da despersonalização. Certos estados de alma,
pensados e não sentidos, sentidos imaginativamente e porisso vividos, tenderão a definir para elle uma pessoa fic-
ticia que os sentisse sinceramente.

equivalent to *feeling in a dramatic way*; that is, it is far from any sentiment originating from the empirical "I."

In this letter, Pessoa not only presents a particular conception of artistic creation, but also foregrounds a criterion of objective value, established in the allusion to Shakespeare. In offering such a conception, Pessoa occasionally defines the sort of poetry he writes in those texts that attempt to theorize literary creation. This is the case of two distinct texts whose titles have been ascribed by their editors after the arrangement of the book in which they appear: "Os heterónimos e os graus de lirismo" ("The Heteronyms and the Grades of Lyricism") (undated) and "Os graus da poesia lírica" ("The Grades of Lyrical Poetry") (possibly from 1930). In both texts, the fluidity between lyrical and dramatic poetry is examined by listing the successive degrees of depersonalization required for the full transition from the first to the second. Following this reasoning, such "desdobramentos de personalidade ou, antes, invenções de personalidades diferentes"[27] would allow the poet to be "vários poetas, um poeta dramático escrevendo em poesia lírica." This would lead to "poesia dramática, sem, todavia, se lhe dar a forma do drama, nem explícita nem implicitamente."[28] Later, Pessoa speculates: "Suponhamos que um supremo despersonalizado como Shakespeare, em vez de criar o personagem de Hamlet como parte de um drama, o criava como simples personagem, sem drama. Teria escrito, por assim dizer, um drama de uma só personagem, um monólogo prolongado e analítico. (Let us suppose that a supremely depersonalized writer such as Shakespeare, instead of creating the character of Hamlet as part of a play, had actually created him as simply a character without a play. He would have written, so to speak, a one-character play, a prolonged analytic monologue.) Não seria legítimo ir buscar a esse personagem uma definição dos sentimentos e dos pensamentos de Shakespeare, a não ser que o personagem fosse falhado, porque o mau dramaturgo é o que se revela."[29]

Even though Pessoa's ideas regarding drama and the dramatic develop in more than one direction, the specific creation of characters deserves a privileged place. This is synthesized in a fragment composed of only two sentences: "O romance é uma explicação dum carácter; o drama é apenas a criação dele."[30] This definition, however, does not dismiss the development of the action nor the building of the plot, for in another text Pessoa would consider inadequate the "introdução em um drama de uma cena em que, por grande que seja a força ou a graça própria, a acção pára ou não progride, ou, o que é pior, se atrasa."[31] The several fragments that constitute his unfinished "Ensaio sobre o drama" ("Essay on Drama") distinguish the foundation of the dramaturgical text within the harmony between the three elements of character, action, and plot: "Toda a obra dramatica, no seu conjuncto organico, se compõe de trez partes: a psychologia das personagens; a psychologia da sua interacção, e a construcção do enredo, por meio, e atravez, da qual essa interacção se produz."[32]

These ideas, however, do not correspond to the ideas Pessoa put into effect. When he claims, to Casais Monteiro, that he is essentially a playwright, this designation refers to the poet, the creator of heteronyms, rather than the artist behind a play such as O Marinheiro. In fact, Pessoa's concept of drama is so ahead of the conventions of the genre that Teresa Rita Lopes, when referring to the writer's relations with symbolist drama, notes that Pessoa tried to distance himself from traditional notions of theater and dramaturgy by committing himself to the creation of a new drama—free, in its structure, from the characteristics common to the dramatic genre.[33] Lopes emphasizes that, regardless of the connection with that movement, O Marinheiro (The Sailor) presents greater formal and psychological refinement than do the plays written by Maeterlinck in this period. Nonetheless, Lopes points out that it is in Pessoa's heteronymic work that his dramatic genius is manifest, not only expressing detachment, but also overcoming the symbolist model. In other words, in Pessoa's work, drama is performed in full "outside" drama. In this sense, the following Pessoan statements are revealing: "Álvaro de Campos é o personagem de uma peça; o que falta é a peça";[34] "Façamos de conta, ao escrever versos, que estamos escrevendo uma peça."[35]

Certainly, in his future work, Pessoa assigned a prominent place to drama itself. O Marinheiro, the only play he finished, highlights the level of importance that the accomplishment of such an extensive theatrical work would assume in his artistic-literary projects. Were this not true, it would make no sense that, almost two decades after publishing the work, Pessoa would see it as "sujeito a emendas";[36] nor would the poet have engaged in writing tens of other dramas if he did not aspire to become a playwright who disrupts the logic of drama "inside" the drama and who, through the creation of heteronyms, redesigns it beyond the drama. Thus, Pessoa's work relativizes the categories "playwright" and "dramatic poet," because he desired both the creation of drama outside drama (the heteronymic and ortonymic production) and the composition of dramas that, being dramas strictly speaking, are not attached to the main conventions of the genre (the action is practically nonexistent, and empty dialogue occurs between characters of little or no distinction).

Here, the paradox is designed as syllabus: the theater of poetry, the poetry of theater; the play whose features are more lyrical than dramatic, the poem whose features are more dramatic than lyrical. Pessoa's ideal of poetic creation, in which the notion of drama is refracted, is guided by a purpose of conjunction based on both the overcoming of clear boundaries between lyrical and dramatic genres and the certainty of the impossibility of giving birth to works perfectly adjusted to the tradition of a genre.[37]

4.

Pessoa makes specific references to Browning in his prose. For example, in "A nova poesia portuguesa sociologicamente considerada" (1912), the Victorian poet integrates, along similar lines with Coleridge and Shelley, the group of "figuras que, sem serem supremas, são [. . .] grandes indiscutivelmente."[38] Around 1916, when proposing the edition of an anthology of Portuguese "sensationist" poetry to an English publisher, Pessoa initially mentions Browning: "Suppose English romanticism had, instead of retrograding to the Tennysonian-Rossetti-Browning level, progressed right onward from Shelley [. . .]." Shortly after this, the "Elegy" of Teixeira de Pascoaes is presented as "certainly transcend[ing] Browning's 'Last Ride Together' as a love-poem."[39] Another unflattering opinion emerges in a recently published note: "Browning parece pensar em voz alta sem ter mais de poeta do que obter rimas."[40] A reference also appears in a letter to João de Castro Osório (then director of Lusitânia Editora), in which Pessoa offers to translate, among many other authors' poems, the "most important poems" of Robert Browning.[41] Although Pessoa claims these translations are in an advanced stage of development, one finds in his files, among several lists of English anthologies, merely a list of five of his poems[42] as well as some sketches of "The Pied Piper of Hamelin." Arnaldo Saraiva argues, however, that Pessoa would also have been responsible for the anonymous translation of "Up at a villa—down in the city" present in the twentieth volume of Biblioteca internacional de obras célebres.[43]

The most significant allusion to Browning is found in a text already mentioned, "Os graus da poesia lírica," in which the degrees of lyric poetry are listed. There, Pessoa elaborates a literary axiology guided by the criterion of depersonalization. Examples in English perpetually recur, and the author asserts that the first degree is characterized by "aquele em que o poeta, de temperamento intenso e emotivo, exprime espontânea ou refletidamente esse temperamento e essas emoções" (the one in which the poet, of intense and emotive temperament, expresses spontaneously or reflectively that temperament and those emotions); this is the "tipo mais vulgar do poeta lírico [. . .] e o seus poemas giram em torno de determinado número, em geral pequeno, de emoções."[44] A range of themes and emotions distinguishes the poet belonging to the second degree, who is still close to the previous one. Despite this specific characterization, the poet of the second degree does not necessarily express how to feel the emotions evoked by the work; Swinburne would represent this category of poet.

Browning arises as the preeminent example of the third-degree poet, in which the depersonalization is already foreseen to the extent that the emotions represented in the poem have their origin in what the poet feels "não já porque sente, mas porque pensa que sente" (no longer because he does feel, but because he thinks he feels). In other words, the poet feels with the imagination, not with the heart. This idea, which aligns with the one Pessoa presented to Francisco Costa, places the drama beyond the dramaturgical structure, propelling the following action: "Estamos na antecâmara da poesia dramática, na sua essência íntima. O temperamento do poeta, seja qual for, está dissolvido pela inteligência. A sua obra será unificada só pelo estilo, último reduto da sua unidade espiritual, da sua coexistência consigo mesmo. Assim é Tennyson, escrevendo por igual 'Ulysses' e 'The Lady of Shalott,' assim, e mais, é Browning, escrevendo o que chamou 'poemas dramáticos,' que não são dialogados, mas monólogos revelando almas diversas, com que o poeta não tem identidade, não a pretende ter e muitas vezes não a quer ter." (We are in the antechamber of dramatic poetry, in its essential intimacy. The poet's temperament, whatever one it is, is dissolved by intelligence. His work will have only the unity of style, the final residue of his spiritual unity, of his coexistence with himself. Thus Tennyson, writing both "Ulysses" and "The Lady of Shalott," and even more so, Browning, writing what he called "dramatic poems," which are not dialogic, but monologues revealing diverse souls with whom the poet neither identifies nor pretends to and many times has no desire to so identify.)[45]

In these statements by Pessoa, only his reference to poems that include no dialogue must be corrected. In the poem "In a Gondola," for example, presented in *Dramatic Lyrics*, voices of a man and a woman alternate and perform a brief, yet tragic love scene. By contrast, in the poem "In a Balcony," published in

Men and Women, the dialogic structure is built in terms that truly resemble a dramaturgical text, presenting not only three characters—Norbert, Constance, and the Queen—but also a love triangle that allows the conflicts among them to develop. This is maintained throughout the nearly 1,000 verses that constitute the text.

When contemplating the fourth degree, "muito mais raro" (a much rarer thing),[46] in which the poet is fully depersonalized, Pessoa mentions Browning once again. However, Pessoa does not necessarily place Browning in the highest rank, because that is reserved for Shakespeare. The fourth-degree poet not only uses the intellect to feel emotions that he does not have, but is also capable of living them—an ability that, in many cases, leads to

> poesia dramática, propriamente dita, como fez Shakespeare, poeta substancialmente lírico erguido a dramático pelo espantoso grau de despersonalização que atingiu [as did Shakespeare, substantially a lyric poet raised to the dramatic level by the astonishing degree of depersonalization he attained]. Num ou noutro caso continuará sendo, embora dramaticamente, poeta lírico. É esse o caso de Browning, etc. (ut supra) Nem já o estilo define a unidade do homem: só o que no estilo há de intelectual a denota. Assim é em Shakespeare, em quem o relevo inesperado da frase, a sutileza e a complexidade do dizer, são a única coisa que aproxima o falar de Hamlet do do Rei Lear, o de Falstaff do de Lady Macbeth. E assim é Browning através dos *Men and Women* e dos *Dramatic Poems*. [No longer does style itself define the unity of the man, but only what the style possesses of intellect. That's how it is with Shakespeare, in which the unexpected exaltation of phrase, the subtlety and complexity of expression, are the only things that link Hamlet's speech with that of King Lear, Falstaff's with Lady Macbeth's. The same is true of Browning's *Men and Women* and his *Dramatic Poems*.]

The fact that Browning is present in both the third (in which the poet "começa a despersonalizar-se" [begins to depersonalizate himself]) and the fourth degree (in which the poet "entra em plena despersonalização" [becomes completely depersonalized])[47] exposes the inconsistency of the system Pessoa proposed. Even though the high ranking assigned to Shakespeare indicates the supremacy of the fourth degree over the third, it is clear that the determining factor in this fourth degree concerns both: "Num *ou noutro caso* continuará sendo, embora dramaticamente, poeta lírico" (emphasis added).

The theoretical inconsistency of this unfinished text, so to speak, can be confirmed even in the following and last degree. Although the fifth degree is not clearly distinguished from the previous degree, the poet, alien to the dramaturgical structure, endeavors a slight tip in the scale of depersonalization: "Certos estados de alma, pensados e não sentidos, sentidos imaginativamente e por isso vividos, tenderão a definir para ele uma pessoa fictícia que os sentisse sinceramente" (Certain states of soul, intellectualized but not felt, felt imaginatively and therefore lived, tend to define for him a fictitious person who feels them sincerely).[48] Other than this distinct last sentence, the others refer to the quality described in the previous degree (the states of the soul, felt by imagination, are vivid to the poet).

Pessoa had already related Shakespeare to Browning. In another recently published text, Pessoa compares them: "Shakespeare é apenas um grande artista porque é um grande poeta; [. . .]; nos modernos da-se a dissociação: ou são, como Browning, grande poetas sem ser grandes artistas."[49] Nevertheless, in "Impermanence," Pessoa praises the ability to create imaginary characters possibly assimilated by Browning from Shakespeare: "We see the same care for universal men in Shakespeare, who penetrates their natures and their waking souls, [. . .] and in Browning, who penetrates their *separate types*."[50] In the same essay, however, Pessoa does not refrain from predicting the poet's future oblivion: "Browning, Byron will disappear altogether, even, perhaps, to the very names."[51]

In a way, Pessoa himself was responsible for the disappearance of Browning's work. In "Os heterônimos e os graus de lirismo" ("The Heteronyms and the Grades of Lyricism"), a text related to "Os graus da poesia lírica" ("The Grades of Lyrical Poetry"), the Portuguese poet clearly elects Shakespeare as a sort of harbinger in relation to the purpose of creating poems that would constitute a "drama de uma só personagem, um monólogo prolongado e analítico" (a one-character play—a prolonged analytic monologue).[52] This time, however, there is no mention of Browning, and this did not go unnoticed by George Monteiro: "Oddly, Pessoa fails to mention the one poet—Robert Browning—who had done exactly, over and again, what Shakespeare had not done, that is, create single-character 'plays.' Browning's creations could be seen—and they probably should be—as the immediate predecessors for Pessoa's heteronymic creations."[53]

In fact, there are affinities between Pessoa's and Browning's poetic projects: both poets were committed to developing a conception of drama that dismantled boundaries between genres. This specific development of drama thus caused

177

dramatic poetry to acquire other features besides the "vulgar or more obvious form of drama—scene & dialogue."[54] In this process, in which the two poets elaborated strategies to relativize the tradition of a specific literary genre, inventing souls was chosen as the privileged way of expression and, therefore, emphasized dramatic monologue.

The use of this form of drama can be identified in hundreds of texts throughout literary history, since, at least, Ancient Greece—hence Pessoa's discovery of "poesia lírica posta na boca de diversos personagens"[55] in Aeschylus's dramas.[56] Specifically concerning the English-speaking tradition, we can refer to this form's beginnings, in poems such as The Wanderer and The Seafarer, and even in the versified stories of The Canterbury Tales by Chaucer.[57] Thus, in a broader sense, the soliloquies in Shakespeare's plays can be likewise understood as dramatic monologues, a notion also suggested by Pessoa when he imagined the hypothetical creation of Hamlet as a "simples personagem, sem drama" (simply a character without a play) and speculated that Shakespeare would have written "um drama de uma só personagem, um monólogo prolongado e analítico."[58]

Studies on the genre of dramatic monologue normally tend to consider Browning's poems as a reference. This is because in his poems, the lyric form is established as self-sufficient and no longer associated with a greater dramatic or narrative context. The principle of dramatic monologue is then set as a technique that allows for the formalization of the discourse of an individual character. However, this character is then made alien to the poet, by addressing one or more people (occasionally itself). Therefore, one finds a moment of communication encapsulated in the text in which the reader has access to a scene that, although independent of a broader context, does not refrain from assuming that context, and thus offers a universe of suggestions from which the "state of soul" of that subject, in Pessoa's terms, is designed.

Through the multiplicity of subjects that arise from Browning's monologues, which cover a wide range of themes and epochs, Browning satisfies the longing for totality already seen in his previous works. Such is the case in Pauline, his first published poem, in which the speaker claims to himself "a centre to all things, / Most potent to create, and rule, and call / Upon all things to minister to it; / And to a principle of restlessness / Which would be all, have, see, know, taste, feel, all—/ This is myself."[59] In Paracelsus, in the moment when the title character asks Aprille to "[t]ell me what thou wouldst be, and what I am," she answers him with a lengthy exaltation of the "eternal, infinite love," in which the desire "to perfect and consummate all" is prominent.[60]

Thus, the many literary masks created by Browning lead the reader through a universe of historical periods as distinct as the Italian Renaissance ("Fra Lippo Lippi"), the English Civil War ("Cavalier Tunes") or the fights for independence in Algeria ("Through the Metidja to Abd-el-Kadr"). Browning mobilizes myths of Ancient Greece ("Artemis Prologizes") and folk tales ("The Pied Piper of Hamelin"); and involves monks ("Soliloquy of the Spanish Cloister"), noble-men ("My Last Duchess"), soldiers ("Incident of the French Camp"), and other poets as well ("Rabbi Ben Ezra").

The reader familiar with Pessoa will be able to recognize, in this wide range of characters, the foreshadowing of the notion "sentir tudo de todas as manei-ras" (to feel everything in every way) discussed by the Portuguese poet. This is not only seen in the words he ascribed to Álvaro de Campos, according to the text signed in his own name, in which he argues to "[a]bolir o dogma da per-sonalidade: cada um de nós deve ser muitos."[61] George Monteiro even identifies in the Pessoan formulation, "um drama em gente, em vez de em actos" (a drama in people, instead of acts),[62] an echo of the expression used in the preface to *Strafford*: "Action in Character rather than Character in Action." This suggests the indebtedness of the heteronymic project to Browning's work.

Despite his speculation about the presence of Browning's dramatic mono-logues in the creation of Pessoa's heteronyms, Monteiro emphasizes the element that distinguishes Pessoa from Browning: Pessoa's characters are writers and, therefore, able to create the poems wherein they will be known. Something sim-ilar can be stated regarding Shakespeare's characters, obviously not outlined as writers, but whose precedence Pessoa claims when he "erases" the reference to Browning in his text on the heteronyms and the degrees of poetry. Although Shakespeare's soliloquies can be read as autonomous poems, they were not written with the intention of being categorized as such: far from being con-ceived as self-centered forms, they guide the action in the play in which they are implemented, presenting a less lyrical purpose than a dramatic one. Browning's poems, in turn, despite functioning as independent plays, refer to the circum-stance wherein they originated and from which it is possible to reconstruct the broader scene in which they are placed. In Pessoa's poetry, however, it is the poem itself that configures the scene.

Pessoa's poetic project also exhibits particular differences in comparison to Browning's. Regarding the position in which the two poets endeavored to situate themselves within the universe they had created, Browning alluded to his dramatic poems as "performances," that is, plays in which he himself would have been the actor.[63] Pessoa, on the other hand, by involving his own name in the context of heteronymy, did not seek to maintain his distance from it, but rather to mingle himself within it, shaping a literary mask with the same physiognomy of the empirical "I."

By radicalizing the procedures of Browning's monologues when creating the heteronyms, Pessoa distanced himself from one of the models that possibly inspired him. It is curious, however, that he comes close to this model in *Mensagem*, exactly the work that, in its appearance, is so distinct from heteronymy, thus demonstrating the true length of the axis of comparison between the two poets.

Mensagem is a rather epic work—whether for its prophetic or messianic tone or for its grandiloquent discourse—in which the lyrical expression is, nevertheless, dramatic in essence. The arrangement of voices continuously staged in the poem brings it closer to the Browning monologue. This occurs when the author employs historical figures that assume the role of speaker and arouse the revision of past events through the outflow of emotions, even when the first person singular is not used. Because the reference in the title to these characters releases the multiplicity of voices that represent ghosts from a glorious past, the characters then enter the discourse of the poem and have a dialogue among themselves.

Therefore, throughout *Mensagem*, both the dissolution of the unity of the speaker, presented in the diversity of personae evoked in the work, and the stability of literary genres is articulated in so far as the epic element is added to the dramatization of the lyrical expression proposed. This articulation thus highlights the reconciliation of the convergence of poetry and drama also desired by Browning. From this perspective, the one collection of verses published by Pessoa in Portuguese can be read as a materialization of his literary project, which, among other factors, is based on a dynamic approach to and detachment from tradition.

NOTES

1. As emphasized by Cabral Martins and Richard Zenith, Pessoa never use the word *heteronymy*. See Fernando Pessoa, *Teoria da heteronímia*, ed. Fernando Cabral Martins and Richard Zenith (Lisbon: Assírio & Alvim, 2012), 111. However, in the famous letter to

Adolfo Casais Monteiro, dated January 13, 1935, he employs "heteronymism." See Fernando Pessoa, *Correspondência 1923–1935*, ed. Manuela Parreira da Silva (São Paulo: Companhia das Letras, 1999b), 341; Pessoa, *Cartas entre Fernando Pessoa e os directores da presença*, ed. Enrico Martines (Lisbon: Imprensa Nacional–Casa da Moeda, 1998), 254. On this matter, see also Jerónimo Pizarro, "Obras ortónimas e heterónimas," in *Pessoa existe?* (Lisbon: Ática, 2012), 73–95.

2. Here is the original verse: "Viviré de olvidarme." Jorge Luis Borges, "Browning resuelve ser poeta," in *Obras completas III, 1975–1985* (Buenos Aires: Emecé, 1989), 82.

3. Adolfo Casais Monteiro, "Pessoa e Pound," in *A poesia de Fernando Pessoa*, 2nd ed., ed. José Blanco. (Lisbon: Imprensa Nacional-Casa da Moeda, 1985), 121–24.

4. Georg Rudolf Lind, "A Hierarquia dos poetas e das artes," in *Estudos sobre Fernando Pessoa* (Lisbon: Imprensa Nacional–Casa da Moeda, 1981), 238–40.

5. Georges Güntert, "Na amaldiçoada sala dos espelhos do eu," in *Fernando Pessoa: O Eu Estranho*, trans. Maria Fernanda Cidrais (Lisbon: D. Quixote, 1982), 124–28.

6. Jacinto do Prado Coelho, "Fernando Pessoa, pensador múltiplo," in *Páginas íntimas e de auto-interpretação*, ed. Georg Rudolf Lind and Jacinto do Prado Coelho (Lisbon: Edições Ática, 1966), xxviii.

7. George Monteiro, "Drama in Character: Robert Browning," in *Fernando Pessoa and Nineteenth-Century Anglo-American Literature* (Lexington: University Press of Kentucky, 2000), 58–66.

8. Odorico Leal de Carvalho Júnior, "Browning, precursor comum: Vereda que se bifurca," in *Lírica impessoal e Modernidade: T. S. Eliot e Fernando Pessoa* (Belo Horizonte: Faculdade de Letras da Universidade Federal de Minas Gerais, 2010), 108–34. Naturally, we do not intend to be exhaustive with these mentionings, but it is necessary to add João Almeida Flor, "Discursos de alteridade," in Robert Browning, *Monólogos dramáticos* (Lisbon: Na Regra do Jogo, 1980), 11–18; and João Barrento, "Monólogos dramáticos: alteridade e modernidade," in *O Espinho de Sócrates: Expressionismo e Modernismo* (Lisbon: Presença, 1987), 103–11.

9. Letter to João Gaspar Simões, dated December 11, 1931. Pessoa 1999b, 255; Pessoa 1998, 178. Translation: Pessoa, Fernando, *The Selected Prose of Fernando Pessoa*, ed. and trans. Richard Zenith (New York: Grove Press, 2001), 235.

10. Charles W. Forward, *Poetical Works of Robert Browning*, intro. (London: Peacock, Mansfield, 1912), 8. Pessoa's private library is currently digitized and accessible at http://casafernandopessoa.cm-lisboa.pt/. A printed version of the catalog may also be consulted: Jerónimo Pizarro, Patricio Ferrari, and Antonio Cardiello, ed., *A Biblioteca particular de Fernando Pessoa I* (Lisbon: D. Quixote, 2010).

11. Robert Browning, *Poetical Works: 1833–1864*, ed. Ian Jack (Oxford: Oxford University Press, 1980), 38.

12. Browning, *Poetical Works*, "Preface," 38.

13. Ibid.

14. Clyde de L. Ryals, *Becoming Browning: The Poems and Plays of Robert Browning, 1833–1846* (Columbus: Ohio State University Press, 1983), 31.

15. A. S. Cook, ed., *Poetry, with Reference to Aristotle's Poetics* (Boston: Ginn, 1891). Quoted in Ryals, *Becoming Browning*, "Paracelsus," 32.

16. *New Monthly Magazine* XLVI (Mar. 1836), 289–308.

17. Robert Browning, *Poems and Plays, 1833–1844*, ed. Ernest Rhys (London: J. M. Dent, 1936), 133.

18. Ibid., "Preface," 133.

19. Years after the first publication of the long poem *Sordello*, in 1840, Browning wrote in the preface to this work, "My stress lay on the incidents in the development of a soul: little else is worth study." In Franklin T. Baker, ed., *Browning's Shorter Poems*, 4th ed. (New York: Macmillan, 1917), xiv.

20. James Patton McCormick, "Robert Browning and the Experimental Drama," *PMLA* 68, 5 (Dec. 1953), 984.

21. Browning, *Poems and Plays, 1833–1844*, "Preface," 133.

22. Forward, *Poetical Works of Robert Browning*, intro., "Dramatic Lyrics," 271.

23. Letter dated Jan. 19, 1915; Pessoa 1999a, 144.

24. Letter dated Dec. 11, 1931; Pessoa 1999b, 255; Pessoa 1998, 178. Translation: Pessoa, *The Selected Prose of Fernando Pessoa*, ed. and trans. Richard Zenith, 235.

25. Letter dated Jan. 20, 1935; Pessoa 1999b, 350; Pessoa 1998, 266. Translation: Pessoa, *The Selected Prose*, trans. Zenith, 250.

26. Letter dated Aug. 10, 1925; Pessoa 199b, 84–85.

27. Fernando Pessoa, *Obras em prosa*, ed. Cleonice Berardinelli (Rio de Janeiro: Nova Aguilar, 1976), 85; *Páginas íntimas e de auto-interpretação*, ed. Georg Rudolf Lind and Jacinto do Prado Coelho (Lisbon: Ática, 1966), 105.

28. Pessoa 1976, "[Os heterônimos e os graus de lirismo]," 87; Pessoa 1966, "[Umas figuras insiro em contos . . .]," 107.

29. Pessoa 1976, 87; Pessoa 1966, 107–8. Translation: Monteiro, "Drama in Character," 58–59.

30. Fernando Pessoa, *Páginas sobre literatura e estética*, ed. António Quadros (Lisbon: Europa-América, 1986), 60.

31. Pessoa 1986, "Introdução à estética," 19.

32. Fernando Pessoa, *Apreciações literárias de Fernando Pessoa*, ed. Pauly Ellen Bothe (Lisbon: Imprensa Nacional–Casa da Moeda, 2013), 58.

33. Maria Teresa Rita Lopes, *Fernando Pessoa et le drame symboliste: Héritage et création*, 2nd ed. (Paris: Foundation Calouste Gulbenkian, 1985), 109.

34. Fernando Pessoa, *Livro de versos: Álvaro de Campos*, ed. Teresa Rita Lopes (Lisbon: Estampa, 1993a), 15.

35. Fernando Pessoa, *Escritos autobiográficos, automáticos e de reflexão Pessoal*, ed. Richard Zenith (São Paulo: A Girafa, 2006), 367.

36. See letter to João Gaspar Simões, dated January 10, 1930: "Respondo agora à sua pergunta sobre o publicarem na *Presença* ou em separata algumas das minhas antigas produções. [. . .] *O Marinheiro* está sujeito a emendas: peço que, por enquanto, se abstenham de pensar nele. Se quiserem, poderei, feitas as emendas, dizer quais são: ficará então ao vosso dispor," in Pessoa 1999b, 190; Pessoa 1998, 115. On the genesis of this play, see Claudia J. Fischer, "Auto-tradução e experimentação interlinguística na génese d' 'O Marinheiro' de Fernando Pessoa," *Pessoa Plural* 1 (Spring 2012), 1–69.

37. On this issue, Kenneth David Jackson's hypothesis is that "Pessoa invented and refined a technique of adverse genres, playing content against formal conventions [. . .] part of a paradoxical juxtaposition whereby poetic genres selected from different historical periods in the Western tradition are filled with an incongruent and inauthentic content, subverting the familiarity of generic expression." In K. David Jackson, *Adverse Genres in Fernando Pessoa* (New York: Oxford University Press, 2010), 15–17.

38. Fernando Pessoa, *Crítica: Ensaios, artigos e entrevistas*, ed. Fernando Cabral Martins (Lisbon: Assírio & Alvim, 2000a), 10.

39. Undated letter, possibly 1916. Pessoa 1999a, 235. In "[Prefácio para uma Antologia de Poetas Sensacionistas]," attributed to Álvaro de Campos, a similar formulation is read. See Pessoa 1966, 145–46.

40. Pessoa 2013, 71.

41. Letter dated June 20, 1923. Pessoa 1999b, 13–15.

42. "Rabbi ben Ezra," "James Lee's Wife," "Prospice," "Evelyn Hope" and "The Pied Piper of Hamelin." See Patricio Ferrari "Meter and Rhythm in the Poetry of Fernando Pessoa," 2012, 385–86.

43. See Arnaldo Saraiva, *Fernando Pessoa poeta-tradutor de poetas: Os Poemas traduzidos e o respectivo original* (São Paulo: Nova Fronteira, 1999), 5–58.

44. Pessoa 1976, 274; Fernando Pessoa, *Páginas de estética e teoria literárias*, ed. Georg Rudolf Lind and Jacinto do Prado Coelho (Lisbon: Ática, 1967), 67. Translation: Monteiro, "Drama in Character," 60.

45. Pessoa 1976, 275; Pessoa 1967, 68. The following quotes refer to the same pages. Translations: Monteiro, "Drama in Character," 61.

46. Translation: Monteiro, "Drama in Character," 61.

47. Translation: ibid., 63.

48. Translation: ibid.

49. Pessoa 2013, 72.

50. Fernando Pessoa, *Heróstrato e a busca da imortalidade*, ed. Richard Zenith (Lisbon: Assírio & Alvim, 2000b), 238.

51. Pessoa 2000b, 243.

52. Pessoa 1976, 87; Pessoa 1966, 108. Translation: Monteiro, "Drama in Character," 59.

53. Monteiro, "Drama in Character," 59.

54. Letter from Browning to John Kenyon, dated October 1, 1855. Quoted in Ryals, *Becoming Browning*, "Afterword," 249.

55. Pessoa 1976, 86; Pessoa 1966, 106.

56. In Pessoa's copy of *The Lyrical Dramas of Æschylus* (1906; repr. Aug. 1917), the translator, John Stuart Blackie, defends "how essentially the lyrical element predominates in their construction [in the construction of the Æschylean pieces]." See John Stuart Blackie, transl., *The Lyrical Dramas of Æschylus*, 6th. ed. (London / Toronto: J. M. Dent, 1917), 17. http://casafernandopessoa.cm-lisboa.pt/bdigital/8–176.

57. See Caroline D. Eckhardt, "Genre," in *A Companion to Chaucer*, ed. Peter Brown (Oxford: Blackwell, 2002), 180–94; C. David Benson, "The *Canterbury Tales*: Personal Drama or Experiments in Poetic Variety?," in *The Cambridge Companion to Chaucer*, 2nd ed., ed. Piero Boitani and Jill Mann (Cambridge: Cambridge University Press, 2003), 127–42; and Barry Windeatt, "Literary Structures in Chaucer" in *The Cambridge Companion to Chaucer*, 214–32.

58. Pessoa 1976, 87; Pessoa 1966, 107–8. Translation: Monteiro, "Drama in Character," 59.

59. Forward, intro., "Pauline: a fragment of a confession," 5.

60. Ibid., "Paracelsus," 37.

61. Pessoa 1993b, "[A sensação como realidade essencial]," 141. Translation: Pessoa, *The Selected Prose*, trans. Zenith, 71.

62. Pessoa 2000a, "Tábua bibliográfica," 405. Translation: Monteiro, "Drama in Character," 64.

63. See the preface to the edition of 1888 of *Pauline*, there designated as "the first of my performances."

WORKS CITED

Baker, F. T. *Browning's Shorter Poems*. 4th ed. New York: Macmillan, 1917.

Barrento, J. "Monólogos dramáticos: Alteridade e modernidade." In *O Espinho de Sócrates: Expressionismo e Modernismo*, 103–11. Lisbon: Presença, 1987.

Benson, C. D. "The *Canterbury Tales*: Personal Drama or Experiments in Poetic Variety?" In *The Cambridge Companion to Chaucer*, 2nd ed., edited by P. Boitani and J. Mann, 127–42. Cambridge: Cambridge University Press, 2003.

Blackie, J. S., transl. *The Lyrical Dramas of Aeschylus.* 6th ed. London / Toronto: J. M. Dent, 1917. <http://casafernandopessoa.cm-lisboa.pt/bdigital/8–176>.

Borges, J. L. "Browning resuelve ser poeta." In *Obras completas III* (1975–1985), 82. Buenos Aires: Emecé, 1989.

Browning, R. *Poems and Plays: 1833–1844.* Edited by E. Rhys. London: J. M. Dent, 1936.

———. *Poetical Works: 1833–1864.* Edited by I. Jack. Oxford: Oxford University Press, 1980.

Carvalho Júnior, O. L. de. "Browning, precursor comum: vereda que se bifurca." In *Lírica impessoal e modernidade: T. S. Eliot e Fernando Pessoa,* 108–34. Belo Horizonte: Faculdade de Letras da Universidade Federal de Minas Gerais, 2010.

Coelho, J. Do P. "Fernando Pessoa, pensador múltiplo." In *Páginas íntimas e de auto-interpretação,* edited by G. R. Lind and J. Do P. Coelho, xxi–xxxvii. Lisbon: Edições Ática, 1966.

Eckhardt, C. D. "Genre." In *A Companion to Chaucer,* edited by P. Brown, 180–94. Oxford: Blackwell, 2002.

Ferrari, P. "Meter and Rhythm in the Poetry of Fernando Pessoa." Unpublished doctoral thesis, University of Lisbon, 2012.

Fischer, C. J. "Auto-tradução e experimentação interlinguística na génese d' 'O Marinheiro' de Fernando Pessoa." *Pessoa Plural* 1 (Spring 2012): 1–69.

Flor, J. A. "Discursos de alteridade." In *Browning, R.: Monólogos dramáticos,* 11–18. Lisbon: Na Regra do Jogo, 1980.

Forward, C. W. Introduction to *Poetical Works of Robert Browning.* London: Peacock, Mansfield, 1912. http://casafernandopessoa.cm-lisboa.pt/bdigital/8–74.

Güntert, G. "Na amaldiçoada sala dos espelhos do eu." In *Fernando Pessoa: O Eu Estranho,* translated by M. F. Cidrais, 124–128. Lisbon: D. Quixote, 1982.

Jackson, K. D. *Adverse Genres in Fernando Pessoa.* New York: Oxford University Press, 2010.

Lind, G. R. "A hierarquia dos poetas e das artes." In *Estudos sobre Fernando Pessoa,* 236–56. Lisbon: Imprensa Nacional–Casa da Moeda, 1981.

Lopes, M. T. R. *Fernando Pessoa et le drame symboliste: Héritage et création.* 2nd ed. Paris: Foundation Calouste Gulbenkian, 1985.

McCormick, J. P. "Robert Browning and the Experimental Drama." *PMLA* 68, no. 5 (Dec. 1953): 982–91.

Monteiro, A. C. "Pessoa e Pound." In *A poesia de Fernando Pessoa,* 2nd ed. Edited by J. Blanco, 121–24. Lisbon: Imprensa Nacional–Casa da Moeda, 1985.

Monteiro, G. "Pessoa: Discípulo de Robert Browning." In *Actas—IV Congresso Internacional de Estudos Pessoanos,* Vol. I, 277–87. Oporto: Fundação Engenheiro António de Almeida, 1990.

————. "Drama in Character: Robert Browning." In *Fernando Pessoa and Nineteenth-Century Anglo-American Literature*, 58–66. Lexington: University Press of Kentucky, 2000.

Pessoa, F. *Páginas íntimas e de auto-interpretação*. Edited by G. R. Lind and J. Do P. Coelho. Lisbon: Ática, 1966.

————. *Páginas de estética e de teoria e crítica literárias*. Edited by G. R. Lind and J. Do P. Coelho. Lisbon: Ática, 1967.

————. *Obras em prosa*. Edited by C. Berardinelli. Rio de Janeiro: Nova Aguilar, 1976.

————. *Páginas sobre literatura e estética*. Edited by A. Quadros. Lisbon: Europa-América, 1986.

————. *Livro de versos: Álvaro de Campos*. Edited by T. R. Lopes. Lisbon: Estampa, 1993a.

————. *Pessoa inédito*. Edited by T. R. Lopes. Lisbon: Horizonte, 1993b.

————. *Cartas entre Fernando Pessoa e os directores da Presença*. Edited by E. Martines. Lisbon: Imprensa Nacional–Casa da Moeda, 1998.

————. *Correspondência 1905–1922*. Edited by M. P. Da Silva. São Paulo: Companhia das Letras, 1999a.

————. *Correspondência 1923–1935*. Edited by M. P. Da Silva. Lisbon: Assírio & Alvim, 1999b.

————. *Crítica: ensaios, artigos e entrevistas*. Edited by F. C. Martins. Lisbon: Assírio & Alvim, 2000a.

————. *Heróstrato e a busca da imortalidade*. Edited by R. Zenith. Lisbon: Assírio & Alvim, 2000b.

————. *The Selected Prose of Fernando Pessoa*. Edited and translated by Richard Zenith. New York: Grove Press, 2001.

————. *Escritos autobiográficos, automáticos e de reflexão pessoal*. Edited by R. Zenith. São Paulo: A Girafa, 2006.

————. *Teoria da heteronímia*. Edited by F. C. Martins and R. Zenith. Lisbon: Assírio & Alvim, 2012.

————. *Apreciações literárias de Fernando Pessoa*. Edited by P. E. Bothe. Lisbon: Imprensa Nacional–Casa da Moeda, 2013.

Pizarro, J. "Obras ortónimas e heterónimas" In *Pessoa existe?*, 73–95. Lisbon: Ática, 2012.

————. Ferrari, P., and A. Cardiello, ed. *A Biblioteca particular de Fernando Pessoa*. Vol. I. Lisbon: D. Quixote, 2010.

Ryals, C. de L. *Becoming Browning: The Poems and Plays of Robert Browning, 1833–1846*. Columbus: Ohio State University Press, 1983.

Saraiva, A. *Fernando Pessoa poeta-tradutor de poetas: Os poemas traduzidos e o respectivo original*. São Paulo: Nova Fronteira, 1999.

Windeatt, B. "Literary Structures in Chaucer." In *The Cambridge Companion to Chaucer*, 2nd ed., edited by P. Boitani and J. Mann, 214–232. Cambridge: Cambridge University Press, 2003.

FLÁVIO RODRIGO PENTEADO wrote a master's dissertation in Portuguese literature at the Department of Vernacular Languages and Literatures at the University of São Paulo. He had a scholarship with the São Paulo Research Foundation (FAPESP) and has published the following articles: "*Salomé* ou uma história em que nos fechemos da vida," in XI SEL—*Seminário de Estudos Literários* (Electronic journals, Assis, UNESP, 2013); and "O teatro da escrita em Fernando Pessoa," in *Itinerários* (Revista de Literatura da UNESP de Araraquara, no. 34, Jan./Jun. 2012).

He can be reached at flaviorodrigo.pc@hotmail.com.

CAIO GAGLIARDI is a professor in the Department of Vernacular Languages and Literatures at the University of São Paulo. His current research area is "Fernando Pessoa: autoria e ironia." He has contributed to many publications to this field, including the books *Mensagem* (São Paulo: Hedra, 2007) and *Teatro do Êxtase* (São Paulo: Hedra, 2010); and the essay "De uma mansarda rente ao infinito: A outra cidade no livro do desassossego," in *Veredas*, Revista da Associação Internacional de Lusitanistas, Vol. 17, 2012.

He can be reached at caiogagliardi@gmail.com.

Pessoa's Walter Pater
Archival Material from a Reading Story

ABSTRACT: In a polemical article Pessoa wrote in 1922 about his close acquaintance the poet António Botto, Walter Pater was identified as a standard of comparison. Two years later, in the second issue of his art and literature review *Athena*, Pessoa became the first translator of Pater's work in Portugal, publishing a brief prose piece, "La Gioconda," extracted from the essay on Leonardo da Vinci in Pater's *The Renaissance*.

However, as the public now knows, after almost eighty years of constantly re-newed posthumous publication, what Pessoa published during his life is just the tip of the iceberg. What he translated and published, together with the reference to Pater in his printed article, is but a dim reminiscence of both a well-informed inter-est, nourished for several years, and a much more ambitious editorial project. Such a project aimed to make Pater's name familiar to a community of readers who would eventually become readers of Pessoa's literary works.

The goal of this essay is to offer the reader a panoramic view of how and in which forms Pessoa's literary production make reference to Pater's, shedding light on both the influence and the instrumental use of tradition in Pessoa's writings.

KEYWORDS: Pessoa, Pater, reading, influence, private library, archive

Fernando Pessoa read Walter Pater's works carefully and perhaps thoroughly. In Pessoa's private library, the presence of a book by Pater with abundant under-lining and other kinds of marginalia supports the claim of careful reading (Ap-pendix I). Further, in Pessoa's archive, many documents that remained unpub-lished after the author's death contain various references to the former don at Oxford University. In some of these documents, Pater is considered one of a triad of Victorian authors to whom Pessoa refers regularly, and not always in flattering terms. The triad consists of Pater, Matthew Arnold, and Oscar Wilde. The joint treatment of these three great Oxonians is not surprising, because of the strong intellectual and biographical links underlying their work. However, the use Pessoa occasionally makes of that joint reference implies a very personal reading, which motivated the outlining of individual characters inside his own literary project. In other cases, Pater appears in Pessoa's texts as a separate, independent reference. Because of this second kind of reference, it seems possible to argue that Pessoa was keen to notice Pater's individuality, even though in some contexts he decided not to emphasize it. The decision of individualizing or not individualizing Pater appears to correlate with the objectives in certain texts, which may vary in others, especially if those texts were signed with different names.

Projects and Lists

Based on the information contained in his archive, it is not clear when Pessoa first became aware of Walter Pater's works. Pater died at age fifty-five in 1894, only six years after Pessoa was born in Lisbon, and less than a year before the infamous trial of Oscar Wilde ended with his condemnation to prison and forced labors for "indecency and sodomy."[1] Wilde's imprisonment encouraged the attribution of a scarlet letter of social disproval to what some artists and art critics were writing in England at that time. The scandal was, in some cases, an appealing form of publicity for the works of some artists, but inside official circles—as in schools and the academic sphere—this same feature could keep books banned and away from young people's access. Pater was a recurrent name in Wilde's works, and the path that could lead from the publicly disgraced man and possible corruptor of minors to his former professor and mentor at Oxford was too visible for any judicious critic. It was evident, for example, that Wilde's description of "Pater's *Renaissance*" in his *De Profundis*, as "that book which has had such a strange influence over my life,"[2] resonated with the effects associated with the mysterious "yellow book" that led to the transformation of Dorian into a murderous hedonist in the novel *The Picture of Dorian Gray*.

Pater enjoyed some recognition during his lifetime, and died just before the scandalous turmoil created around Wilde could reach him. For this reason, and for the obvious sympathetic stance toward male homosexuality implied by Pater's works, these could not be swiftly integrated into the pedagogical reading lists for British schools for the generations immediately following his death. Even though the worst part of the scandal began only after his death, Pater endured some negative labeling of his works. His individualistic ideas of human perception and sensibility building, supposedly at stake in the appreciation of any art form, provoked instantaneous questioning about their moral implications. The most direct exposition of these ideas appeared in the conclusion of *The Renaissance*, ending with the following statement: "For art comes to you, proposing frankly to give nothing but the highest quality to your moments as they pass, and simply for those moments' sake."[3]

Criticisms arose immediately after the first edition of this book was published under the title *Studies in the History of the Renaissance* in 1873. As a result, the book was later republished as *The Renaissance: Studies in Art and Poetry*, with the original conclusion removed—a defensive act by Pater, who sought to protect his career as professor at Oxford. Pater reintegrated his conclusion into the book, in a slightly modified version, only after having published his historical and philosophical portrait titled *Marius the Epicurean: His Sensations and Ideas* in 1885, and after renouncing his professorship. As he asserted in a note added to the reprinting of his conclusion in 1893, he thought that in his portrait of the life of a young man in Rome during the rule of Marcus Aurelius, he had successfully explained the difference between the meditation on the perpetually changing world of impressions and sensations, and the mere apology of egotistical, irresponsible, and antisocial hedonism.[4] For that purpose, the character Marius was portrayed as an ascetic, humanitarian, and courageous man capable of admiring the simplicity of the animistic local religion of his native village as well as the rising affective power present in the beginnings of Christianity in the outskirts of Rome.

Given this context, it is possible that Pessoa did not come across any of Pater's books as part of his curriculum, and that Pater's work would not commonly be recommended to a schoolboy by teachers at Durban High School. But the existence in Pessoa's archive of a project for a dramatic piece titled "Marino the Epicure," in a notebook used between 1903 and 1904 (Appendix II, 1)—before his definitive return to Lisbon—appears as an indicative but inconclusive hint. In this early list of projects attributed to a fictional author named David Merrick,[5] the title of the piece offers no additional information. Afterward, Pessoa seems to have carried on with this dramatic project, writing some fragments of it during the first decade of the twentieth century, although calling it "Marino: A Tragedy." The similarity between the first title of Pessoa's project and Pater's *Marius the Epicurean* is evident. Considering some fragments of Pessoa's play (or plays) with the note "Marino"—not edited, and of which a sequential reading is not feasible—similarities that could be mentioned do not appear as proof of a clear and direct relationship between the two works.

In Pessoa's play, Marino interacts with other male characters—Vincenzo, Antonio, and Terentio—thus an Italian or Roman context is suggested by the names. The trait that would more directly relate "Marino" to Pater's *Marius* seems to be the presence, in both stories, of the sickness and death of a beloved friend provoking a sentimental meditation on the fragility of life and its impermanency.[6] It is clear that, even though Pessoa might have been thinking of *Marius the Epicurean* when he thought of writing "Marino the Epicure," at age fifteen or sixteen, this possibility is just a vague hypothesis. Other sources to support an informed consideration of Epicureanism were available to him at that time.

After his return to Lisbon, in 1905, Pessoa had direct contact with French symbolist literature, together with works that described in accusatory terms the state of art, perceived as "decadent" by the end of the nineteenth century in Europe. Perhaps the most important of these works was Max Nordau's *Entartung*, which Pessoa read in a French translation around 1907 (*Dégénérescence*). Authors who defended the autonomy and self-justifying property of art provoked a major concern in critics such as Nordau. All kinds of aestheticism would seem to those critics to be an egotistical and potentially antisocial influence being spread in modern society by corrupted art forms. This historical context was favorable for Pessoa discovering Pater's work in a broader context of European literature and art criticism outside England's shores and colonial extension, even if these works had a negative label. This also seems to be the context in which Pessoa for the first time was able to read about Oscar Wilde, an author who was constantly ridiculed and abhorred by Nordau.[7] The corrupted nature of Wilde, accused and censored by Nordau—and with this criticism extendable to Pater—would be resignified by Pessoa in his own texts. He would maintain the idea that Wilde and Pater were morbid artists, but he would characterize their illness as a lack of completeness, an incapacity to realize a much more radical project that he intended to lead in modern art.

A concrete trace of what became Pessoa's attentive reading of Pater dates from approximately 1913, in a vast and pluralistic editorial plan. Simply titled *Anthology* (Appendix II, 2), this list of projects features titles from English-language authors from different periods, such as Wordsworth, Shakespeare, Poe, and Coleridge, side by side with such contemporary and older Portuguese authors as Camilo Pessanha and Soares de Passos, and also with non-European references, such as Omar Khayyam and even a selection of Japanese haiku. The list does not seem to have been created under a single criterion for uniting such diverse authors, but when a reference to Pater's conclusion to *The Renaissance* appears translated into Portuguese as "Epilogo da 'Renascença'" just after the translation of two titles from Wilde—*Prose Poems* and *De Profundis*[8]—some associative continuity may be recognized. The proximity of Wilde to Pater, and especially of his *De Profundis* with the conclusion to *The Renaissance*, is emphasized in this ordering. Publishing these two authors would prove a more relevant project when the reference to them became pivotal in texts where Pessoa intended to introduce the public to the more original aspects of his own literary production by contrasting his ideas with a biased characterization of his predecessors.

In another list, written probably in the second decade of the twentieth century (Appendix II, 3), a reference to Pater appears without a corresponding title. In this document, Pater is again listed immediately after Wilde, but here the Irish author is represented by his novel *The Picture of Dorian Gray*. In contrast to the list for the *Anthology*, noted earlier, all the names mentioned in this document have much in common. Besides Pater and Wilde, the list includes G. B. Shaw, G. K. Chesterton, Max Stirner, Remy de Gourmont, Maurice Barrès, Rudolf Euken, J. M. Robertson, Friedrich Nietzsche, and Jules Gaultier.[9] All these authors could be considered bibliographical references for developing an encompassing argument on art and religion, the moral implications of individualism, or the value of Christianity by the end of the nineteenth century and the beginning of the twentieth. This list does not have a title or general designation, and the fact that only Stirner's title *Der Einzige und sein Eigentum* was translated into Portuguese, simply as "O Unico," suggests that this was not necessarily a list of translation projects. Instead, this could be a reading list Pessoa was organizing, having in mind a project for an essay or article. Pater in this case could serve as a reference for argument in a case study.

A significant list from around 1915 (Appendix II, 4) is also difficult to classify. The document presents the titles "Studies in the History of the Renaissance," "Imaginary Portraits," "Appreciations," and "Marius the Epicurean," under the heading "W. H. Pater." On the left side of the page, Pessoa added the word "Chief" joining, with a line, both *The Renaissance* and *Imaginary Portraits*. Hesitating about the correct order of enumeration, which is revealed as hierarchical, Pessoa first wrote "Marius," and then crossed it out and replaced it with a reference to *Appreciations with an Essay on Style*, putting Marius at the bottom of the list. This document contains Pater's most important works, leaving aside only his later *Plato and Platonism*. It is not clear if this was some kind of wish list of books Pessoa wanted to read or purchase, not having read them before, or if the list was created after a first reading of the works mentioned in it. In that case, the hierarchical order would be a product of Pessoa's reflection after reading those books instead of a guideline suggested by some other source. The appearance of the title "Studies in the History of the Renaissance" in order to refer the book *The Renaissance* makes it difficult to understand what Pessoa's knowledge of Pater was at the moment he made this list, particularly when we remember that in 1913, he had probably already used the later and definitive title for that book when he projected a translation of its conclusion. These are not questions that these lists alone may resolve. More relevant is the fact that every direct reference to Pater that Pessoa integrated into his writings is a reference to *The Renaissance*. The unique appearance of other titles of Pater's works in Pessoa's documents are contained in this list. Nevertheless, it is difficult to imagine Pessoa voluntarily ignoring other works of an author that impress him so deeply, especially because those other books were also clearly dedicated to subjects of interest to him.

Pessoa bought a copy of *The Renaissance* after October 1916, evidenced by the fact that he wrote on the cover pages of that book, printed in 1915, the signature "Fernando Pessoa" and not "Pessôa" as he had done before that date (Appendix I, 1.). The pages of the book are filled with underlining and other reading notes, and the references to Pater become more noticeable in Pessoa's writing after 1916. And yet, even if it were possible that Pessoa might have read some parts of *The Renaissance*, as is suggested by the 1913 project for a translation of the conclusion, he made an attentive reading or rereading in his own copy of the book and left plenty of annotations. *The Renaissance* would become Pater's emblematic book for Pessoa, but this does not necessarily mean that his knowledge of the author was limited to this book only.

Two other lists in Pessoa's archive, clearly called translation projects, were created closer to the 1920s (Appendix II, 5 and 6). In these lists, Pater appears side by side with Wilde and Matthew Arnold, and in one case he shares a page with the heteronym Ricardo Reis, assigned as a translator of poems from the *Greek Anthology*. In the first of these lists, the project of translating Pater consists of a selection of some excerpts from *The Renaissance*, and in the second list, the project seems to be a complete translation of the book. Therefore, Pessoa seems to have extended his initial interest in the conclusion to other parts of Pater's book, after purchasing his copy. Both these projects include content similar to the editorial lists of Olisipo, the publishing house Pessoa founded in the beginning of the 1920s, where Botto, Almada Negreiros, Raul Leal, and Pessoa were able to publish, before some of the books were seized by the police in 1923 and Olisipo went out of business. One of the most detailed plans for Olisipo also contains a reference to a translation of The Renaissance (Appendix II, 7).

Chronologically, the last list of projects identified in Pessoa's archive as containing a reference to Pater was certainly written after 1923 (Appendix II, 8). In this list, two different projects related to Pater were noted. The first was a complete translation of the essay dedicated to Leonardo da Vinci in Pater's The Renaissance, and the second was a translation of the conclusion.

Translations

Pessoa's project of translating Pater turned into concrete action and development in the 1920s. For that purpose, he wrote a detailed list containing the precise pages from which he would extract the excerpts to translate (Appendix III, 1). The pages correspond to those in his copy of the book. As part of this project, Pessoa began a translation of the preface (Appendix III, 2). Narrowing his efforts, Pessoa concentrated on the translation of an excerpt from Pater's chapter on Leonardo da Vinci, which he simply titled "La Gioconda," carefully choosing words and syntax. Two complete versions of the excerpt were redacted with some differences between them (Appendix III, 3, 4). This excerpt was finally published in the second issue of Athena (Appendix III, 5), the review Pessoa directed for five issues between 1924 and 1925, with some alteration from the previous drafts. This became Pater's first translation published in Portugal, and it is possible that many of the readers of Athena had never heard of Pater.[10]

Having the opportunity to publish an excerpt from The Renaissance, Pessoa opted, significantly, for "La Gioconda" instead of some lines from the conclusion or the preface, as he had many times considered. In this decision he would anticipate W. B. Yeats, who in 1936 included a verse rendering of Pater's prose on Da Vinci's painting as part of The Oxford Book of Modern Verse.[11] "La Gioconda" features Pater's prose in action: not making general judgments about the purpose of art, or reflecting on its consequences, but passionately describing Pater's own impressions of an object he contemplates. The last lines of Pater's excerpt were also adequate for a review such as Athena, with no avant-garde pretensions

expressed by Pessoa in an introductory text included in the first issue of the review, titled "Athena." Pater's final assertion on Da Vinci's painting could easily
reinforce the ideas Pessoa had already presented: "modern philosophy has conceived the idea of humanity as wrought upon by, and summing up in itself, all
modes of thought and life. Certainly Lady Lisa might stand as the embodiment
of the old fancy, the symbol of the modern idea."[12] The publication of those
lines, translated into Portuguese, was also part of an anticipatory excitement
that Pessoa wanted to create before finally publishing, after almost ten years
of judicious preparation, some poems of Alberto Caeiro in the fourth and fifth
issues of the review.

References

In Pessoa's archive, the presence of Pater is not merely an occasional token either of his self-taught erudition or of his instructed acquaintance, in Durban,
with the critical and poetical traditions of nineteenth-century English literature.
The author of The Renaissance, together with the authors that were closer to his
works, played an instrumental and performatory role in the heart of Pessoa's
understanding of his own literary project. Therefore, having a broader comprehension of what Pessoa found in Pater may help us grasp the meaning of some
texts that, at first sight, could appear as being isolated or containing needlessly
conflicting ideas.

Probably the most significant reference that Pessoa made to Pater in his texts
can be found in a notebook annotation in which he associates Pater's description of "La Gioconda" with a project for a new kind of literature that would
contain and supersede the arts of architecture, music, and painting (Appendix
IV, 1). Characterizing Pater's critical effort as a supporter of Wilde's description of the critic's objective "to see the object as in itself it really is not,"[13] Pessoa
celebrates Pater's capacity of seeing in "La Gioconda" "things that are not
there." The text, written around 1916, also recalls the content of Pater's essay
included in The Renaissance on the eighteenth-century art historian Johann Wick-
elmann. Pater created a bridge between romantic authors such as Goethe—
Winckelmann's admirer—and the study of classical Greece, arguing that Winckelmann offered Goethe the experience of a time not his own. The implications
of Pessoa's take on Pater's description of Winckelmann as a post-Christian
return to some constituent elements of "Greek modelling" were identified by
António Feijó in a seminal article on Pessoa's systematic creation of fictional

authorships, in which Pater is recognized as a source for Pessoa's architectural understanding of his own literary project.[14] Pessoa's descriptions of his fictional authors, as personalized poetical styles, owe much to the "Classical" and "Romantic" elements and their complementary dynamics in modern art as postulated by Pater. Those terms are explored with detail in the postscript with which he concludes his book *Appreciations with an Essay on Style*.[15]

The acknowledgment of Pater as a precursor of the literary movement of which *Orpheu* was the first manifestation was explicit in a text in which Pessoa intended to foretell the sociological consequences of World War I on the future of the arts (Appendix IV, 2). In this case, "Pater or Wilde" or Mallarmé were described as interchangeable parts of a dual heritage from the nineteenth-century artistic movements. That heritage, together with the influence of Verlaine, would offer models to modern literature for responding to the need for introspection and the cultivation of social indifference that would be awakened by the devastation of the war. The text affirms that *Orpheu* had brought something new to literature because it could be seen as a synthesis of the influence of those four authors.

Until this point Pessoa's texts are unambiguously apologetic of Pater's importance for literature in the beginning of the twentieth century, but this same feature does not reveal itself univocally in Pessoa's archive.

After the publication of the two issues of *Orpheu* in 1915, one of Pessoa's main objectives was to publish the works of Alberto Caeiro, whose writings had been partially conceived in 1914. Pessoa intended Caeiro to be at the center of his literary works, representing the return of a pagan *Weltanschauung* into the modern world. In order to guarantee the attention to Caeiro's poems that Pessoa thought they deserved, he also found it necessary to create some presentation texts for the poems that could explain to the public Caeiro's revolutionary nature, which Caeiro as a non-self-conscious poet would not explain for himself. One of those texts was an extended preface authored by Caeiro's self-proclaimed disciple Ricardo Reis. Pessoa never finished this task, but he produced abundant material relating to it.[16]

In some of the preparatory documents for the preface, Reis expresses with vehemence his own opinions on Pater. For example, he unites Wilde, Pater, and Arnold, calling them "Christian waste with pagan pretensions" (Appendix IV, 3), with clearly derogatory intent that benefitted his exalted object, that is, Caeiro. In still another text that was also meant to be integrated into the preface, Reis

accuses "the aesthete Wilde" and "his master Pater" of being completely ignorant of the moral substance of Greek paganism, equating non-Christian principles with straightforward immorality (Appendix IV, 4). In yet another contemporary draft for the same preface, Reis refers to Pater separately, in terms that
are less caustic but not free of reproach: he calls Pater's understanding of paganism "perfect"—in direct opposition to the ignorance he attributed to Pater
when considered next to Wilde—but he still characterizes him as a "morbid
Christian with pagan aspirations" (Appendix IV, 5).

These slight variations of tone and the moderation of caustic language could
seem to be consequences of an ingratitude Pessoa felt toward his predecessors,
poorly disguised under the name Ricardo Reis. But it has become clear, for
some of Pessoa's critics, that even when he was not eulogistic about some authors he had read carefully, for his own work, Pessoa did not always deny the
importance of those authors.[17] The fundamental point about Pater in Reis's
preface is that Reis is supposed to write about him in a certain manner, because
that manner represents who he *becomes* in his writing. The variation in the form
of a reference can be read as Pessoa's way of calibrating the voice that was to be
Reis's voice. This idea becomes much clearer when reading another text, which
began as being written by Reis, as part of his preface on Caeiro; but at some
point in its development, it changed from being *by* Reis to being *about* Reis, ac-
quiring a new authorship under the signature António Mora (Appendix IV, 6).
As surprising as it may seem, after the harsh judgment Pessoa made about Pater
under Reis's authorship, Mora makes a harsh criticism of Reis and Caeiro as
well, accusing them of acting like Pater and Wilde in an aspect of their understanding of paganism. The authorship of the text changed when Pessoa understood that it was necessary to affirm a new individuality that could be responsible
for a particular assertion that had Pater as a reference point.

In yet another text, Mora corrects what were Pessoa's own projects. After the
publication of *Orpheu*, Pessoa planned to develop a "Portuguese Neo-Pagan"
movement led by the figures of Ricardo Reis, Caeiro, Mora, and himself. The
name of the movement appears in numerous texts and editorial lists.[18] In a moment of extreme orthodoxy, Mora attacks the use of that name, considering it
an absurd label, acceptable only in the cases of some "Christian rebels" such as
Pater and Swinburne (Appendix IV, 7). Pessoa's *coterie* of writers takes advantage
of constant opposition, using Pater and other authors' names as a vertex point
toward delineating each signature's autonomy. Then, a negative reference to

Pater in a certain text should not be merely understood as Pessoa's erratic un-derestimation of the author. Rather, it should be recognized as a calculated rad-icalism that benefits from a predecessor's achievements and reputation in order to note its own independence.

In other texts not attributed to any fictional author, Pessoa seems to be more at ease with the extravagant assessment of Pater's importance. For example, in a text in which he reflects on how to write commercial publicity, he considers Pater and Arnold as paradigms for brilliant prose writing (Appendix IV, 8). More directly, on the back of a page used for redacting a text for an essay titled "Im-permanence," dedicated to "[t]he problem of the survival of literary works and of the permanent elements of literature,"[19] Pessoa presented Pater in a short note as the most enduring element of his epoch: "Of all that modern times have said, only Pater will remain" (Appendix IV, 9). Finally, inserted in a critical con-sideration of Anatole France, written after the French author's death in 1924, Pessoa intended to quote Pater as the author that defined "once and forever" the meaning of humanism (Appendix IV, 10). In that text Pessoa left a blank space where he would, most likely, transcribe from his edition of The Renaissance a sentence he had underlined in Pater's essay about Pico della Mirandola: "For the essence of humanism is that belief [. . .] that nothing which has ever interested living men and women can wholly lose its vitality."[20]

Continuing this apologetic line, the most noticeable reference to Pater in what Pessoa published during his lifetime appears in his essay on António Botto's poetry (Appendix IV, 11). The meaning of that reference can be better under-stood in relation to the constant presence of the author of The Renaissance in the construction and reformulation of Pessoa's literary project. After publishing Botto's second edition of the book Canções through Olisipo, Pessoa wrote an ar-ticle for the literary review Contemporanea in 1922. In this article, he suggested a paraphrasing of Winckelmann by Pater as a perfect preface for the book Canções, and he also argued, subtly, that Botto was a lower degree of aesthete on a scale ranking Winckelmann and Pater at the top. This kind of positioning should be seen precisely as another version of the instrumental use Pessoa made of Pater's reference in order to compose individualized characters inside his own works. Giving Botto a place on this scale, Pessoa could feel closer to what he thought were the adequate conditions for presenting his own works to the public, by preparing a standard of comparison. The consequences of his article were different: Olisipo's books were seized by the police in 1923, after a group of

Catholic students saw them as an immoral insurrection that one of the supporters of the group baptized "Literature of Sodom."[21]

By the end of the 1920s, and after the not immediately successful publication of Caeiro poems in *Athena*, Pessoa reflected in a short note on the possibility of maintaining an ironic stance toward life to endure suffering. In that reflection, Pater reappeared in order to remember the condition of criticism in life as a perpetual appreciation of values (Appendix IV, 12). The presence of the author of *The Renaissance* cuts across Pessoa's life, leaving the mark of a conscious recognition of influence. Pater was thus summoned to be part of a literary project that required him as a character.

NOTES

I would like to thank Giulia Bossaglia and Michael Daily for reviewing this article.

1. Another version of the pledge of charges against Wilde states "gross indecency with other men." Cf. Ellmann, *Oscar Wilde* (London: Penguin Books, 1988), 431; and J. Bristow, "Biographies," in *Palgrave Advances in Oscar Wilde* (London: Palgrave MacMillan, 2004), 7.

2. Oscar Wilde, *De Profundis and The Ballad of Reading Gaol* (Leipzing: Taunichtz, 1908), 45. This book belongs to Fernando Pessoa's private library, and a digital copy is available online at the Casa Fernando Pessoa website: http://casafernandopessoa.cm-lisboa.pt. In these notes, when quoting books from the private library, the abbreviation CFP will be used with the number in the catalog of reference: *De Profundis*, CFP 8–583.

3. Walter Pater, *The Renaissance* (London: Macmillan, 1915), CFP 8–425, 252.

4. Pater's disclaimer in the republishing of the conclusion: "This brief 'Conclusion' was omitted in the second edition of this book, as I conceived it might possibly mislead some of those young men into whose hands it might fall. On the whole, I have thought it best to reprint it here, with some slight changes which bring it closer to my original meaning. I have dealt more fully in *Marius the Epicurean* with the thoughts suggested by it." Pater, CFP 8–425, 246. About the reception of *The Renaissance* when it was first published, see Donald L. Hill, "Notes," in Pater, *The Renaissance: Studies in Art and Poetry, the 1893 Text* (Berkeley: University of California, 1980), 443–58.

5. About David Merrick's projects and figure, see Pessoa, *Eu sou uma antologia* (Lisbon: Tinta-da-China, 2013), 126–33.

6. The incomplete fragments for the drama *Marino* can be found in Pessoa's archive, in the envelope BNP/E3, 11¹⁰MA, and a plot resume can be found in BNP/E3, 13–1ᵛ. It is not clear if all the material corresponds to only one play, or even if *Marino: A Tragedy* has any correspondence with the project titled *Marino the Epicure*. The fragment on the lament of the death of a friend is related to the character Vincenzo (cf. BNP/E3, 11¹⁰MA–11), a

name that would also be used by Pessoa as the title for another dramatic project. In BNP/
E3, 13–1ᵛ Marino has leprosy. In *Marius the Epicurean*, Pater dedicated a long chapter to
describing the friendship of Marius with the young poet Flavian, who dies of plague,
provoking in Marius a sentimental understanding of life as a continuous flux. I'm grateful to Richard Zenith, who gave me the references on *Marino*, and who explained some
details on the development of the plays.

7. The relationship of Pessoa with Nordau's works has been studied in detail by
some critics, namely Jerónimo Pizarro, *Fernando Pessoa: Entre génio e loucura* (Lisbon: Imprensa Nacional–Casa da Moeda, 2007) and Keneth Krabbenhoft, *Fernando Pessoa e as
doença do fim de século* (Lisbon: Imprensa Nacional–Casa da Moeda, 2011). From 1907,
Pessoa kept a reading diary that mentioned his first reading of Nordau. This diary was
transcribed in Pizarro, 2007, 57. Max Nordau dedicated a chapter of his *Dégénérenscence*
to Wilde, portraying him as the English rendering of a French decadent artist. Nordau
accused Wilde of being unconscious of his actions and took Wilde's works as proof of
his morbid deviation; cf. Nordau, *Dégénérescence* (Paris: Felix Alcan, 1894), 131–41. No reference to Wilde has been found in Pessoa's archive prior to 1911. About the first contact
Pessoa had with French Symbolism, see Pessoa, *Correspondência 1923–1935* (Lisbon: Assírio & Alvim, 1999), 279.

8. Pessoa's projects of translating Wilde were ambitious and numerous, and covered
all the genres of Wilde's works, from drama to critical writing. However, the concrete
development of those projects was limited. Pessoa actually translated some of Wilde's
Prose Poems, without publishing them. Those translations were edited by Richard Zenith,
in "A Importância de não ser Oscar? Pessoa tradutor de Wilde," *Egoísta* (June 2008). Pessoa also translated one initial page of *De Profundis* (BNP/E3, 23–66ʳ) that has been erroneously published by some editors as Pessoa's original production.

9. Books by Robertson, Shaw, Chesterton, Gourmont, and Gaultier belong to Pessoa's private library, and books about Nietzsche and Barrès as well. These names were
of interest for Pessoa from the first years of his return to Lisbon, and they reappear in his
papers regularly.

10. In a book dedicated to Walter Pater's reception in Europe, Teresa Malafaia and
Jorge da Silva confirmed this information; cf. Malafaia and Silva, "Fernando Pessoa and
the Reception of Walter Pater in Portugal," in *The Reception of Walter Pater in Europe* (London: Thoemmes Continuum, 2004), 224–26.

11. Yeats was also an author deeply influenced by Pater. The way that the Irish author
and Pessoa took advantage of and characterized the influences of English aestheticism in
their works has been explored by Patricia Silva McNeill in a comparative study titled *Yeats
and Pessoa: Parallel Poetic Styles* (London: Legenda, 2010).

12. Pater, *The Renaissance*, CFP 8–425, 130.

13. Oscar Wilde, "The Critic as Artist," in *Complete Works* (London: Harper Collins, 2003), 1128. Pessoa here radicalized Pater's famous take on Matthew Arnold's definition of the objective of criticism, leaving Pater closer to Wilde than to Arnold.

14. See António Feijó, "Fernando Pessoa's Mothering of the *Avant-garde*," *Stanford Humanities Review* VII, 1 (1999).

15. Walter Pater, "Postscript," in *Appreciations with an Essay on Style* (London: Macmillan, 1924).

16. The most complete edition of the remains of this project in Pessoa's archive can be consulted in Pessoa, *Ricardo Reis: Prosa* (Lisbon: Assírio & Alvim, 2003). The editor of that volume, Manuela Parreira da Silva, decided to title the section dedicated to Reis's preface "Notas para um prefácio a Alberto Caeiro," higlightening the unfinished and disorganized state of the documents.

17. One of the first critics to notice this particular condition of Pessoa's critical prose was Orietta Del Bene, in an article about Walter Pater. See Orietta Del Bene, "Vivências de Walter Pater en Fernando Pessoa," *Separata da Revista "Occidente"* LXXIV (1968), 296. Del Bene's article concentrates on a detailed reading of Pessoa's essay on António Botto and the genealogy of what she calls, following Jacinto do Prado Coelho, Pessoa's Anglo-Saxon anti-Christian feeling.

18. At least three editions of Pessoa's works concentrate partially on the project that Pessoa baptized "Neo-paganismo Portugués," and reproduce several texts and project lists under that category: Pessoa, *Ricardo Reis: Prosa*; Pessoa, *Obras de António Mora* (Lisbon: Imprensa Nacional–Casa da Moeda, 2002); and more recently, Pessoa, *O Regresso dos deuses e outros escritos de António Mora* (Lisbon: Assírio & Alvim, 2013).

19. Pessoa, *Heróstrato e a busca da imortalidade* (Lisbon: Assírio & Alvim, 2000), 231.

20. Pater, *The Renaissance*, CFP 8–425, 51.

21. The article originally titled "Literatura de Sodoma: O Sr. Fernando Pessoa e o ideal estetico em Portugal" was also published in *Contemporanea*, written by a Catholic journalist named Álvaro Maia. About the polemics awakened by the article and its consequences, see José Barreto, "Fernando Pessoa e Raul Leal contra a campanha moralizadora dos estudantes em 1923," *Pessoa Plural* 2 (Fall 2012).

WORKS CITED

Barreto, José. "Fernando Pessoa e Raul Leal contra a campanha moralizadora dos estudantes em 1923." *Pessoa Plural* 2 (Fall 2012).

Bristow, Joseph. "Biographies." In *Palgrave Advances in Oscar Wilde*, edited by Frederick S. Roden. London: Palgrave MacMillan, 2004.

Del Bene, Orietta. "Vivências de Walter Pater en Fernando Pessoa." *Separata da Revista "Occidente"* LXXIV, 1968.

Ellmann, Richard. *Oscar Wilde*. London: Penguin Books, 1988.

Feijó, António. "Fernando Pessoa's Mothering of the *Avant-garde*." *Stanford Humanities Review* VII, no. 1, 1999.

Ferreira, António Mega. *Fernando Pessoa: O Comércio e a publicidade*. Lisbon: Cinevoz, 1986.

Krabbenhoft, Kenneth. *Fernando Pessoa e as doença do fim de século*. Lisbon: Imprensa Nacional–Casa da Moeda, 2011.

Malafaia, Teresa, and Jorge da Silva. "Fernando Pessoa and the Reception of Walter Pater in Portugal." In *The Reception of Walter Pater in Europe*, edited by Stephen Bann. London: Thoemmes Continuum, 2004.

McNeill, Patricia da Silva. *Yeats and Pessoa: Parallel Poetic Styles*. London: Legenda, 2010.

Nordau, Max. *Dégénérescence*. 2nd ed. Translated by Auguste Dietrich. Paris: Félix Alcan, 1894.

Pater, Walter. *The Renaissance*. London: Macmillan, 1915. CFP 8–425.

———. *Appreciations with an Essay on Style*. London: Macmillan, 1924.

———. *The Renaissance: Studies in Art and Poetry, the 1893 Text*. Edited with explanatory notes by Donald L. Hill. Berkeley: University of California, 1980.

Pessoa, Fernando. "Antonio Botto e o ideal esthetico em Portugal." *Contemporanea* 3, Lisbon, 1922.

———. *Páginas íntimas e de auto-interpretação*. Edited and introduced by Georg Rudolf Lind and Jacinto do Prado Coelho. Lisbon: Ática, 1966.

———. *Páginas de estética e de teoria e crítica literárias*. Edited and introduced by Georg Rudolf Lind and Jacinto do Prado Coelho. Lisbon: Ática, 1967.

———. *Poemas completos de Alberto Caeiro*. Edited by Teresa Sobral Cunha. Lisbon: Editorial Presença, 1994.

———. *Correspondência 1905–1922*. Edited by Manuela Parreira da Silva. Lisbon: Assírio & Alvim, 1998.

———. *Correspondência 1923–1935*. Edited by Manuela Parreira da Silva. Lisbon: Assírio & Alvim, 1999.

———. *Heróstrato e a busca da imortalidade*. Edited by Richard Zenith. Lisbon: Assírio & Alvim, 2000.

———. *Obras de António Mora*. Edited and introduced by Luís Filipe Teixeira. Fernando Pessoa's Critical Edition, Major Series, Vol. VI. Lisbon: Imprensa Nacional–Casa da Moeda, 2002.

———. *Escritos autobiográficos: Automáticos e de reflexão Pessoal*. Edited by Richard Zenith, with the collaboration of Manuela Parreira da Silva. Lisbon: Assírio & Alvim, 2003.

———. *Ricardo Reis: Prosa*. Edited by Manuela Parreira da Silva. Lisbon: Assírio & Alvim, 2003.

————. *Cadernos*. Edited by Jerónimo Pizarro. Critical edition of Fernando Pessoa's Works. Lisbon: Imprensa Nacional–Casa da Moeda, 2009.

————. *Sensacionismo e outros ismos*. Edited by Jerónimo Pizarro. Fernando Pessoa's Critical Edition, Major Series, Vol. X. Lisbon: Imprensa Nacional–Casa da Moeda, 2009.

————. *Livro do desasocego*. Edited by Jerónimo Pizarro. Edição Crítica de Fernando Pessoa. Lisbon: Imprensa Nacional–Casa da Moeda, 2012.

————. *Eu sou uma antologia: 136 autores fictícios*. Edited by Jerónimo Pizarro and Patricio Ferrari. Lisbon: Tinta-da-China, 2013. Pessoa Collection coordinated by Jerónimo Pizarro.

————. *O Regresso dos deuses e outros escritos de António Mora*. Edited by Manuela Parreira da Silva. Lisbon: Assírio & Alvim, 2013.

————. *Apreciações literárias de Fernando Pessoa*. Edited by Pauly Ellen Bothe. Fernando Pessoa's Critical Edition, Collection "Studies." Lisbon: Imprensa Nacional–Casa da Moeda, 2013.

Pizarro, Jerónimo. *Fernando Pessoa: Entre génio e loucura*. Fernando Pessoa's Critical Edition, Collection "Studies," Vol. III. Lisbon: Imprensa Nacional–Casa da Moeda, 2007.

Uribe, Jorge. "Oscar Wilde, educação e teoria aristocrática: Um texto que era três." *Pessoa Plural* 2 (Fall 2012).

Wilde, Oscar. "The Critic as Artist." In *Complete Works*. London: Harper Collins, 2003.

————. *De Profundis and The Ballad of Reading Gaol*. Leipzing: Taunichtz, 1908 [1910]. CFP 8–583.

Zenith, Richard. "A Importância de não ser Oscar? Pessoa tradutor de Wilde." *Egoísta*. Casino de Estoril, Casino de Lisboa, Casino da Póvoa, June 2008.

JORGE URIBE has a PhD in theory of literature from the University of Lisbon and a bachelor's degree in literature from the University of the Andes. His doctoral dissertation explored the works of Fernando Pessoa in relation to his readings of Oscar Wilde, Walter Pater, and Matthew Arnold, focusing the topics of aesthetic criticism and dramatic depersonalization. Uribe has organized and collaborated on several editions of Pessoa's works, including *Sebastianismo e Quinto Império* (Ática, 2011) and *Obras Completas de Álvaro de Campos* (Tinta da China, 2014). He has held grants from the Fundação Calouste-Gulbenkian (FCG) and the Fundação para a Ciência e a Tecnologia (FCT). He is a member of the research project *Estranhar Pessoa*, at the Universidade Nova de Lisboa.

Appendix I: A Book

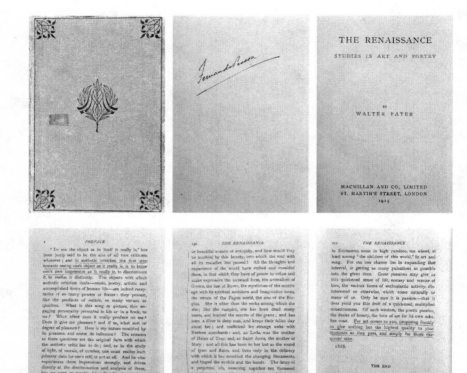

Walter Pater, *The Renaissance*, London: Macmillan, 1915. *Top row (left to right):* cover; Pessoa's signature in his copy; title page from Pessoa's personal copy; *second row (left to right):* preface, with underlining by Pessoa; chapter on Leonardo Da Vinci, with reading marks; conclusion, underlined by Pessoa.

❖ This book was purchased by Pessoa, probably after September 1916. The attribution of this date is associated with information contained in a letter Pessoa wrote to his friend Armando Côrtes-Rodrigues. On October 4, 1916, Pessoa communicated his decision to change the former spelling of his name "Pessôa," used in his published works until that date, by removing the circumflex. Pessoa, *Correspondência 1905–1922* (Lisbon: Assírio & Alvim, 1999), 222.

Appendix II: Projects and Lists

1. BNP/E3, 153–8ᵛ [1903–1904] ❖

David Merrick

Books to Come

"Sub /Umbrâ/" (Book of Poems) Must be ready on May 31st, 1904 to consist
  only of short, pretty poems.

"Martin Kéravas" (A novel) Must be ready anytime before June 30th, 1905. In
  plead for peace. Length, about from 120.000 to 150.000 words.

"Simple Tales" (Stories) Must be ready on July 31st, 1904. Short and pathetic.
  From 5000 to 7000 words each. Number about 20 or more.

"Longer Tales" (Stories) Must be ready by December 31st, 1904. 4 or 5 tales
  each of 30.000 words being: 1. "The Atheist," 2. "The Philanthropist," etc.

"Seared Leaves (?)" (Book of Plays) Must be ready by □

Plays: 1. "Marino the Epicure"; 2. "The Savages"; 3. "Doctor □"; 4. "Inez de
  Castro; 5. "□

❖ Published in Pessoa, *Cadernos* (Lisbon: Imprensa Nacional–Casa da Moeda, 2009), 111. The
editor, Jerónimo Pizarro, presented arguments for the attribution of this date: Pessoa, *Cadernos*, 105.

2. BNP/E3, 48–4ʳ and 5ʳ [1913?] ❖

Project for a
world literature
"Anthology"
in Portuguese,
manuscript,
BNP/E3, 48–4ʳ.

"Anthology"
in Portuguese,
manuscript,
BNP/E3, 48–5ʳ.

Anthologia

Shakespeare: A Tormenta

S[amuel] Johnson: Carta ao Conde de Chesterfield

J[ean] B[Pèrés]: Como Napoleão nunca existiu.

Amiel: excerptos do "Diario Intimo"

/Maupassant: Madame Baptiste./

Antonio Molarinho: Maria Manuela.

Soares de Passos: O Firmamento.

Manuel da Veiga; a "Ode" da "Laura de Anfriso."

Edgar Poe: O Corvo.

O'Shaugnessy: Ode

Wordsworth: Ode sobre as Intimações de Inmor[talida]de.

Coleridge: Trova do /Velho Marinheiro/.

José Anastacio da Cunha: □

Oscar Wilde: Poemas em Prosa.

Oscar Wilde: De Profundis.

Walter Pater: Epilogo da "Renanscença."

Rivarol: Dictos.

Sappho: Poemas extantes. (juntos ou separados).

Haikai japonezes.

Omar Khayyam: O Rubaiyat.

Keats: Ode a um Rouxinol.

Petronio: A Matrona de Epheso.

Swift: Conto de uma Celha

Schiller: O Sirio

(Camillo Pessanha: Poemas varios)

Vigny: Moisés.

❖ The project for this anthology was written on the same type of paper used by Pessoa in a personal diary, developed between February and March of 1913. See Pessoa, *Escritos autobiográficos, automáticos e de reflexão Pessoal* (Lisbon: Assírio & Alvim, 2003), 110–33 In this diary, some references to projects for editing Camilo Pessanha were included, together with notes describing the chronological progress of what Pessoa meant to be an extended article about Oscar Wilde. On Pessoa's production about Wilde between February and March of 1913, see Jorge Uribe, "Oscar Wilde, educação e teoria aristocrática: Um texto que era três," *Pessoa Plural* 2 (Fall 2012), 282–85; and Pessoa, *Apreciações literárias* (Lisbon: Imprensa Nacional–Casa da Moeda, 2013), 300–308.

3. BNP/E3, 48B–103ʳ [191-?]

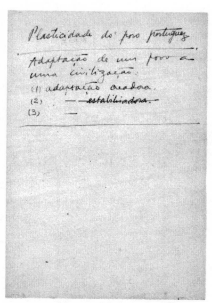

List of authors, manuscript, BNP/E3, 48B–103ʳ.

"Plasticidade do povo portuguez," manuscript, BNP/E3, 48B–103ᵛ.

G[eorge] B[ernard] Shaw: "Man and Superman."
Oscar Wilde: "Picture of Dorian Gray."
Walter Pater: □
G[ilbert] K[eith] Chesterton: "Heretics."
Remy de Gourmont: "Une nuit au Luxembourg."
Maurice Barrès: □
Rudolf Eucken: □
J[ohn] M[ackinon] Robertson: "Rationalism."
F[riedrich] Nietz[s]che:
Max Stirner: (O Unico)
Jules Gaultier: □
[. . .]

4. BNP/E3, 144D²–99ʳ [1915?] ❖

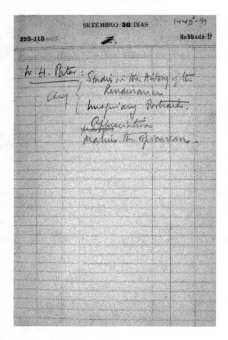

W. H. Pater's list of works, manuscript, BNP/E3, 144D²–99ʳ.

W. H. Pater:

Chief ⎰ Studies in the History of the Renaissance
⎱ Imaginary Portraits

~~Marius~~ Appreciations

Marius the Epicurean

❖ The notebook identified with the reference 144D² was considered by some editors as datable between 1914 and 1916. Pessoa, *Sensacionismo e outros ismos* (Lisbon: Imprensa Nacional–Casa da Moeda, 2010), 337. Moreover, the fact that in this list Pessoa writes the title that Pater only used in the first edition of *The Renaissance* could suggest that the list was written before Pessoa purchased his copy of the book.

5. BNP/E3, 55I–5ᵛ [1918–1921?] ❖

1. "A Decadencia da Mentira"—Oscar Wilde.

2. "Os Principais poemas de Edgar Poe."

3. "De 'A Renascença' de Walter Pater." Trechos Selectos.

/4. Selecta de Dryden./

5. Alguns Poemas de Matthew Arnold.

6. Os Poemas de José Anastacio da Cunha.

7. Selecta on "Phenix Renascida."

8. Da Anthologia Grega—(Ricardo Reis)

9. Wordsworth.

10. □

❖ Even though Pessoa probably had known the *Greek Anthology* since his school years in Durban, the acquisition, sometime after 1918, of an edition of that book seems to have enhanced the appearance of projects for translating that title. See Pessoa's copy of the *Greek Anthology* in his library, CFP 8–235. The occurrence of Ricardo Reis as translator is also found in Pessoa editorial projects of the period of Olisipo (Appendix II, 7).

6. BNP/E3, 481–9ʳ [1918–1921?] ❖

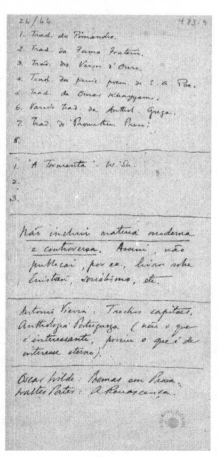

Editorial projects, manuscript, BNP/E3, 481–9ʳ.

1. Trad[ucção] do Pimandro.
2. Trad[ucção] da Fama Fraterni[tatis].
3. Trad[ucção] dos Versos d'Ouro.
4. Trad[ucção] dos princ[ipais] poem[as] de E[dgar] A[llan] Poe.
5. Trad[ucção] de Omar Khayyam.
6. Varias trad[uções] da Anthol[ogia] Grega.
7. Trad[ucção] do "Prometheu Preso."
8. □

Não incluir materia moderna ou controversa. Assim, não publicar, por
ex[emplo] livros sobre Einstein, socialismo, etc.

Antonio Vieira: Trechos Capitaes.
Anthologia Portugueza (não o que é interessante, porém o que é de interesse
eterno).

Oscar Wilde: Poemas em Prosa.
Walter Pater: A Renascença.

❖ Some of the titles in this list were also mentioned in Pessoa's editorial projects during the lifespan of his publishing company Olisipo, between 1920 and 1923 (Appendix II, 7). Pessoa actually published some translations of the *Greek Anthology* in *Athena*, but without authorial attribution. This could suggest that the lists mentioning that project were prior to that publication.

7. BNP/E3, 137A–21ʳ and 22ʳ [c. 1921] ❖
"Canções" (Antonio Botto), 2ª ediçaõ, augmentada.
"A Tormenta" (Shakespeare), trad[ucção], Fernando Pessoa.
[. . .]
Poemas de Sappho e de Alceu. Trad[ucção] Ricardo Reis.
"Trovas do Bandarra," com commentario interpretativo de Raphael Baldaya.
Poemas Anthologia Grega. (Sel[ecção]). Trad[ucção]. Ricardo Reis.

Poemas Principais de Edgar Poe. Trad[ucção] Fernando Pessoa.

"A Politica" (Aristoteles). Trad[ucção] Ricardo Reis.

[. . .]

"Mar Portuguez" (Fernando Pessoa).

"Cancioneiro, Liv. I e II." (Fernando Pessoa).

"Cancioneiro, Liv. III e IV." (Fernando Pessoa).

"Auto das Bacchantes" (Fernando Pessoa).

"Arco do Triumpho" (Alvaro de Campos).

"A Invenção do Dia Claro" (José de Almada-Negreiros).

"Indicios de Ouro" (Mario de Sá-Carneiro). Ed[ição] Fernando Pessoa. (ou "Poemas Completos," incluindo aquelle livro inedito, e outro ineditos que haja). (ou "Obras Completas de Mario de Sá-Carneiro," sendo o primeiro volume o dos "Poemas Completos," ut supra).

"A Idéa de Progresso" (J. B. Burry). Trad[ucção]

"Historia do Christianismo" (J. M. Robertson). Trad[ucção]

"A Renascença" (Walter Pater). Trad[ucção]

"Historia da Liberdade de Pensamento" (J. B. Burry). Trad[ucção]

"A Fabula das Abelhas" (Mandeville). Trad[ucção]

"Octavio." (Victoriano Braga).

❖ These titles are part of the extended list of editorial projects considered for Olisipo at the time of its foundation. The complete list was published for the first time in Ferreira, *Fernando Pessoa: O Comércio e a publicidade* (Lisbon: Cinevoz, 1986), 159–62.

8. No call number [after 1923] ❖

Traducções, typescript, Manuela Nogueira's private collection.

Printed copy of Alvaro de Campos's "Aviso por causa da moral," Manuela Nogueira's private collection.

Traducções.

O CORVO, de Edgar Poe.

ODE, de O'Shaughnessy.

A CIDADE NO MAR, de Edgar Poe.

A ULTIMA CAVALGADA, de Robert Browning.

O HOMEM E A COBRA, de Ambrose Bierce.

POEMAS EM PROSA, de Oscar Wilde.

A DECADENCIA DA MENTIRA, de Oscar Wilde.

EPILOGO, da "Renascença," de Walter Pater.

LEONARDO DA VINCI, de Walter Pater.

CARTA AO CONDE DE CHESTERFIELD, do Dr. Johnson.

DESCIDA AO MAELSTROM, de Edgar Poe.

A CAVALGADA ATÉ O MAR, de J. M. Synge.

A TERRA DOS CEGOS, de H[erbert] G[eorge] Wells.

A PORTA NO MURO, de H[erbert] G[eorge] Wells.

O SENHOR DO CASTELLO NEGRO, de Sir A[rthur] Conan Doyle.

A SOMBRA, de Edgar Poe.

STROPHES DA GRANDE CHARTREUSE, de Matthew Arnold.

ODE Á IMORTALIDADE, de William Wordsworth.

DE COMO NAPOLEÃO NUNCA EXISTIU, de J[ean] B[aptiste] Pérès.

MAXIMAS, de La Rochefoucauld.

O.Henry Caminhos do Destino.

❖ This list was written on the back of a printed page of "Aviso por causa da moral," a pamphlet signed by Álvaro de Campos and published in 1923, as a response to the confiscation by the police of Antonio Botto's and Raul Leal's books. Manuela Nogueira's private collection.

Appendix III: Translations

1. BNP/E3, 133F–90ᵛ [after Sept. 1916] ❖
Preface—beginning to middle p. XII.
La Gioconda—128–130
Conclusion—all

> ❖ The pages referred to in this project for an anthology of *The Renaissance* correspond to the exact pages of the book Pessoa purchased.

2. BNP/E3, 14⁵–79 [c. 1924] ❖
PAGINAS DE "A RENASCENÇA"
DE WALTER PATER

PREFACIO

Muitas são as tentativas, que teem feito os que escreveram sobre a arte e a poesia, de definir a belleza em abstracto, de exprimil-a em os termos mais ger-aes, de encontrar para ella uma formula universal. O valor d'estas tentativas tem sido principalmente o das cousas suggestivas e penetrantes dictas pelo caminho. Taes discussões muito pouco nos conduzem a gosar o que foi bem feito em arte ou em poesia, a distinguir o que em ellas é mais ou menos excellente, ou a usar de palavras como belleza, excellencia, arte, poesia com uma significação mais exacta do que antes para nós tiveram.

> ❖ This document and the following two were written with material characteristics similar to those that resulted in the more definite draft for the translation of Pater, which Pessoa published in *Athena*.

3. BNP/E3, 113P²–18ʳ and 19ʳ [c. 1924]
La *Gioconda* é, no mais verdadeiro dos sentidos, a obra prima de Leonardo, o exemplo revelador do seu modo de pensamento e de trabalho. Em suggestão, só a Melacholia de Dürer lhe é comparavel; e não ha rudeza de symbolismo que perturbe o effeito do seu mysterio esbatido e gracil. Todos nós conhecemos o rosto e as mãos da figura, posta na sua cadeira de marmore, naquelle circulo de rochedos fantasticos, como numa vaga luz de debaixo do mar. De todos os quadros antigos é talvez aquelle que o tempos menos esfriou. Como muitas

vezes acontece com as obras, em que a invenção parece chegar ao limite, he nella um elemento dado ao mestre, não inventado por elle. Naquelle inappreciavel folio de desenhos, em tempo possuido por Vasari, havia certos esboços de Verrochio, rostos de tão impressiva belleza que Leonardo na sua mocidade os copiou muitas vezes. É difficil não relacionar com estes desenhos do mestre mais velho, já do passado, como com o seu principio germinador, sorriso impenetravel, sempre laivado de qualquer cousa de sinistro, que paira por sobre toda a obra de Leonardo. Além d'isso, o quadro é um retrato. Desde a infancia vemos esta imagem definindo-se na materia dos seus sonhos; e se não fora o expresso testemunho historico, poderiamos crer que esta não passava de a sua dama ideal, corporizada e vista por fim. Que relação houve entre uma florentina real e esta creatura dos seus sonhos? Por que estranhas affinidades tinham o sonho e a pessoa crescido assim tão afastados, e todavia um do outro? Presente desde o começo incorporeamente no cerebro de Leonardo, esboçada vagamente nos desenhos de Verrochio, ella aparece por fim na casa de Il Giocondo. Que no quadro é muito que é simplesmente retrato, testifica-o a lenda de que por meios artificiaes, a presença de mimicos e de tocadores de flauta, aquella expressão subtil se demorou no rosto. E, ainda, seria em quatro annos e por um labor renovado que nunca na verdade completou, ou em quatro mezes e como por um golpe de magia, que a imagem se projectou?

A presença, que assim tão estranhamente surgiu de ao pé das aguas, é expressiva de aquillo que nos caminhos de milhares de annos os homens tinham vindo desejar. Aquella é a cabeça sobre a qual todos "os fins do mundo tinham vindo," e as palpebras estão um pouco cansadas. É uma belleza trabalhada de dentro sobre a carne, o deposito, cellula a cellula, de pensamentos estranhos e sonhos fantasticos e paixões exquisitas. Collocae-a um momento ao pé de uma d'aquellas brancas deusas gregas ou mulheres bellas da antiguidade, e como as perturbaria esta belleza, na qual entra já a alma com todas as suas doenças! Todos os pensamentos e a experiencia do mundo alli modelaram e gravaram, no que teem de poder de afinar e tornar expressiva a forma externa, o animalismo da Grecia, a luxuria de Roma, o mysticismo da edade media com a sua ambição espiritual e os seus amores imaginativos, o regresso do mundo pagão, os peccados dos Borgias. Ella é mais velha que os rochedos entre os quaes se senta; como o vampiro, morreu já muitas vezes, e aprendeu os segredos do tumulo; e mergulho em mares profundos e guarda em torno a si o seu dia morto; e trafficou em tecidos estranhos com os mercadores do Oriente; e, como Leda, foi a mãe de Helena de Troia, e, como Santa Anna, a mãe de Maria; e tudo isto não foi para ella mais que um som de lyras e de flautas, e vive apenas na delicadeza com que modelou as feições instaveis, e coloriu as palpebras e as mãos. É antiga a fantasia de uma vida perpetua, ajuntando dez mil experiencias; e a philosophia moderna concebeu a idéa da humanidade como trabalhada por, e congregando em si, todos os modos de pensamento e de vida. Porcerto a dama Lisa poderia valer como a personificação da antiga fantasia, o symbolo da idéa moderna.

Walter Pater, "A Renascença"

4. BNP/E3, 30A–9ʳ and 8ʳ [c. 1924]
LA GIOCONDA

DE WALTER PATER

(Traducção de Fernando Pessoa)

La Gioconda é, no mais verdadeiro dos sentidos, a obra-prima de Leonardo, o exemplo revelador do seu modo de pensamento e de trabalho. Em suggestão, só a Melacholia de Dürer lhe é comparavel; e não ha symbolismo cru que perturbe o effeito do seu mysterio esbatido e gracioso. Conhecemos todos o rosto e as mãos da figura, posta em sua cadeira de marmore, naquelle circulo de rochedos fantasticos, como em vaga luz submarina. Talvez de todos os quadros antigos seja aquelle que o tempos menos desbotou. Como muitas vezes acontece com obras em que dir-se-hia que a invenção parece chegou ao seu limite, he nella um elemento dado ao mestre, que não inventado por elle. Naquelle inestimavel folio de desenhos, que um tempo Vasari possuiu, havia certos esboços de Verrochio, rostos de belleza tão impressiva que Leonardo, jovem, muitas vezes os copiou. É difficil não relacionar com estes esboços do mestre preterito, como com seu principio germinal, o sorriso insondavel, sempre como tocado de qualquer cousa de sinistro, que paira por sobre toda a obra de Leonardo. Além d'isso, o quadro é um retrato. Desde a infancia vemos esta imagem definindo-se no estofo de seus sonhos; e, se não fôra o testimunho expresso da historia, puderamos pensar que esta não era esta mais que a sua dama ideal, por fim corporizada e vista. Que parentesco teve uma florentina real e esta creatura do seu pensamento? Por que estranhas affinidades assim cresceram separados o sonho e a pessoa, ainda que ligados de tão perto? Presente desde o principio incorporeamente no cerebro de Leonardo, delineada vagamente nos desenhos de Verrochio, ella encontra-se por fim presente na casa d' *Il Giocondo*. Que ha muito de simples retrato no quadro, attesta-o a lenda de que por meios artificias, a presença de mimos e de tocadores de flauta, se prolongou no rosto aquella expressão subtil. E, ainda, seria em quatro annos e por um trabalho renovado nunca em verdade findo, ou em quatro mezes e como por um golpe de magia, que a imagem se projectou?

A presença que assim tão estranhamente se ergueu de ao pé das aguas é expressiva d'aquillo que os homens, nos caminhos de um milhar de annos tinham chegado a desejar. Aquella é a cabeça sobre a qual "vieram todos os fins do mundo," e as palpebras estão um pouco cansadas. É uma belleza trabalhada de dentro sobre a carne, o deposito, cellula a cellula, de pensamentos estranhos, e devaneios fantasticos, e paixões exquisitas. Collocae-a um momento ao pé de uma d'essas brancas deusas da Grecia ou mulheres bellas da antiguidade, e como ellas se turbariam d'esta belleza, para onde entrou já a alma com todas as suas doenças! Todos os pensamentos e experiencia do mundo alli gravaram e modelaram, no que teem de poder de afinar e tornar expressiva a fórma exterior, o animalismo da Grecia, a luxuria de Roma, o mysticismo da Edade Media com a sua ambição espiritual e seus amores imaginativos, o regresso do mundo pagão, os peccados dos Borgias. Ella é mais velha que os rochedos entre os quaes se assenta; como o vampiro, morreu já muitas vezes, e apprendeu os segredos do tumulo; e mergulho em mares profundos, e guarda, cercando-a ainda, o seu dia morto; e trafficou em tecidos estranhos com os mercadores do Oriente; e, como Leda, foi mãe de Helena de Troia, e, como Santa Anna, a mãe de Maria; e tudo isto não foi para ella mais que um som de lyras e de flautas, e vive apenas na delicadeza com que lhe modelou as feições instaveis, e coloriu as palpebras e as mãos. A fantasia de uma vida perpetua, congregando dez mil experiencias, é antiga; e a philosophia moderna concebeu a idéa da humanidade como trabalhada por, e resumindo em si, todos os modos de pensamento e de vida. Porcerto a dama Lisa poderia valer como a incarnação da fantasia antiga, o symbolo da idéa moderna.

5. [published in *Athena* 2, Dec. 1924]

LA GIOCONDA

DE WALTER PATER

(Traducção de Fernando Pessoa)

La Gioconda é, no mais verdadeiro dos sentidos, a obra-prima de Leonardo, o exemplo revelador do seu modo de pensamento e de trabalho. Em suggestão, só a *Melancholia* de Durer lhe é comparavel; e não ha symbolismo crú que perturbe o effeito do seu mysterio esbatido e gracioso. Conhecemos todos o rosto e as mãos da figura, posta em sua cadeira de marmore, naquelle circulo de rochedos fantasticos, como em vaga luz de sob o mar. Talvez de todos os quadros antigos seja aquelle que o tempo menos desbotou. Como muitas vezes acontece com obras em que dir-se-hia que a invenção chegou a seu limite, ha nella um elemento dado ao mestre, que não inventado por elle. Naquelle inestimavel folio de desenhos, que um tempo Vasari possuiu, havia certos esboços de Verrocchio, rostos de belleza tão expressiva que Leonardo, jovem, muitas vezes os copiou. E' difficil não relacionar com estes esboços do mestre preterito, como com seu principio germinal, o sorriso insondavel, sempre como tocado de qualquer cousa de sinistro, que paira em toda a obra de Leonardo. Além d'isso, o quadro é um retrato. Desde a infancia vemos esta imagem definindo-se no estofo de seus sonhos; e, se não fôra o testimunho expresso da historia, puderamos pensar que não era esta mais que a sua dama ideal, por fim corporizada e vista. Que parentesco teve uma florentina real com esta creatura de seu pensamento? Por que extranhas affinidades assim cresceram separados o sonho e a pessoa, ainda que ligados de tão perto? Presente desde o principio incorporeamente no cerebro de Leonardo, delineada vagamente nos desenhos de Verrocchio, ella encontra-se por fim presente em casa d'*Il Giocondo*. Que ha muito de simples retrato no quadro, attesta-o a lenda de que, por meios artificiaes, a presença de mimos e de tocadores de flauta, se prolongou no rosto aquella expressão subtil. E, ainda, seria em quatro annos e por um trabalho renovado nunca em verdade findo, ou em quatro mezes e como por um golpe de magia, que a imagem assim se projectou?

A presença que assim tão extranhamente se ergueu de ao pé das aguas é expressiva d'aquillo que os homens, nos caminhos de um milhar de annos, tinham chegado a desejar. Aquella é a cabeça sobre a qual «vieram todos os fins do mundo», e as palpebras estão um pouco cansadas. E' uma belleza trabalhada de dentro sobre a carne, o deposito, cellula a cellula, de pensamentos extranhos, e devaneios fantasticos, e paixões exquisitas. Collocae-a um momento ao pé de uma d'essas brancas deusas da Grecia ou mulheres bellas da antiguidade, e como ellas se turbariam d'esta belleza, para onde entrou já a alma com todas as suas doenças! Todos os pensamentos e experiencia do mundo alli gravaram e modelaram, no que teem de poder de refinar e tornar expressiva a forma exterior, o animalismo da Grecia, a luxuria de Roma, o mysticismo da Edade Media com sua ambição espiritual e seus amores imaginativos, o regresso do mundo pagão, os peccados dos Borgias. Ella é mais velha que os rochedos, entre os quaes se assenta; como o vampiro, morreu já muitas vezes, e apprendeu os segredos do tumulo; e mergulhou em mares profundos, e guarda, cercando-a ainda, o seu dia morto; e trafficou em tecidos extranhos com os mercadores do Oriente; e, como Leda, foi mãe de Helena de Troia, e, como Santa Anna, foi mãe de Maria; e tudo isto não foi para ella mais que um som de lyras e de flautas, e vive apenas na delicadeza com que lhe modelou as feições instaveis, e lhe coloriu as palpebras e as mãos. A fantasia de uma vida perpetua, congregando dez mil experiencias, é antiga; e a philosophia moderna concebeu a idéa da humanidade como trabalhada por, e resumindo em si, todos os modos de pensamento e de vida. Por certo que a Dama Lisa poderia ficar como a incarnação da fantasia antiga, o symbolo da idéa moderna.

58

"La Gioconda de Walter Pater," printed version in *Athena* 2, 1924.

Appendix IV: References

1. BNP/E3, 144C–12 and 13ᵛ [1916?] ❖

A descripção de uma estatua, feita em linguagem bella, é absolutamente essa estatua, com toda a sua belleza plastica *mais* o movimento, o rhythmo vivo, o *som* correspondente ao rhythmo, na pedra parada e morta, das suas linhas.

Todos os assumptos são bons—tanto os modernos como os antigos, os naturaes como os artificiaes, os do exterior como os da alma.

A literatura antiga é por vezes bella, mas sempre insufficiente. É, sobretudo, sempre antiga.

Dar á literatura o seu papel de arte unica e absoluta, fazendo-a ter: *architectura* na perfeita e bella estructura e construcção do *todo* da obra literaria e no arranjo constructivo das partes e das partes para com o todo; *esculptura* no perfeito recorte dos periodos e das idéas dadas; *pintura* na energia-côr com que as suggestões são insinuadas; *musica* no rhythmo das phrases componentes da obra, no rhythmo dos versos ou da prosa em que está escripta; *metaphysica* nas idéas—todas ellas cheias, inevitavelmente, porque são idéas, de theorias das cousas que a obra tem.

Quando Walter Pater descreve a Gioconda vê n'ella cousas que lá não estão. Mas a sua descripção é mais bella do que a Gioconda porque é *Gioconda + musica* (rhythmo da prosa) + *idéas* (as contidas nas palavras da descripção) + □

Todo o exhibicionismo é ordinario e vulgar. Cultivamos o aristocratismo do desprezo.

A pintura, a musica, etc. são confissões de impotencia artistica, porque não são a literatura.

❖ Published in Pessoa, *Sensacionismo e outros ismos* (Lisbon: Imprensa Nacional–Casa da Moeda, 2009), 282–84. Jerónimo Pizarro argued that the notebook 144C was used between 1914 and 1916. See Pessoa, *Sensacionismo e outros ismos*, 279. Pizarro also divided the text in two parts, separating the paragraph that is explicitly about Pater from the one that is implicitly about him. Here the entire text is presented as continuous.

2. BNP/E3, 20–100ʳ [1916?] ❖

[. . .]

Como expressão da dysgenica da guerra, apparecerão correntes ultra-decadentes, interpretativas do abatimento em que grande parte ficará. São trez essas correntes, consoante reajam contra o spirito de organização, contra o spirito revolucionario, ou contra os dois simultaneamente. O primeiro typo de decadentismo será uma continuação, differente por novas individualisações apenas, d'aquella parte do decadentismo que representa uma revolta contra as regras, uma introspecção excessiva. O segundo typo de decadentismo será uma continuação d'aquelle typo de decadentismo que mais se occupa em crear uma indifferença aos problemas do meio, do que em se entregar á introspecção propriamente. O primeiro partirá de Verlaine, como o segundo de Mallarmé ou dos chamados esthetas ingleses, Pater ou Wilde. O terceiro typo de decadentismo é que trará novidades; será uma exacerbação dos dois reunidos: qualquer prenuncio d'elle surgiu, de resto, já antes da guerra, na corrente portugueza que viu [veio] depois a manifestar-se em ORPHEU.

[. . .]

❖ Published in Pessoa, *Páginas íntimas e de auto-interpretação* (Lisbon: Ática, 1966), 176. This document was also published with corrections and improvements in Pessoa, *Sensacionismo e outros ismos*, 420. In both editions the date "1916?" was considered as a hypothesis for the text.

3. BNP/E3, 21–10 [c.1917] ❖
Prefacio de Ricardo Reis:

[. . .]

Reconstruir o paganismo involve, pois, como primeira acção intellectual, fazer renascer o objectivismo puro dos gregos e dos romanos. Tudo o mais que se tente não passa de reproducção esteril dos elementos secundarios ou mesmo acessorios do paganismo antigo. Porisso nunca houve, adentro da civilização christan, tentativa alguma que de pagan mereça o nome, embora varias tenha havido com sobradas pretensões nesse respeito. Não exemplifiquemos exhaustivamente, que a tarefa, sobre ser inutil, seria penosamente longa. Enumerar todo o lixo christão com pretensões pagans dos Matthew Arnolds, dos Oscar Wildes e dos Walter Paters do baixo-christismo, seria enfadonho e desolador. Esta gente julgava estar com os antigos quando ia de encontro ao christismo por o que ellas [elles] chamariam razões estheticas; não passam de discipulos christãos, nem sequer do paganismo, mas apenas de certas escolas philosophias que o paganismo produziu. Epicuristas christãos, hedonistas catholicos, stoicos de um portico judeu, deixemol-os na podridão estulta dos que quizeram acceitar os deuses sem saber de que materia elles eram feitos, dos que quizeram seguir os philosophos da antiguidade, no que elles tinham de essencial, sem saber o que é que elles tinham de essencial, nem por que caminho iam.

[. . .]

❖ Published in Pessoa, *Poemas completos de Alberto Caeiro* (Lisbon: Presença, 1994), 186–87.

4. BNP/E3, 21–16 and 17 [c. 1917] ❖

Prefacio de Ricardo Reis:

[. . .]

Encaremos, agora, o paganismo greco-romano do ponto de vista em que é vulgar comparal-o ao christismo: isto é, da sua pretensa amoralidade, ou im-moralidade mesmo. Esta immoralidade, a que a ignorancia moderna se atém, apoiada ou em cultos que contrastam com a severidade do culto cristão, ou em que a expressão da moral pagan é, no geral, menos severa e menos espiritual que a cristista, provém simplesmente de que se considera moral o christismo, passando, portanto, a serem immorais os não-christismos todos. No erro teem cahido, com um descuido systematico, quantos, quer propondo-se ser christãos, quer propondo-se ser anti-christãos, quer defendendo a moral christã, quer procurando defender a immoralidade suposta anti-christan. É um erro crasso que subjaz os debeis pensamentos de tais como o "estheta" Wilde ou o seu mestre Pater; a ignorancia da substancia do paganismo basta para explical-a.

❖ Published in Pessoa, *Páginas íntimas e de auto-interpretação* (Lisbon: Ática, 1966), 245.

5. BNP/E3, 21–91^r [c. 1917] ❖

R[icardo] Reis on Caeiro.

Das tentativas de paganismo, que o seculo passado produziu, não ha uma que não sofra de ser cristã. Mesmo Walter Pater, que unia a um perfeito enten-dimento do paganismo, um perfeito desejo de ser pagão, não passou de um cristão doente com ansias de paganismo.

A compreensão do paganismo, e o amor das verdades pagãs não bastam para fabricar um pagão. Um homem pode compreender por optima a profissão mil-itar, e sentil-a por magnifica; e contudo ser falho de spirito de comando e de coragem physica. Ha uma sensibilidade da inteligencia, e ha uma sensibilidade de temperamento. Podem estar em desacordo, embora em geral o não estejam.

❖ Published in Pessoa, *Páginas íntimas e de auto-interpretação* (Lisbon: Ática, 1966), 352. The date attributed to the text was "1916?." The present hypothesis considers that choice, but also accepts an approximation of this document to others texts and projects from a later period, even from the be-ginning of 1918. This same argument applies to the two following documents, related with Ricardo Reis's preface to the works of Alberto Caeiro.

6. BNP/E3, 12A–16[c. 1918]

Prefacio ~~Ricardo Reis~~ Antonio Móra

Ad Finem

[. . .]

Não nos deixemos, porém, arrastar pela comprehensão de quanto o nosso spiritu se não com a nossa epocha. É justo que nos isolemos, porque o que podemos dar a este mundo, ello não o quere; nem elle nos pode dar aquillo que, se pedissemos, lhe pediriamos. Não podemos, pois, como pagãos participar da vida da cidade, ou das cousas da epocha activamente. Até este punto é justa e propria a nossa attitude negativa [. . .]

De outro modo não seremos dignos da statura de pagãos, nem do nome, que devemos merecer, de servos dos Deuses, de escravos submissos do universal Destino. Seremos apenas homens de um periodo de decadencia, superiores pelo instincto da libertação, mas /não/ pela practica, dentro em nós, d'esse instincto.

Digo isto porque tão altos e claros spriritus como Caeiro e Ricardo Reis não deixaram de peccar neste poncto. A que fim supremos serve dizer—e antes de dizer, pensar—como Caeiro □

Que nobreza ha na frase impia de Ricardo Reis:

Prefiro rosas, [meu amor, á] patria?

ou no estulto e jactancioso epodo em que se vangloria de não se importar com as guerras e as crises dos homens, antepondo-lhes um jogo de xadrez?

Em que se distinguem estas □ das mais characteristicas efusões dos baixos "decadentes" do christismo, dos Paters, dos Wildes da nossa Bizancio universal? [. . .]

❖ Published in Pessoa, *Obras de António Mora* (Lisbon: Imprensa Nacional–Casa da Moeda, 2002), 242. The editor does not offer a possible date for the text. However, keeping in mind that this text seems to constitute an evolution from Ricardo Reis's original point of view, an approximate date of 1918 seems plausible.

7. BNP/E3, 21–43ʳ [c. 1918] ❖

Antonio Mora

Não somos, na verdade, neo-pagãos, nem pagãos novos. O paganismo é a religião que nasce da terra, da natureza direitamente—que nasce da attribuição a cada objecto da sua realidade verdadeira. [. . .]

Que se designassem, a si-mesmos, neo-pagãos aquelles christãos rebeldes, como Pater e Swinburne, que nada tinham de pagãos, senão o desejo de o ser— conceda-se porque não é falta de razão que se dê um nome impossivel a uma coisa absurda. Mas nós, que somos pagãos, não podemos usar um nome que indique que o somos como "modernos," ou que viemos "reformar" ou "recon-struir" o paganismo dos gregos. Viemos ser pagãos. Renasceu, em nós o pagan-ismo. Mas, o paganismo que renasceu em nós é o paganismo que sempre houve, a subordinação aos deuses como a justiça da Terra para consigo mesma[.] [. . .]

❖ Published in Pessoa, *Páginas íntimas e de auto-interpretação* (Lisbon: Ática, 1966), 286; and with corrections and improvements in Pessoa, *Obras de Antonio Mora* (Lisbon: Imprensa Nacional–Casa da Moeda, 2002), 210–11.

8. BNP/E3, 14⁴–47ʳ [192-?] ❖

[. . .]

Literary finish is not indispensable α [and] a catalogue written in the style of Arnold or of Pater would presumably be, not be bad, but unnecessarily good. Still there is a limit to the non-literary element admissible in these cases, [and] that limit is *intensified by grammatical and idiomatic accuracy and clearness and flow in style. The best descriptions of goods or medicines [and] the best advertisements of them, are breed on no other principle.

❖ The transcription of this text is offered by Pauly Ellen Bothe. The hypothetical date for the document is related to the presence, on the back of the page, of a project for a "Commercial Guide," also part of Olisipo's projects. However, on the same page, notes are present for what seems to be an article, or even a detective story, about the authorship of Shakespeare's *Sonnets*, perhaps associat-ing this text with several periods of Pessoa's writing, between the 1910s and 1930s.

10. BNP/E3, 133J–9ᵛ [1918?] ❖
Pater

Of all that modern times have said, only Pater will remain, [because] he tells us why it was said.

❖ This text was written on the same sheet of paper that contains a fragment belonging to the essay "Impermanence," and it was included as a note in an edition of the drafts for that essay re-united by Richard Zenith, in Pessoa, *Heróstrato e a busca da imortalidade* (Lisbon: Assírio & Alvim, 2000), 245. Zenith has remarked that the essay was developed during the second half of the decade beginning in 1910, and some lists of projects that mention it can be dated to 1918.

10. BNP/E3, 19–106ʳ [after Oct. 1924] ❖
Anatole France

Não, não era um diletante. Prouvera aos deuses que o fôra! Anatole France era apenas um dilletante amador. Tinha do dilletante (excepto no que diz respeito á doença cancerosa, o communismo, de que soffria) o scepticismo, que nasce de se saber que todas as doutrinas são igualmente defensaveis, valendo cada uma, não o que vale, senão o que vale o defensor; a curiosidade, que sabe que em tudo ha tudo; e, aquella flôr suprema da cultura a que se chama o humanismo, assim definido, uma vez para sempre, por Pater □

O dilletantismo verdadeiro vae, porém, adeante da simples curiosidade pela superficie de tudo: desce á essencia das cousas, e é passageiramente intenso e sincero com cada uma d'ellas. O grande dilletente vive profundamente, com o pensamento e com a emoção, todos os aspectos que pode da realidade illusoria. Dilletanti foram Goethe e Shakespeare, nem ha dilletante maior que este, que viveu os typos mais differentes de humanidade com egual esplendor de imaginação e de intelligencia.

[. . .]

❖ Published in Pessoa, *Páginas de estética e de teoria e crítica literárias* (Lisbon: Ática, 1967), 345. The first editors attributed it to 1914, perhaps by typographical mistake. The text was written after the death of Anatole France, in October of 1924.

11. ["Antonio Botto e o ideal esthetico em Portugal," *Contemporanea*, nº3, 1922]

[. . .] Como se guia, pois, só pela belleza o estheta canta de preferencia o corpo masculino, por ser o corpo humano que mais elementos de belleza, dos poucos que ha, pode accumular.

Foi assim que pensaram os gregos; foi esse pensamento que Winckelmann, fundador do esthetismo na Europa, descobrindo-o nelles, reproduziu, como no passo celebre que Pater transcreveu, e que parece feito para servir de prefacio a um livro como *Canções*:

"Como é confessadamente a belleza do homem que tem de ser concebida sob uma idéa geral, assim tenho notado que aquelles que observam a belleza só nas mulheres, e pouco ou nada se commovem com a belleza dos homens, raras vezes teem um insitnto imparcial, vital, innato da belleza na arte. A pessoas como essas a belleza da arte grega parecerá sempre falha, porque a sua belleza suprema é antes masculina que feminina."

[. . .] o apparecimento na Europa moderna de um typo integro de estheta só pode dar-se por um desvio pathologico, isto é, por uma inadaptação estructural aos principios constitutivos da civilização europeia, em que vivemos.

Este desvio pathologico é, porém, no caso dos grandes esthetas europeus o elemento predisponente, se bem que, por isso mesmo, radical, do seu esthetismo; a elle se accrescenta uma mergencia prolongada do espirito na atmosphera da cultura hellenica, que lhe cria um perpetuo contacto, ainda que só intellectual, com a Grecia antiga e os seus ideaes. Da acção d'este segundo elemento sobre o primeiro o estheta desabrocha. São d'esta origem os esthetismo de Winckelmann e de Pater, quasi, em verdade, os unicos typos exactos do estheta que a civilização europeia pode apresentar. Como, porém este esthetismo tem uma base cultural, resulta que tem a plenitude e a largueza que distinguem todos os productos culturaes, em contraposição aos naturaes seus similhantes, e porisso de algum modo transcende a estreiteza especifica do ideal esthetico, sem todavia deixar de lhe pertencer.

[. . .]

A dentro do ideal esthetico, os casos de Winckelmann e de Pater representam o genio, porque a tendencia para a realização cultural immanente no seu esthetismo ingenito é, por sua natureza, synthetica; o caso de Antonio Botto representa o talento, porque o ideal esthetico, dada a sua estreiteza e vacuidade, represente já o senso esthetico isolado de todos os outros elementos psychicos, e, no caso de Antonio Botto, estheta simples, esse isolamento não se modifica, como no esthetismo culto, pelo reflexo nelle da multiplicidade dos objectos de cultura. [. . .]

12. BNP/E3, 138A–11ʳ [c. 1929] ❖

Uma interpretação ironica da vida, uma acceitação indifferente das cousas, são o melhor remedio para o soffrimento, posto que não sejam para as razões que ha para soffrer.

Walter Pater.—A vida [humana] é um tumulto de valores. A critica é uma appreciação de valores.

❖ This text has been associated by some editors with *Livro do desassossego*, and was published in Pessoa, *Livro do desasocego* (Imprensa Nacional–Casa da Moeda, 2012), 513. But the editor, Jerónimo Pizarro, has explained that the text should not be considered part of that work.

Appendix V: Varia

1. BNP/E3, 14⁴–55ʳ and 56ʳ [after 1915] ❖

List of authors, including ages at their death, manuscript, BNP/E3, 14⁴–55ʳ.

List of authors, including ages at their death, manuscript, BNP/E3, 14⁴–56ʳ.

❖ The year 1915 is part of a bibliographic reference on the other side of the paper. This is a list of famous men and their ages when they died. The purpose of a list of this kind is not clear.

PATRICIO FERRARI AND CARLOS PITTELLA-LEITE

Four Unpublished English Sonnets
(and the Editorial Status of Pessoa's English Poetry)

ABSTRACT: We present a brief account of the publication history of Pessoa's English poetry, along with four unpublished sonnets (1907, 1914, 1921, and 1933), each dating from a different decade and accompanied by a corresponding facsimile from the archive at the National Library of Portugal. This evidence dispels the mistaken assumption that Pessoa had discontinued writing English verse by 1920 and enables us to make a strong case for the need to produce a complete critical edition of the unpublished English poems.

KEYWORDS: Fernando Pessoa, critical edition, unpublished English poetry, sonnet

Referring to Pessoa as the "Rei da nossa Baviera"[1] ("King of Our Bavaria"[2]) Eduardo Lourenco captures the essence of what our greatest poet since Camões has become. Although the expression may be half serious, half humorous, the fact remains that Pessoa's literary estate was finally accorded the status of Portuguese national treasure in 2009.[3] Today, eighty years after his death, interest in his works continues to grow, within and beyond the Iberian Peninsula.

It was Pessoa's Portuguese works that led Harold Bloom to include the author's name in The Western Canon.[4] Yet, when juxtaposing Pessoa with such paragons of modernism as Borges, Neruda, and Whitman, Bloom underscored this facet of the Portuguese poet's early life: "Pessoa, born in Lisbon and descended on the paternal side from Jewish conversos, was educated in South Africa and, like Borges, grew up bilingual. Indeed, until he was twenty-one, he wrote poetry only in English."[5]

There is growing evidence that Pessoa wrote in multiple languages before 1909, and not "only in English" (as Bloom asserts). Indeed, by the end of 1908 he had produced more lines of verse in English (and French)[6] than in his native Portuguese—a fact that remains largely unknown, since Pessoa's English poetry is still largely unpublished.

Publication of Pessoa's English Poetry: A Brief Overview

Most readers would agree that Pessoa wrote his best poetry in Portuguese. Nonetheless, the first book he submitted for publication was *The Mad Fiddler*, a collection of English poems that the London publisher Constable and Company turned down in 1917. Disappointed, though not discouraged, Pessoa reacted quickly and, within a year, self-published two chapbooks of English poetry in Lisbon: *Antinous* and *35 Sonnets*. Three years later, in 1921, he published *English Poems I–II* (a revised version of *Antinous* plus *Inscriptions*) and *English Poems III* (*Epithalamium*). These two slim volumes were issued by Olisipo, the publishing house founded by Pessoa that same year. In addition to these works, and in spite of his vast English output, Pessoa published only two other English poems in his lifetime, one in London and the other in Lisbon.[7]

Following publication of these works, only in the second half of the twentieth century did more of his English poetry become available. The most important editorial contributions are listed here,[8] chronologically:

Fernando Pessoa. *Obra poética*. Intro. and annot. Maria Aliete Dores Galhoz.
    Rio de Janeiro: José Aguilar, 1960.
Georg Rudolf Lind. "Die englische Jugenddichtung Fernando Pessoas." In
    Aufsätze zur portugiesischen Kulturgeschichte, comp. Hans Flasche. Bd. 6
    (Westfalen: Aschendorffsche Verlagsbuchhandlung, 1966), 130–63.
———. "Descobertas no espólio de Fernando Pessoa." In *Separata da Revista
    "Ocidente"* 70 (334) (Lisbon, Feb. 1966): 57–62.
———. "9 unbekannte englische Gedichte F. Ps, Diskussion und
    Kommentar von Ulrich Suerbaum und Vf." In *Poetica* 2 (2) (Munich, Apr.
    1968): 229–36.
———. "Oito poemas ingleses inéditos de Fernando Pessoa." In *Ocidente* 74
    (362) (Lisbon, June 1968): 266–90.
———. "Fernando Pessoa perante a primeira guerra mundial." In *Ocidente*
    72 (405) (Lisbon, Jan. 1972): 425–58.
Pessoa, Fernando. *Poemas ingleses: Antinous, inscriptions, epithalamium, 35
    Sonnets e dispersos*. Bilingual edition. Ed. and annot. Jorge de Sena, Trans.

Jorge de Sena, Adolfo Casais Monteiro and José Blanc de Portugal. Lisbon: Ática, 1974.

———. *O Louco rabequista*. Trans. and annot. José Blanc de Portugal. Lisbon: Presença, 1988.

———. *Il violinista pazzo*. Ed. Aminadi Munno. Rome: Lucarini, 1989.

Crespo, Ángel. "El último amor de Fernando Pessoa." *Revista de Occidente* 94 (Madrid, Mar. 1989): 5–26.

———. *Pessoa inédito*. Ed.. Teresa Rita Lopes. Lisbon: Livros Horizonte, 1993.

———. *Poemas ingleses: Antinous, inscriptions, epithalamium, 35 sonnets*. Ed. João Dionísio. Fernando Pessoa Critical Edition. Lisbon: Imprensa Nacional–Casa da Moeda, Major Series, 1993, Vol. V, Part I.

———. *Poesia inglesa*. Ed. and trans. Luísa Freire. Lisbon: Livros Horizonte, 1995.

———. *Poemas ingleses. Poemas de Alexander Search*. Ed. João Dionísio. Fernando Pessoa Critical Edition. Lisbon: Imprensa Nacional–Casa da Moeda, Major Series, 1997, Vol. V, Part II.

———. *Poemas ingleses: The Mad Fiddler*. Ed. Marcus Angioni and Fernando Gomes. Fernando Pessoa Critical Edition. Lisbon: Imprensa Nacional–Casa da Moeda, Major Series, 1999, Vol. V, Part III.

———. *Poesia inglesa II*. Ed. and trans. Luísa Freire. Lisbon: Assírio & Alvim, 2000.

———. *Obra essencial de Fernando Pessoa: Poesia inglesa*. Ed. Richard Zenith, trans. Luísa Freire. Lisbon: Assírio & Alvim, 2007, Vol. VI.

———. *Cadernos*. Ed. Jerónimo Pizarro. Fernando Pessoa Critical Edition. Lisbon: Imprensa Nacional–Casa da Moeda, Major Series, 2009, Vol. XI, Part I.

———. *No Matter What We Dream: Selected English Poems*. Edited and selected by Patricio Ferrari and Jerónimo Pizarro. 2nd ed. Lisbon: Tell-a-Story, 2015.

In the introduction to the first part of Pessoa's *Poesia inglesa* (English Poetry), published in 1993 by the Imprensa Nacional–Casa da Moeda (INCM), João Dionísio, the editor, presented a plan for the systematic publication of Pessoa's

English poetry: "A parte da obra poética de Fernando Pessoa escrita em língua inglesa é tão extensa que não cabe nos limites de um livro, por grande que seja. Assim, o volume V da Edição Crítica, dedicado aos *Poemas ingleses*, será dividido em vários tomos, dos quais este é o primeiro. Nos tomos subsequentes, prevê-se a publicação de *Mad Fiddler*, dos poemas de Search e da restante poesia inglesa." (The number of English poems in Pessoa's overall output is so vast that it would not fit within the confines of a single book, however large it might be. Thus, Volume 5 of the critical edition, dedicated to the *English Poems*, will be divided into various parts, of which this is the first. In the subsequent parts, we expect to publish *The Mad Fiddler*, the poems by Search, and Pessoa's remaining English poetry.)[9]

As of 1999, INCM had published three English parts (under Vol. 5), but none contained "Pessoa's remaining English poetry." It is noteworthy that more than 50 percent of Pessoa's English poems remain unpublished. The number of texts represented by this percentage is by no means insignficant, given that the English poetry published to date (both during Pessoa's lifetime and posthumously) amounts to approximately 240 poems.[10]

Luísa Freire's 2000 edition *Poesia inglesa II* constitutes the only significant editorial attempt at publishing this corpus with ninety-six poems, forty-nine of which were previously unpublished.[11] Since 2000, other previously unpublished English poems have been printed: five in Zenith's edition dating from 2007; and eight by Ferrari and Pizarro in 2015.

In spite of these editorial efforts, much of Pessoa's English poetry remains unpublished. As Jerónimo Pizarro observed in 2012: "Estamos a falar de um total de 1338 originais [em Inglês], de acordo com o *Inventário* do espólio de Fernando Pessoa, que não tem, infelizmente, perdido grande actualidade: na verdade, quase toda a poesia inventariada como inédita em 1986 continua hoje, em 2012, ainda sem publicação"[12] (We are talking about a total of 1,338 originals in English. This is in accordance with the 1986 inventory of Pessoa's estate. Unfortunately, very little has changed with regard to the English poetry, since nearly all of it remains unpublished as of 2012).

This number provided by Pizarro takes into account only the documents grouped under the category "Poemas inéd[itos] ingl[eses]" (unpublished English poems), labeled by the Biblioteca Nacional de Portugal (BNP [National Library of Portugal]), where Pessoa's estate is housed.[13] We should note that other unpublished English poems have been found in other parts of Pessoa's estate, separate from this labeled group (for example, "There Was a Wonderful . . ."[14] and "The Real Nature of the Universe").[15]

Regarding Pessoa's Condemning "his English self to total literary silence after 1921"

In 1963, the American poet and translator Edouard Roditi said the following about Pessoa as an English poet: "Had he continued to express himself in English after 1920, he might well have become one of the more outstanding English poets of our age. Instead, he seems, a kind of Rimbaud, to have condemned his English self to total literary silence after 1921 and to have then expressed himself, until his death in 1935, only in Portuguese."[16]

In 2000, almost half a century later, Luísa Freire undermined Roditi's claim by publishing an edition of Pessoa's English poems, nine of which were dated between 1922 and 1935. In fact, a thorough examination of the BNP documents labeled "unpublished English poems" proves that a posthumous publication of Pessoa's English poetry would far exceed the nine poems published by Freire.

By presenting four unpublished sonnets of Pessoa, one for each decade in which he wrote English poetry, we intend both to illustrate that Pessoa continued writing in English after 1921 (as opposed to what Roditi and Lind[17] affirmed) and to suggest that one can still find poems that advance our understanding of his work as a whole. These four sonnets, none of which is attributed to any fictitious authors, are a microcosm of Pessoa's unpublished English poetry: they are mostly (but not exclusively) composed of documents difficult to decipher, somewhat incomplete, but rich in poetic motifs, rhythms, and literary influences.

The first sonnet (datable to 1907) is remarkably legible in comparison to the average manuscript in the Pessoa archive. It is a Petrarchan sonnet (an octave followed by a sestet), a form that Pessoa likely encountered while reading Milton's sonnets in Durban. This unfinished piece is reminiscent of John Keats's "When I have fears that I may cease to be,"[18] in which the speaker's fears of not fulfilling his life as a writer are intertwined with the idea of losing his beloved.[19] Though both poets develop a meditative soliloquy on mortality, Keats's sonnet ends in defiance, and Pessoa's in pessimism.

Written seven years later, the second poem is a Shakespearean sonnet (three quatrains followed by a final couplet). In the opening line it addresses the reader in a game of pretense that echoes Pessoa's famous poem "Autopsycographia" ("Autopsycography").[20] Both the faked "dor" (pain) of "Autopsycographia" and the "bitterness" expressed in this unpublished sonnet are suggestive of Pessoa's poetics of feigning, central to the heteronymic scheme.

The third sonnet, dating from 1921 (also in the Shakespearean form), is a virtuosic play on the word *hope* (occurring eight times in the poem). The labyrinthine syntax evokes both the "ultra-Shakespearianisms"[21] of Pessoa's 35 *Sonnets* and the "conceptism"[22] of the baroque tradition in Spanish and Portuguese.

The last sonnet presented here, dating from 1933, also Shakespearean in form, depicts a theme that reverberates in Pessoa's mystic fable "Eros e Psyque," poem published in 1934[23]—another path for exploration, because Pessoa could have been drafting ideas in English to develop a year later in Portuguese. Playing with the verb *to know*, the sonnet ends in a way that invites comparison with the poet's last known phrase, penned on November 29, 1935, at the French S. Luis Hospital: "I know not what to-morrow will bring."[24] The tone of this sonnet is different from that of the previous three. The language is devoid of awkward compound word coinages and the speaker no longer constructs a complex web of word play and paradoxical conceits. Whether these traits become a pattern in the later English poems, only a complete transcription and further study of the unpublished English verse will confirm or disprove such a reading.

Four Unpublished Sonnets by Fernando Pessoa

Were I to die even upon this day
2   What would I leave in this great world & vain
   That looking once upon it men might say,
   Here is a thing to lessen our deep pain?

5   I would leave nothing. Men have had no gain
   From the brief while that I on earth did stay.
7   Within the sea I was a drop of rain
8   A useless wanderer on life's common way.

   I have come here to suffer and to die
10 To seek for things the world containeth not
   And having [   ]

12 Like worms and beasts to [   ] & to rot
   And fill some poet's mind that wanders by
14 With a face-saddening most use-painless thought.

"Were I to die even upon this day," manuscript, BNP/E3, 49A¹–32ʳ.

The bitterness thou readest on my lips
That seemeth yet a salt of bitterness
3 Like the faint trace of longing's finger-tips
4 On the touched soul Time-dust-strewn with Distress—

5 This sad expression of not saying aught
6 Which does perplex thee as if aught it said,
7 I bear it not as banner of my Thought,
8 Nay, nor as ship's trail of a far-off Dread.

No. I myself know not what cares I bear,
10 *Some that a deep, life-seated weary sense
11 Of life doth show me that all in me is care,
And show of too much a small care pretense

For neither doth my care have *measure size
14 Nor doth its mere pretense deceive my eyes . . .

"The bitterness thou readest on my lips," manuscript, BNP/E3, 49A³–58ʳ.

Hope without means to hope is drunkard's ease.
Who (like a prisoner in a time-shut cell
3   That does by sleep, not flight, obtain release)
Hopes but by hope, hopes too exactly well.

5   Our human law cannot put flesh & fact
In the corner of having. We must keep
7   With carnal earth a presence of contact
8   And give away again the gifts of sleep.

Some substance, if hope fail of being more,
10   Let us give hope by will, thus ourselves making
11   The reason to hope, our act being the shore
Where to return from too adventurous seeking.

13   Our purpose shall supply what the world lacks
And print its sign on its own prepared wax.

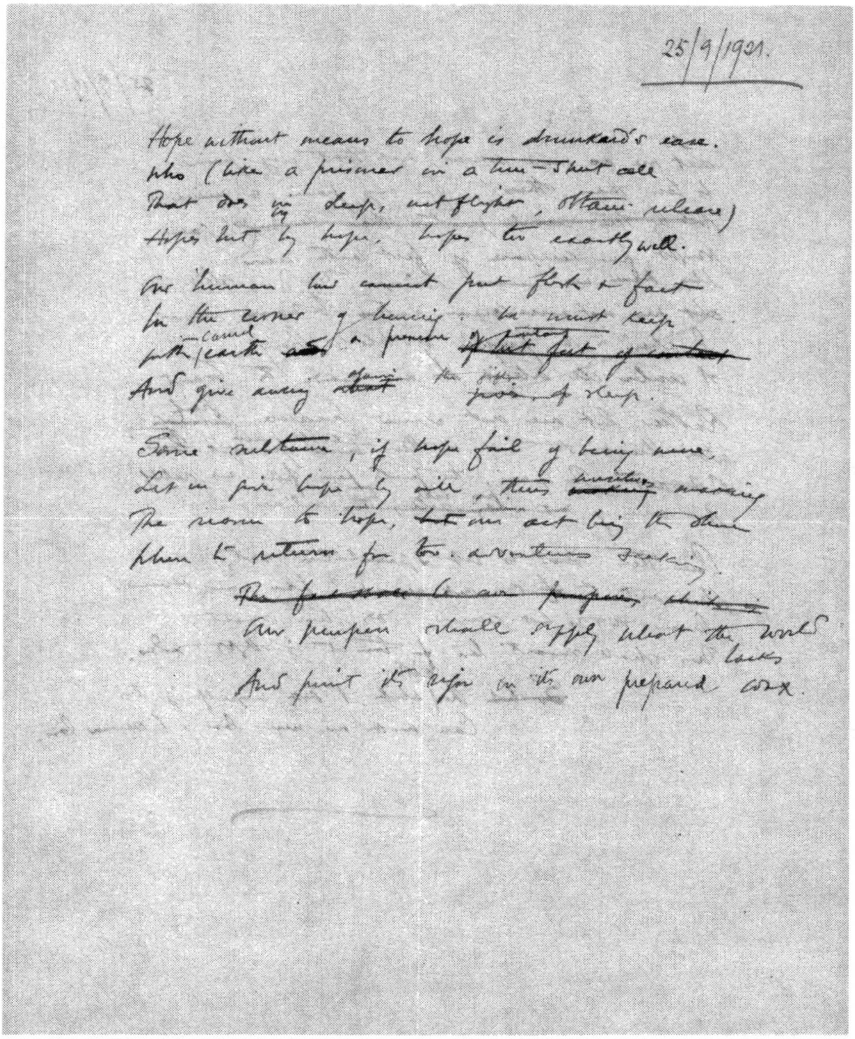

25/9/1921.

Hope without means to hope is drunkard's ease.

[handwritten draft manuscript, largely illegible]

"Hope without means to hope is drunkard's ease," manuscript, BNP/E3, 49A[6]–42[v].

Tell me again that story of the Prince,—
2   That fairy tale of when I was a child.
It cannot now sustain me nor convince
4   But it can make my sullen soul feel wild.

5   The improbable is ours because we love.
6   Awake in me once more the sleeping tale
That my old heart its stubborn youth may prove.
8   Who finds the Prince may find the Holy Grail.

9   Tell me again the story. He was bold,
10   He fought against bad giants and at last
11   That princess cloistered since old age was old
12   Was wakened by him and won. This is the past.

What the blind future holds let us forget,
14   Knowing it or not knowing, we regret.

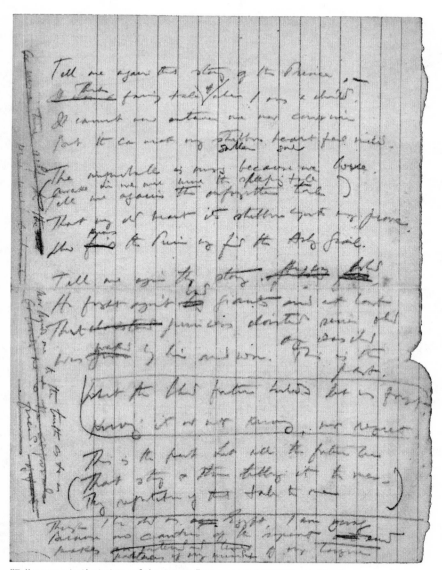

"Tell me again that story of the Prince," manuscript, BNP/E3, 49A⁷–9ᵛ.

*

Were I to die even upon this day

[BNP/E3, 49A^I^–32^r^]. *Datable to March–April, 1907. Unpublished. Written in black ink on lined paper; additions with a finer writing instrument (also black ink) and violet pencil. Above the opening line, we read the following two dates canceled out: ?<March 1907.> <April [19]07.> The additions in violet pencil date from a later period, possibly c. 1910. Facsimiled with the transcription of the opening verse in Carlos Pittella-Leite,* Pequenos Infinitos em Pessoa: Uma aventura filológica-literária pelos sonetos de Fernando Pessoa *(unpublished doctoral thesis, PUC-Rio, 2012), 22. On the verso we read* Sonnets, *an indication certainly serving for sorting out poems written in this form.*

Notes

2 /<dark> [↑ great] world & vain/] [→ ? Milton's ?]] *The adjective* great *was added in black ink, but seemingly with a finer writing instrument; the doubting concerning* dark [. . .] vain, *as well as the marginal note were done in violet pencil.*

7 I was a mouth [↑ thing] to eat and to retain] *In violet pencil (starting on the verse underneath, and extending to the bottom of the page) an arrow points downward where, also in the original black ink, we read the variants for lines 7–8. Both variants are preceded by the number of the lines in question: 7. and 8.*

8 *Line before the variant:* Things which for others had had use and way.

12 Like <ants> worms and bea[→s]ts to

14 With a most usual of a [↑ & most] painful thought.] *With the same finer writing instrument used for the intervention in line 1, the author added the following variant:* [↓ face-saddening <a> [↑ most] use-painless]; *written between the closing line and the variant for line 7, we read* <the sin> / <Of living & the curse [↑ sin] of having thought.>

The bitterness thou readest on my lips

[BNP/E3, 49A³–58^r^]. *Dated 23 September 1914. Unpublished. Written in blank ink on a thin, loose sheet of paper.*

Notes

3 Like the faint <† where> [↑ trace of] longing's finger-tips

4 <Another soul that was †> [↓ On the touched soul <that> Time coated [↓ Time dust-strewn] with <d>/D\istress–]

5 <This bitterness dwells not with me like> [↓ This sad expression of not saying aught]

6 does] *in the ms.*

7 </Like a mind passing through the rooms of Thought/> [↓I bear it not as banner of my Thought,]

8 </At *weight flies the [   ]at [   ] dread/> [↓ Nay, nor as ship's trail of a far-off Dread.]

11 care<.>/,\

14 its eyes . . . [↑ my size]] *this line is doubted*

Hope without means to hope is drunkard's ease.

[49A^{6-}42^v]. *Dated 25 September 1921. Unpublished. Written in blank ink on a thin loose, sheet of paper.*

Notes

3 in [↓ by]

7 With [↑ carnal] earth <and> a pressure <if but feet of contact> [↑ of contact]] *Occupying positions 9–10, the noun* contact *requires an unnatural delivery to match the realization of the iambic pentameter.*

8 And give away <what> [   ] <gives,> [↑ again the gifts of sleep.]

10 <making> [↑ ourselves] making

11 to hope, <but> our act being the shore

13 <The fact shall be our purpose, which is> [↓ Our purpose shall supply what the world lacks]

Tell me again that story of the Prince,—

[BNP/E3, 49A^7–9^v]. *Dated 22 October 1933. Unpublished.*

Notes

2 <It was a> [↑ That] fairy tale [↑ of] when I was a child.

4 stubborn heart [↓ sullen soul]

6 Tell me again the unforgotten tale [↑ Awake in me once more the sleeping tale]

8 Who <finds> [↑ finds] the Prince may find the Holy Grail.

9 Tell me again the story. <of how †> [↑ He was bold],

10 <big> [↑ bad] giants

11 That <cloistered> princess cloistered

12 Was <grieved> [↑ wakened]

14 *The author wrote other lines serving as the couplet, finally drawing a rectangle around the one we edit. The alternative couplet reads thus:* This is the past. Let all the future be / That story & story telling it to me. [↓ Thy repetition of that tale to me]; *in the left margin we also read the following lines:* <Or mine True self to the <†> wise world contact> / <Or binds me to the corporal of fact> [↑ Nor binds me to the truth as to a friend.]

NOTES

1. Eduardo Lourenço, *Fernando, rei da nossa Baviera* (Lisbon: Imprensa Nacional–Casa da Moeda, 1993).

2. All translations of titles and quotes are by Susan M. Brown.

3. The official decree 21/2009 by the Portuguese Ministry of Culture, issued on September 14, 2009, declared the literary estate of Fernando Pessoa a national treasure; this estate includes all of Pessoa's papers, documents, and private library.

4. Harold Bloom, *The Western Canon: The Books and School of the Ages* (New York: Hartcourt, 1994).

5. Ibid., 485.

6. Besides Portuguese and English, Pessoa also composed French verse. Though his literary relationship with French began in Durban, his first French poems date from 1906. The approximately 200 verse French texts were written during three specific periods: 1906–1908, the 1910s, and 1933–1935. See Fernando Pessoa, *Poèmes français* (Paris: Éditions de la Différence, 2014).

7. Fernando Pessoa, "Meantime," *Athenaeum* (Jan. 30, 1920, London), 136; Pessoa, "Spell," *Contemporanea* III, 9 (Jan.–Mar. 1923, Lisbon), 150. For the English poems Pessoa published under different names during his last years in Durban, South Africa, see Pessoa, *Eu sou uma antologia: 136 autores fictícios* (Lisbon: Tinta-da-China, 2013).

8. The significance of the edition *Il violinista pazzo* is that it included seventeen previously unpublished poems. The advantage of the edition *Poemas ingleses: The Mad Fiddler* lies in its critical apparatus. It should be noted, however, that the fifty-three poems included here have been published previously: two poems during Pessoa's life (in *Athenaeum* and *Contemporanea*); the others by Galhoz (three poems), Lind (six poems), Blanc de Portugal (twenty-five poems), and Di Munno (seventeen poems). Angioni and Gomes,

in their edition, did not include a complete breakdown of first publications of the poems that constitute *The Mad Fiddler*. The volume edited by Pizarro (Pessoa, *Cadernos*, I [2009]) is a transcription of ten notebooks that include, among other writings, several English poems written in the first decade of the twentieth century.

9. João Dionísio, "Introdução," in Fernando Pessoa, *Poemas ingleses*, I, ed. João Dionísio (Lisbon: Imprensa Nacional–Casa da Moeda, 1993), 7.

10. In his lifetime, Pessoa published seventy-three English poems (this number does not include those he published under the names Karl P. Effield and Charles Robert Anon); see Pessoa, *Eu sou uma antologia: 136 autores fictícios* (Lisbon: Tinta-da-China, 2013). Regarding the estimated number of posthumously published poems, our intention is only to be approximate.

11. Although the number of English poems in Freire's edition amounts to ninety-six, the actual number should be ninety-five: the poem "The Day Is Sad as I Am Sad," inaccurately transcribed in *Pessoa inédito* (Lisbon: Horizonte, 1993), 194, and subsequently included by Freire in *Poesia inglesa II* (Lisbon: Assírio & Alvim, 2000), 32–34, 238, is part of an earlier draft of a poem pertaining to *The Mad Fiddler*. Both this and the later versions were accurately reproduced in Pessoa, *Poemas ingleses: The Mad Fiddler* (Lisbon: Imprensa Nacional–Casa da Moeda, 1999), 52, 155.

12. Pizarro, *Pessoa existe?* (2012), 158.

13. BNP/E3, 49A^1 to 49D^3.

14. Pessoa, *Obra essencial*, Vol. 6 (Lisbon: Círculo de Leitores, 2007), 498.

15. Pessoa, *No Matter What We Dream: Selected English Poems* (Lisbon: Tell-a-Story, 2014), 78.

16. Edouard Roditi, "Fernando Pessoa: Outsider among English Poets," *Literary Review* 6, 3 (1963), 380–81.

17. Although always a proponent of the complete publication of Pessoa's dispersed English poems, Lind believed that Pessoa was not prolific in English in the second half of his life. Not counting the poems of *The Mad Fiddler* and *35 Sonnets*, Lind held that only about thirty poems written after 1911 remained to be published: "existem ainda umas 30 poesias dispersas, escritas entre 1911 e 1935, de valor desigual, não redigidas definitivamente pelo poeta, fragmentárias umas, acabadas e belas outras" ["there are still 30 dispersed poems, written between 1911 and 1935, of unequal value, some not finished, some fragmentary, some completed and beautiful"]; in Lind, "Descobertas no espólio de Fernando Pessoa" (*Separata da Revista "Ocidente,"* 1966), 59.

18. John Keats, *The Poetical Works* (London: Frederick Warne, 1898), 336. In Pessoa's copy in his private library, we read the following marginal note: "good; very painful, very sad." Keats's sonnet is a Shakespearean sonnet (three quatrains and a couplet, and the usual rhyme scheme *ababcdcdefefgg*). For the influence of this sonnet on a Portuguese poem composed by Pessoa in 1908, see Mariana de Castro's "Pessoa and Keats," in this issue.

19. The proximity of these two topoi is common in the Romantic period. As Catherine Bates has pointed out, "The experience of not having the Lady [e.g., in Petrarch's sonnets] is essentially the same as the experience of not persuading or of not writing great poetry." Bates, "Desire, Discontent, Parody: The Love Sonnet in Early Modern England," in A. D. Cousins and Peter Howarth, eds., *The Cambridge Companion to the Sonnet* (London: Cambridge University Press, 2011), 117.

20. Pessoa. "Autopsycographia," *Presença* 36 (Nov. 1932, Coimbra), 9.

21. We are quoting the *Times Literary Supplement* (TLS) of September 19, 1918, which stated, "Mr. Pessoa's command of English is less remarkable than his knowledge of Elizabethan English. He appears to be steeped in Shakespeare [. . .] The sonnets, on the other hand, probing into the mysteries of life and death, of reality and appearance, will interest many by reasons of their ultra-Shakespearianisms, and their Tudor tricks of repetition, involution and antithesis, no less than by the worth of what they have to say." Reproduction in Américo da Costa Ramalho, "Fernando Pessoa e o 'Times' de Londres," *Revista de História Literária de Portugal* 1, 1 (Coimbra, 1962), 281–82.

22. "Conceptism" is a baroque literary style that started in the mid-fifteenth century in Spain, subsequently reaching Portugal and Brazil. Conceptist writers, such as Francisco de Quevedo and Gregório de Mattos, would play with *concepts*, generating poems featuring logical arguments, embedded in refined rhetoric.

23. Pessoa, "Eros e Psyque," *Presença* 41/42 (May 1934, Coimbra), 13.

24. See Pizarro, Ferrari, and Cardiello, "Introduction," in *A Biblioteca particular de Fernando Pessoa I* (Lisbon: D. Quixote, 2010), 13.

WORKS CITED

Bates, Catherine. "Desire, Discontent, Parody: The Love Sonnet in Early Modern England." In *The Cambridge Companion to the Sonnet*, edited by A. D. Cousins and Peter Howarth. London, Cambridge University Press, 2011.

Bloom, Harold. *The Western Canon: The Books and School of the Ages*. New York: Hartcourt, 1994.

Costa Ramalho, Américo da. "Fernando Pessoa e o 'Times' de Londres." *Revista de História Literária de Portugal* 1, 1 (Coimbra, 1962): 281–82.

Ferrari, Patricio. "Meter and Rhythm in the Poetry of Fernando Pessoa." Unpublished doctoral thesis, University of Lisbon, 2012.

Keats, John. *The Poetical Works of John Keats*. With memoir, explanatory notes, portrait, and illustrations. London / New York: Frederic Warne, 1898. CFP 8–294.

Lind, George Rudolf. "Descobertas no espólio de Fernando Pessoa." *Separata da Revista "Ocidente"* LXX, 334 (Lisbon, Feb. 1966): 57–62.

Lourenço, Eduardo. *Fernando, rei da nossa Baviera*. Lisbon: Imprensa Nacional–Casa da Moeda, 1993.

Pessoa, Fernando. *No Matter What We Dream: Selected English Poems*. Selected and edited by Patricio Ferrari and Jerónimo Pizarro. 2nd ed. Lisbon: Tell-a-Story, 2015.

———. *Poèmes français*. Edition established and annotated by Patricio Ferrari with the collaboration of Patrick Quillier. Preface by Patrick Quillier. Paris: Éditions de la Différence, 2014.

———. *Eu sou uma antologia: 136 autores fictícios*. Edited by Jerónimo Pizarro and Patricio Ferrari. Lisbon: Tinta-da-China, 2013. Pessoa Collection coordinated by Jerónimo Pizarro.

———. *Cadernos*. Edited by Jerónimo Pizarro. Fernando Pessoa's Critical Edition, Major Series, Vol. XI, Tome I. Lisbon: Imprensa Nacional–Casa da Moeda, 2009.

———. *Obra essencial de Fernando Pessoa: Poesia Inglesa*. Edited by Richard Zenith; translated by Luísa Freire. Lisbon: Assírio & Alvim, 2007.

———. *Pessoa inédito*. Edited by Teresa Rita Lopez. Lisbon: Livros Horizonte, 1993.

———. *Poesia Inglesa II*. Edited and translated by Luísa Freire. Lisbon: Assírio & Alvim, 2000.

———. *Poemas Ingleses: The Mad Fiddler*. Edited by Marcus Angioni and Fernando Gomes. Fernando Pessoa's Critical Edition, Major Series, Vol. V, Tome III. Lisbon: Imprensa Nacional–Casa da Moeda, 1999.

———. *Poemas Ingleses: Poemas de Alexander Search*. Edited by João Dionísio. Fernando Pessoa's Critical Edition, Major Series, Vol. V, Tome II. Lisbon: Imprensa Nacional–Casa da Moeda, 1997.

———. *Poesia Inglesa*. Edited and translated byLuísa Freire. Lisbon: Livros Horizonte, 1995.

———. *Poemas Ingleses: Antinous, inscriptions, epithalamium, 35 Sonnets*. Edited by João Dionísio. Fernando Pessoa's Critical Edition, Major Series, Vol. V, Tome I. Lisbon: Imprensa Nacional–Casa da Moeda, 1993.

Pittella-Leite, Carlos. "Pequenos infinitos em Pessoa: Uma aventura filológica-literária pelos sonetos de Fernando Pessoa." Unpublished doctoral thesis, PUC-Rio, 2012.

Pizarro, Jerónimo. "Pessoa bilingue." *Pessoa existe?*, 151–69. Lisbon: Ática, 2012.

———. Patricio Ferrari, and Antonio Cardiello. *A Biblioteca particular de Fernando Pessoa*. Vol. I. Fernando Pessoa's House Collection. Bilingual edition. 3 vols. Lisbon: D. Quixote, 2010.

Roditi, Edouard. "Fernando Pessoa, Outsider among English Poets." *Literary Review* 6, 3 (Spring 1963): 372–85.

CARLOS PITTELLA-LEITE is a poet, researcher, and educator; author of the poetry book *Civilizações volume dois* (Coimbra, Palimage 2005); doctor of literature with a thesis on the sonnets of Pessoa (PUC-Rio 2012). From 2012 to 2014, he worked as curriculum chair at Global Citizenship Experience, Chicago. In 2012, he received a scholarship from the Biblioteca Nacional de Portugal and the Fundação Luso-Americana para o Desenvolvimento to do research on Pessoa's unpublished sonnets. Along with Ferrari, he is currently preparing a critical edition of Fernando Pessoa's complete English sonnets.

He can be reached at cpittella@gmail.com.

Fiction

Introduction to "A Very Original Dinner" by Fernando Pessoa

ABSTRACT: "A Very Original Dinner" is a horror short story written in 1907 by Alexander Search, a fictional author created by Fernando Pessoa around 1906. In the story, Herr Prosit, a coarse but merry man, president of the Gastronomical Society of Berlin, invites all the members of the society to a very original dinner. Each member is challenged to discover the originality: Is it in a sauce? Is it in a new ingredient? Is it in the lighting of the room or arrangement of the tables? Originality could be in anything. The members, barely containing their fever of expectation, take each detail into account as they try to discover the originality in the banquet. Even though they have some hypotheses—sufficiently ridiculous—none of them imagines how far Prosit's joke has gone this time.

KEYWORDS: Alexander Search, short story, originality, banquet

In June 1907, under the name Alexander Search, Fernando Pessoa wrote a short story titled "A Very Original Dinner"[1] about a very special banquet. The story is divided into two parts: the first concerns the invitation to this dinner, and the second describes how the dinner unfolds.

The first part introduces the main character of the story, Herr Prosit, president of the Gastronomical Society of Berlin, who invites all the members of the society to dine at his home. The purpose of the dinner is stated at the beginning by the president, who proclaims it will be a dinner like no member has attended before.

Prosit is quite a character; he is clever and cheerful, and has a unique sense of humor. At the same time, he can be coarse and impulsive, but he never behaves like a brute: he is impervious to anger and is always ready to please everyone. These features make him very popular among the members of the Gastronomical Society and his friends.

Prosit's characterization is essential to the facts presented in the second part of the story, the celebration of *a very original dinner*, during which the guests must discover where the originality lies. Every aspect of the banquet—the dishes, the way the table is laid, the servants, the lightning, and so on—is taken into consideration by the members of the society in order to find an answer to Prosit's challenging test. Some of the guests put forward their hypotheses, but the president just laughs, proud of his ability to ensure that the mystery remains unsolved. On this occasion, Prosit's joke goes much farther than anyone expects.

With detailed descriptions, dialogues, and discussions about society, the arts, and mankind, Pessoa presents a story of mystery, suspense, and horror—certainly a very original one.

The story was first published in 1988 in Portuguese by Maria Leonor Machado de Sousa, even though it was written in English. It first appeared in English in 2010, in David Jackson's book *Adverse Genres in Fernando Pessoa*.

The present version was compared with Jackson's transcription and revised, including some unpublished sentences,[2] and was published in 2014 by Tragaluz Editores in Medellín, Colombia, as part of the bilingual anthology of Alexander Search's texts *Un libro muy original (A Very Original Book)*.

NOTES

1. BNP/E3, 79A-1ʳ to 70ʳ; Pessoa, *Um jantar muito original seguido de A porta*, ed. Maria Leonor Machado de Sousa (Lisbon: Relógio d'Água, 1988).

2. For instance, Jackson makes changes to the punctuation of the text by adding or deleting commas, separating paragraphs, and eliminating quotation marks throughout the text; and he substitutes some words from the manuscript, such as "appearing" (BNP/E3, 79A-4ʳ), which is replaced by "seeming" in his transcription (191). In these cases, the substitution of the words does not affect the reading of the story in a broad sense due to the use of synonyms; but in other cases, this substitution is more problematic because it subtly alters the author's prose, as when changing from "it is as of *ought impossibly true*" in the manuscript (BNP/E3, 79A-65ʳ) to "it is as of *a sight devily seen*" (203) in his version (emphasis added). Besides this, in Jackson's version of the manuscript, several omissions of phrases are particularly confusing. One of these is what is written in the middle of the front and back of page 52 of the manuscript: "The elaborate seasoning of the dishes, their superficial newness of presentation—if that these were not legitimate in the President as culinary artist apart from the end of the dinner—[. . .] (52ᵛ) No one, I may add, after considering them, really took them for important" (BNP/E3, 79A-52ʳ and 52ᵛ). Another example of these omissions can be found at the end of the story, on page 69 of the manuscript: "They had been in everything the President's coadjutors"; the word *coadjutors* was very difficult to read, and Jackson's version eliminated the phrase entirely.

WORKS CITED

Jackson, K. David. *Adverse Genres in Fernando Pessoa*. New York: Oxford University Press, 2010.

Pessoa, Fernando. *Um Jantar muito original seguido de A porta*. Edited by Maria Leonor Machado de Sousa. Lisbon: Relógio d'Água, 1988.

NATALIA JEREZ QUINTERO earned a BA in literature from University of Los Andes in Bogotá, Colombia. Since 2011, she has been working in the publishing industry as a copyeditor and a professional grammar and stylistic proofreader. Her areas of interest are Portuguese and Latin American literature. She has selected and translated into Spanish Alexander Search's texts included in *Un libro muy original* (*A Very Original Book*) published by Tragaluz in 2014.

She can be reached at njerezq@semana.com.

"A Very Original Dinner"

Tell me what thou eatest and I'll tell thee what thou art.
—SOMEBODY

I.

It was during the fifteenth annual session of the Gastronomical society of Berlin that the President, Herr Prosit, made the famous invital to its members. The session was of course a banquet. During the dessert a very great discussion had arisen concerning originality in the art of cooking. The period was bad for all arts. Originality was in decay. In gastronomy also there was a decay and a weakness. All productions of the cuisine which were called "new" were but variations on dishes already known. A different sauce, a slightly diverse way of spicing or of seasoning—in this way the latest dish was different from the one before it. There were no real novelties. There were but innovations. These things were all deplored at the banquet in a unity of voices, with a variety of intonations and with various degrees of vehemence.

While warmth and conviction were poured into the discussion, yet there was among us one man who, although he was not the only man who was silent, was nevertheless the one man who noticeably did not speak; for from him, most of all, intervention might have been expected. This man was of course Herr Prosit, president of the Society, chairman at this meeting. Herr Prosit was the only man who gave no heed to the discussion—he was quiet more than inattentive. His voice's authority was lacking. He was thoughtful—he, Prosit; he was silent—he, Prosit; he was serious—he, Wilhelm Prosit, president of the Gastronomical Society.

The silence of Herr Prosit was, for most men, a rare thing. He resembled (let the comparison pass) a storm. Silence was not of his essence. Quietness was not his nature. And like a storm (to follow the simile), if silence were ever with him, it was as a rest and as a prelude to an outburst greater than all. Of him was this opinion held.

The President was a man remarkable in many ways. He was a merry man and a social, yet all this with an abnormal vivaciousness, with a noisiness of bearing

First manuscript page, "A Very Original Dinner," BNP/E3, 79A–2ʳ.

that seemed a perpetual unnaturalness of disposition. His socialness seemed pathologic; his wit and jokes, while appearing not in any way forced, seemed compelled from within by a faculty of the spirit which is not the faculty of wit. His humour seemed falsely true, his restlessness naturally assumed.

In the society of his friends—and he had many—he kept up a steady current of mirth, he was all joy and all laughter. Yet it is remarkable that this strange man should not bear in his habitual countenance an expression of mirth or of joy. When he ceased to laugh, when he forgot to smile, he seemed to fall, by the contrast which his face betrayed, into an unnatural seriousness, as of something sister to pain.

Whether this were due to a fundamental unhappiness of character, or to sorrows of earlier life, or to any other ill of the spirit—I who tell this could hardly presume to say. Besides, this contradiction in his character, or, at least, in its manifestations, was perceived only by the observant; the others did not see it, nor was there any need that they should.

As in a night of storms following one upon another yet with intervals, he who is witness calls the whole night a night of storm, forgetting the stops between the outbursts, and naming the night after that character of it which struck him most; even so, following an inclination of mankind, men called Prosit a merry man because what struck most in him was his noisiness in mirth, the uproar of his joy. In the storm the witness forgot the deep silence of the intervals. In this man easily did we forget, in his wild laughter, the sad silence, the sullen heaviness of the intervals of his social nature.

The President's countenance, I repeat, also bore and betrayed this contradiction. That laughing face lacked animation. Its perpetual smile seemed the grotesque grin of those on whose faces the sun is striking; the natural contraction there of the muscles before a strong light; here, as a perpetual expression, most unnatural and most grotesque.

It was commonly said (among those who knew him to be thus) that he had taken to a merry life to escape a kind of family nervousness of nature, or, at most, morbidness, for he was the son of an epileptic and had had as forefathers, not mentioning many over-extravagant rakes, several unmistakable neurotics. He himself might have been a sufferer by his nerves. But of this I speak with no certainty.

What I can give as true beyond doubt is that Prosit had been brought into the society of which I speak by a young officer, also a friend of mine and a merry fellow, who had picked him up somewhere, having been extremely amused at some of his practical jokes.

This society—that in which Prosit moved—was, truly to speak, one of those dubious side-societies, which are not uncommon, formed of high and of low elements in a curious synthesis, ever of the nature of a chemical change, for they have often a new character, of their own, different from that of their elements. This was a society whose arts—arts they must be called—were that of eating, that of drinking, and that of making love. It was artistic, no doubt. It was coarse, less doubt. And it united these things without discord.

Of this group of people, socially useless, humanly rotting, Prosit was the leader, because he was the coarsest of them. I cannot enter, obviously, into the psychology, simple yet intricate, of this case. I cannot explain, here, the reason of the fact that the leader of such a society should have been chosen from its lowest part. All through literature much subtlety, much intuition has been spent over cases of this kind. They are manifestly pathologic. Poe gave to the complex sentiments that inspire them, thinking they were but one, the general name of *perverseness*. But this case I chronicle, and no more. The feminine element of the society came, conventionally speaking, from below; the masculine element from above. The pillar of this arrangement, the hyphen of this compound,—nay, better, the catalytic agent of this chemical change, was my friend Prosit. The centres, the meeting-places of the society were two: a certain restaurant or the respectable X hotel, accordingly as the feast was a revel empty of thought, or was a chaste, masculine, artistic session of the Gastronomical society of Berlin. As to the first, suggestion is impossible; not a hint is possible within a hair's breadth from indecency. For Prosit was not normally coarse, but abnormally; his influence lowered the aim of his friends' lowest desiring. As to the Gastronomical society, that was better; it represented the spiritual side of that group's concrete aspirations.

I have just said that Prosit was coarse. It is true; so he was. His exuberance was coarse, his humour coarsely manifested. I inform of all this with care. I write neither praise nor calumny. I am sketching, as neatly as I can, a character. As well as my mind's vision permits, I follow on the tracks of truth.

But Prosit was coarse, no doubt. For even in the society where, by being in touch with elements socially high, he was sometimes forced to live, he did not lose much of his native brutality. He indulged in it half with consciousness. His jokes were not always inoffensive nor pleasant, they were almost all coarse, though, to those who could appreciate the "point" of such performances, they were funny enough, witty enough, sufficiently well contrived.

The better aspect of this vulgarity was its impulsiveness, in so far as it was ardour. For the President entered with ardour into all things which he undertook, especially into culinary enterprises and into love affairs; in the first he was a poet of gustation, daily gaining inspiration; in the last his lowness of character was ever at its horrible best. Nevertheless his ardour, as the impulsiveness of his mirth, could not be doubted. He carried others along with him by the violence of his energy, created ardour in them, animated their impulse without consciousness that he did so. Yet his ardour was for himself, to himself, was an organic necessity; it was not meant for a relation with the world outside. This ardour could not, it is true, be long sustained; but, while it lasted, its influence as an example, however unconscious, was immense.

But, let it be noticed, though the President was ardent, impulsive, at bottom coarse and rude, yet he was a man who was never cross. Never. No man could put him into a rage. Besides, he was always ready to please, always ready to avoid a quarrel. He seemed ever to desire everybody to be well with him. It was curious to observe how he restrained his ire, how he held it in hand with a firmness no one had given him credit for, least of all those who knew him impulsive and ardent, his most intimate friends.

It was chiefly on account of this, I conjecture, that Prosit was such a favourite. Perhaps, indeed, taking into consideration the fact that he was coarse, brutal, of impulse, yet never behaving brutally in the showing of rage and of aggressiveness, never impulsive in ire—perhaps we, unconsciously considering this laid on this the basis of our friendliness. Besides, there was the fact that he was always ready to please, to be pleasant. As for being rough, with men that mattered little, for the President was a good fellow.

It is obvious therefore, and now, that Prosit's attractiveness (so to call it) was in this: in his being unsusceptible to rage, in his earnestness to please, in the peculiar fascination of his coarse exuberance, perhaps even, ultimately, also in the unconscious intuition of the slight enigma which his character presented.

Enough! My analysis of Prosit's character, perhaps excessive in details, is nevertheless defective, because, as I suppose, it has missed or left inevident the elements that point to a final synthesis. I have ventured beyond my ability. My comprehension cannot be matched to the clearness that is my desire. Wherefore I shall say no longer.

One thing remains nevertheless, on the superficies of all I have said: the external view of the President's character. It remains clear that, for all conceivable intents, for all imaginable purposes, Herr Prosit was a merry man, an odd fellow, a man who was merry habitually, who impressed other men with his mirth, a man prominent in his society, a man who had many friends. His coarse tendencies, as they gave the character to the society of men in which he lived, that is to say, as they were creators of environment, disappeared by excessive obviousness, passed gradually into the domain of the unconscious; became unperceived, ended imperceptible.

The dinner was already at an end. The conversation grew, in the number of those who spoke, in the noise of their combined, discordant, interpenetrated voices. Prosit was still silent. The principal speaker, Captain Greiwe was discoursing lyrically. He insisted on the lack of imagination (so he called it) improductive of modern dishes. He grew enthusiastic. In the art of gastronomy, he observed, new dishes were always needed. His manner of comprehending was narrow, restricted to the art he knew. He contended falsely, gave to understand, that in gastronomy alone newness was of preëminent value. And this may have been a subtle way of saying that gastronomy was the only science and the only art. "Blessed art," the Captain cried, "whose conservatism is a perpetual revolution!" "Of it I could say," he continued, "what Schopenhauer says of the world, that it preserves itself by its destruction."

"Why, Prosit," said a member from the extreme end of the table, noticing the silence of the President; "Why, Prosit, you have not yet given your opinion! Say something, man! Are you absent-minded? Are you melancholy? Are you ill?"

Everybody looked towards the President. The President smiled upon them in his usual way, his usual smile, malicious, mysterious, half-humourless. Yet this smile had a meaning; it foreboded in some way the strangeness of the President's words.

The President broke the silence which was made for his expected answer.

"I have a proposal to make, an invital," he said. "Have I your attention? Can I speak?"

As he said this, silence seemed to grow more profound. All eyes looked towards him. All actions, gestures, stopped where they were, for attention seized upon all.

"Gentlemen," began Herr Prosit, "I am about to invite you to a dinner, the like of which, I contend, none of you have ever attended. My invital is at the same time a challenge. Afterwards I shall explain."

There was a slight pause. No one moved, except Prosit, who finished a glass of wine.

"Gentlemen," he repeated in a manner eloquently direct, "my challenge to any man is contained in this, that, ten days from now, I shall give a new sort of dinner, *a very original dinner.* Consider yourselves invited."

Murmurs for explanation, questions, poured in from all sides. Why that sort of invital? What did he mean? What had he proposed? Why that obscurity of expression? What, clearly speaking, was the challenge which he had made?

"At my house," said Prosit, "in the square."

"Good."

"You are not going to transfer to your house the meeting-place of the society?" inquired one member.

"No; it is only on this occasion."

"And is it going to be something so very original, Prosit?" inquired obstinately a member who was inquisitive.

"Very original. A complete novelty!"

"Bravo!"

"The originality of the dinner lies," said the President, as one speaking an after-thought, "not in what it conveys or appears, but in what it means, in what it contains. I defy any man here (and I could say "any man anywhere," for the matter) to say, having finished it, in what it is original. No one, I assert, will guess. This is my challenge. Perhaps you thought it would be that no man could give a more original banquet. But no, that is not it; it is as I have said. As you see it is much more original. It is original beyond your expectation."

"May we know," a member asked, "the motive of your invital?"

"I am urged to this," Prosit explained, and his face was sarcastic in its determined look, "by a discussion which I had before dinner. Some of my friends here present may have heard the dispute. They can inform those who desire to know. My invital is made. Do you accept?"

"Of course! of course!" came in shouts from all parts of the table.

The President nodded, smiled; nursing amusement at some inner vision, he relapsed into silence.

When Herr Prosit had made his astonishing challenge and invital, conversations, separately maintained among the members, fell upon the real motive thereof. Some were of the opinion that this was another joke of the President's; others that Prosit had desired to make another assertion of his culinary skill, rationally gratuitous, since (said these) no one had challenged it, but pleasant to any man's vanity in his art. Others again were certain that the invital was indeed made because of certain young men of the city of Frankfort between whom and the President there was a rivalry in gastronomy. It turned out soon, as those who read this will see, that the end of the challenge was certainly this third—the immediate end, I mean, for, as the President was a human being, and, especially, a very original one, his invital bore psychologically traces of the three intentions that were imputed to him.

The reason why it was not immediately believed that Prosit's true reason for the invital was the dispute (as he himself had said) was that the challenge was too vague, too mysterious, to seem but a reply to a provocation, to appear a vengeance and no more. At last, however, it had to be believed.

The discussion the President had mentioned had been (said those who knew) between him and five young men from the city of Frankfort. These were no particular young men, except that they were gastronomers; that was, I believe, their only title to our attention. The discussion with them had been long. Their contention had been, as far as was remembered, that some dish which one of them had invented, or some dinner which they had given, was superior to some gastronomic performance of the President's. Over this the dispute had come; round this centre the spider of contention had spun with industry its web.

The discussion had been hot on the young men's part; soft and moderate on Prosit's. It was his custom, as I have said, never to yield to rage. On this occasion, however, he had been almost angry on account of the heat of his opponents' retorts. But he remained calm. It was thought, now that this was known, that the President was about to play some gigantic joke on the five young men, to have in his usual manner the revenge of that harsh dispute. On this account expectation soon was high; whispers of a giant joke were set running, tales of a striking originality in the vengeance. Given the case, and the man, these rumours suggested themselves; they were built clumsily upon truth. They were all, sooner or later, told to Prosit; but, as he heard them, he shook his head and, while seeming to do justice to their intention, lamented their coarse appearance.

No one, he said, had guessed aright. It was impossible, he said, that anyone should guess aright. All was a surprise. Conjecture, guess, hypothesis were ridiculous and without use.

These rumours, of course, were of later occurrence. Let us return to the dinner at which the invital had been made. It had just ended. We were going towards the smoking room when we came across five young men, of fairly refined appearance, who saluted Prosit with some coldness.

"Ah, my friends," the President explained turning to us, "these are five young gentlemen of Frankfort whom I once defeated in a challenge in matters gastronomical . . ."

"I hardly think you defeated us, you know," retorted one of the young men, with a smile.

"Well, let that be as it is, or as it was. As a matter of fact, my friends, the challenge which I have now made before the Gastronomical Society" (with a wide sweep of his hand he designated us) "is of a much larger import and of a nature much more artistic." He explained it to the five. They listened as impolitely as they could.

"When I made this challenge, just now, gentlemen, I was thinking of you!"

"Oh! you were, were you? And what have we got to do with it?"

"Oh, you'll soon see! The dinner is on the week after next, on the seventeenth."

"We don't wish to know the date. We don't need to."

"No; you are right!" chuckled the President. "You don't. It won't be necessary. Nevertheless," he added, "you will be present at the dinner."

"What!" cried one of the three young men. Of the other two, one grinned and the other stared.

The President grinned back.

"Ay, and you will contribute to it most materially."

The five young men manifested physiognomically their doubt of this and their half-interest in the matter.

"Come, come!" said the President as they were going. "When I mean a thing I mean it, and I mean you to be present at the dinner, I mean you to contribute to its appreciation."

This was spoken in a tone of such obvious and pointed sneering that the young men were angered and hastened down stairs.

The last one turned round.

"We will be there in spirit, perhaps," he said, "thinking of your failure."

"No, no; you will be there right-enough. You will be there in body—in body, I assure you. Don't trouble about that. Leave everything to me."

A quarter of an hour after, all proceedings being over, I followed Prosit downstairs.

"Do you think you can make them be present, Prosit?" I asked him as he put on his overcoat.

"Certainly," he said, "I am sure of it."

We went out together—I and Prosit—parting at the hotel-door.

———

II.

The day soon came when Prosit's invital was to be fulfilled. The dinner took place at Prosit's house at half-past-six in the evening.

The house—that of which Prosit had spoken as being "in the square"—was not, properly speaking, his house, but was of an old friend of his who lived out of Berlin and who lent the house to Prosit when the President desired. It was always at his disposal. Yet he rarely needed it. Some of the earliest banquets of the Gastronomical Society had been held there, until the superior convenience of the hotel—comfort, appearance, locality—had been ascertained. In the hotel Prosit was well known; it was after his directions that the dishes were made. His inventive skill had there as much scope as at the house, with cooks either of his, or of the members, or imported from some restaurant; and not only had his skill as much scope, but the execution of his designs was prompter, better; they were more neatly and more accurately accomplished.

As to the house in which Prosit lived—no one knew it, nor did any one care to know. For some banquets the house was used of which I have just spoken, for love affairs he had a small suite of rooms; he had a club—nay, two clubs—, and he was often to be seen at the hotel.

Prosit's house, I say, none knew; that he had one, apart from the places mentioned, which he frequented, was a matter of vulgar certainty. But where the house was, none suspected. The people with whom he there lived were also unknown to us. Who the associates of his retirement were, Prosit had never given us to understand. That they existed, not even this had he said. It was merely the conclusion of our reasoning, simple and homely in the matter. Prosit had been, we knew—though I remember not by whom—in the Colonies—in Africa, or in India, or elsewhere—and had there made a fortune upon which he lived. Thus much being known, the rest only idleness could research.

The reader now knows sufficiently the state of things to dispense my further observations, either on the President or on the house itself. I pass on therefore to the scene of the banquet.

The room in which the banquet table had been spread was large and long, though not lofty. On the sides there were no windows but only doors, leading off to several rooms. At the top, on the side facing the street, a high and wide window was cut, splendid, that of itself seemed to breathe the air it allowed to enter. It took the place of three ordinary large windows and filled it well. It was divided into three parts by mere partitionings of its casement. Though the room was large this window was sufficient; it gave light and air to the whole; every corner was not robbed of Nature's most natural things.

In the middle of the dining-hall a long table had been set for the banquet; at the head of this the President sat with his back turned to the window. I, who write, as the oldest member, sat at his right hand. Other details are inessential. The attendance was fifty-two.

The room was lighted by chandeliers placed above the table, three in number. By a skilful arranging of their ornaments, the lights were singularly concentrated on the table, leaving rather in the dark the spaces between it and the walls. It seemed, by its effect, the lighting arrangement over billiard tables. However as here it was not obtained, as there, by a device the end of whose use was manifest, what existed in the mind, at most, was a sensation of strangeness with regard to the lights in the dining-hall. Had there been other tables, collaterally, the sense of the darkness between them had been of something obtrusive. As there was but one table no such thing happened. I myself only noticed this later, as the reader who follows me will see. Although I, as all who were there, when I first entered looked everywhere for strangeness, yet this was unperceived, somehow.

How the table was laid, dressed, ornamented, partly I cannot remember, partly it needs not to remember. What difference there may have been from other dinner-tables was a difference within normalness, not a difference because of originality. Description in this case were sterile and to no end.

The members of the Gastronomical Society—fifty-two, as I have said—began to turn up at a quarter to six. Some three, I remember, came only within a minute of the dinner hour. One—the last one—appeared as we were sitting down to the table. In these things, in this part of the session, as was proper among artists, all ceremonial was set aside. By this late coming no one was offended.

We sat down to the table in a contained fever of expectation, of inquiry, of intellectual suspicion. This was to be, each man remembered, a *very original dinner*. Each man had been challenged—this to discover in what was the originality of the dinner. This was the difficult point. Was the originality in something inapparent, or in an obvious thing? Was it in some dish, in some sauce, in some arrangement? Was it in some trivial detail of the dinner? Or was it, after all, in the general character of the banquet?

As is natural, being every one of us in this state of mind, every possible thing, everything vaguely probable, everything sanely improbable, impossible, was a cause of suspicion, of self-inquiry, of bewilderment. Was the originality in that? Did that contain the joke?

Thus all of us, the guests, as soon as we had sat down to dinner, began minutely, curiously, to scan the ornaments and flowers on the table, nay, not only these, but also the patterns of the plates, the disposition of the knives and forks, the glasses, the bottles of wine. Several had already examined the chairs. Not a few had, with the appearance of unconcern, paced round the table, round the room. One had looked under the table. Another had felt with his fingers, rapidly and carefully the under side of the same. One member dropped his table-napkin and bent very low to pick it up, which he did with half ludicrous difficulty; he had wished to see, he told me afterwards, whether there were not a trapdoor which, at a given moment of the banquet, might not swallow us up, or the table only, or us and table together.

I cannot now accurately call to mind what my suppositions were, or my conjectures. I remember distinctly however that they were sufficiently ridiculous, of the same kind as I have shown in others. Fantastic and extraordinary notions succeeded each other in my mind by a purely mechanical association of ideas. Everything was, at the same time, suggestive and unsatisfactory. Well considered everything contained a singularity (so will anything anywhere contain). But no one thing presented clearly, neatly, indubitably, the sign of its being the key to the problem, the hidden word of the enigma.

The President had defied any of us to find the originality in the dinner. Given this challenge, given the capacity for jokes for which Prosit was renowned, no one could say how far the confounding went, whether the originality was ridiculously insignificant, on purpose, or hidden in excessive obtrusiveness, or, for such a thing was possible, consisting in there being no originality at all. This was the state of mind in which the guests in their totality—I say it without boldness of expression—sat down to the eating of *a very original dinner*.

Attention was on all things.

The first thing to be noticed was that the service was done by five black servants. Their countenances could not be well seen, not only on account of the somewhat extravagant costume in which they were dressed (which included a peculiar turban), but also on account of that singularity in the light-arrangement by which, as in billiard saloons, though not by the same device, the light was turned upon the table and left darkness all around.

The five black servants were trained well; not excellently, perhaps, but well. They betrayed this in many things, perceptible most especially to men such as we who were in relation with such people daily and importantly, on account of our art. They seemed to have been very well trained, outside, for a dinner which was the first at which they served. This was the impression which their serving made on my experienced brain; but I, for the moment, dispelled it, seeing in it nothing extraordinary. Servants could not be found anywhere. Perhaps, I thought, on the moment, Prosit had brought them with him from where he had been, abroad. That I did not know them would be no reason to doubt this, because, as I have said, Prosit's more intimate life, as well as his place of dwelling, were not known to us, were kept private by him, for reasons which he probably had and which it was no business of ours to search for or to appreciate. My thoughts of the five dark servants, when first I noticed them, were these.

The dinner was then begun. It puzzled still more. The peculiarities which it offered were before reason so meaningless that it was in vain that an interpretation of any kind was put upon them. The observations which one of the guests made, humorously, towards the end of the dinner, gave fit expression to all this.

"The only thing which my attentive and acute mind can perceive here of original," said, with assumed pompousness, a titled member, "is, primò, that our attendants are dark, and more or less in the dark, though it is we that are decidedly so; secundò, that this, if it mean[t] anything, means nothing at all. I see nowhere anything fishy, unless, in a decent sense, the fish."

These light-minded observations met with approval though their wit was poorer than poor. Everybody, however, had noticed the same things. But no one believed—though many were vague in mind—that Prosit's joke was this and no more. They looked towards the President to see if his smiling countenance betrayed any sentiment, any indication of a sentiment, anything—but the smile was on it, usual and inexpressive. Perhaps it grew slightly wider, perhaps it implicated a wink, when the titled had made those observations, perhaps it grew more sly; but there is no certainty of this.

"In your words," Prosit said at length, to the member who had spoken, "I am pleased to see an unconscious recognition of my ability in concealing, in making a thing appear other than it is. For I see that you have been deceived by appearances. I see that you are yet far from knowing the truth, the joke. You are far from guessing the originality of the dinner. And I may add that if there be anything fishy in it—which I do not deny—it is certainly not the fish. Nevertheless I thank you for your praise!" And the President bowed in mockery.

"My praise?"

"Your praise, because you did not guess. And, not guessing, you proclaim my ability. I thank you!"

Laughter put an end to this episode.

Meanwhile I, who had been reflecting during the whole time, arrived suddenly at a strange conclusion. For, as I considered the reasons of the dinner, calling to mind the words of the invital and the day on which it had been made, I remembered suddenly that the dinner was considered by all as the result of a discussion of the President's with the five gastronomers from Frankfort. I recalled Prosit's expressions of the time. He had told the five young men that they would be present at his dinner, that they would contribute to it "*materially*." This was the very word he had used.

Now these five young men were not guests . . . At this moment the sight of one of the black servants put me naturally in mind of them and immediately after of the fact that they were five. The discovery startled me. I looked up to the places where they were, to see if their faces betrayed anything. But the faces, themselves dark, were in darkness. It was at this moment that I perceived the extreme skill with which the lighting arrangement threw the whole glare upon the table, leaving in comparative night the room around, most especially at the height from the floor at which were the heads of the five servants who attended. Strange, bewildering as the matter was, no doubts remained with me. I was absolutely certain that the five young gentlemen of Frankfort had become, for the moment, the five black servants at the dinner. The entire incredibility of the whole thing detained me awhile, but my conclusions were too well-drawn, too obvious. It could not be but as I had found.

Immediately did I remember that, five minutes or so before, at the same banquet, the black servants having naturally attracted attention, one of the members, Herr Kleist, an anthropologist, had asked Prosit what was their race (he being entirely unable to see their countenances), and where he had got them from. The contrariety which the President had shown may not have been absolutely manifest; nevertheless I saw it clearly, perfectly, though I had not yet then the stimulus to attention of the discovery which afterwards I made. But I had seen Prosit's confusion, and had wondered. Shortly afterwards—as I had subconsciously noticed—one of the servants holding the dish by Prosit, the latter had said something in a low voice; the result of this had been the five "blacks" keeping further in the shadow, exaggerating perhaps the distance, to one who paid attention to the stratagem.

The President's fear was, of course, quite natural. An anthropologist like Herr Kleist, one familiar with human races, with their types, with their facial characteristics, would, perforce, were he to see the faces, discover at once the imposture. Hence Prosit's extreme unrest at the question; hence his order to the servants to keep well in the darkness. How he evaded the question I forgot; I have suspicions, however, that it was by declaring the servants not his and protesting his ignorance of their race and of their manner of coming to Europe. In making this reply he was, however, as I noticed, considerably ill at ease; this with the fear that Herr Kleist might, precisely to know the race, wish suddenly to examine the blacks. But he could not, obviously, have said not denying that they belonged to him: "this race" or "that race," for being ignorant of races, and knowing himself to be so, he might venture on a type one of whose most elementary and most apparent characteristics, as, for instance, stature, might be in open contradiction to that of the five black attendants. I remember vaguely that, after this reply, Prosit had covered it with some material incident, by diverting attention to the dinner, or to gastronomy,—to something, I know not what, which was not the servants.

The elaborate seasoning of the dishes, their superficial newness of presentation—if that these were not legitimate in the President as culinary artist apart from the end of the dinner—I regarded as trifles made on purpose to turn aside the attention, so manifest was, I considered, their character of petty absurdity,

the five black attendants. I remember
vaguely that, after this reply, Prost
had covered it with some material
incident, by diverting attention to
the dinner, or to gastronomy, — to
something (which was not the servants.

The elaborate seasoning of the
dishes, then   I regarded
as trifles made on purpose
to turn aside the attention, so manifest was, I considered, their character
of petty absurdity, of striking littleness of willed unconvention
The fact in itself was, it is true,   (Verso)
exceedingly, unutterably strange; the
more reason then, I said to myself,
to contain the originality of Prost's.

"The five black attendants," manuscript page, "A Very Original Dinner,"
BNP/E3, 79A–52ʳ.

"No one, I may add, after considering them, really took them for important,"
manuscript page, "A Very Original Dinner," BNP/E3, 79A–52ᵛ.

of striking littleness, of willed unconvention. No one, I may add, after considering them, really took them for important.

The fact in itself was, it is true, exceedingly, unutterably strange; the more
reason then, I said to myself, to contain the originality of Prosit's. It was indeed
bewildering, I reflected, that it should have been accomplished. How? How
could five young men absolutely hostile to the President be induced, trained,
obliged to act the part of servants at a dinner, a thing repugnant to every man of
a certain social condition? It was a thing that startled grotesquely like the reality
of a woman's body on a fish's tail. It made, in the mind, the world to tread on
its own heels.

As to their being black, that was easily explained. Obviously Prosit could not
present the five young men, before the members of the Society, with their own
countenances. It was natural that he should avail himself of the vague knowledge which he knew we had of his having been in the Colonies to cover his joke
with their blackness. The torturing question was how this had been done; and
that only Prosit could reveal. I could understand—and yet could not very well—a
man acting a servant's part, for a great friend and in a joke, and as a very great
favour. But in this case!

The more I reflected the more extraordinary the case appeared, but, at the
same time, given all the proofs it had, given the character of the President, the
more probable, the more certain that Prosit's joke was contained therein. Well
might he challenge us to discover the originality of the banquet! The originality,
as I had found it, was not, it is true, properly in the dinner; still it was in the
servants, in something connected with the dinner. At this point of my reasoning
I wondered that I had not seen this before: that the banquet being given on account of the five young men (as was now known) could not but bear upon them,
as a revenge, and bearing upon them obviously could not do so in anything more
directly connected with the dinner than in the servants.

These arguments, reasonings, which I have here taken a few paragraphs to
set forth passed in a few minutes through my mind. I was convinced, bewildered, satisfied. The rational clearness of the case dispelled its extraordinary
nature from my brain. I saw lucidly, accurately in the matter. Prosit's challenge
had been won by me.

The dinner was almost at an end, on the before-side of the dessert.

I resolved, that my ability might be recognized, to tell Prosit of my discovery.
I re-considered, that I might make no failure, no mistake; the strangeness of the

matter, as I conceived it, creeping through my sureness of fact. At length, I bent my head towards Prosit and said in a low tone:

"Prosit, my friend, I have the secret. These five *black people* and the five young men from Frankfort . . ."

"Ah! You have guessed that there is some connection between them." He said this half sneeringly, half in doubt, yet I could see that he was put out and inly irated by the acuteness of my reasoning, which he had not expected. He was ill at ease and looked on my face with attention. "Certainty," I thought, "is mine."

"Of course," I replied, "they *are* the five. Of that I have no doubt. But how on earth did you do it?"

"Brute force, my dear fellow. But don't say anything to the others."

"Of course not. But how by brute force, my dear Prosit?"

"Well, that's a secret. It cannot be told. It's as secret as death."

"But how do you manage to keep them so quiet. I am astonished. Won't they get away or revolt?"

The President was convulsed inwardly with laughter. "There's no fear of that," he said, with a wink that had more than meaning. "They won't run away—not they. Absolutely impossible." And he looked at me quietly, slyly, mysteriously.

At length the end of the dinner was reached—no, not the end of the dinner—another singularity, apparently purposed for effect—when Prosit proposed a toast. Everybody was astonished at this toast just after the last dish and before the dessert. All wondered, excepting myself, who saw in this another eccentri[ci]ty, meaningless in itself, to divert the attention. Nevertheless the glasses were all filled. As they were being filled, the President's bearing was extremely altered. He shifted about in his chair in great excitement, with the ardency of a man who *will* speak, of one who must reveal a great secret, who must make a great revelation.

This demeanour was at once noticed. "Prosit has some joke to reveal—*the* joke. It's Prosit all through! Out with it, Prosit!"

As the moment of the toast approached the President seemed to go mad with excitement; he moved about in his chair, he writhed, he grinned, smiled, made faces, chuckled meaninglessly and without end.

The glasses had all been filled. Every man was ready. A profound silence was made. In the tension of the moment I remember hearing two footsteps in the street and feeling angry at two voices—one a man's, another a woman's—that held converse in the square below. I lost them from attention. Prosit rose to his feet; nay, rather, he bounded, almost upsetting the chair.

"Gentlemen," said he, "I am going to reveal my secret, the joke, the challenge. It's very amusing. You know how I said to the five young men of Frankfort that they would be present at this banquet, that they would aid it most materially? The secret's there, in this, I mean."

The President spoke hurriedly, incoherently, in his haste to arrive at the point.

"Gentlemen, this is all I have to say. Now the first toast, the great toast. It concerns my five poor rivals . . . Because none guessed the truth, not even Meyer (this is I); not even he."

The President paused; then, lifting his voice into a shout; "I drink," said he, "*to the memory of the five young gentlemen of Frankfort, who have been present in body at this dinner and have contributed to it most materially.*"

And haggard, savage, *completely* mad, he pointed with an excited finger to the *remains of flesh in a dish* which he had caused to be left upon the table.

These words had no sooner been spoken than a horror that laughs at expression fell with weird coldness upon all. All were for the moment crushed by the unthinkable revelation. It seemed, in the intensity of horror, in its silence, as if no one had heard, no one understood. Madness above all dreams was horrible in the nest of reality. A silence that lasted a moment yet seemed by sentiment, by significance, by horror, to have the duration of ages, was on all, a silence the like of which has never been dreamt nor thought. I conceive not with what expression each one was, all of us were. But those faces must have had looks such as no vision has yet met.

This for a moment—short, aging, profound.

My own horror, my own commotion cannot be conceived. All the humorous expressions and innuendoes, which I had naturally, innocently connected with my hypothesis of the five black servants, yielded now their deeper, their most horrible meaning. All the malicious undertone, all the suggestiveness of Pros-it's voice—all this, I say, appearing now to me in its true light, thrilled and shook me with a fear that cannot be spoken. The very intensity of my terror seemed to prevent me from fainting. For a moment I, like the others, but with greater fear, and with more reason sat back in my chair and stared at Prosit with a horror no words can express.

For a moment this, for a moment and no more. Then, excepting some of us, the weaker-hearted, who had fainted, the guests all, beside themselves with a just and uncontrollable rage, rushed maniacally at the cannibal, at the mad author of this more than horrible exploit. It must have been, to a pure spectator, a horrible scene, these well-bred, well-dressed, refined, semi-artistic men animated by a fury of more than beasts. Prosit was mad, but, at that moment we were mad also. He had no chance against us—none at all. Indeed, at this instant, we were madder than he. Even one of us, in the rage we were, had sufficed to punish horribly the President.

Myself, first of all, bore a blow against the offender. With a rage so terrible it seemed some one else's, and seems now so, for my memory of it is as of ought impossibly true I seized the wine-decanter which was near me and hurled it, with a horrible exultation of ire, at Prosit's head. It struck him full in the face, mixing blood and wine upon it. I am mild, sensitive, abhorrent of blood. Thinking upon it now, I cannot realise how it is possible that I should have done an act to my usual self of such dreadful cruelty, however just, for, mostly by the passion that inspired it, it was a cruel, a most cruel deed. How great then must have been my rage and my madness! And that of the others, how great!

"Out of the window!" cried a terrible voice. "Out of the window!" shrieked a formidable chorus. And it is characteristic of the brutality of the moment that the way of opening the window was by breaking it entirely. Someone put a strong shoulder to it and dashed the central part (for the window was divided in three) into the square below.

More than a dozen animal hands were eagerly, disputingly laid upon Prosit, whose madness was thrilled by his ill-speakable fear. With a nervous motion he was hurled towards the window, but he did not pass it for he contrived to hold on to one of the partitions of the casement.

Again those hands clutched him, more firmly, more brutally, more savagely still. And with a Herculean joining of strength, with an order, with a combination perfectly diabolic in such a moment, they swung the President in the air and hurled him from them with incalculable violence. With a thud that had sickened the strongest, but which was the maker of calm in our eager and expecting hearts, the President fell into the square, four or five feet beyond the pavement.

Then no word, no sign exchanged, each man locked in the horror of himself, each of us departed from the house. Once outside, the fury past and the horror that made it like a dream, we experienced the inenarrable horror of meeting naturalness again. All without exception were turned sick and many fainted soon or late. I fainted at the very door.

The five dark servants of Prosit—they were really dark, being old Asiatic pirates, of a murderous and abominable tribe—these, who, understanding the affair, had fled during the fray, were caught—all with the exception of one. It appears that Prosit, for the consummation of his great joke, had, with an adroitness perfectly diabolic, bit by bit awakened in them their brutal instincts which slumbered in civilization. They had been in everything the President's coadjutors. They had been ordered to stand as far as they could from the table in dark places, on account of Prosit's ignorant and criminal fear of Herr Kleist, the anthropologist, who, for all Prosit knew of his science, might have been able to see in the black faces the ill-determined stigmas of criminality. The four of them who were caught were punished fitly and well.

June, 1907

Essay

Excerpts from "Erostratus" by Fernando Pessoa

The principal content of Fernando Pessoa's "Erostratus" is his reflection on the quest for immortality or, more specifically, the desire for celebrity. "The proper reward of genius is therefore immortality,"[1] Pessoa wrote in a fragment of the essay, and almost immediately added, "The proper reward of talent is therefore what we have called fame."[2] As a man and a writer, Pessoa strove to examine several points connected with the concept of celebrity: its meaning, the different ways of achieving it, its connection with other notions—inspiration, genius, sincerity, and so on—and with more concrete instruments, such as literary critique, propaganda, and language; he also explored its relevant relation with literature. However, Pessoa's fragments are not only devoted to theoretical or even philosophical considerations. They are filled with examples of other authors' works through which Pessoa attempted to understand and confirm his own ideas. We find observations about Shakespeare, Chesterton, Goethe, Huxley, Milton, and Dante, among many others. Shakespeare is seen as an "example of great genius and great wit linked to insufficiency of talent. He is a supreme in the intuition that constitutes genius and in the quickness of strangeness that constitutes wit as he is deficient in the constructiveness and the coordination which constitute talent."[3] Milton "is the example of the union of great genius and great talent. He has the intuition of genius and the formative power of talent. He had no wit; he was, in fact, a pedant. But he had the pedant's firm, though heavy, will."[4] Victor Hugo's works, however, "fill fifty large volumes, yet each volume, each page almost, contains all Victor Hugo. The other pages add up as pages, not as genius. There was in him no productivity, but prolixity."[5]

For Pessoa, the justification is clear: "No man should leave twenty different books unless he can write like twenty different men."[6] This fragment is pertinent if we consider the fact that Pessoa created 136 fictional authors,[7] from poetry to prose, giving each a different point of view. It is enough to recall the multiplicity we can find in Alberto Caeiro, Álvaro de Campos, Ricardo Reis, Bernardo Soares, António Mora, Barão de Teive, and so on. Although the heteronyms may show similar characteristics, there is no doubt that each reveals a singular world, giving Pessoa the authority to criticize other authors. As Pessoa

277

clearly reveals in his poem "Eu sou uma antologia" ("I Am an Anthology"), the poet is someone who should be universal, that is to say, a person who can compose in a way that reflects the world and its infinity. The poem that Pessoa wrote on December 17, 1932, states it clearly: "Sou como o mundo"[8] (I am like the world). In his famous letter to Adolfo Casais Monteiro dated January 13, 1935, Pessoa tries to explain this peculiar ability of multiplying himself, something he displayed as a child and that would remain a part of him throughout his life, leading to his well-known multiple fictional work: "E assim arranjei, e propaguei, varios amigos e conhecidos que nunca existiram, mas que ainda hoje, a perto de trinta annos de distancia, oiço, sinto, vejo. Repito: oiço, sinto vejo . . . E tenho saudades d'elles."[9] (And so I created and propagated several friends and acquaintances that never existed, but to this day, after almost thirty years, I hear, I feel, I see. I repeat: I hear, I feel, I see . . . and I miss them.)

"Erostratus" was first published by Georg Rudolf Lind and Jacinto do Prado Coelho (in *Páginas de estética e de teoria e crítica literárias*, 1967), and later completed by Richard Zenith (in *Heróstrato e a busca da imortalidade*, 2000). Jerónimo Pizarro also published a few fragments in *Escritos sobre génio e loucura* (*Writings on Genius and Madness*, 2006), and found one unpublished document. It is not certain when "Erostratus" was written, because the texts are not dated, but according to Richard Zenith, it was probably written around 1930, in light of the texts' material characteristics (for example, several fragments were written on the same type of paper and with the same ink as in fragments of the *Livro do desassossego* [*Book of Disquiet*], dating between 1929 and 1934; the 1929 stamp on the envelope on which Pessoa wrote one of the "Erostratus" fragments; or the reference to the death of Sir Henry Segrave[10] in 1930, and so on).

Although "Erostratus" is a fragmentary work and not a complete theoretical system, it allows us to understand Pessoa's ideas about such a complex theme as celebrity, and his desire to comprehend or even achieve the path to immortality. As a poet who fulfilled his own literary potential and created a multiplicity of worlds, Pessoa seemed to be following his own belief: "a genius is a man who does a difficult thing, even when it is easy."[11] In fact, the tendency to understand the meaning of celebrity or immortality is not only presented in "Erostratus." We can also find fragments related to the idea of fame in Ricardo Reis and *Fausto*, for example. But it is interesting to see that Pessoa shows an apparent detachment from the desire for fame through some of these texts. Or so it seems, according to Reis: "Não quero a fama, que comigo a têm / Erostrato e o pretor"[12] (I do not want the fame attributed to me / Erostrato and the pretor)—or *Fausto*— "Outrora quis a fama—e não a quis, / Que a fama, a popularidade, o ser / Conhecido, falado—quando não visto—/ Confrange-me dum terror que não compreendo"[13] (Once I wanted fame—and I did not want it, / that fame, popularity, being, / Known, spoken of—when not seen—/ distresses me with a terror which I do not understand).

The importance of literature in achieving fame, or as the necessary instrument for the survival of an author's name, is also present in Pessoa's texts. For example, one fragment attributed to Barão de Teive declares the undeniable relationship between the writer and the writing: "Seria o fogo em minha casa? Corriam risco de arder todos os meus manuscriptos, toda a expressão de toda a minha vida?"[14] (Could my house be on fire? Were my manuscripts, all the expression of my life, at risk of burning?). Or when Bernardo Soares says, "A literatura, que é a arte casada com o pensamento, e a realização sem a macula da realidade, parece-me ser o fim para que deveria tender todo o exforço humano"[15] (Literature, which is art married to thought, and realization without the imperfection of reality, seems to be the purpose toward which every human effort should tend). These few examples are sufficient to elucidate the relevance of some concepts and relations in Pessoa's thoughts. He tries to analyze and explore them throughout his writing, signed by himself or by one of his literary figures.

NOTES

1. BNP/E3, 19–44^r. First published in Fernando Pessoa, *Páginas de estética e de teoria e crítica literárias*, ed. Georg Rudolf Lind and Jacinto do Prado Coelho (Lisbon: Ática, 1967), 189.

2. BNP/E3, 19–44^r. Pessoa, *Páginas de estética*, 189.

3. Ibid., 185.

4. BNP/E3, 19–41^r.

5. BNP/E3, 19–61^r, 208–9.

6. BNP/E3, 19–61^r, 208.

7. Pessoa, *Eu sou uma antologia: 136 autores fictícios*, ed. Jerónimo Pizarro and Patricio Ferrari (Lisbon: Tinta-da-China, 2013).

8. Pessoa, *Poemas 1931–1933*, ed. Ivo Castro (Lisbon: Imprensa Nacional–Casa da Moeda, 2004), 109.

9. Pessoa, *Cartas entre Fernando Pessoa e os directores da presença*, ed. Enrico Martines (Lisbon: Imprensa Nacional–Casa da Moeda, 1998), 255.

10. Henry Segrave (1896–1930) was an English racer who established several land and water speed records. He was knighted by the king in 1929.

11. BNP/E3, 19–74^r. Pessoa, *Páginas de estética*, 220.

12. Pessoa, *Poemas de Ricardo Reis*, ed. Luiz Fagundes Duarte (Lisbon: Imprensa Nacional–Casa da Moeda, 1994), 93.

13. Pessoa, *Fausto: Tragédia subjectiva*, ed. Teresa Sobral Cunha (Lisbon: Presença, 1988), 134.

14. Pessoa, *A Educação do stoico*, ed. Jerónimo Pizarro (Lisbon: Imprensa Nacional–Casa da Moeda, 2007), 44.

15. Pessoa, *Livro do desassossego*, ed. Jerónimo Pizarro (Lisbon: Tinta-da-China, 2013), 361.

WORKS CITED

Pessoa, Fernando. *A Educação do stoico*. Edited by Jerónimo Pizarro. Lisbon: Imprensa Nacional–Casa da Moeda, 2007.

———. *Cartas entre Fernando Pessoa e os directores da presença*. Collection "Studies." Edited by Enrico Martines. Lisbon: Imprensa Nacional–Casa da Moeda, 1998.

———. *Escritos sobre génio e loucura*. Edited by Jerónimo Pizarro. 2 vols. Lisbon: Imprensa Nacional–Casa da Moeda, 2006.

———. *Eu sou uma antologia: 136 autores fictícios*. Edited by Jerónimo Pizarro and Patricio Ferrari. Lisbon: Tinta-da-China, 2013.

———. *Fausto: Tragédia subjectiva*. Edited by Teresa Sobral Cunha. Lisbon: Presença, 1988.

———. *Heróstrato e a busca da imortalidade*. Edited by Richard Zenith. Lisbon: Assírio & Alvim, 2000.

———. *Livro do desassossego*. Edited by Jerónimo Pizarro. Lisbon: Tinta-da-China, 2013.

———. *Páginas de estética e de teoria e crítica literárias*. Edited by Georg Rudolf Lind and Jacinto do Prado Coelho. Lisbon: Ática, 1967.

———. *Poemas de Ricardo Reis*. Edited by Luiz Fagundes Duarte. Lisbon: Imprensa Nacional–Casa da Moeda, 1994.

———. *Poemas 1931–1933*. Edited by Ivo Castro. Lisbon: Imprensa Nacional–Casa da Moeda, 2004.

FILIPA DE FREITAS earned a master's degree in Portuguese studies with the thesis "Comparative Analysis of Four Versions of 'The Foreigners' by Francisco Sá de Miranda" and a master's in philosophy with the thesis "Baron of Teive: Emotion and Lucidity in the 'Education of the Stoic,'" at the Faculty of Social Sciences and Humanities of the New University of Lisbon. She is currently pursuing PhD research in philosophy there for the thesis "Universalite ou a doença do poeta: O ponto de vista de Álvaro de Campos e o conceito de Poeta em Søren Kierkegaard" (Universalite or the poet's disease: Álvaro de Campos' point of view and the concept of poet in Søren Kierkegaard), financed by the Foundation for Science and Technology. She has participated in projects related to Portuguese Theater and Fernando Pessoa.

She can be reached at filipasf2@gmail.com

"Erostratus"

1.

[BNP/E3, 19–38ʳ]

ER.[1]

[. . .]

I purpose to examine the problem of celebrity, both occasional and permanent, to investigate in what conditions either sort has happened to men, and to foresee, as far as can be, in what conditions either sort is likely to happen in the future. Celebrity is the acceptance of any man or of any group of men as in some way valuable to mankind. To investigate the problem we shall have to define value.[2] We shall also have to define mankind.

(1) Celebrity may be of things or of men. There are celebrated crimes, battles, novels, empires; there are celebrated authors of these. We shall not concern ourselves with the things, but with the men. It is the conditions that produce celebrity that interest us.

(2) Celebrity may be incidental or fundamental. A man who is killed in a particularly mysterious manner becomes celebrated by his death. If the case is important, he may live[3] through history as a corpse.[4] We are not interested in incidental but in fundamental celebrity, however unjust it may happen to be.

(3) Celebrity may be artificial and natural. A king is naturally famous. He is born into that with the kingdom. We shall not concern ourselves with this sort of celebrity. It varies with manners and customs, with institutions. We shall examine only the problem of natural[5] celebrity.

(4) Celebrity may be good or bad, the second sort being generally called notoriety. The shifting ideas of good and evil sometimes complicate the problem; they are even superimposed in some cases. Where one sees a murderer, another will see a bold man. Where one sees a martyr, another will see a fool. The difficulty of the point has been given, with no intention of giving it, in Proudhon's famous phrase: "After the tyrants, I know nothing more hateful than the martyrs."

ER.

They do not fall in some silly corner of duty, but in the sillier open spaces of vanity. They have no status above the dandy and the swaggerer except the bad taste of the daring and the impudence of the height of the swagger (vanity)(impudence). They lose their lives not like heroes but like animals; as these blunder into danger, those blunder into chance. Cowardice seems a virtue when courage is hidden under these. (thus defiled)

Except the Germans and the Russians, no one has as yet been able to put anything like art into the cinema. The circle cannot be squared there.

I purpose to examine the problem of celebrity, both occasional and permanent, to investigate in what conditions either sort has happened to men, and to foresee, so far as can be, in what conditions either sort is likely to happen in the future. Celebrity is the acceptance of any man as in some way valuable to mankind. To investigate the problem we shall have to define value. We shall also have to define mankind.

Celebrity may be of things and of men. There are celebrated crimes, battles, novels; there are celebrated authors of these. We shall not concern ourselves with the things, but with the men. It is the conditions that produce celebrity that interest us.

Celebrity may be natural and artificial. A king is naturally famous. He is born into that with the kingdom. We shall not concern ourselves with this sort of celebrity. It varies with manners and customs, with institutions. We shall examine only the problem of natural celebrity.

Celebrity may be incidental or fundamental. A man who is killed in a particularly mysterious manner becomes celebrated by his death, if the case is important, he may live through history as a corpse, (an interesting corpse). We are not interested in incidental but in fundamental celebrity, however unjust it may happen to be.

Celebrity may be good or bad, the second sort being generally called notoriety. The shifting ideas of good and evil sometimes complicate the problem; they are even superimposed in some cases. Where one sees a murderer, another will see a bold man. Where one sees a martyr, another will see a fool. The difficulty of the point has been given, with no intention of giving it, in Proudhon's famous phrase: "After the tyrants, I know nothing more hateful than the martyrs".

"I purpose to examine the problem of celebrity,"
manuscript page from "Erostratus," BNP/E3, 19–38^r.

2.

[BNP/E3, 19–39^r]

ER.

There are only two types of constant mood with which life is worth living—with the noble joy of a religion, or with the noble sorrow of having lost one. The rest is vegetation, and only a psychological botany can take interest in such diluted mankind.

Yet it is admissible to think that there is one sort of greatness in Erostratus—a greatness which he does not share with lesser crashers into fame. He, a Greek, may be conceived as having that delicate perception and calm delirium of beauty which distinguishes still the memory of his giant clan. He may therefore be conceived as burning Diana's temple in an ecstasy of sorrow, part of him being burnt in the fury of his wrong endeavour. We may fitly conceive him as having overcome the toils of a remorse of the future, and facing a horror within himself for the stalwartness of fame. His act may be compared, in a way, to that terrible element of the initiation of the Templars, who, being first proven absolute believers in Christ—both as Christians, and in the general tradition of the Church, and as occult Gnostics and therefore in the great particular tradition of Christianity, had to spit upon the Crucifix in their initiation. The act may seem no more than humanly revolting from a modern standpoint, for we are not believers, and, when, since the romantics, we defy God and hell, defy things which for us are dead and thus send challenges to corpses. But no human courage, in any field or sea where men are brave with mere daring, can compare with the horror of that initiation. The God they spat upon was the holy substance of Redemption. They looked into hell when their mouths watered with the necessary blasphemy. Thus may be conceived Erostratus, save that the stress of the love of beauty is a lesser thing than the conviction of a sentimental truth. Thus let us conceive him, that we may justify the remembrance.

For if Erostratus did this, he comes at once into the company of all men who have become great by the power of their individuality. He makes that sacrifice of feeling, of passion, of □ which distinguishes the path to immortality. He suffers, that his name may enjoy.[6]

ER.

constant mood
There are only two types of xtnt with which life
is worth living - with the noble joy of a religion, or
with the noble sorrow of having lost one. The rest is
vegetation, and only a psychological botany can take interest in such diluted mankind.
so general a fungus.

- - - - - - - - - - - - -

Yet it is admissible to think that there is one
sort of greatness in Erostratus - a greatness which he
does not share with lesser crabbers into fame. He, a
Greek, may be conceived as having that delicate perception and calm delirium of beauty which distinguishes
still the memory of his giant xxxxx clan. He may therefore be conceived as burning Diana's temple in an ecstasy
of sorrow, part of him being burnt in the fury of his
wrong endeavour. We may fitly conceive him as having overcome the toils of a remorse of the future, and facing a
horror within himself for the stalwartness of fame. His
act may be compared, in a way, to that terrible element
of the initiation of the Templars, who, being first proven
absolute believers in Christ - both as Christians, and
in the xgxnstx general tradition of the Church, and as
occult Gnostics and therefore in the great particular tradition of Christianity, had to spit upon the Crucifix in
their initiation. The act may seem no more than humanly
revolting from a modern standpoint, for we are not believers,
and, when, since the romantics, we defy God and hell, defy
things which for us are dead and thus send challenges to
corpses. But no human courage, in any field or sea where
man are brave with mere daring, can compare with the horror of thatinitiation. The God they spat upon was the
hóly substance of Redemption. They looked into hell when
their mouths watered with the necessary blasphemy. Thus
may be conceive Erostratus, save that the stress of the
love of beauty is a lesser thing than the conviction of
a sentimental truth. Thus let us conceive him, that we
may justify the remembrance.

For if Erostratus did this, he comes at once into
the company of all men who have become great by the power
of their individuality. He makes that sacrifice of feeling,
of passion, of   which distinguishes the path to
immortality. He suffers, that his name may enjoy.

like Christ who dies astheman that he may prove himself
the Word.

"There are only two types of constant mood with which life is worth living,"
manuscript page from "Erostratus," BNP/E3, 19–39[r].

3.

[BNP/E3, 96–32^r]

Erostratus

We meet then that peculiar thing called inspiration—a meaningless name and a reality. It is that strange accident that breaks like a day out of the night of Wordsworth's dullness. It is the strange gleam on those strange sonnets which Gerard de Nerval got from outside the world. Blake stretched out his hand and received it through the curtain. Shakespeare had it perpetually[7]—and[8] was his own daemon.

A great rise and swell in the verse of Homer, Virgil or Milton can be understood with reason; it is a quickening of what is. But how is this[9] quickening of what is not to be gathered into understanding? Not a light that rises into a flame, but a log that is kindled with an outer light that becomes its own—this inspiration is . . .

"We meet then that peculiar thing called inspiration,"
manuscript page from "Erostratus," BNP/E3, 96–32ʳ.

4.

[BNP/E3, 96–23^r]

ER

Not sincerity in the absolute, but some sort of sincerity, is required in art so that it may be art. A man can write a good love sonnet in two conditions—because he is greatly in love, or because he is greatly in art. He must be sincere in the love or in the art; he cannot be great in either, or in anything, otherwise. He may burn inwardly not thinking of the sonnet he is writing; he may burn outwardly not thinking of the love he is figuring. But he must be on fire somewhere. Otherwise he will not cook the goose of his human inferiority.[10]

"Not sincerity in the absolute," manuscript page from "Erostratus," BNP/E3, 96-23ʳ.

5.

[BNP/E3, 19–46ʳ]

ER.

In the arts which are not literature, we have a universal speech and there is no misunderstanding, except each man's insensibility. But in literature, in this matter of fame and extension of fame, we are met at the corner of speculation by the problem of language and come into a different landscape of conjecture.

There is a dead and a living fame, and each is fame; there is a fame that works and delves, and a fame that is like a statue, or an inscription on a tomb, a survival without life. Shakespeare lives and works; Spenser is a name without force. No one (perhaps not even Spenser) ever read the *Faerie Queene* with a through[11] thoroughness. Even the great complete epics have sinned against interesting always. The ideal is an epic that shall wear like Milton and interest like Conan Doyle. That is not an impossibility, for there are no impossibilities; even contradictions in terms have been freed by Hegel from being such.

How shall a man survive if he survive but as the name he had. How much of the fame of Homer comes from men who have read him in the original? Frenchmen have been known to be moved by Shakespeare, yet no French mind can ever grasp the mental rhythm of phrase and the sudden complexity of meaning that only a knowledge of English from the soul side can allow or concede.

ER.

In the arts which are not literature, we have a
universal speech and there is no misunderstanding, except each man's insensibility. But in literature, in
this matter of fame and extension of fame, we are met
at the corner of speculation by the problem of language
and come into a different landscape of conjecture.

There is a dead and a living fame, and each is
fame; there is a fame that works and delves, and a fame
that is like a statue, or an inscription on a tomb, a
survival without life. Shakespeare lives and works;
Spenser is a name without force. No one (perhaps not
even Spenser) ever read the Fearie Queene with a through
thoroughness. Even the great epics have sinned against
interesting always. The ideal is an epic that shall
wear like Milton and interest like Conan Doyle. That
is not an impossibility, for there are no impossibilities; even contradictions in terms have been freed by
Hegel from being such.

How shall a man survive if he survive but as the
name he had. How much of the fame of Homer comes from
men who have read him in the original? Frenchmen have
been known to be moved by Shakespeare, yet no French
mind can ever grasp the mental rhythm of phrase and
the sudden ~~springing~~ of meaning that only a knowledge
of English from the soul side can allow or concede.

"In the arts which are not literature," manuscript page
from "Erostratus," BNP/E3, 19–46ʳ.

6.

[BNP/E3, 19–70^r]

Er.

He may not be intelligent, but he must be intellectual.

Art is the intellectualization of sensation[12] through expression. The intellectualization is given in, by and through the expression itself. That is why great artists—even great artists in literature, which is the most intellectual of the arts—are so often unintelligent persons.

"He may not be intelligent, but he must be intellectual,"
manuscript page from "Erostratus," BNP/E3, 19–70ʳ.

NOTES TO TEXT 1

1. The text preceding the dashed line is excluded.
2. value [↑ celebrity]
3. live [↑ be immortal]
4. The author's variant is in parentheses: "a corpse" / "(an interesting corpse)."
5. By mistake, the author wrote "natural" instead of "artificial."
6. that his name may enjoy [↓ like Christ who dies as the man that he may prove himself the Word]
7. perpetually [↑ inhabitantly]
8. and [↑ he]
9. this [↑ a]
10. human inferiority [↓ natural humanity]
11. By mistake, the author wrote "through" instead of "thorough."
12. The author's variant is in parentheses: "sensation (feeling)."

Translation

CLAUDIA J. FISCHER
Translated by Carole Garton

Dryden, Keats, Tennyson, and Browning
Unpublished Translations by Fernando Pessoa

ABSTRACT: Reading, writing, and translating were three interconnected activities for Pessoa. Although some of his translations were brought to light in Portugal during his own lifetime, a great number of them remained unpublished. This chapter provides a transcription of lines from Dryden, Keats, Tennyson, and Robert Browning, along with brief comments on each of the translations.

KEYWORDS: unpublished translation, Dryden, Keats, Tennyson, Robert Browning

---

As numerous fragments in the archive demonstrate, for Pessoa readings and rereadings of his favorite English poets were a continual inspiration for his own poetry and for critical reflection, as well as an impetus for his translations.

In a monograph from 1996 on poetry translated by Fernando Pessoa,[1] Arnaldo Saraiva revealed some poems, generally in English, that the young Pessoa had translated for the *Biblioteca internacional de obras célebres*, an anthology of world literature in twenty-four volumes that came out in the first decade of the twentieth century and was made available chiefly in Brazil.[2]

As for editorial projects undertaken throughout Pessoa's life (for example, Olisipo in 1921), a significant number were devoted to translations of works in different languages, with Pessoa as the main translator of the English. In June 1923, disheartened over the Olisipo project, Pessoa suggested to João Castro Osório, a manager of and partner in a publishing house, a Herculean plan for translations. The plan included ten plays by Shakespeare, as well as major works by Poe, Robert Browning, Wordsworth, Coleridge, Arnold, Shelley, Keats. In addition, Pessoa planned to include in volumes of the same set some minor English Restoration poets (for example, Sir Charles Sedley, Suckling, and Lovelace), as well as late Victorian poets (O'Shaughnessy, Dowson, and Lionel Johnson, among others).[3] The sense of urgency and some megalomania in the letter to

297

Osório, in which Pessoa asks for an advance of 2,000 escudos, indicate that there was also a financial motivation. The idea failed to lead to any published results; however, it contributed to translations extant in Pessoa's archive, "prontas, e sujeitas apenas à necessária revisão final" (ready and subject only to the need of a final revision),[4] as he optimistically announced in the letter.

Saraiva, in the appendix to his book, presents facsimiles of five fragments of translations, together with the passages in the original, but not the transcription of Pessoa's manuscripts. These are verses by Dryden (taken from "The Hind and the Panther," *Aureng-Zebe, The Conquest of Granada,* and *Don Sebastian);*[5] Keats (from "Ode on a Grecian Urn"); Poe (from "Annie" and "The Haunted Palace"); Tennyson (from "Break, Break, Break"); and Robert Browning (from "The Pied Piper of Hamelin: A Child's Story"). Apart from Poe's verses, transcribed by Margarida Vale de Gato and subsequently published in 2011,[6] all these translations have remained unpublished. This material, transcribed here, provides the reader with one more insight into the translation methods used by Pessoa, a poet who defined poetry as "obra litteraria em que o sentido se determina *atravez do* rhythmo" (a literary work in which sense is determined through rhythm)[7] and asserted that this was "[o] primeiro elemento a fixar" (the first element to consider)[8] when translating a poem. In the paragraphs that follow, I briefly comment on some of the translations presented here for the first time.

The title of the manuscript that contains his translations of John Dryden's lines—"Dryden (LOWELL)"— suggests that Pessoa used a selection of poems from *Literary Essays* by James Russell Lowell,[9] especially those in his essay on Dryden on pages 95 to 180 of the third volume.[10] In his translation of "The Hind and the Panther," for instance, written in heroic couplets by the only Restoration poet included in this set, Pessoa opted for the decasyllable (mixing sapphic and heroic rhythmical patterns) and respected the rhyme scheme.[11]

A copy of *The Complete Works of John Keats* extant in Pessoa's private library[12] dates back to his South African days. It was one of the books Pessoa selected on winning the Queen Victoria Memorial Prize for best English essay when he took the entrance examination for the University of the Cape of Good Hope.[13] Pessoa considered Keats a master for his "line perfection"[14] and even coined the Portuguese adjective *sensuoso*[15] (sensuous) to describe the quality distinguishing Keats from his contemporary Shelley. Keats, one of the English lyrical poets Pessoa wrote most about, appears repeatedly in several of his editorial projects. Although Pessoa considered "Ode to a Nightingale" to be "the best of all odes of

Keats,"[16] it was "Ode on a Grecian Urn," expressing "so human an idea as the heart-rending *untimeness* of beauty,"[17] that he selected for a poetry anthology project[18] datable to 1917–1923. Keats's ode is in rhymed iambic pentameter, meter that Pessoa rendered by using the decasyllable (mixing for the most part Sapphic and heroic rhythmical patterns).

A copy of *The Complete Works of Alfred Tennyson*[19] also figured on the list of books Pessoa chose on winning the prize mentioned earlier. "Break, Break, Break," a poem by Tennyson, "the greatest artist of modern times," according to Pessoa,[20] was also to be included in the anthology he envisioned. Tennyson's lines are in ictic verse. In his translation, Pessoa managed to reproduce the number of beats of the original (three beats per line become three stresses in the Portuguese text) and respect the rhyme scheme.[21]

Pessoa owned at least two books by Browning: *Poems of Robert Browning* (1907) and *The Works of Robert Browning* (1912).[22] Pessoa, in keeping with his obsession with comparing poets, defines the greatness of Browning and Tennyson by placing them in opposition: "There's a disassociation among the moderns: they are either like Browning, great poets without being great artists, or like Tennyson, great artists without being great poets."[23] This "dramatically lyrical poet,"[24] as he calls Browning in another critical reflection, is presented here in a partial translation of the first stanzas of "The Pied Piper of Hamelin." In this poem, Browning mostly combines the four-beat dolnik, a ballad meter known as *long measure*, with the three-beat dolnik.[25] In Pessoa's translation, we observe many decasyllabic and octosyllabic lines.

299

John Dryden: Lines from "The Hind and the Panther," *Aureng-Zebe*, *The Conquest of Granada*, and *Don Sebastian*

Prompt to assail, and careless of defense,
Invulnerable in his impudence,
He dares the world; and, eager of a name,
He thrusts about, and jostles into fame.
Frontless, and satire-proof, he scours the streets,
And runs an Indian-muck at all he meets.
So fond of loud report, that, not to miss
Of being known, (his last and utmost bliss,)
He rather would be known for what he is.
"The Hind and the Panther," Part Third, lines 1184–92

Death, in it self is nothing; but we fear
To be we know not what, we know not where.
Aureng-Zebe, Act IV, Scene 1, lines 3–4

Forgiveness to the injur'd does belong;
But they ne'r pardon who have done the wrong.
The Conquest of Granada, Part II, Act I, Scene 2, lines 5–6

The secret pleasure of a generous Act,
Is the great minds great bribe.
Don Sebastian, Act V, Scene 1, lines 316–317

With open Arms, loose vayl, and flowing Hair,
Just flying forward from my rowling Sphere.
The Conquest of Granada, Part I, Act III, Scene 1, lines 233–34

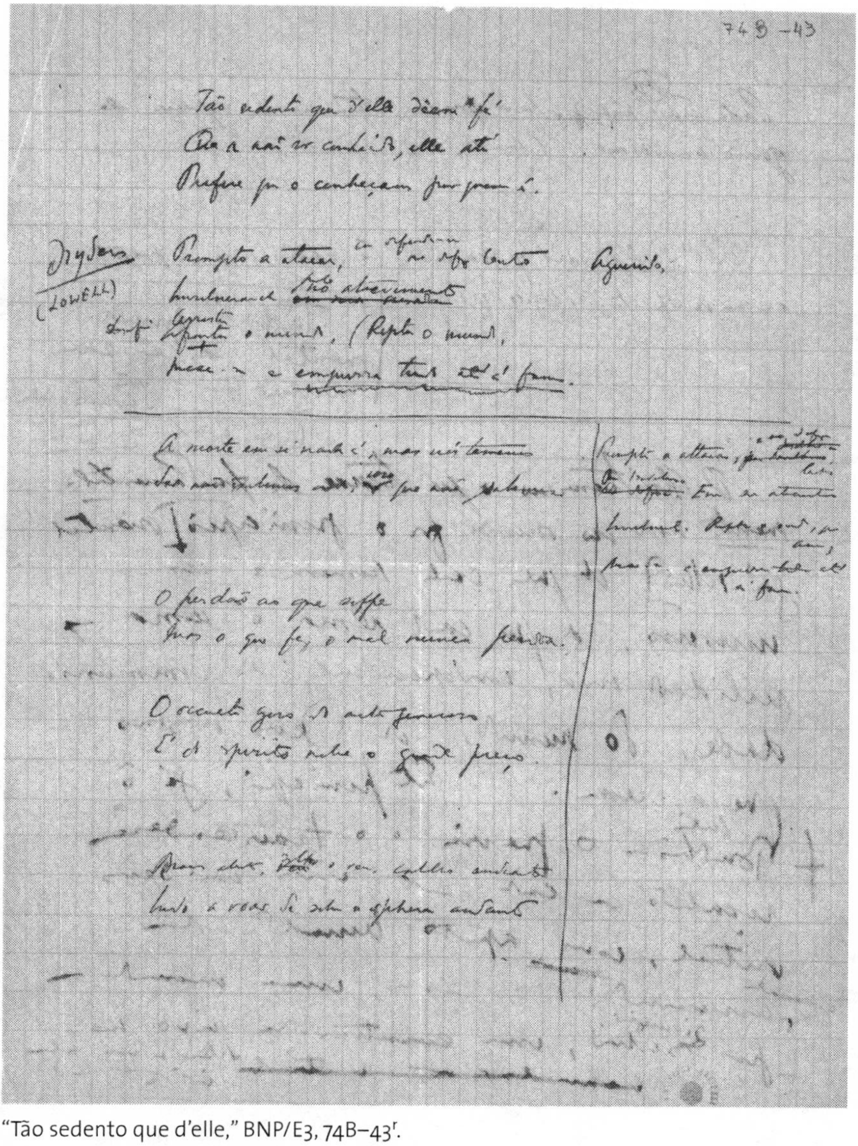

74B-43

Tão sedento que d'elle dêem fé
Que a não ser conhecido, elle até
Prefere que o conheçam por quem é.

"Tão sedento que d'elle," BNP/E3, 74B–43r.

¹ Prompto a atacar, em defender-se lento
² Invulneravel pelo atrevimento
³ Repta o mundo, [   ]
   Mexe-se e empurra tudo até á fama.
   [

                                      ]
   Tão sedento que d'elle dêem fé
   Que de não ser conhecido, elle até
   Prefere que o conheçam por quem é.

---

¹ᵇ Prompto a attacar, e na defeza lento
²ᵇ Por *desdenhoso. Em ser atacante
   Invulneravel. Repta o mundo, que ama;
   Mexe-se e empurra tudo até á fama.

   A morte em sinada é, mas nós tememos
²ᶜ Ser não sabemos onde; isso que não sabemos.

   O perdão ao que soffre [   ]
   Mas o que fez o mal nunca perdoa.

   O occulto goso do acto generoso
   É do spirito nobre o grande preço.

---

¹ᵈ Braços abertos, solto o veu, cabello ondeante
   Indo a voar de sobre a sphera andante

John Keats: "Ode on a Grecian Urn"

II.

1   [   ] mas aquellas
        Que não se ouvem, são mais; trilam, pois,
3   Não ao ouvido sensual; mais bellas,
        Cantae-me á alma musicas sem som!
5   Tu, jovem, sob as arvores, [   ]
6   Teu canto, nem os ramos [   ]
            Tua bocca, amante nunca a beijará,
8   Sempre perto do beijo—mas não chores
9   Ella não morre, inda que tu não
10   Sempre amarás e ella bella será.

III

Ramos felizes! Nunca o vosso braço
12   Perde as folhas ou [   ]
    E feliz melodista, [   ]
14   Trilando enfim canções sempre novas.
15 E amor feliz! Oh mais feliz amor!
16   Sempre em calor e para ser gosado
            Sempre apaixonado e jovem, e a querer;
18 Além do humano respirado ardor
        Que deixa o coração triste e cançado
20   A bocca senão a doer e a fronte a arder.

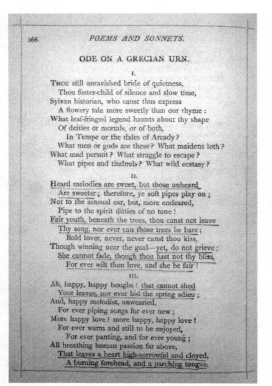

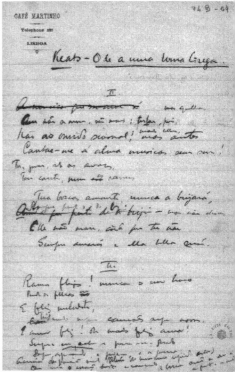

Keats, "Ode on a Grecian Urn," *The Poetical Works*, 1898, 266. CFP 8–294.

"Mas aquellas," manuscript of Pessoa's translation of "Ode to a Grecian Urn," BNP/E3, 74B–54ʳ.

Alfred, Lord Tennyson: "Break, Break, Break"

[BNP/E3, 19–70^r]

"Break, break, break," Alfred Tennyson, *The Poetical Works of Alfred Tennyson*, London: Macmillan, 1902, 124. CFP 8–541.

Bate, bate, bate
Nessas rochas [   ] do mar
Ai que eu dizer pudesse
4   O que eu me sinto pensar.

"Bate, bate, bate," BNP/E3, 74B–28^r.

Robert Browning: "The Pied Piper of Hamelin: A Child's Story"

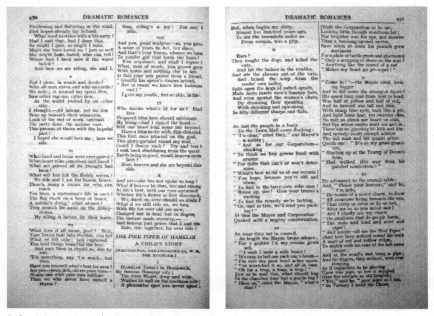

Robert Browning, *The Poetical Works of Robert Browning*, London: Peacock, Mansfield, [1912], 430–31. CFP 8–74.

[I]

Ao pé de Hanover, em Brunswick
    É a villa de Hamelin
O Weser, longo e fundo rio,
Banha-a do sul [   ]
5 Mas o que me importa a mim
    É que ha uns quinhentos annos, quando
    Se passou o que irei contando
    Estava uma praga a villa infestando
        De rataria sem fim.

[II]

10   Ratos!
        Mordiam os cães, matavam os gatos,
        [   ]
        Comiam cousas dos proprios pratos
        Lambiam sopa até das colheres,
15   Abriam barricas, roiam fatos
        Faziam ninhos em sapatos
                E até as conversas de mulheres
                Interrompiam fazendo-as dar
                Pulos e porem-se a chiar
20 Com e [   ] e flatos.

[III]

        Por fim o povo em procissão
        Chegou aos paços do concelho
        Dizendo "O alcaide é um toleirão
        E os outros não valem um prego velho."
25   Pensar a gente que paga bem
        As vestes reais do cargo que tem
27   A gente que não sabe que tratos
        Dar para nos livrar dos ratos!
        Então vocês por serem velhos
30   Julgam só fallar em conselhos?
31   Acordem! E um remedio dêem
32   Ou então não *pisem nos pés sem †["]
33   E com isto o alcaide e o outro
        [   ]

[IV]

35   Uma hora estiveram em conselho,
        Por fim o alcaide [   ]
37   "Trocaria o cargo p'r um tostão velho
        Só para me ver longe de aqui!"

³⁹ É fácil dizer á gente que pensa
⁴⁰ Mas já me doe a cabeça
⁴¹ Tanto a cocei [   ]
    Ah uma ratoeira, uma ratoeira"
    E estando elle fallando d'esta maneira
    Bate á porta uma mão ligeira.
⁴⁵ "Santo Deus" disse o alcaide, "o que é

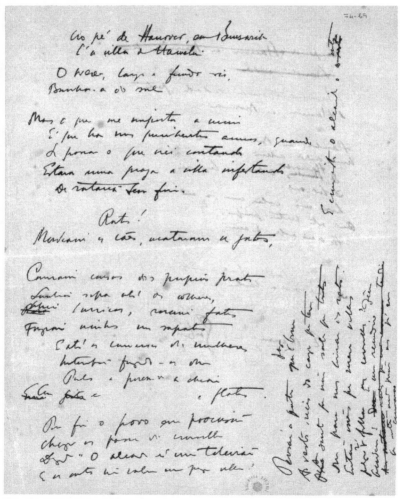

"Ao pé de Hanover, em Brunswick / É a villa de Hamelin," BNP/E3, 74–69^r.

*

Prompto a atacar, em defender-se lento

[BNP/E3, 74B–43ʳ]. *Datable from 1910s. Written in blank ink on ruled paper. By the second stanza, we read the following indication:* Dryden (Lowell); *On the verso (43ᵛ) Pessoa notes:* Cada Era [↑ Age] (Epocha), disse Dryden, tem uma especie de genio universal. (Lowell, 5) / J. C. Scaliger said of Erasmus: "Ex alieno ingenio poeta, ex suo versificator." (Lowell, 13)

Notes to "Prompto a atacar"

1 na defeza [↑ em defender-se] lento   Aguerrido,
2 <em sua ousada> [↑ no ↑ pelo] atrevimento
3 /Afronta/ [↑ Arrosta ← Desafia] o mundo, / Repta o mundo,
1b <por *desdenhoso> [↑ <*desdenho> ↑ e na defeza lento]
2b <Na defeza.> [↑ Por *desdenhoso]
2c onde; [↑ isso] que não
1d abertos, <veu> [↑ solto] o veu,

*

[   ] mas aquellas

[BNP/E3, 74B–54ʳ]. *Datable to c. 1911. Written in black ink on a lined sheet of paper from the Café Martinho. This is Lisbon's oldest coffeehouse (Fernando Pessoa called it Café da Arcada), located at 3 Terreiro do Paço (Praça do Comércio). The city was rebuilt after the Great Lisbon Earthquake of 1755 by the Marques de Pombal, who opened it as Café da Neve on January 7, 1782. It was only officially named Martinho around 1845, when Martinho Bartolomeu Rodrigues owned it. At the top of the fragmentary translation, Pessoa left the following indication:* Keats—Ode a uma Urna Grega. *(underlined). This autograph document was facsimiled, without a transcription, in* Fernando Pessoa: Poeta tradutor de poetas, *edited by Arnaldo Saraiva (Lisbon: Lello Editores, 1996), 217. Translations for Parts I–II and IV–V of this ode have not been located in Pessoa's archive. In document* [BNP/ E3, 74B–54ᵃʳ] *we find a translation from two different lines of Keats's "Ode to Psyche":* Da do Olympo fanada hierarchia. [↑ gerarchia] *"Of all Olympus' faded hierarchy!"(line 23);* Em vez de pinheiraes murmuração.*"Instead of pines shall murmur in the wind:" (line 53) (Keats,* The Poetical Works, *1898), 268–69.* The Poetical Works of John Keats *(London: Frederick Warne, 1898) is part of Pessoa's private library. The call number is* [CFP 8–294].

Notes to "[   ] mas aquellas"

1 <A musica que se ouve é> [   ] mas aquellas
3 mas antes [↑ ; mais bellas,]
6 nem<ess> [↑ os] ramos
8 <Ainda que perto de a beijar> [↑ Sempre perto do beijo]
9 Elle] *in the ms.*
12 as folhas ao [↑ ou]
14 <Cant> [↑ Trilando]
16 /em calor/
18 Acima da paixão real (Além do humano respirado ardor)] *the variant appears in parenthesis.*

*

Bate, bate, bate,

[74B–28ʳ]. Datable to 1908. Fragment of a sheet of paper handwritten in blue ink. The last verse of the stanza was added in black ink, possibly at a later time. On top of the verses, we read the indication Tennyson. These Portuguese lines are the translation of the first stanza of Tennyson's "Break, Break, Break," adm[irable] according to Pessoa, as he wrote in his own copy still existing in his private collection. This marginal note certainly dates from 1904, the year he won this book in Durban.

The book can be consulted online; the call number is [Casa Fernando Pessoa, 8–541]. This autograph document is facsimiled, without a transcription, in Fernando Pessoa: Poeta tradutor de poetas, edited by Arnaldo Saraiva (Lisbon: Lello Editores, 1996), 225. It is transcribed in Patricio Ferrari, "Meter and Rhythm in the Poetry of Fernando Pessoa," unpublished doctoral thesis (University of Lisbon, 2012), 371.

Notes to "Bate, bate, bate,"
4 <Os> O que eu me sinto [↓ O que em mim sinto pensar.]

*

Ao pé de Hanover, em Brunswick

*[BNP/E3, 74–69ʳ and 70ʳ]. Datable to post-1911. Written in black ink on thin paper. We find translations of the beginning of the poem in two different documents: [I.] <Ao pé de Hanover, em Brunswick *fica> / <Hamelin, cidade> / Hamelin é uma cidade perto / De Hanover, *ou, Brunswick / Hamelin em Brunswick é / Uma cidade allemã ao pé / De <Brunswick> [↑ Hanover], o Weser, hoje rio / Do lado sul /*

Lugar mais calmo nunca se viu / Quando esta historia principia / Ha meio seculo de annos, / [I.] O Weser, largo e fundo rio, / Do lado sul a banha | E chamam-no o *Gaiten. [BNP/E3, 74B–69ᵛ]; [I.] O rio Weser largo e fundo / [   ] / Mas quando<a> [↑ esta] historia <começa> [↑ principia] / Ha uns quinhentos annos eram [   ] /Da rataria [   ] // [II.] Ratos! / Lutavam com cães, matavam os gatos, / Mordiam nos berços as creanças / Comiam os queijos sem os pratos // [III.] Por fim o povo veio em massa / Á Camara [   ] / E disse é claro: <O Presidente> / O Presidente é um besta / E quanto aos *meandros, esta / Palavra nem sequer lhes calha. / Talvez alli e perto de alli / Que *nada sabem que fazer / Para nos livrar d'este *moer / <De> Ratos, ratinhos, ratazanas, [BNP/E3, 74B–68ʳ]. *A copy of Robert Browning,* The Poetical Works of Robert Browning, *Centenary Edition, with introductory note by Charles W. Forward (London: Peacock, Mansfield [1912]), exists in Pessoa's private library; the call number is [CFP 8–74].*

Notes to "Ao pé de Hanover"

15 <Roia> [↑ Abriam]
20 <Em jeitos> [↑ Com e]
25 que [↑ paga] bem] *Quotation marks are missing between lines 25–32.*
27 <P'ras> [↑ A]
30 Julgam [↑ só] fallar
31 Acordem! <Deem> [↑ E] um remedio [↑ dêem]
32 <Ao † † que não † tedio>
33 e o <resto> [↑ outro]
37 <Daria> [↑ Trocaria] o <meu>cargo
39 *Quotation marks are missing between lines 39–42.*
41 Tanto a <†> [↑ cocei]
45 *Question and quotation marks are missing at the end of the line.*

NOTES

I thank Patricio Ferrari and Jerónimo Pizarro for their help on the transcription of the documents here published. I also extend my acknowledgments to Ivan Moody and Susan Brown for revising Garton's English translation.

1. Arnaldo Saraiva, *Fernando Pessoa: Poeta tradutor de poetas* (Lisbon: Lello Editores, 1996).

2. Pessoa mentions this anthology in his notes on the Olisipo project, and presents it as a model for the editorial section of Olisipo (BNP/E3, 137D–44 to 47; *O Comércio e a publicidade,* ed. António Mega Ferreira. [Lisbon: Cinevoz/Lusomedia, 1986]).

3. Letter to João Castro Osório dated June 20, 1923, in Fernando Pessoa, *Correspondência 1923–1935*, ed. Manuela Parreira da Silva (Lisbon: Assírio & Alvim, 1999), 14.

4. Pessoa, *Correspondência*, 14–15.

5. As a source for the two final verses in Pessoa's manuscript, Saraiva mistakenly indicates four verses of Dryden's *Cleomenes* instead of the two verses from *The Conquest of Granada* translated by Pessoa ("With open arms, loose veil, and flowing hair, / Just flying forward from my rolling sphere"). See Saraiva, *Fernando Pessoa: Poeta tradutor de poetas*, 214.

6. Cf. Fernando Pessoa, *Principais poemas de Edgar Allan Poe*, ed. Margarida Vale de Gato (Lisbon: Babel, 2011). Pessoa's fragmentary translations are completed in this edition by Vale de Gato's translation. The exact transcriptions can be found on pages 179–80 and 170–71 respectively.

7. BNP/E3, 14D–13^r; Fernando Pessoa, *Apreciações literárias*, ed. Pauly Ellen Bothe (Lisbon: Imprensa Nacional–Casa da Moeda, 2013), 215.

8. Ibid. Pessoa's comments are precisely about translating Poe's work.

9. James Russell Lowell, *Literary Essays* (Boston / New York, Cambridge University Press, 1890).

10. This book is not in Pessoa's private library; see Pizarro, Ferrari and Cardiello, *A Biblioteca particular de Fernando Pessoa* (Lisbon: D. Quixote, 2010).

11. The complete lines in Pessoa's translation have either a sapphic (mandatory stresses fall on positions 4, 8, and 10) or a heroic (positions 6 and 10) rhythmical pattern.

12. Call number: CFP 8–294.

13. Although the prize was designated for 1903, it was awarded on February 24, 1904. In fact, one of the books chosen is by Johnson and dates from 1904. The other volumes selected were by Keats, Poe, and Tennyson.

14. BNP/E3, 49B^5–35^r; Pessoa, *Apreciações literárias*, 171.

15. BNP/E3, 14^4–80; Pessoa, *Apreciações literárias*, 82.

16. BNP/E3, 14C–81^r; Pessoa, *Apreciações literárias*, 159.

17. BNP/E3, 19–98^r; Pessoa, *Apreciações literárias*, 158.

18. BNP/E3,48–8; Patricio Ferrari, "Meter and Rhythm in the Poetry of Fernando Pessoa," (unpublished doctoral thesis, University of Lisbon, 2012), 385.

19. Call number: CFP 8–541.

20. BNP/E3, 14E–24 and 25; Pessoa, *Apreciações literárias*, 273.

21. This is what metrists consider a true dolnik. According to Martin Duffell, "56 per cent of intervals [in this poem] are disyllabic, a significantly higher proportion than that found in normal speech, a difference that may also be mimetic, since waves break irregularly, and at what sometimes seem longer intervals." Duffell, *A New History of English Metre* (London: Legenda, 2008), 173. Editors' note.

22. CFP 8–73 and 8–74.

23. BNP/E3, 14²–81ʳ; Pessoa, *Apreciações literárias*, 71.

24. Pessoa, *Páginas de estética e teoria e critica e literárias*, ed. Georg Rudolf Lind and Jacinto do Prado Coelho (Lisbon: Ática, 1967), 67.

25. For an account of this terminology borrowed from Russian metrics, see Duffell, *A New History of English Metre*. Editors' note.

WORKS CITED

Browning, Robert. *The Poetical Works of Robert Browning*. Centenary edition. With introductory note by Charles W. Forward. London: Peacock, Mansfield [1912]. CFP 8–74.

Dryden, John. *The Works of John Dryden*. Cambridge: Chadwyck-Healey, 1992.

Duffell, Martin. *A New History of English Metre*. London: Legenda, 2008.

Ferrari, Patricio. "Meter and Rhythm in the Poetry of Fernando Pessoa." Unpublished doctoral thesis, University of Lisbon, 2012.

Keats, John. *The Poetical Works of John Keats*. With memoir, explanatory notes, portrait, illustrations. London / New York: Frederic Warne, 1898. CFP 8–294.

Pessoa, Fernando. *Apreciações literárias de Fernando Pessoa*. Edited by Pauly Ellen Bothe. Fernando Pessoa's Critical Edition, Collection "Studies." Lisbon: Imprensa Nacional–Casa da Moeda, 2013.

———. *O Comércio e a publicidade*. Edited by António Mega Ferreira. Lisbon: Cinevoz/Lusomedia, 1986.

———. *Correspondência 1923–1935*. Edited by Manuela Parreira da Silva. Lisbon: Assírio & Alvim, 1999.

———. *Principais poemas de Edgar Allan Poe*. Edited by Margarida Vale de Gato. Lisbon: Ática, 2011.

Pizarro, Jerónimo, Patricio Ferrari, and Antonio Cardiello. *A Biblioteca particular de Fernando Pessoa*, Vol. I. Lisbon: D. Quixote, 2010.

Saraiva, Arnaldo. *Fernando Pessoa: Poeta tradutor de poetas*. Lisbon: Lello Editores, 1996.

Tennyson, Alfred. *The Works of Alfred Tennyson*. London: Macmillan, 1902. CFP 8–541.

CLAUDIA J. FISCHER (PhD, University of Lisbon, 2007) is associate professor of German and translation at the University of Lisbon, where she also coordinates the German language courses. As researcher at the Center for Comparative Studies of the University of Lisbon, she collaborates on a project dealing with theater translation in Portugal. She has published translations of Rilke, Thomas Mann, and W. Benjamin, and translated Brecht and Fassbinder for the National Theater of Oporto. Her research interests lie mainly in the area of translation studies and German literature from the eighteenth and early nineteenth century. Many of her recent publications (for example, in Ática's Pessoa Nova Série and the *Pessoa Plural* journal), international talks, and research also involve Fernando Pessoa both as playwright and translator. Her book concerning the concept of grace in Friedrich Schiller and Heinrich von Kleist has just been published (2015).

She can be reached at c.fischer@flul.pt.

Interview and Reviews

An Interview with Margaret Jull Costa

Margaret Jull Costa is a renowned translator of Portuguese, Spanish, and Brazilian authors (mainly prose writers). She has translated Eça de Queirós, Fernando Pessoa, José Régio, José Saramago, Lídia Jorge, António Lobo Antunes, Teolinda Gersão, Javier Marías, Bernardo Atxaga, Julian Ayesta, and Luis Verissimo, among others.

Margaret Jull Costa has won various prizes, including the 2008 PEN/Book-of-the-Month Club Translation Prize and the 2008 Oxford Weidenfeld Translation Prize for her version of *The Maias*. In 2012, she won the Calouste Gulbenkian Prize for her translation of *The Word Tree* by Teolinda Gersão. In Portugal and in the Lusophone world, she is mostly known for her translations of Eça de Queiroz and José Saramago (for which she has won various prizes).

Recently, Jerónimo Pizarro asked Margaret Jull Costa to revisit *The Book of Disquiet*, a posthumous fragmentary work by Pessoa, which has been edited by various editors since 1982. She sat down with Maria de Lurdes Sampaio to answer some questions about the experience of translating Fernando Pessoa's work. We are extremely grateful to Margaret for her generosity.

MLS: You were the author of one of the four translations of *Livro do desassossego* (LdD) that appeared in English in 1991, and "your" *The Book of Disquiet* (published by Serpent's Tail) was joint winner of the Portuguese Translation Prize in 1992. Your translation remains in print. Was Fernando Pessoa the first Portuguese author you translated? And how would you describe your relationship with Pessoa?

MJC: Yes, he was the first Portuguese author I translated. I had translated three Spanish novels already when Pete Ayrton of Serpent's Tail asked if I would be interested in translating LdD. I immediately said yes, blissfully (or perhaps foolishly) unaware of the difficulties ahead. Before this, I had translated (purely for myself) some of FP's writings (that is, some of those he did not attribute to any of his heteronyms) poems, because I loved them so much, especially "Chuva oblíqua," maybe because the title is so hard to translate! LdD chimed perfectly with my own feelings of melancholy at the time, and while I did find the text extraordinarily difficult to render into English—and sometimes doubted I could do it—I also found the whole experience an extremely companionable one, as if Pessoa himself were there with me. I think many people feel that same sense of companionship when they read the book.

MLS: Your translation of LdD opens a door not only to Pessoa's universe but also to Portuguese literature and culture, as well as to the city of Lisbon. Besides footnotes concerning certain foreign books and authors, you added crucial information about major Portuguese writers, such as Francisco Sanches, Frei Luis de Sousa, Father António Vieira, Camilo Pessanha, Cesário Verde, and Fialho de Almeida.

And most interestingly, you also inserted explanations and information about some emblematic places in Lisbon (often referenced in the "book"), such as the Baixa, the Rotunda, Café Leão, Cais do Sodré. Why these footnotes? Do they have to do with your view of the translator as a bridge between cultures?

MJC: I very rarely use footnotes, but I did feel it necessary to explain briefly who or what these people and places were and, in a way, what they meant to Portuguese readers. Translators, by the very nature of their work, do provide a bridge between cultures, and so, yes, I felt that was part of my role in this case.

MLS: Many years have passed since you translated LdD, but you doubtless often return to it as a reader and rewriter of some passages of your own translation. Do you feel it is the gloomy book some people consider it?

MJC: I have occasionally dipped into my own translation, and recently, Jerónimo Pizarro asked me to translate some extra passages for a brief selection of Pessoa's most Lisbon-centered pieces (for which he was using other texts from my translation). I was astonished at how difficult it was (a) to understand precisely what Pessoa meant (always assuming he knew!) and (b) to capture the density, compactness, and eccentricity of his language. I was amazed, too, at my own audacity, as a translator at the beginning of my career, in undertaking such a task in 1991. I did then go on to reread my original translations of the other texts, and there were a few places that needed a little adjustment, but not that many, which was encouraging! Perhaps I've become another heteronym.

As for the book's supposed gloominess, there were times when I felt like telling Bernardo Soares/Vicente Guedes to cheer up, but then Pessoa/Soares/Guedes are often very funny, and there is something very English about the self-deprecation at which he so excels. He speaks to us as a fellow failure, and perhaps therein lies that companionableness I mentioned earlier.

MLS: Fernando Pessoa published his first poems in English (in England), and his language was accused of being archaic (the same accusation was made of Ezra Pound's first books of poetry), but he was not accused of writing bad English. Up until his death, Pessoa went on writing in English, although his heteronymic work and LdD were written in Portuguese. As a native English speaker and as a skilled *reader*, how English does Pessoa's work in Portuguese sound to you?

MJC: Apart from that very English tendency to self-mockery and self-deprecation I mentioned earlier, Pessoa feels entirely Portuguese to me, even though he's using the Portuguese language as no one else does or has. It occurs to me that perhaps his other languages, especially English, did influence his use of Portuguese, but only in the sense that, being bilingual, his linguistic world and his perception of the possibilities of language are that much wider. Joseph Conrad, writing in his third language, produces wonderful English, but I sometimes think that the vividness and quirkiness of it comes about because it isn't his first language. Perhaps the same degree of fruitful alienation is there in Pessoa too.

MLS: There are some passages in your translation of LdD in which one seems to hear some Shakespearean echoes (more than in the Portuguese text). For instance, a passage that begins as follows: "To cease, to sleep . . ." [frag, 49 (99)] inevitably reminds anyone acquainted with Shakespeare of *Hamlet*. And there are many passages that seem (at least to me) to echo Shakespeare, perhaps the English author Pessoa most loved. Did you feel any Shakespearean undertones when you translated LdD?

MJC: I'm not sure this was deliberate, and I have no idea if those echoes are in the original Portuguese, but English is shot through with Shakespeare's language and imagery. It's very hard to avoid. Also, any Portuguese text is full of literary allusions that will get lost in translation, so perhaps I was trying to fill in those gaps with English literary allusions. I don't think Pessoa would have minded.

MLS: One of the most quoted passages from LdD is "A minha pátria é a língua portuguesa." But there is another in the same "book" that, from a literary point of view, is more important: "Eu não escrevo em português. Eu escrevo eu mesmo." Can you comment on this last statement?

MJC: I agree absolutely with both statements. I think that, for both writers and translators, their mother tongue is their one true homeland, and the best writers do write *themselves* when they write. Mediocre writers use language; the best writers use language in ways it has never been used before, and their language is crammed full of a lifetime of linguistic memories and echoes.

MLS: As someone who knows Pessoa from the inside (you are an insider in Kermode's sense of the term), do you feel there is some kind of unity or design behind or beneath Pessoa's heterogeneous work (the heteronyms and the ortonyms)?

MJC: I have no idea, although my feeling is that Pessoa had no grand plan for his work; he simply wrote and wrote using as many different personae as he could muster. Perhaps he was an actor manqué . . .

MARIA DE LURDES SAMPAIO is professor at the University of Oporto (FLUP) and research fellow at the Institute of Comparative Literature Margarida Losa.

Fernando Pessoa.
Apreciações literárias de Fernando Pessoa.
ed. Pauly Ellen Bothe

"I have outgrown the habit of reading," declares Fernando Pessoa in a text in English estimated to be from 1910, justifying his assertion with the claim, "I am now in full possession of the fundamental laws of literary art." As shown by the 372 documents spanning 1904 and 1935 that comprise Pessoa's aesthetic appreciations collected in this volume, this was hardly the case. Pessoa's pronouncement should thus be read as an act of mystification, signifying the coming-of-age assertiveness of a budding poet who, conversely, declared himself "a reader voracious and ardent" in the same text. Nonetheless, it reveals the principal motivation underlying Pessoa's copious readings and critical responses to those readings, notably the desire for knowledge and mastery of the essence of literary processes. Guided by this view of aesthetic knowledge as creative empowerment, Pessoa read extensively from a mainly Western canon, as this volume attests.

With the explicit intention of giving continuity to the two closing chapters of *Páginas de estética e de crítica e teoria literárias* (1967), which Georg Rudolf Lind and Jacinto do Prado Coelho have devoted to fragments about European and Portuguese literatures, this thoroughly researched and carefully edited book substantially expands the corpus of Pessoa's aesthetic appreciations, including 240 previously unpublished documents. Increasing to ninety-eight the number of authors about whom Pessoa wrote appreciations, the volume is organized in a reader-friendly format as a dictionary of authors in alphabetical order and with an index. The editor went to great lengths to determine the dates of the documents based on examination of physical carriers and various complementary sources, including Pessoa's archives and contemporary newspaper articles, presenting the texts in chronological order, whenever it has been possible to date them, to provide some idea of the development of Pessoa's taste.

As with other volumes of the critical edition of Pessoa's works, *Apreciações literárias de Fernando Pessoa* is divided into two sections: the first comprises the critical text accompanied by footnotes providing information about the editions of works by the author in question in Pessoa's private library; the second consists of a critical apparatus of variants, including detailed topographic and genetic information about the autograph or typescript and appendices with transcriptions of fragments about different topics from the critical text featured in the document. Given its content, consisting of Pessoa's own writings, and its organization according to critical-genetic principles, this latest volume of the critical edition of Pessoa's works belongs to the Série Maior of the Edição crítica da obra completa de Fernando Pessoa carried out by Equipa Pessoa, but it has been erroneously published with a cover belonging to the Coleção "Estudos" (Collection "Studies"), which is devoted to scholarly studies of problems related to Pessoa's archive and the edition of his works. This does not, however, detract from the scholarship with which the volume has been edited.

Pauly Ellen Bothe's judicious cross-referencing of authors mentioned in the same document allows the reader to realize that Pessoa often recorded reflections about different authors on the same piece of paper, which both confirms the avowed voraciousness of his readings and reveals the obsessive manner in which he wrote his aesthetic appreciations. Additionally, by quoting specific passages of works referenced in Pessoa's aesthetic appreciations and indicating reading marks in the existing editions in Pessoa's private library (for example, p. 134), she retraces the poet's dialogue with the author he was reading and writing about, providing valuable information for critical exegesis. According to the editor, Pessoa's aesthetic appreciations consisted mostly of fragmentary and unfinished essays on individual authors that he planned to publish (some of which correspond to titles listed in publication projects in his archive), brief critical pronouncements, and drafts of texts that Pessoa published in his lifetime. Although some of these texts were published as reviews in Portuguese periodicals and magazines, including the influential cultural magazines *Contemporânea* (1922–1923) and *Athena* (1924–1925, founded by Pessoa), and as prefaces to books by other writers, the bulk of Pessoa's aesthetic appreciations remained unpublished at the time of his death.

As indicated in the introduction, the majority of the texts were written in Portuguese and in English, and some are bilingual. That English was as important a vehicle of expression of his aesthetic thought as his mother tongue can be gathered from the fact that Pessoa alternated between the two languages when writing about most of the authors with whom he engaged critically. His dual linguistic and cultural heritage also explains the high incidence of Anglophone authors, as well as the bias of some of his comments, for instance, his claim that English literature is the greatest of all literatures save the Greek (frag. 70, p. 100), which undoubtedly owes much to his familiarity with it through his formal English education. Elsewhere Pessoa identifies English as one of the three European languages that display the greatest degree of pure lyrical poetry, the other two being German and Portuguese (frag. 120, p. 139). Accordingly, he writes about major poets of the English canon, such as Shakespeare, Milton, and the romantics, as well as American poets such as Poe and Whitman. Within a Lusophone context, despite expressing the intention of examining the works of Portuguese and Brazilian poets he thought "worthy of analysis" (frag. 137, p. 149), Pessoa's appreciations comprise exclusively Portuguese poets. These include significant figures from the Portuguese canon, such as Camões—whom he praises for his lyrical epopee (frag. 48, p. 85)—as well as Antero de Quental, Cesário Verde, and Camilo Pessanha—his avowed nineteenth- and twentieth-century "masters" (frag. 207, p. 211)—and contemporary poets, such as Mário de Sá-Carneiro and António Botto. However, his appreciations also include novelists, dramatists, and essayists, although these are less numerous.

Pessoa's aesthetic appreciations of poets are particularly revealing because, while appraising their works and reflecting on their poetic practices, he often expounds his views on poetry. Hence, his appraisal of Shakespeare elicits a definition of lyricism as "o poder de exprimir intensamente (pela fala) emoções e estados de alma concretizando-os o mais possível" (the power to intensely express [through speech] emotions and states of soul rendering them as concrete as possible) (frag. 266, p. 243). Accordingly, supreme lyricism, of the kind he ascribed to Shakespeare, consists of the perfect expression of a great number of "states of soul" in this fashion (frag. 266, p. 243). These pronouncements about Shakespeare reveal the continuities between Pessoa's aesthetic appreciations and his own poetic practices, in this instance the deployment of a "drama em almas" (drama in souls) through the heteronyms, which allowed him to lyrically express multiple states of soul rendered concrete.

In other cases, an appreciation about a specific poet rehearses or echoes Pessoa's theoretical formulations about his own practices, as illustrated by the claim that Victor Hugo "is always outside himself, but that in the person of another; but that other is no person: he is no more than an artificial V[ictor] H[ugo]. [. . .] a dramatic mind would have othered itself in more ways than one [. . .] and better" (frag. 125, p. 142; emphasis added). The English turns of phrase Pessoa uses here recur in statements in Portuguese about his own poetic depersonal-ization, namely his claim that the work "Caeiro-Reis-Campos" was "sentido na pessoa de outro" (felt in the person of another) in a letter to Armando Côrtes-Rodrigues from January 19, 1915, and his remark, "Em prosa é mais difícil de se outrar" (It is much harder to other oneself in prose), when comparing Livro do desassossego by Bernardo Soares with the works of the heteronyms in a preface for the anthology Ficções do interlúdio. These statements show the reciprocity, even across different languages, between Pessoa's criticism and his own aesthetic thought and poetic praxis.

These aesthetic appreciations also reveal the extent of Pessoa's critical inter-est in formal aspects of the structure and composition of a poem. He defined lyrical verse as a compound of words and music (frag. 121, p. 139) and ascribed substantial importance to the melodic quality of the lyric and to rhythm, which he believed could determine the meaning of a poem (frag. 223, pp. 218–19). Hence, his aesthetic appreciations included remarks about several poets in rela-tion to these issues, notably his praise of Tennyson's "fine music of paragraph" and "melody of line" (frag. 313, p. 274) and of Poe's (frag. 215, p. 215) and Swin-burne's (frag. 309, p. 272) poetry as rhythmic. Pessoa's definitions of lyricism and lyrical verse proposed in these passages illustrate Jacinto do Prado Coelho's claims that Pessoa's reasoning was scholastic and largely based on definitions with the rigor of mathematical demonstrations ("Sobre as ideias estéticas de Fernando Pessoa," in A Letra e o leitor, Oporto: Lello & Irmãos, 1996, 265).

Coelho also notes Pessoa's tendency to distinguish, isolate, and classify ("Sobre as ideias estéticas," 270); this is corroborated by Pessoa's claim that there are visual and aural poets, such as Victor Hugo and Antero de Quental re-spectively (frag. 116, p. 136). In this tendency to elaborate typologies of poets, Pessoa resembled other major modernist writers such as W. B. Yeats, whose po-etic system expounded in A Vision hinges on two types of poets—the objective and subjective—a polarization that also underpins Pessoa's typologies, as shown by his comments about the "radically objective" nature of Hugo's "mind" (frag. 125, p. 143). Nonetheless, the expanded corpus collected in this volume shows that Pessoa did not abstain from posing questions and problems about the works he analyzed, particularly in relation to the author's "temperament" or "mind," contradicting Coelho's assertion about the dogmatic quality of Pessoa's essay-istic style ("Sobre as ideias estéticas," 265).

This critical inquisitiveness, which often led Pessoa to counter the views of other critics regarding the authors he was writing about, is in accordance with the deductive reasoning that Georg Rudolf Lind considers both Pessoa's greatest strength and his weakest point, as he notes in the introduction to his and Coelho's edition of *Páginas de estética e de crítica e teoria literárias* (Lisbon: Ática, [2nd ed. 1973, repr. 1994], xv). And indeed, if on the one hand, the speculative quality of Pessoa's criticism allowed him to make insightful deductions about certain works and authors, particularly those with whom he felt greater aesthetic affinity, on the other hand, the abstract nature of his reasoning prevented him from examining structural and contextual aspects in detail and at length, which, in Coelho's view, makes him more of a theorist than a literary critic ("Sobre as ideias estéticas," 265). Despite this, a more pragmatic facet of Pessoa's criticism emerges in the form of observations about the translation of poetry that recur in the appreciations collected in this volume. Although Pessoa believed that it was nearly impossible to translate lyrical poetry (frag. 119, p. 138), this edition features introductions to his translations of Shakespeare's *The Tempest* (frag. 288–89, pp. 260–61) and of poems by Poe (p. 480), and a preface to a collection of Portuguese poets and foreign poets in translation that he intended to call "Anthology" (p. 482). His comments about this subject show that he was familiar with translation theory and terminology and, according to information provided in the critical apparatus, he did, at one time, contemplate establishing a "publishing house in Britain for translations of foreign books and 'continental' publications of English ones" (p. 506), referring to an "Olisipo in London" (p. 505).

Apreciações literárias de Fernando Pessoa provides an invaluable record of Pessoa's literary aesthetic thought, which surveyed the Western canon and his contemporaries, focusing to a large extent on poetry. The appreciations collected in this volume show that Pessoa reflected assiduously on literary matters, and they feature some of his key aesthetic concerns: mystical nationalism, transcendental pantheism and neopaganism, and his obsessive interest in the expression of literary genius, which underlies the often comparative nature of his criticism of major authors. Hence, the critical portraits collected in this edition can also be regarded as portraits of Pessoa the critic and literary theorist.

Fernando Pessoa.
Eu sou uma antologia: 136 autores fictícios.
ed. Jerónimo Pizarro and Patricio Ferrari

Edgar Allan Poe, one of Pessoa's two great American masters (the other being Walt Whitman), begins his tale "The Man of the Crowd" with the mysterious statement that "it was well said of a certain German book that '*er lasst sich nicht lesen*'—it does not permit itself to be read." That's not entirely true of the book under review, but, modifying what Poe's narrator said about that German book, I would come close to saying that it "does not permit itself to be reviewed"—at least not readily.

From childhood, Pessoa was the creator of fictitious beings. In his famous letter to Adolfo Casais Monteiro, dated January 13, 1935, he named the Chevalier de Pas "o meu primeiro heteronymo, ou, antes, o meu primeiro conhecido inexistente." He also recalled that the Chevalier had a rival, though he could not at the moment recall his name. Interestingly, this hinted-at interplay between these childhood nonexistent acquaintances seems to foreshadow what would become, for the adult Pessoa, the fruitful way of extending his notion of "drama-em-gente" to a "drama entre" those fictitious beings. As he wrote in "Tábua bibliográfica" (1928), prepared at the request of José Régio in his capacity as one of the editors of *Presença*, "As obras heterónimas de Fernando Pessoa são feitas por, até agora, trez nomes de gente—Alberto Caeiro, Ricardo Reis, Alvaro de Campos. Estas individualidades devem ser consideradas como distinctas da do auctor dellas. Fórma cada uma uma espécie de drama; e todas ellas juntas formam outro drama." Let us single out the words *até agora*. Never mind that here, Pessoa chooses to ignore his numerous other heteronyms, such as Alexander Search, Antonio Mora, or the Barão de Teive, to name but three. What stands out for me is the hint that besides the possibility that other heteronyms might participate in the drama that has been created by the big three, there may be other heteronyms whose individual dramas might form a separate cluster, that is, a drama played out among themselves.

There's a chicken-and-egg question here. Given Pessoa's lifelong fascination with the names and signatures of all sorts of fictitious beings of his own making, along with multiple and varied signatures of those names (including his own), one can legitimately ask if the existence of a given heteronymous being preceded his naming, or vice versa. I suspect that it could go either way. Yet an answer to this mystery might well contribute to our understanding of how the complex creative mind of Pessoa actually worked, especially given the all-but-professional interest Pessoa took in the character analysis of signatures and all handwriting. Recognizing this, the editors of *Eu sou uma antologia* reproduce such signatures, sometimes, when available, in generous quantities.

One hundred thirty-six fictitious authors. That is the number the editors have settled on as the so far identifiable body of writers barely named, shadowy, sketchy, or, in the cases familiar to all of Pessoa's readers, bodied forth substantially with a body of writing of their own. Besides presenting the facts and comments that give the "fictitious author" an identity, the editors offer samples (when they exist) of that author's writing. This combination of biographical dictionary and anthology makes *Eu sou uma antologia* a valuable resource for future scholarly work on the nature and extent of Pessoa's heteronymous project.

There have been other compilations of the names of Pessoa's fictitious persons, but the authors of this "anthology" have honored the listings of those predecessors by applying a simple test. Was the fictitious name that of a "writer"? The editors allow, moreover, that their list (or compiled evidence) is not to be considered definitive. After all, in many cases, there is presented no more than a name and the title of a work that was merely projected and, as far as anyone knows (at least *até agora*), not even begun. No doubt Pessoa, despite the sheer quantity of his writing that has survived, was the victim of the old adage: "His eyes were bigger than his belly."

Well, I must confess that, despite my initial reservations about the possibility, this is a book that can be read. In fact, this part reference book, part anthology made for compelling reading. Its length militated against my usual sort of sit-down, straight-ahead reading, yet my gradual fascination with this anthology kept me interested in just what name, old or new, would be considered next, all the way through its more than 600 pages. For the scholar, moreover, *há pano p'ra mangas*—that is, leads that call for further exploration. I am grateful once again to Jerónimo Pizarro and Patricio Ferrari for coming up with the idea for this book and then providing scholars with such an excellent tool for future research into this phenomenon that is Fernando Pessoa.

Fernando Pessoa.
No Matter What We Dream: Selected English Poems.
ed. Patricio Ferrari and Jerónimo Pizarro

No Matter What We Dream is a surprising little book of Fernando Pessoa's poetry in English precisely because it is *not* one more book of translations into English. Rather, it is a carefully complied anthology of poetry written by Pessoa himself. Anyone seriously interested in Pessoa cannot afford to ignore it, for it is the first book to give readers the opportunity to become acquainted with the full range of his poetic practice in English. Until now, the English poems have been largely overlooked. Discounted as second-rate or simply neglected altogether, they have remained in the shadow of his seemingly endless output in Portuguese. The irony is that these poems have waited so long to be discovered, for they offer us an invaluable window from which to glimpse Pessoa at work during his early years of apprenticeship. We see him in these pages experimenting with voices, meters, moods. Particularly in the poems of Alexander Search, we discern a young Pessoa at the frontiers of his mind, on the verge of mapping out the unknown territory that would soon become the heteronyms, particularly the voices of Caeiro and Campos. One cannot put the book down without having gained a keener awareness of the significance and even prophetic value of these early English poems.

Editors Patricio Ferrari and Jerónimo Pizarro form the ideal team to take on the challenges of this book. Renowned within the world of Pessoan scholarship for their thorough and accomplished work—both holding doctorates in linguistics—they are particularly suited to delve into areas that involve a bilingual interest in Pessoa's poetry. Pizarro and Ferrari (who is currently at work on Pessoa's unpublished English poetry) are the dreamers that matter, for they, along with Antonio Cardiello, engineered the monumental project of digitizing Pessoa's private library, begun in 2008 and completely online since 2010. Subsequently and in connection with that project, the same trio co-authored the voluminous catalog of *Fernando Pessoa's Private Library (A Biblioteca particular de Fer-*

nando Pessoa, Lisbon: D. Quixote 2010), which categorizes and at least minimally describes all 1,311 items—*more than half of which are in English!*—acquired by the poet between 1898 and the year of his death, 1935. In addition to this, Ferrari and Pizarro have also co-edited two other works: *I Am an Anthology: 136 Fictitious Authors* (*Eu sou uma antologia: 136 autores fictícios*, Lisbon: Tinta-da-China, 2013) and a book of Portuguese proverbs that Pessoa compiled, translated, and sent to a publisher in England in 1914, but never saw published due to the outbreak of war in late 1914 (*Provérbios Portugueses: Seleccionados e traduzidos por Pessoa*, Lisbon: Ática, 2010).

All of this should provide more than ample reason to trust that this unique anthology of selections—culled from each of Pessoa's various English-speaking preheteronymic authors (Karl P. Effield, Charles Robert Anon, Alexander Search, and Frederick Wyatt) as well as from his English poems written under his own name (the astonishing Shakespearean sonnet series; the other-worldly collection of poems titled *The Mad Fiddler*; the long "cathartic" poems, *Antinous* and *Epithalamium*, that Pessoa reputedly wrote to relieve himself of certain sexual tendencies; plus eight English poems published for the first time)—will be another dream come true that matters.